GERMANS AND TEXANS

Walter Struve

GERMANS
&
TEXANS

Commerce

Migration

and Culture

in the Days

of the

Lone Star

Republic

UNIVERSITY OF TEXAS PRESS, AUSTIN

Requests for permission to reproduce material from this work should be sent to Permissions, University of Texas Press, P.O. Box 7819, Austin, TX 78713-7819.

The paper used in this publication meets the minimum requirements of American National Standard for Information Sciences—Permanence of Paper for Printed Library Materials, ANSI Z39.48-1984.

LIBRARY OF CONGRESS CATALOGING IN PUBLICATION DATA

Struve, Walter
    [Republik Texas, Bremen und das Hildesheimische. English]
    Germans and Texans : commerce, migration, and culture in the days of the Lone-Star Republic / by Walter Struve.
        p.   cm.
    Includes bibliographical references and index.
    ISBN 0-292-77700-0 (cloth:alk. paper). — ISBN 0-292-77701-9 (pbk.:alk. paper)
    1. German Americans—Texas—History—19th century.   2. Texas—History—Republic, 1836–1846.   3. Giesecke family.   4. Texas—Commerce—Germany—Bremen.   5. Texas—Commerce—Germany—Hildesheim.   6. Bremen (Germany)—Commerce—Texas.   7. Hildesheim (Germany)—Commerce—Texas.   I. Title.
    F395.G3S7713   1996
    305.831'0764—dc20   96-11036

TO THE MEMORY OF MY PARENTS
LOUIS WILLIAM STRUVE
(1905–1980)
MARY LA FORGE RUSSELL STRUVE
(1909–1980)

CONTENTS

Tables and Illustrations / ix
Abbreviations / xi
The Lure of an Heirloom: In Place of a Preface / xiii
Introduction / 3

PART ONE. WORLD OF ORIGIN:
NORTH GERMANY IN THE BIEDERMEIER ERA / 11

1. German Patricians and Merchants in Crisis / 13
2. The Homeland of the Gieseckes / 17
3. Bremen and Its Hinterland / 27

PART TWO. ENMESHMENT:
NORTH GERMANY AND THE AMERICAS / 37

4. The Lure of Mexico, Texas, and the United States / 39
5. Galveston and Its Hinterland / 54

PART THREE. WORLD OF DESTINATION:
MERCHANTS AND IMMIGRANTS IN THE REPUBLIC OF TEXAS / 57

6. North German Arrivals / 59
7. Brazoria / 67
   Rise and Fall of a Town / 67
   Agriculture and Slavery in Brazoria County / 73
8. The Many Worlds of the Gieseckes in Texas / 79
   Export, Import, Agriculture, and Retail Business / 79

Cotton and Bremen / 86
"Plantation," Slavery, and the Tobacco Trade / 92
Distilling in Texas / 100
Craftsmen and Emigration / 101

EPILOGUE: REFLECTIONS ON MIGRATION / 109

APPENDIX 1: LETTERS FROM TEXAS, 1844–1845
The Merchant and Farmer Charles A. Giesecke in Brazoria, Republic of
Texas, to His Brother, the Merchant Friedrich Giesecke in Elze, AMT
(Subdistrict) Gronau-Poppenburg, Kingdom of Hannover / 117

APPENDIX 2: CHART OF THE GIESECKE FAMILY:
Some Relationships among the Giesecke, Sander, Basse, and Struve
Families / 139

Notes / 145
Glossary of Weights, Measures, and Monetary Units / 197
Bibliographical Essay and Bibliography / 199
Index / 245

TABLES AND ILLUSTRATIONS

Table 1: Factory Employees in Bremen, 1842–1847   34

Table 2: Ships from Bremen and Other Weser Ports Arriving at Selected U.S. Ports, 1841–1847   49

Table 3: Value of Imports and Exports of the Republic of Texas, 1842–1845 (in Dollars)   52

Table 4: Cotton (in Bales), 1840–1846   90

ILLUSTRATIONS
(following p. 262)

1. Map of Germany in 1815

2. Map of Northwestern and North Central Germany Showing Many Places Discussed in the Text

3. Bockenem. The St. Pankratius Church before the Great Fire of 1847

4. Elze. Engraving of 1736 after a Drawing by Johann Friedrich Haarstick

5. The Giesecke-Sander House in Elze ca. 1910

6. The Main Marketplace in Hildesheim

7. The Horns of Gronau. Photographs of Oil Portraits

7.1. Henriette Sophie Horn, née Sander (1780–1858), Aunt of Charles A. Giesecke and His Brothers

7.2. Her Husband, Johann Alhardt Horn (1767–1851)

8. Large German Freight Wagon on the Bremen Route, 1853

9. Emigrant Ships in Bremerhaven ca. 1840

10. Giant Crane in Bremerhaven (mid-nineteenth century)

11. Bremen ca. 1852

12. German Caricatures of Emigration and Commerce

12.1. 1847

12.2. 1848

13. Map of Texas ca. 1830–1845

14. Areas of Origin of German Settlers in Texas

15. The Eastern German Settlements in Texas in the Nineteenth Century

16. German-Born as a Percentage of Total Free Population Not Born in Texas

17. Galveston ca. 1839

18. Galveston ca. 1846

19. From Charles A. Giesecke's Correspondence with His Brother Friedrich

19.1. Address Fold of Letter of March 16, 1844, Transmitted from Texas to Elze via Bremen

19.2. Address Fold of Letter of February 18, 1845, from Texas to Elze via New Orleans, Liverpool, and Le Havre

19.3. First Page of the Letter of February 10, 1845

19.4. Preliminary Conclusion of the Letter of February 10, 1845, with a Fine Example of Charles A. Giesecke's Signature

ABBREVIATIONS

NA   National Archives and Record Service of the United States. Washington

NHH   Nidersächsisches Hauptstaatsarchiv. Hannover (Lower Saxon Central State Archives. Hannover)

SAE   Stadtarchiv Elze (Municipal Archive Elze)

SB   Staatsarchiv der Freien Hansestadt Bremen (Archives of the Free Hanseatic City Bremen)

THE LURE OF AN HEIRLOOM:
IN PLACE OF A PREFACE

THE RESEARCH LEADING TO THIS BOOK began more than twenty years ago as a quest for background material for a chapter in a projected historical novel. I had just published a long scholarly work on German political culture during the nineteenth and twentieth centuries, and before completing the research for my next book, I intended to write an installment of the novel. The idea for the chapter had been suggested to me by some letters sent from Texas to Germany in the 1840s. This small packet had been handed down on my father's side of the family for three generations. I knew virtually nothing about the author of these letters, Charles A. Giesecke, except what could be derived from the letters themselves.

Soon the research for the novel became the tail that wagged the dog. My desire to understand the worlds Charles Giesecke inhabited led me ever farther into the history of the period. Finding the composition of another scholarly work more congenial than writing an historical novel, I postponed the latter task indefinitely.

Encouraged by the late Dr. Manfred Hamann, director of the Lower Saxon State Archives in Hannover, I wrote a book in German drawing on my research on Texas and Germany during the period of the Republic of Texas. This publication, which appeared in 1983,[1] includes in an appendix an edited transcription of the letters of Charles A. Giesecke in the original German. I planned to follow up the German work shortly with one in English that would pursue many of the same issues but would be designed for an English-speaking audience. Other research and writing prevented me for years from fulfilling my pledge to myself. In the interim, many people in Texas who knew no German but were fascinated by the subject of Germans in Texas pleaded with me to give them something they could read. With the exception of a lecture in Houston and copies of a paper from a conference, I had to disappoint them for a long time. At last in the late 1980s I found an opportunity to get out an installment on my promises in the form of an article exploring further some of the issues I had raised in the German book.

Several years later I was finally able to return for a sustained period to the material on Texas and Germany. The present work is the result. Far from being a mere translation, it is a new book. It has benefited from the opportunity to incorporate the fruits of new research by myself and others. I have been able to enrich the work in numerous areas with additional perspectives and details, most notably those relating to the migration of German craftsmen. I am now able to document Charles Giesecke's presence in Texas some years earlier than I was able to do previously, and this is simply one of numerous major and minor additions.

In the preface to the German book I remarked how much I had enjoyed doing the research. For the first time, my research led me to interact extensively with people other than scholars, librarians, and archivists in order to obtain sources, since significant portions of the material came from private individuals. In the interim since I began working on the German study, I have had extensive experience with oral sources for a long study of Nazism that also draws heavily on conventional sources. I see now more clearly than ten years ago how my research on Texas and Germany emboldened me to leave my desk and rely increasingly on the assistance of other people, whether scholars, officials, or just plain citizens. If I mentioned the names of everyone who aided significantly in the creation of the present book, the list would prolong this preface beyond the publisher's, if not the reader's, patience.

These generous people are concentrated in Lower Saxony, Bremen, New York, and Texas, with one important exception, a resident of the Rheinland, Jürgen Huck. The retired director of the municipal archives in Neuss, and for several decades the honorary director of the small municipal archive in his home town of Elze, he has been of inestimable assistance. One of the most selfless people I have ever known, he had responded generously to dozens of queries and supplied me with much material long before we at last met personally in Germany.

In the Lower Saxon communities of Alfeld, Bockenem, Bremen, Elze, Hannover, Hildesheim, and Wolfenbüttel, I found help not only in the archives, but also from what the Germans call *Heimatforscher*, a term that loses its folksy flavor when translated as "local historians." I am especially indebted to a chemist and *Heimatforscher*, the late Professor Georg Haeseler of Bockenem, for several critical bits of information. My friend and colleague Klaus J. Bade of the University of Osnabrück, one of the world's foremost experts on migration, has been a source of encouragement for twenty years now.

When I was preparing the first transcription of Charles Giesecke's old handwritten letters, Vernon Nelson, director of the Moravian Archives in Bethlehem, Pennsylvania, and his associate Dr. Lothar Madeheim gave me sound advice that facilitated the deciphering of symbols and letters. Dr. Walter L. Robbins, now at the University of Kentucky in Lexington, put at my disposal his rich knowledge of nineteenth-century German-American literature when I was entering a field largely new to me. Our conversations in a little town in Maine impelled me to look farther for material in unexpected places. Early versions of some of my findings were commented on helpfully by colleagues in New York: Emmanuel Chill, Judith Stein, and Michael Weisser. My dear friend and colleague Martin Waldman was, as always, generous with time and advice.

In Texas I received the most assistance from people in Angleton, Galveston (principally the archives of the Rosenberg Library), and Austin (especially from Dr. Michael Dabrishus prior to his retirement as head of the Texas State Archives). Theodore Gish of the University of Houston's program in Texas German Studies kindly helped me with several scholarly inquiries.

I would never have had the courage to continue the research necessary for this study without the easy availability of the enormous resources of the New York Public Library and its splendid collections pertaining to Germany and Texas. Its staff and that of the City College Library were ever ready to try to obtain material for me via interlibrary loan. During the past several summers, the personnel of the marvelous public library in the small community of Springvale, Maine, have been unstinting in their willingness to request old and obscure publications for me, even when those works bore seemingly endless German titles.

I am grateful to the Dun & Bradstreet Corporation in Wilton, Connecticut, for permission to cite the records of its predecessor, R. G. Dun & Company. This collection is housed in Historical Collections, Baker Library, Harvard University Graduate School of Business Administration in Boston; I would like to thank also Baker Library for its permission to cite these same records. The editors of the *Yearbook of German-American*

Studies have allowed me to utilize material I published in its pages.[2] I am indebted to Professor Terry G. Jordan for graciously permitting me to reproduce three charts from his *German Seed in Texas Soil.*[3]

New York
March 1995

GERMANS AND TEXANS

LOOK NOT FOR THREE THINGS, for you will not find them:
A person of knowledge whose deeds measure up to his knowledge,
A person of action whose heart is in accord with his deeds,
And a fellow human without faults.

> "Fozeil Ayâz" in *Quellen persischer Weisheit*
> (2. Aufl., St. Gallen, n.d.).

CONSTANT REVOLUTIONIZING OF PRODUCTION, uninterrupted
disturbance of all social conditions, everlasting uncertainty and
agitation distinguish the bourgeois epoch from all earlier ones. All
fixed, fast-frozen relations, with their train of ancient and venerable
prejudices and opinions, are swept away, all new-formed ones
become antiquated before they can ossify. All that is solid melts
into air, all that is holy is profaned, and man is at last compelled to
face with sober senses his real conditions of life and his relations
with his kind.

The need of a constantly expanding market for its products
chases the bourgeoisie over the whole surface of the globe. It must
nestle everywhere, establish connections everywhere.

> Karl Marx and Friedrich Engels,
> *The Communist Manifesto* (1848).

INTRODUCTION

DURING THE TEN-YEAR EXISTENCE of the Republic of Texas (1836–1846) the number of Germans in the population increased rapidly, mostly as a result of immigration. As the nineteenth century wore on, Germans, many of them relatives and acquaintances of people already living in Texas, continued to arrive, but in smaller numbers. The further settlement of Texas was accomplished primarily by migrants from the United States, supplemented during the twentieth century by Mexican immigrants. These late-coming Mexicans enlarged the indigenous Spanish-speaking segment of Texas inherited from the state's past as a part of Mexico.[1] Most people think correctly of Texas as an "Anglo" state with a large Mexican American minority and a smaller African American minority. European emigration to nineteenth-century Texas is still, despite some attention during recent decades, largely ignored, at least outside Texas.[2] Most European migrants to Texas were Germans, although significant numbers of other Central Europeans, such as Czechs and Wends, eventually arrived. The Wends, a small minority speaking a Slavic language in addition to German, came mainly from Saxony. The Germans in Texas and their descendants remained concentrated in two major areas: first, in Galveston, Houston, and generally along the eastern coast of south Texas; second, farther inland in the eastern and central regions of Texas, above all in the Hill Country along the Guadalupe, Colorado, and Brazos rivers.

Differences among the Germans in these two regions have resulted in misconceptions persisting to this day. Whatever else one may think of James Michener's *Texas*, for example, its treatment of Germans perpetuates a common misconception. Michener portrays Texas Germans as people who quickly adopted Anglo-American culture and speech.[3] It would be more historically accurate to depict the Germans near the coast as assimilating rapidly, and the Germans of the Hill Country as doing so slowly. The coastal Germans accepted the dominant culture, and English became their primary, soon only, language. However, the Germans of the Hill Country tended to retain German ways, including their language, and many continued to speak German into the twentieth century. As had occurred in some other sections of the United States, such as the Pennsylvania "Dutch" region, non-Germans in the area often learned German. Thus future President Lyndon Baines Johnson, scion of an "Anglo" family on his father's side, learned Texas German from his playmates.[4]

This book is about the short period during the 1830s and 1840s when it appeared to many people in America and Europe that Texas would harbor a large, permanent German colony. As has often been pointed out,[5] American scholars have concentrated on a single phase of the vast international migration of the past two centuries, the phase of immigration.[6] Even the recent revival of interest in the Germans of Texas has led to little research examining the emigrants in their homelands before departure.[7] The present work makes extensive use of primary sources from both sides of the Atlantic in examining the international movement of people and goods. The pages that follow bring together findings from several types of inquiries that are seldom combined in studies of American immigration. The basic objective has been to explore the interrelated processes of migration from one continent to another and the rooting of immigrants in the new continent. In recent years several works about Germans have successfully challenged older views stressing either the ease of migration or its difficulties.[8] Innovative studies of German migration to the United States have included analyses not only of the role of social class, but also of the importance, within the German diaspora, of regional and local identities derived from the homeland.[9] Stanley Nadel's excellent book on New York's "Little Germany" in the nineteenth century is one of a number of such studies. Nadel, however, overstresses the prototypical quality of this particular settlement.[10]

Germans have long had a romantic interest in Texas. This passion arose in the 1820s and intensified during the 1830s and 1840s. One of the early literary promoters of this enthusiasm was a renegade, German-speaking, former monk from Bohemia who, under the pen name Charles Sealsfield, became famous in both the United States and German-speaking Europe.[11] Down to the present day an intermittent fascination with Texas and Texas Germans has been manifest in Germany.[12] This fascination, however, has seldom led to detailed examinations of the fate of German immigrants there. The exception is the attention that has been given to the "Adelsverein," the association of German princes in the 1840s that sought to develop a German colony in Texas[13]. American research on Germans in Texas has been preoccupied with peasants and farmers, with the *Adelsverein*, with a handful of eccentrics such as that organization's commissioner-general, Prince Carl of Solms-Braunfels, and with the few highly educated men nicknamed "Latin farmers."

The present work deals with two important but largely neglected segments of the German populace: people from the numerous artisan occupations, and those from the much smaller group of merchants. This study is also intended to cast light on several aspects of the relationship between Texas and Germany. Among them are the social and economic conditions in Germany and Texas that induced many Germans to go to Texas and that structured the development of commerce between Germany and the Republic of Texas.

We shall often encounter striking differences between the society the Germans left and the one they entered, but this discovery should not obscure the basic similarities between the two worlds. Capitalism was well established in both of them. Both were developing and expanding bourgeois societies. A bourgeoisie rooted in the owners and managers of profit-making ventures and institutions was accumulating wealth and power. However, both societies harbored institutions and social arrangements that, perhaps falsely, appeared to many observers, both then and later, incompatible with the success of capitalism and with a bourgeois social order. In Texas these limitations or anomalies centered in the institution of slavery, which the Anglo-American colonists had imported from the United States despite its prohibition by the new Republic of Mexico. In Germany the limitations and anomalies consisted above all of two overlapping institutions: the survival of a legally privileged, landholding nobility with special rights in society and over peasants; and a web of restrictions upon the pursuit of business, of which some of the most visible were the maintenance of artisan guilds, often with exclusive commercial and production rights in a territory or in a branch of economic activity. Although Germany was almost invariably seen as part of an "Old World," and Texas as part of a "New World," this distinction was misleading. Both belonged to an expanding world of bourgeois societies that interacted with each other with increasing intensity. For example, the port of Galveston and the modern port of Bremen developed, as we shall see, through interaction with each other.

The objectives of our study will be pursued by examining the activities of three brothers who were merchants in Germany and Texas. The middle brother was eventually to become principally a farmer, although he preferred, pretentiously, to describe himself as a planter. This preference reflected the vanity of Charles A. Giesecke, as Anton Carl Giesecke (1811–1864/65) rechristened himself in America. The appendix contains a selection from his correspondence in 1844–1845 with his brother Fritz (Friedrich) in Germany. Born in a small town in the Hildesheim district of northern Germany, in what is today the German state of Lower Saxony, the three Giesecke brothers played a modest but noteworthy role in the development of commerce between Germany and Texas, as well as in furthering emigration from Bremen and the southern section of the Kingdom of Hannover to Texas.

If we are to understand the Gieseckes and many other Germans like them, we must put aside rigid preconceptions about immigrants in nineteenth-century America. One widely held notion is that immigrants were poor, but this is not true of the Giesecke brothers. They came from the upper, although not the uppermost, strata of society. Another preconception is that, until the days of transatlantic steamers and the mass migration of people back and forth across the ocean seeking jobs during the later nineteenth and early twentieth centuries,[14] immigrants arrived in America and stayed there. The Giesecke brothers did not stay put until they married in 1844–1845. Although there is no evidence that Edward (Eduard), the youngest of them, ever went back to Germany, Charles and Fritz crossed the Atlantic more than once. Fritz returned to Germany, married there, and remained in his mother's home town of Elze with her and his sister, Riecke (Friederike).

Like many merchants, Charles and Edward did not emigrate officially. Merchants often do not appear in German emigration statistics, although they generally appear in American immigration statistics — even if, like Fritz Giesecke, they returned to Europe. Later, during the period of rapid industrialization in the United States following the Civil War, returnees became commonplace. Many German and other European immigrants sought work, not a new home across the seas, and when they had saved up sufficient money, or the business cycle turned downward, they returned to their homelands, some permanently, others temporarily.[15] At the turn of the century, return migration rates soared; each year about half as many members of some southern European nationalities returned from the United States to their homelands as sailed in the opposite direction.[16] Reliable data on return rates for the first half of the nineteenth century is lacking. The proportion of returnees was not then as great as during the later years, but it was certainly far from negligible. Industrialization and improvements in transportation such as railways and steamships enabled faster transatlantic trips, but the biggest savings in travel time were effected by inland railways and waterways, which shortened the time required to reach ports or inland destinations. By the 1840s the traveler could already reckon with a fourteen-day passage across the Atlantic if sailing on a superior vessel, such as an American clipper ship with an experienced captain and crew. That is one reason why wind remained the principal means of transatlantic propulsion long after the development of steam-powered vessels suitable for the high seas. Even with the advent of the age of steamships in the late nineteenth century, travelers could not do much better than ten to fourteen days to Central European ports. Of course the bulk of the emigrant trade traveled with the slower ships. During the 1840s many a trip from Germany to a North American port lasted six to eight weeks.

The notion of nineteenth-century European immigrants as people who came intending to stay and carried out that resolve has not been as strong in Europe as in the United States. Returned "emigrants," often termed "Americans" in their home areas, were common in many parts of Europe by the latter half of the century. Some had become "rich uncles," while others were less fortunate or even broken men. One part of the European scholarly literature on emigration has emphasized the travails of the less fortunate immigrant. The great, but romantically distorted, work of the American historian Oscar Handlin, *The Uprooted*, also conveys forcefully the notion that acculturation and assimilation have been torturous processes for most immigrants.[17] This "European" perspective has otherwise been more likely to be found in studies by European scholars, although it is common in literary works, including some by European immigrants in America. Rølvaag's *Giants in the Earth* stands at the pinnacle of these literary works.[18] The novel follows a Norwegian couple from their home village on a fjord to their settlement in a remote section of the Midwest. The transition from the affluent peasant home of the woman's parents to the isolation and rigors of the prairie proves more than she can endure. Her psychic balance tips fatefully. Her optimistic husband is the opposite type of emigrant. He withstands every challenge until the ever-worsening illness of his wife and the raw power of nature on the frontier combine to kill him. The novel implies that, while the children and grandchildren of immigrants may complete the transition to America through acculturation and assimilation, immigration destroys the first generation and deforms subsequent generations.

The Gieseckes have little in common with either Rølvaag's Norwegians or the North German peasant from Mecklenburg, Jürnjakob Swehn, who is the central figure in a popular German novel based on the actual letters of an emigrant to America.[19] Granted, Swehn, like Charles and Fritz Giesecke, sails eastward as well as westward across the Atlantic, but under entirely different circumstances. Like Rølvaag's characters, Swehn belongs to a social stratum and an era different from those of the Gieseckes. The upright farmer Swehn, who is compelled to emigrate by the overcrowding of his homeland, recognizes toward the end of his life that he has always been dissatisfied in America. When World War I begins, he and his son set out for Germany. There the father can die in the comforting surroundings of his native village and the son can bear arms for his true Fatherland. Although the nationalistic bathos of this wartime German novel distorts Swehn's characteristics as an historical type, the core of the novel provides a simple poetic description of the inability of a rural North German emigrant to take root in America.

When Charles Giesecke returned to Germany, it was to pursue business affairs. Evidently, he experienced no significant problems of acculturation or assimilation. He knew how to do business in two worlds. He accommodated himself to America. In this respect he had much in common with the industrial worker of a later age who earned a livelihood both in Europe and in the United States. But more than the abysses of era and social position separated Charles from that worker. Charles had, or quickly gained, a knowledge of languages that enabled him to conduct his affairs easily in Texas.

Cultural differences other than language existed between Texas and Charles Giesecke's homeland, or more precisely between the life of a German burgher of the *Biedermeier* era and that of a member of the propertied classes in America during the 1830s and 1840s. These differences, however, were not so imposing that Charles was devastated or alienated by them. The middle-class world of merchants and landowners was already largely internationalized. He belonged to a social group possessing a similar culture, whether in Germany or America. This is not to deny the presence of cultural differences or to claim the existence of a single, uniform culture. Differences in language alone precluded that. Yet crucial common elements in the two worlds predominated. As best we can surmise, Charles experienced none of the culture shock or other agonies of migration that are documented in the works of writers, sociologists, and historians. He encountered more prosaic difficulties in the "New World" — business problems. They had little or nothing to do with psychic malaise triggered by migration, and everything to do with the search for profit. Existence near the American frontier and life in *Biedermeier* Germany were in many ways more similar than we might assume. The letters of Charles Giesecke reveal a Texas in which the merchant with his ledger and his stock was a familiar sight. We gain a perspective that counterbalances the fabled Texan of Walter Prescott Webb's frontier, with his horse and six shooter.[20] The merchant did not simply follow the cowboy; often the merchant preceded him. Charles Giesecke serves to remind us that, as Webb certainly recognized, before the growth of the great herds in the latter half of the nineteenth century, and before the human social order that created them, a commercial culture existed in Texas. Although Webb saw clearly that the frontier played a dynamic role in the development of capitalism, he entrapped himself in a romantic preoccupation with one aspect of Texan history. A study investigating the activities of the Gieseckes can contribute to a better understanding of the place of German merchants in the development of America and Germany in the nineteenth century.

We want to ascertain how it was possible for the Gieseckes to adapt themselves to business in Texas. Herbert G. Gutman writes suggestively about the ability of American immigrants during the industrial era preceding World War I to utilize customs from their old culture to forge weapons enabling them to assert themselves against both their employers and agencies of the state.[21] Gutman tries to show that these immigrants did not disappear into a "melting pot," but rather drew upon their culture to forge tools and weapons in the new country for their lives as industrial workers. His thesis can be applied *mutatis mutandis* to other groups. The German merchant in the antebellum period could derive much support from the culture in which he had grown up, even if he did not live in a German enclave in America. In addition, he was able to obtain information, equipment, workers, goods, and much else from his homeland, as did Charles Giesecke.

The Germany Charles left, as well as the Texas he settled in, were developing bourgeois societies. Neither was in every respect more advanced than the other, and often they complemented each other. The tempo of change differed, but the direction was similar. The initial encounter with several of the similarities came as a surprise to me — all the more because I was raised neither in Texas nor in Germany. Like most other historians I had no idea that the great ports of Galveston and modern Bremen emerged contemporaneously, as did the development of their hinterlands. What I learned pursuing the history of the Gieseckes first called my attention to the many ways in which the growth of the two harbors was intertwined.

The life of the merchant and "planter" Charles Giesecke is no exceptional case in the history of Texas during his era. This is not to contest his pronounced individuality. A restless man driven by a passion to succeed in business, he wielded a caustic pen. He felt no compunction about offering his opinion on virtually any matter. His self-assertiveness was that of the man who welcomes decisive action, attempts to master the determinants of his life, and seeks to shape his age. This description begins to suggest a larger-than-life Balzacian character, but there is another side to Charles's personality. Tempered by the frustrations of existence on both sides of the Atlantic, he exhibited more mundane qualities. Thus on a chilly day in March 1844 he sits down to write to his older brother in Germany. Charles's cheek is puffed out by a bad tooth, but for the moment he is distracted by his vituperative recounting of their younger brother's business dealings in Texas. Then, seemingly oblivious to the vast expanse separating him from Germany, he requests his brother in Germany to dispatch a time-tried nostrum for tooth aches. Was Charles vainly clutching at hope, as he so often had? We trust that the physical pain subsided before the soothing lilac arrived — if it ever came.

PART 1

World of Origin:

NORTH GERMANY IN THE BIEDERMEIER ERA

1

GERMAN PATRICIANS AND MERCHANTS
IN CRISIS

GERMANY HAD A SURPLUS of merchants during the first half of the nineteenth century. Population growth, the consequences of the industrial revolution in Britain, and the degradation of old methods of production reduced the occupational prospects for merchants. Their opportunities constricted. Many markets disappeared. Until well into the middle of the century, the situation of the small merchant deteriorated due to the rise of large commercial firms.

In the Kingdom of Hannover one of the advocates of traditional economic protectionism was the prominent scholar Gustav von Gülich. His was one of many voices calling for measures to limit the number of merchants, or people in the "selling estate [*Kaufmannsstand*]."[1] Despite the influence of the French Revolution, most of Germany remained a status society. Changes in the social and economic situation of families and individuals were assumed to occur slowly over the course of generations. There was no dearth of proposals for reform, whether to promote industrialization or to inhibit its development. Although conservative and reactionary forces opposed to rapid industrial development had the upper hand throughout Germany, no state adopted a consistent economic policy. The situation in the Kingdom of Hannover was typical of the impasse. Attempts to establish uniform regulations for the varied territories in Hannover had been stymied by 1831.[2] Even proposals for minor changes were regarded as dangerous precedents by many artisans and those wishing to avoid civic strife. Although Germans did not anticipate sudden riches and rapid social ascent, they expected state and society to protect their places in the community. Yet many were faced with a precipitous decline in their station in life. Within the ranks of the bourgeoisie, which consisted mainly of merchants, other businessmen, and university-trained professionals, this crisis offered both dangers and grounds for optimism. Although the recurrent problem of providing for the future of the progeny of the bourgeoisie intensified after the defeat of Napoleon and the initiation of the Restoration in 1815, promising solutions beckoned. Many merchants with only modest or little capital determined to try their luck overseas and took ship for North or South America. There they expected to utilize their connections, skills, and material resources in a desperate effort to increase their economic chances.[3] Writing in the mid-1830s after a visit to Missouri, Nicholas Hesse cautiously appraised the prospects for merchants in the United States:

> Merchants, who possess adequate means, and have the necessary business experience, who are able to acquaint themselves with the peculiarities of the local trade, and who are good salesmen of the goods they have, will certainly not prove failures if they have a thorough knowledge of English and know how to find the right location. Of course, they must not be too conservative in starting a new venture. Only he who takes a chance in America, can gain something worthwhile, like the gambler with his 'quit or double!' . . . In this land of speculation not much is gained without daring, and he who is too cautious may be compared to a creature suspended between heaven and earth, without being able to descend or ascend. The golden mean is never observed.[4]

Other sons of the bourgeoisie, rather than leaving their homeland, attempted to improve their situation by becoming citizens of neighboring or distant towns, or even moving to large cities. However, the last alternative required substantial capital. In Alfeld, a small town in the Duchy of Hildesheim in the south of the Kingdom of Hannover in the immediate area where the Gieseckes lived, the fees necessary to become a full-fledged citizen had reached 31 *Reichstaler* by the nineteenth century. This amount was necessary simply to acquire the highest level of citizenship, the so-called *große Bürgerrecht*, which entitled its holder to conduct business. German towns retained many elements of a status society that had no place for the concept of the "rights of man" or general citizenship. By 1859 the price of citizenship in Alfeld had risen to 39 Reichstaler.[5] The significance of such sums becomes clear when we find that the entire annual cost of maintaining an artisan family of four to five people in a small town in 1820 was estimated at one hundred Reichstaler.[6] Moreover, the cost of acquiring citizenship in a town was only a small part of the expenditures required to become a merchant there. The highest level of citizenship necessitated ownership of a house with "brewing rights." The candidate for this level of citizenship had to inherit or purchase property to which the medieval householder's privilege of brewing beer was attached. The acquisition of a lower level of citizenship such as the *kleines Bürgerrecht* and a less favored property, a *Kleinbürgerhaus*, was cheaper, but the applicant obtained fewer rights and privileges and had to be entitled to engage in an artisan trade. In little Elze, the birthplace of the mother of the Giesecke brothers, the distinction between different types of citizenship did not exist; citizenship cost fifteen Reichstaler uniformly in 1817. A few years later the cost had decreased. When the father of the Giesecke brothers became a citizen of Elze in 1824, he paid eleven Reichstaler, including one as a contribution to fire equipment.[7]

Opportunities may have been greater in large towns and cities, but the costs of becoming a merchant were considerably greater. After 1820 the acquisition of the highest level of citizenship (*das Große Bürgerrecht mit Handlungsfreiheit*) in Bremen cost four hundred Reichstaler in gold.[8] With this purchase came the privilege of pursuing a wholesale trade, but that was only the beginning of the expenditures required for founding a firm. The merchant still needed to establish a household and open an office. A major factor in the increase in opportunities was the revival of Bremen's overseas trade following the Napoleonic era, which propelled a stream of merchants to the United States.[9] This relocation of merchants opened up opportunities in North German towns for the remaining merchants who could raise enough capital to found a firm or — as was often common among merchants from the hinterland — to join an existing firm.[10] Little wonder that only about one-tenth of the ten thousand people who became citizens of Bremen from 1840 to 1862 acquired the highest level of citizenship.[11] In view of the substantial capital outlays, powerful family connections, and good business ties that were the ordinary prerequisites to becoming a big merchant, many a son of the bourgeoisie was attracted to the idea of working overseas. After all, he normally did not expect to stay there permanently. Firms from the Hanseatic cities — Hamburg, Bremen, and Lübeck — sent abroad employees, who did not have to possess capital of their own. Although the number of such positions remained modest until the end of the nineteenth century,[12] the overseas firms created a large network of German merchants.

Limits on opportunities for members of the bourgeoisie to work for big firms abroad arose from the nature of the parent firms. Even the big firms were still family businesses through the middle decades of the century, and their branches overseas were small. Generally, they had only a partner and one or two clerks. For example, a study of the period 1844–1845 ascertained that nine firms had branches in New Orleans. These branches employed a total of only 17 partners and 25 clerks.[13] The pattern in other American ports was similar. In New York, the port with, by far, the most German branches, there were 62 firms with 64 partners and 132 clerks. The German firms abroad could absorb only a fraction of the many young sons of the bourgeoisie who went overseas. Most had to find other employment for themselves.

Conditions in Germany encouraged people with little or no capital to start a business abroad, where there were fewer restrictions on business, in the hope that orders from other German merchants could be obtained. A goodly number of opportunities for such orders resulted from the expansion of German firms; the commercial houses liked to work with German merchants abroad. Businessmen from the same hometown as that of the German firm were preferred.[14] It was legally much easier to found a firm in America than in Germany. Of course many American firms were short lived. Only a small minority of the German merchants going to America could reasonably hope to support themselves through dealings with German firms. Nicholas Hesse, a well-informed German visitor to the United States, estimated in the mid-1830s that a family of six could travel from their home in Germany to St. Louis via Bremen for 549 Reichstaler, including living costs. He stressed that his calculations were for a family accustomed to frugality and that his estimate for passage across the Atlantic presupposed sailing third class with reduced fares for children under twelve.[15] A merchant traveling alone would have been likely to pay considerably more than a sixth of this sum, primarily because he would book better accommodations and would not be able to effect the savings in living costs obtainable by several people traveling together.

Before the 1840s the situation of many a German bourgeois had already become precarious. Old families accustomed for generations to prestige, wealth, and power had to exert themselves if they were to have any chance of retaining their property and social rank. The beginnings of industrialization, still lagging far behind Britain's development, were exerting a leveling effect upon society. Many a measure to rescue position and wealth began as a family endeavor and ended as a medley of individual efforts. Old bourgeois families succeeded or fell apart in the course of these exertions. The response of the Giesecke family to this situation was to lead to its disintegration.

2

THE HOMELAND OF THE GIESECKES

HEINRICH FRIEDRICH GIESECKE, father of Charles A. Giesecke, was born in 1776 in Gittelde, a small community of about a thousand people close to the Harz Mountains in northern Germany. Near the junctures of several states in the patchwork quilt of eighteenth-century Germany, Gittelde belonged to the Duchy of Brunswick. Although Heinrich Friedrich's mother came from a nearby community, his father was a "farmer and businessman [*Acker-und Handelsmann*]" with deep family roots in Gittelde.[1]

Several branches of Gieseckes resided there when Heinrich Friedrich was growing up. Members of one of these lines hauled freight on the route from Bremen to Nürnberg. Several decades later, when the Gieseckes in Texas and Elze shipped goods in both directions on this same route, one of these other Giesecke families in Gittelde was still serving as carters to and from Bremen.[2] Gittelde had some metallurgical industries as well as agriculture, and Heinrich Friedrich's ancestors included both smiths and farmers. He was the youngest of three sons who reached adulthood. His older brother became a citizen and master baker in Gandersheim, a small town and administrative center belonging also to the Duchy of Brunswick. The second brother became a storekeeper in Gittelde; he was the only one of the three to remain in the town of their birth. The practice of moving to establish a career elsewhere had long been common among bourgeois families, especially those in small communities and with more than one male heir. Prudence — and ambition — dictated the geographical dispersal of the bourgeoisie, but in the nineteenth century the numbers of people as well as the distances involved increased, often dramatically.

Heinrich Friedrich Giesecke and his family found a niche for him outside Gittelde. He became an enterprising businessman in Bockenem, another small town in the area. Although not far from Gittelde, Bockenem had belonged, politically, to the Bishopric of Hildesheim until the secularization of the Bishopric under Napoleon. The bishop failed to regain his temporal powers with the Restoration 1814–1815; the new Kingdom of Hannover absorbed most of the Bishopric's former territory. Located near the northwestern rim of the Harz Mountains, Bockenem had about 1800 inhabitants in the early nineteenth century.[3] This approached twice as many as Gittelde, which, unlike Bockenem, was a mere *Flecken*, a designation for a community that was neither a *Stadt* (town, city) nor a village. Towns and cities — the German language has only one word for both — had charters, often going back to grants of liberties from medieval princes, conceding economic privileges and the right of self-government or self-administration.

Bockenem was what the Germans appropriately call an *Ackerbürgerstadt*. It depended mainly on agriculture. Even its full citizens (*Bürger*) engaged in farming; a number of them were "gentlemen" farmers who directed the cultivation of their own or leased land while engaging also in other economic pursuits. More important economically than Gittelde, Bockenem was the principal town in the Ambergau, an agriculturally rich area on the Nette River southeast of the city of Hildesheim.[4] As occurred in countless other small German towns, many of Bockenem's residents supported themselves partly or entirely through handicrafts and cottage and textile industries. Textile production in Bockenem consisted mainly of spinning yarn from flax. An official report of 1808 confirms Heinrich Friedrich Giesecke's residence there and lists him as the owner a "horse[-powered] oil mill."[5] This installation pressed oil from flax or rape seeds. According to the report, Bockenem had in addition to this oil mill two other "sizable" undertakings of note: a potash works and a tobacco factory.[6] The latter belonged to a patrician, municipal Senator Christian August Giesecke, who had been born in nearby Peine. Despite the shared surname, he and Heinrich Friedrich were not closely related.[7]

Heinrich Friedrich's position as a well-established citizen of Bockenem is attested to by his civic activities as well as his position as a merchant. In 1808 he had led a group of fellow citizens in the town council and successfully pursued a complaint against the mayor. The grievance hinged on a situation easily imagined in an agricultural community. The mayor had sold the second crop of hay from a community meadow to obtain cash for his salary; the complainants wanted to uphold their custom of using the meadow to graze their animals.[8] Although in 1813 Heinrich Friedrich advertised rum of his own making,[9] his principal occupation in Bockenem was the cloth trade. He was one of the refounders of the local merchants' guild in 1817. The guild's objectives included the introduction of means to combat peddling.[10] In the future only those possessing both a guild master's certificate and municipal citizenship would be permitted to sell cloth. These demands were among the many attempts to roll back reforms of the era of the French Revolution and Napoleon, when freedom of trade had been introduced into the entire area of Lower Saxony. A series of government decrees in 1817 reestablished guilds in the Hildesheim district.[11]

Heinrich Friedrich had married well in 1808. His bride was Luise *Amalie* Sander, a "young lady [*Demoiselle*]" from a patrician family in Elze.[12] With some 1,800 inhabitants Elze was about the same size as Bockenem, but Elze had the distinction of being one of the oldest communities in the district.[13] Charlemagne had designated Elze in 796 the seat of a bishopric that a quarter century later, however, was transferred to Hildesheim. For generations the male members of Amalie Sander's family had been pastors, other university-educated professionals, landowners, and businessmen. Her mother's father had been the proprietor of Elze's principal inn, the "Golden Star [*Der Güldene Stern*]," as well as the owner and administrator of various agricultural lands in the area. Her father, Anton Christian Sander, was serving as deputy mayor of Elze at the time of her marriage. He was to become mayor in 1815.

Born in the Brunswick town of Wolfenbüttel in 1752, then still the seat of government of the Duchy of Brunswick-Wolfenbüttel, Anton Christian Sander was the son of a court apothecary. In the last decades of the preceding century the famous philosopher G. W. Leibniz had been the librarian of the extraordinary ducal library in Wolfenbüttel, even today one of Europe's most famous collections of books and manuscripts. Before Anton Christian Sander reached his majority, the classic German writer, dramatist, and critic G. E. Lessing became one of Leibniz's successors as librarian.

As possessions of the Bishopric of Hildesheim, until its secularization and inclusion in the new Napoleonic Kingdom of Westphalia in 1808, Elze and Bockenem had shared a common history during the Middle Ages and the Reformation very different from that of the neighboring Brunswick territories, which included Gittelde, Gandersheim, and Wolfenbüttel. To be sure, most of northwestern Germany was united briefly in the Kingdom of Westphalia, but the Restoration of 1814–1815 redivided Brunswick and Hannover. The revived Duchy of Brunswick received most of the old Brunswick towns, while the newly created Kingdom of Hannover obtained territories of the pre-Napoleonic Electorate of Hannover as well as some new possessions, including the lands of the former Bishopric of Hildesheim. Elze and Bockenem remained politically under the aegis of authorities in an office in Hildesheim, now known as a *Landdrostei*, which governed the Hildesheim area reorganized into a Hannoverian administrative district.

Like most North Germans, the Gieseckes and Sanders were Protestants in an overwhelmingly Protestant region of the country. Their hometowns had few Catholics. The Kingdom of Hannover that emerged from the Napoleonic Wars was a Protestant state. However, the religious situation in the Hildesheim district was more complicated than that in most of North Germany. The outcome of the struggles of the Reformation era had left the Bishopric of Hildesheim Catholic. Not until 1711, and only under pressure from the Elector of Hannover, did Protestants in the lands of the Bishopric receive guarantees of religious freedom. The Protestants of Elze, Bockenem, and the remainder of the Hildesheim district were governed after 1814, as they had been since before the Reformation, from the historically Catholic city of Hildesheim. The city of Hildesheim and some of the communities surrounding it continue down to the present to be heavily or predominantly Catholic. Despite the increasing secularization of institutions in the early nineteenth century, Hildesheim's continuation as an island of Catholicism still posed a threat in the eyes of the Protestants of the district. To be sure, the situation was radically different from that endured by their ancestors after the Reformation, when the Catholic bishop of Hildesheim had continued to serve also as a temporal ruler. This arrangement continued until the dissolution of the Holy Roman Empire under Napoleon's influence in 1806. The temporal powers of the bishop of Hildesheim were not restored in 1815 after the fall of Napoleon. The Kingdom of Hannover was dominated by Protestants. It was ruled by the King of England under the personal union with Great Britain that had begun in 1714 when the Elector of Hannover ascended the English throne as George I. Despite many changes favorable to Protestantism, the Protestants of the Hildesheim area remained apprehensive about the Catholicism of the district capital and their neighbors after 1815, when the generation of Gieseckes who later became involved with Texas was growing up in Bockenem.

Their grandfather Anton Christian Sander, unlike his ancestors for generations, had not become an apothecary or a pastor. Upon his marriage in 1779 Anton Christian had moved to Elze, the hometown of some of his Sander ancestors. Indeed, his wife, Sophia Dorothea, had been born in

Elze: her maiden name was Sander, and she was a distant cousin. Like many a carefully contracted bourgeois marriage, this union brought the groom the prospect of a substantial addition to his resources. For generations Sanders from the various lines in Elze had held municipal offices and intermarried with other patrician families from Elze and other towns in the region. Both Anton Christian and Sophia Dorothea were related to the Falcke family, the source of several of the highest judicial officials serving the government in Hannover during the eighteenth and nineteenth centuries.

In Elze Anton Christian Sander became an *Ackerbürger*, a gentleman farmer. He had a large house and administered 17 *Morgen* of farmland that had belonged to Lieutenant Colonel Sander. This Hannoverian officer, who died in 1800 in Harburg, then in Hannoverian territory and today part of Hamburg, was a brother of his mother-in-law. As early as 1769 another brother of Anton Christian's mother-in-law had been in America as a soldier,[14] but nothing has turned up to suggest any direct link between this experience overseas and her Giesecke grandsons' trips to Texas more than half a century later. It is noteworthy that the mother-in-law, too, had been born a Sander and married a relative, although in this instance one from Elze.

Anton Christian Sander and Sophia Dorothea Sander had four children who survived childhood, but their only son died in 1803 at the age of 20. This gap in the Sander family was filled years later by the Gieseckes from Bockenem. Only one of the Sander daughters remained in Elze after marriage. The oldest married a country doctor, the surgeon (*Landchirug*) Johann Alhardt Horn from the neighboring town of Gronau.[15] The youngest daughter married the scion of another patrician family in Elze, Christoph *Carl* Basse, who at the time of his marriage was already a member of the town council, and the couple remained in their hometown. Their nuptials were celebrated in 1808, the same year as Amalie Sander's marriage to Heinrich Friedrich Giesecke. Both events were recorded in a beautiful hand in the new local civil marriage register of the Kingdom of Westphalia. The names and personal data of the prominent guests and relatives were carefully noted.[16]

Heinrich Friedrich Giesecke and Amalie Sander also had four children. Their three sons and only daughter were born in Bockenem during the first two decades of the nineteenth century: Friedrich (Fritz), the oldest, in 1809; Anton Carl, who was to anglicize his name to Charles A. Giesecke in Texas, in 1811; Ernst *Eduard* (Edward) in 1815; and, finally, their sister

Friederike, known to family and friends as "Riecke," in 1819. Friedrich, or Fritz, was given his father's first name; the future Charles had the same initials as his maternal grandfather Sander, A. C., but only the first name derived from his grandfather Sander. The second name came from his uncle Carl Basse.

In the fall of 1820 grandfather Anton Christian Sander died in Elze. Long ailing, grandmother Sander had predeceased him by several years. These deaths opened the possibility of the Gieseckes retaining one of the Sander family's houses in Elze. From the available records it is not clear who administered Anton Christian's estate. However, Anton Christian's son-in-law in Elze, Carl Basse, who was to become treasurer of Elze in 1821, was often entrusted with matters concerning inheritances.[17] Basse and his wife were childless after twelve years of marriage; nor did they have any children subsequently. Although Basse's own financial situation later became precarious,[18] he and his wife were well situated during the 1820s to look benevolently upon the children of their close relatives. In 1824 Heinrich Friedrich Giesecke became a citizen of Elze,[19] although he continued to maintain his household in Bockenem. His sons were confirmed in the Protestant Church in Bockenem during the mid-1820s. After Heinrich Friedrich died in January 1831, his widow Amalie eventually returned to live in her birthplace.

In addition to Amalie's inheritance of the house in Elze, conditions in both Elze and Bockenem may well have contributed to the move and its timing. Only two months after her husband's death a terrible fire in Bockenem destroyed sixteen large buildings and many smaller ones. This great fire of 1831 was merely one of several major fires there during the 1830s and 1840s. Those of 1832 and 1833 were almost as bad as that of 1831; the fire of 1834 was even worse.[20] Bockenem deserved its nickname "the town of many fires." Although many other small towns, including Elze, were known by this same designation, the fires of the early 1830s in Bockenem may have provided another impetus for the Gieseckes to move to Elze. On the other hand, their settlement there may have been postponed by the great fire that ravaged more than half of Elze in 1824.[21]

Frau Giesecke had other reasons to be discouraged by the initial results of her endeavor to establish her family in Elze. In 1832 she requested a concession to run a textile store in the old family house. In her application to the municipal authorities she listed the address of her sister and brother-in-law only a few doors away. Perhaps she was living temporarily with them, or perhaps she continued to reside in Bockenem while awaiting the outcome of her request. The district authorities in Hildesheim, whose approval was necessary, viewed her application skeptically. The royal officials feared that granting her a concession in a town of only 1800 inhabitants would diminish unduly the orders obtained by other local businesses.[22] The town officials, however, supported her throughout a long, wearisome correspondence with Hildesheim. Whether potential competitors contacted the authorities in Hildesheim is uncertain from the records. The primary justification offered by the town officials for her petition was the lack of a textile shop at the one end of the town. Hildesheim queried suspiciously if Elze did not already have too many textile dealers, whether the house did not actually belong to the Giesecke children, and whether the proposed business was really necessary for the support of the widow. The town officials sought to undercut these objections: her resources were modest; the major part consisted of seven *Morgen* (less than five acres)[23] of garden, farming, and meadow land; the Widow Giesecke intended eventually to yield her municipal citizenship to "her son," who had "learned the trade."[24] In other words, her oldest son, Fritz, would take over the business. The town reported eventually that other people who had submitted similar applications had withdrawn or altered them. Finally, in September 1832 the authorities in Hildesheim granted her request.

Elze's census of 1833 listed none of the Gieseckes, but the next census, that of 1836, lists the Widow Giesecke.[25] She was living in the house inherited from her father; the household consisted of two other females and a male. These three must have been her son Fritz, her daughter, and a servant. In 1839, according to the census of that year, the Basses continued to live nearby in Elze, and another male, aged 20 to 45, was living in Amalie's household. This person is likely to have been another servant or an apprentice, rather than her youngest son, Edward, who arrived that year in New Orleans en route to Texas.[26]

Elze suffered, as did Bockenem and many other towns, from the competition its artisans faced from local nonguild craftsmen. Although Elze remained an agricultural town, its development depended upon its favorable location astride trade routes. East-west trade from the Rheinland went through or near Elze. In 1841 a municipal report complained that as a consequence of concessions in the surrounding villages, the once numerous shoemakers of Elze had been badly hurt. Almost fifty master shoemakers had been forced out of business.[27] The next year the town officials justified their opposition to the settling of Jews in Elze with the explanation that commerce and crafts were already oversaturated. In 1847 the officials reported to Hildesheim that many artisans were now producing only for the markets of cities and led miserable existences. The attempt by the mayor to get a factory to locate in town fell through when the entrepreneur settled in Bremen. The only larger undertaking in Elze, that of the clock-maker and organ builder Philipp Furtwängler, an ancestor of the renowned conductor and composer Wilhelm Furtwängler, was still modest before the middle of the century. With the exception of agriculture and commerce there was only one other trade that brought substantial income to Elze. This was tanning, which supplied leather to the many local shoemakers. In 1848 municipal officials reported that the two tanneries produced some fifty to sixty thousand pounds (500 to 600 *Zentner*) of leather per year. Raw leather for soles was obtained from South America. The finished leather was sold locally or sent to Hannover. It was estimated that the annual wages of the workers employed by the tanneries totaled 2000 Reichstaler. Expenditures for raw material for the tanneries came to roughly the same amount. Although no weaving establishment was located in Elze, spinning linen yarn was a secondary occupation engaged in by many inhabitants.[28]

Neither Bockenem nor Elze were towns of importance for the production of textiles, but Alfeld (not to be confused with Alsfeld in Hessen), a larger town close to Elze, had a well-known linen industry. On the instructions of the authorities in Hildesheim, a linen standard office (*Linnen-Legge*) was opened in Alfeld in 1829.[29] Linens made in Alfeld, Elze, and the Bilderlahe and Gronau-Poppenburg subdistricts (*Ämtern*) were brought there to be measured and stamped. The Gronau-Poppenburg subdistrict (*Amt*) included villages and other communities in the Elze area. The purpose of the linen office was to raise the quality of linens in the region and standardize them in order to facilitate their sale in larger and more distant markets. In the course of the 1830s additional linen standard offices for "Alfeld Linens" were opened in several other communities.[30] During the mid-1840s Charles Giesecke was ordering Alfeld linens to sell in Texas.

The prolonged difficulties of the German textile industry in the first half of the nineteenth century led many people to emigrate.[31] The spinning of flax and the weaving of linens had been a seasonal and part-time occupation of the rural populace since the Middle Ages. This highly elastic, often marginal segment of the linen industry was extremely sensitive to changes in demand. Prior to the Napoleonic Wars there had been a large market for coarse linens from European countries for use as slave clothing in the Americas. Napoleon's continental system and the British blockade temporarily closed off the entire overseas market, but the end of these barriers to exports in 1814–1815 brought no great upswing to the traffic in German linens. Britain's victory over its rivals in the battle for world empire and the success of industrial capitalism with its effective application of new technology created the preconditions for the worldwide triumph of English cotton goods. They began to supplant linens even on the German market. It has been argued that the prices of Hannoverian linens fell 50 to 80 percent from 1819 to 1821.[32] Russian and Prussian tariffs increased the difficulties of the North German linen industry in the European market. Then in 1824 the protectionist "American System" of Henry Clay achieved its first legislative victory when higher duties were imposed on textiles. The increases in U.S. tariffs reached a pinnacle in 1828 with the "Tariff of Abominations." Although the American tariff law of 1833 initiated a tendency toward lower duties that was sustained through the next two decades, the U.S. market would never again look as promising as it had immediately following the Peace Settlement of 1814–1815. To be sure, the revolt of Latin America against European domination and the Mexican declaration of independence from Spain in 1821 had greatly improved the prospects for overseas' markets, but these openings were offset by increased competition from England and France.[33]

Baron von Reden, general secretary of the Business Association for the Kingdom of Hannover, was optimistic in 1839 and expected access to large new markets.[34] He described the flax and linen industry as the most important in the entire Kingdom of Hannover.[35] Yet the linen crisis refused to go away. The poorest strata of the rural populace were hardest hit. Many businessmen and other bourgeois were partly shielded from its effects during the 1820s and 1830s. They had time to withdraw their capital from the linen industry and reinvest it elsewhere. The most favored investments were the costs of relocating within Europe and those of emigration overseas. This was the case in the Kingdom of Hannover, where industrialization was not encouraged by state policy as it was in Prussia's Rhine Province. Having been a nonindustrial segment of the British Empire through the personal union of the Hannoverian and British crowns, Hannover did not initiate basic policy changes when Queen Victoria's accession to the British throne compelled the dissolution of this union. Like most German states Hannover limited freedom of occupation, preserved guilds, and curtailed the free movement of the population.[36]

Agriculture provided another source of capital for new investments.[37] Reforms facilitating the extraction of capital from agriculture were initiated during the late eighteenth century in the Bishopric of Hildesheim, to which Elze as well as Bockenem then belonged.[38] These reforms encouraged the development of capitalistic relations in agriculture. The changes included the conversion of old obligations of the rural populace into money payments to the holders of seigneurial rights. Further reforms were carried out under the Kingdom of Westphalia during the Napoleonic era, but many of the innovations were undone by the Restoration beginning in 1814. The next important reforms came with the Hannoverian decrees of 1824 and 1825 permitting the division of common lands. The transformation of service and other obligations into money rents also was promoted. The measures of 1824 and 1825 generally favored the operations of the larger landholders, while the poorest strata of the rural populace were adversely affected. Further laws in 1831 and 1833 had a similar impact and hastened the termination of many old obligations by permitting a one-time money payment in their stead. Although some larger property owners opted to collect regular rents in place of single payments, many others preferred a one-time payment whereby they obtained substantial capital for agricultural or other investments. Since the agrarian reforms of the 1820s and 1830s had unfavorable consequences for much of the rural populace and coincided with the crisis of the artisan system, these reforms served to increase the flow of poor emigrants.[39] Much of the capital generated or freed by agrarian reform was invested elsewhere in Germany, often in rapidly developing areas such as Prussia's Rhine Province or Bremen's new harbor, known as Bremerhaven, which was opened in 1830. However, the possibility of investing money overseas was attractive to many of the more affluent people who were being adversely affected by the decline of old trades and businesses.

3

BREMEN AND ITS HINTERLAND

ONE OF THE EARLIEST GERMAN BOOKS about Texas, published in 1834 when Texas still belonged to Mexico, cautioned against viewing Texas as an "El Dorado."[1] The author, long known only by his pseudonym, Detlef Dunt, warned his readers not to think they could become rich effortlessly in Texas. However, Dunt went on to suggest that immigrants could improve their economic situation in Texas. Later in the book he was more concrete: "Young, robust people, who can do good work and have only about seventy to eighty Reichstaler in resources with which to get here [Texas], will find that with only a bit of luck their fortunes are made."[2] We can begin to measure the value of eighty Reichstaler if we recall that full citizenship in a small German town cost about half this amount. A few other statistics will make clear why Dunt regarded emigration to Texas so favorably. An assistant bookkeeper at a savings bank in Bremen received 100 to 150 Reichstaler annually in 1831, while the head bookkeeper received 400. The twenty-two-year-old German Ferdinand Freiligrath, later famous as a political poet, received what he termed "a moderate salary" corresponding to 340 to 396 Reichstaler for his services as a commercial clerk in Amsterdam in 1832. Twenty-eight-year-old Johann Höpken managed to establish himself as a merchant in Bremen with 500 borrowed Reichstaler in 1830, although generally a merchant needed an initial capital of several thousand. Yet a small shopkeeper in a provincial town had annual gross sales of less than 3,000 Reichstaler.[3]

German emigration to America began in the seventeenth century at the same time that the English and Dutch were founding permanent, lasting settlements.[4] From the late seventeenth to the late eighteenth century many German emigrants to America were Pietists, Anabaptists, and other members of small sects located in the Rhenish Palatinate and elsewhere along the Rhine. Never again in the history of German emigration would such a large proportion belong to small sects. Many of these emigrants left a region where the farmland had been so subdivided that few peasants had enough property to live off their own holdings. Often lacking passage money, German settlers of that era chose to become indentured for several years to pay off their passage. They became virtual slaves in America for up to seven years, if they lived that long—for not a few perished sooner. These "redemptionists" settled primarily in Pennsylvania in the region from Philadelphia to the line of European settlement east of the Allegheny Mountains. Large numbers of Germans spilled over into adjoining areas in the present states of West Virginia, Maryland, and New York. Smaller settlements were founded in the eighteenth century in locations as widely distant as Waldoboro in Maine, several sites in Georgia, and Winston-Salem in the Carolinas. Waldoboro was settled mostly by peasants from Brunswick, adjoining Hannover, and from other parts of North and Central Germany. Among the sites in Georgia, Ebenezer was settled by some of the Protestants expelled by the Archbishop of Salzburg in 1731. Winston-Salem in today's North Carolina was settled by the United Brethren, more familiar in English as the "Moravians." During the American Revolution still other Germans fought in mercenary regiments sent across the Atlantic by the British. Known to Americans as "Hessians," these soldiers were not all from Hessen, although the overwhelming majority were from North Germany. Not a few of them became unexpected immigrants as thousands of German soldiers were enticed to flee their colors and stay in the former colonies. The areas of Germany supplying large numbers of immigrants thus expanded to the north and east, although eastern Germany itself was still among the significant sending areas.

A hiatus in German emigration ensued as a result of the wars of the French Revolution, Napoleon's Continental System, and the British blockade of the Continent. During the first few years after 1815 the heaviest German migration flowed eastward to Poland, Russia, and southeastern Europe. However, when emigration to America gradually resumed after 1818, the new emigrants came in large numbers not only from the old supply regions along the Rhine, but also from Hessen and other areas, especially those such as Brunswick and Hannover that had provided troops for the British forces in North America. Emigration mounted as the 1820s and 1830s progressed. The new supply areas also included other northern and northwestern parts of Germany, especially Nassau, Waldeck, Oldenburg, the Münsterland, and southern Hannover. These were all districts with conditions conducive to emigration, and all were near established emigration routes to French, Dutch, and English ports. Bremen would soon become the great port of embarkation for Central Europe. During the 1830s and 1840s, however, Bavarians and many Rhinelanders continued to use French, Belgian, and Dutch ports. Bremen, or, strictly speaking, Bremerhaven, would not be overtaken by Hamburg as an emigrant port until the late nineteenth and early twentieth centuries. By that time the bulk of the passengers were non-Germans from Eastern and East Central Europe. Hamburg dominated German commerce with South America and England throughout most of the nineteenth century, while Bremen dominated both commerce and the passenger trade with North America. At critical points in the development of its commerce, Bremen lacked the substantial exports, whether man-made goods or agricultural products, that supported the growth of other major international ports. Its hinterland did not manufacture the industrial goods that Liverpool's did. Nor did the agricultural products of Bremen's hinterland rival those of Odessa, America's Great Lakes ports, or even Hamburg at their highpoints. Human beings provided Bremen with a convenient, self-loading substitute for exports.

But we have gotten ahead of our story. Several changes had to come about before the great wave of emigration from Northern Germany from the 1830s through the 1850s gathered strength. Bremen built a deeper harbor downstream on the Weser in what would be called "Bremerhaven" (literally, "Bremen's Harbor"). The opening of Bremerhaven in 1830 provided superior emigration facilities. Ships loaded with human beings bound for America would have to take on ballast overseas or, preferably, find return cargoes that could be carried profitably. People had to be familiarized with the idea of going to America. Conditions had to ripen that would make emigration appear enticing, and, often, inevitable.

As the volume of the emigrant trade grew during the late 1820s and early 1830s, a constellation of forces favoring emigration began to affect the southern portions of the Kingdom of Hannover. Widely circulated letters from Germans abroad, reports by emigrants in newspapers, and handbooks for prospective emigrants appeared in ever-multiplying numbers, as they did in other regions of western Germany. Shipping lines, emigrant agents, and the projects of some German merchants and princes promoted emigration.[5] At the same time, most state barriers to emigration remained, and an entire literature condemning emigration arose.[6] German-language novels and other works of fiction set in America became an enduring craze in nineteenth-century Germany.[7] The forces conducive to emigration to America evidently were stronger than the barriers, and from 1832 to 1843 the number of emigrants leaving every year from Bremen, most of whom came from North Germany, fluctuated between 6,000 and over 13,000. Next the numbers increased exponentially: almost 20,000 in 1844, almost 32,000 in 1845, over 32,000 in 1846, and almost 33,000 in 1847. The numbers then fell temporarily.[8]

After a slow start, emigration from the Hildesheim district followed a similar pattern. According to district records for 1834, only one person emigrated from the town of Alfeld, no one from the rural subdistrict of Alfeld, two people from the Gronau-Poppenburg subdistrict, and no one from Elze or Bockenem.[9] A total of 240 emigrants left the entire Hildesheim district that year.[10] It must be acknowledged that these official statistics may well understate the amount of emigration. Because of government restrictions on emigration, some emigrants may have neglected to inform the authorities of their intentions. Ten years later, however, the official count had risen dramatically. In 1845, a total of 1437 people were listed as emigrants, six times as many as in 1834. Although annual figures for the intervening years are lacking, the data for 1845 indicate that emigration had increased in some places in the Hildesheim district and commenced in others. The town of Alfeld had four emigrants, the rural subdistrict of Alfeld sixty-two, Bockenem now had twelve, Elze thirteen, and the Gronau-Poppenburg subdistrict twenty-five. Many more people emigrated in 1845 simply from the subdistrict and town of Hildesheim — 334 — than the mere 240 who had emigrated officially from the entire Hildesheim district in 1834.[11]

In an article entitled "The Emigration Issue," a major Hildesheim newspaper solemnly wished the emigrants well in 1844. "Also in our area," wrote the newspaper, "ever more people are preparing for their departure and are often taking significant amounts of money with them. One might complain of the loss of industrious hands and of business for the fatherland. [Implied is the Hildesheim district or the Kingdom of Hannover, as well as, perhaps more than, Germany.] It seems to us the duty of periodicals that wish not merely to entertain, but also instruct and be of service to their readers, to communicate to those desiring to emigrate that which is important to them."[12] The paper exhorted the German governments to concern themselves more with the process of emigration.

Unfortunately, we have no occupational statistics for pre-1848 emigrants from the entire Kingdom of Hannover. The general studies of German migration during the period from 1815 to the middle of the century agree that emigrants were neither the wealthiest nor the poorest people.

They were mainly from "the food-consuming lower middle class."[13] They were "neither great landowners nor harvest hands, but small farmers who cultivated their own land; not apprentices, nor unskilled laborers, nor great merchants, but independent village shopkeepers and artisans. . . . They traveled on their own resources. They were people who had something to lose, and who were losing it."[14]

Before the generation of Gieseckes that grew up in Bockenem, the Giesecke and Sander families already had personal and business contacts with Bremen. What we can reasonably conclude about these contacts is confined mostly to the position of the Gieseckes as merchants in Gittelde and Bockenem and to relatives of the Sanders in Bremen, for the relationship of the Bockenem Gieseckes to the Gittelder teamsters of the same name during the 1830s and 1840s has not been reconstructed. The sister of Charles Giesecke's mother had married into the Basse family of Elze, and that family had members in Bremen. Friedrich Heinrich Basse, the brother of the sister's husband, had settled in Bremen. Acquiring the highest form of citizenship there (the *große Bürgerrecht mit Handlungsfreiheit*) in 1815, he owned a white lead factory.[15] In 1820 he married Antoinette Achelis, a woman from a family of Bremen businessmen.[16] Her father, Thomas Achelis (1766–1841), owned a tannery and sat in Bremen's parliament. Her half-brother, also named Thomas Achelis (1807–1872), went to New York in 1833 and became a partner in the firm Viëtor & Achelis there.[17] This firm and its branch in Bremen engaged in the cotton and tobacco trades, as did the Gieseckes in Texas, but no positive evidence has come to light indicating that the Gieseckes in Texas had business dealings with Viëtor & Achelis.

The close family ties between Basses and Gieseckes were compounded during the mid-1840s through marriage between the Basses in Bremen and the Gieseckes in Elze. Often it is impossible to ascertain whether the frequent allusions to the Basses in Charles Giesecke's letters pertain to the Elze or the Bremen branch. Marie Basse, the daughter of Friedrich Heinrich Basse and his wife Antoinette née Achelis, married Friedrich Giesecke in 1844. Several Basses from Bremen and one of their relatives acted as the godparents of the young couple's children in Elze. For example, at the christening of the first child, who was named after his uncle Christoph Carl Basse, Tilman Gloystein, also from Bremen, served as the second godfather. Gloystein was an older half-brother of the infant's grandmother, Antoinette Basse.[18] He was a businessman who became the executive secretary of a fire protection service in Bremen.[19]

Charles Giesecke manifests much familiarity with Bremen in his letters. Both he and one or more of his brothers probably served a merchant apprenticeship there, but conclusive evidence is lacking even for Charles.[20] However, we know with certainty that both Friedrich and Edward Giesecke embarked at least once in Bremerhaven.[21]

When the thirteen British North American colonies won their independence, the prospects for trade between the Hanseatic cities and North America became favorable. However, a short upturn in this commerce was terminated by the British blockade of the European continent during the Napoleonic wars. The peace settlement of 1814–1815 did not herald the reinvigoration of trade with the Americas. Only the attainment of independence by most of Spain's American colonies in the 1820s stimulated its rapid expansion. These were the days when a partisan of German commerce announced triumphantly: "Hamburg has acquired colonies!"[22] The Hanseatic cities of Bremen, Hamburg, and Lübeck concluded a commercial treaty with the United States in 1827. Trade between America and Germany was carried at this time mainly by American ships. With the opening of Bremerhaven in 1830 Bremen's vessels overtook those of the United States in less than a decade. From 1836 to 1840 four-fifths of the trade between Germany and the United States was carried by Hanseatic ships.[23]

In view of the meager beginnings of the America trade, its rapid growth during the 1830s and 1840s is as astounding as is Bremen's development into the greatest continental distribution center for tobacco, coffee, and cotton. During the first half of the nineteenth century, Bremen remained a port without a developed hinterland to supply export goods. There was no agricultural or industrial counterpart to the grain that had been shipped down the Weser River during the Middle Ages and the early modern period. Physically and legally the Weser had to be made navigable again. The many obstructions in the waterway had to be cleared, and agreements had to be forged with the states through which it flowed.[24] But none of these obstacles was the primary reason for the continuing weakness of Bremen's trade after the conclusion of the Napoleonic wars. For example, the river-passage problems could be circumvented in part by the great wagons that were used to haul goods overland to and from Bremen. As observers during the first half of the nineteenth century recognized, Bremen had to create a hinterland in order to become a major port.[25] Bremen's ships usually went to sea with ballast as late as 1840 because they lacked cargoes.[26] Ballast, or extra ballast, was necessary because otherwise the ships would be top-heavy and unstable. Outgoing cargoes had to be found, not simply goods overseas to bring back to Europe. Neither Bremen nor Germany as a whole had large quantities of raw materials or foodstuffs to export, even if there had been a demand for all of these products in America. Unlike the British, the Germans did not produce large quantities of industrial products that could be marketed abroad.

The solution to the problem of inadequate exports came gradually with a phase of the trade in human beings that we are accustomed to labeling "emigration" from Europe. Significantly, only in 1840 was the number of Africans arriving in the Americas surpassed permanently by the number of European immigrants disembarking.[27] The waves of emigration that brought and ensured Bremen's salvation began with Germans from Hessen, the northwest, and the Kingdom of Hannover. Subsequent waves included Germans from areas farther north such as Schleswig-Holstein as well as Mecklenburg and northeastern Germany. Still later, toward the end of the century, Jews and Slavs from East Central and Eastern Europe provided the bulk of the emigrants. From 1832 to 1905 four million human beings passed through Bremen on their way overseas.[28] These people provided a voluminous and well-paying freight. Like the products of the Americas — hides, tobacco, cotton, and coffee — they required much space. A perspicacious British observer wrote as early as 1846: "Germany is the only other country, besides Great Britain, from which emigration takes place on a large scale, and is likely to lead to important results." He went on to describe in detail the areas from which the emigrants came and the European harbors from which they embarked. He commented that until then comparatively few North Germans had departed for overseas from Bremen.[29]

A German-American partisan of Bremen had attempted three years earlier to justify the already considerable beginnings of the city's trade in human cargoes. Seeking to undercut the still resonant mercantilist belief that subjects constituted an invaluable resource for the state, he argued that emigrants were no loss to the fatherland. For "the Germans in America consume yearly a mass of German products and thereby have a very positive effect on trade with the fatherland. Without the German emigrants neither the commerce nor the shipping of Hamburg and notably Bremen would have expanded so much, and without the emigrants Bremen's ships would not be in a position to earn money on over half their freight."[30] This astute observation about earnings from passages to America turned out to be a far more compelling argument than the claim that German-Americans would buy German goods.

TABLE 1

Factory Employees in Bremen, 1842–1847*

	1842	1843	1844	1845	1846	1847
In Cigar Factories	515	717	922	1,037	1,154	1,245
In All Factories	2,836	2,984	3,362	3,620	3,849	4,315

*Source: Data derived from Schaefer, Bremens Bevölkerung, p. 115.

With the early rise in the numbers of emigrants traveling via Bremen, it was possible as early as 1826 to initiate the first liner service from Germany to North America.[31] However, the majority of German emigrants long continued to sail to America from ports in France, the Low Countries, or Britain. By 1846 the ratio was 49 to 51 in favor of non-German harbors. A few years later the ratio had worsened to 38 to 61 against ports in Germany. The balance shifted at last in favor of German ports, primarily Bremen, in 1853. The shift was dramatic. The ratio became 59 to 30 to the benefit of the Germans.[32]

The development of Bremen's population reflected the city's success. In 1823 there were under 40,000 inhabitants, in 1842 over 50,000, and in 1855 over 60,000.[33] During the 1830s the emigrant trade had already enabled Bremen to overtake its rivals Amsterdam and Rotterdam and become the world's greatest transshipment center for tobacco.[34] Little wonder that a German writer at the time described Bremen as "one enormous tobacco factory."[35] Until midcentury the tobacco trade remained at the center of Bremen's commerce with North America.[36] In 1852 every sixth resident of Bremen derived his or her living directly or indirectly from cigarmaking.[37] In the decades since 1815 the rolling of cigars had displaced the production of pipe tobacco as the most important component of the tobacco trade.[38] Statistical data from the 1840s shows clearly the rapid proliferation of cigarmaking in Bremen. The number of employees in cigar factories rose with greater rapidity than did the number of employees in all of Bremen's factories, as shown in Table 1, above.

Before the middle of the century Bremen was taking one-half the tobacco exports of the United States. The principal American port in this trade long remained Baltimore.[39] Bremen's rise to the world's tobacco emporium depended upon the endeavors of numerous businessmen, most of them operating on a small scale. No aspect of the tobacco business was industrialized. The manufacture of tobacco products was carried on by handicraft methods. Merchants on both sides of the Atlantic expanded their activities until they supplied tobacco for Germany, Austria, Switzerland, and, eventually, all of Central Europe. An army of merchants and traveling salesmen was satisfied only when they furnished tobacco even to the smallest community.[40] Much of the tobacco consumed in the Kingdom of Hannover had still been harvested in the kingdom itself as late as the 1830s. Most of this tobacco would soon be supplanted by American tobacco, especially among the wealthier and more discerning consumers. Baron von Reden, in his 1839 description of the Kingdom's economy, declared that the most important tobacco factories were in the city of Hannover, in Hildesheim, and in Bockenem. He noted that the smoking of cigars was becoming more common. He also mentioned "smoking tobacco," still an omnibus term for pipe tobacco, tobacco plugs for chewing, and snuff.[41] In 1833 the tobacco connoisseur and economic geographer G. C. Bocris had been more detailed in his sovereign guide to the subject of tobacco. The triumph of American tobacco standards is clear in his work:

> In the Kingdom of Hannover the cultivation of tobacco has been undertaken for many years, especially in Nienburg, from Northeim to Göttingen, in Liebenau, and in Stolzenau on the Weser. All of these types, planted from the same seeds, are always inferior [abweichend] in quality, odor, and taste. The tobacco in the vicinity of the last two towns, planted with American seeds, provides, with the benefit of a hot summer, a type of smoking [i.e., pipe] tobacco similar to that of the [Rhenish] Palatinate, and the fat leaves can be utilized for good snuff better than the tobacco plugs of the Palatinate."[42]

For Bocris most Hannoverian varieties of tobacco were mediocre compared to American tobacco. He favored tobacco from the Palatinate among German varieties, and he classified tobacco from Nürnberg, Hanau, the Rheingau, and part of Hessen as on the next lower level.[43] Importers of American tobacco could invoke such judgments to help develop a market for their products.

During the mid-1840s Bremen's tobacco merchants celebrated another success. Cheap cigars, rolled in Germany from West Indian, American, and German tobacco, began to displace American-made cigars on the U.S. market itself.[44] Most of these German cigars were rolled in Bremen, or at least exported via Bremen. A portion of them were produced in Bremen's expanding hinterland. Significantly, at this time Charles Giesecke urged his brother in Elze to undertake cigarmaking.[45] Unfortunately for the Gieseckes—and soon to be felt by Charles—the tendency for the largest of Bremen's tobacco firms to dominate the market was already established. This tendency appeared in Bremen first in the wholesale trade in unmanufactured tobacco. The reasons lay partly in the volume of this trade and partly in the large, expensive warehouses required to store the easily damaged product until the opportune time came to sell it.[46] Despite the large numbers of cigar and other tobacco factories, the wholesale tobacco business in Bremen was already securely in the hands of a few. The business was dominated in 1847 by fourteen firms engaged exclusively in the wholesale tobacco and cigar trades, and by another six firms dealing also in other wares.[47] The separation of the import of tobacco from its manufacture had been far advanced as early as the beginning of the nineteenth century.[48]

Although the cotton trade was as important as the tobacco trade to the Gieseckes in Texas, we shall touch only briefly here on the development of the cotton trade in Bremen. This is because the pioneering role of the Gieseckes in the cotton trade is manifest in the available sources and will be discussed in Part Three. The role of the Gieseckes in the history of the tobacco trade was historically less innovative. We must be aware that Bremen's trade in cotton lagged far behind that of Hamburg until well into the century. Hamburg's lead in this endeavor reflects its much stronger ties to Britain, the world's principal importer of cotton. The basis for the emergence of Bremen as the world's second largest cotton-importing harbor, following Liverpool, was laid in the 1840s, but that spectacular future could hardly then be foreseen. Not until a few decades later did Bremen become the primary intermediary between American cotton and the Central European textile industry.[49]

Enmeshment:

NORTH GERMANY AND THE AMERICAS

THE LURE OF MEXICO, TEXAS, AND THE UNITED STATES

LATIN AMERICA'S SUCCESSFUL WARS of liberation against European colonial domination sparked the interest of German merchants in the possibilities of commerce with the region after 1815. By 1820, even before Mexico proclaimed its independence from Spain, a large number of Hanseatic merchants and shippers had taken up places there, as well as in the already independent countries of Colombia and Chile. Mexico's declaration of independence from Spain in early 1821 preceded by a year and a half Brazil's declaration of independence from Portugal. The vast realms of Brazil and Mexico excited Hanseatic businessmen's imaginations as markets for goods and as trading partners. By 1824 German commerce with Mexico far exceeded in volume and significance that of all other countries with Mexico except other American states. Mexico's demand for manufactured goods appeared insatiable to German merchants. Linens constituted the principal of these export commodities, which also included iron wares and musical instruments. Germany imported from Mexico in increasing volume silver, cochineal (a red dye derived from insects), vanilla, indigo, medicinal herbs, and stirring poles for dyeing vats.[1]

Contacts between the German states and Latin America for the purpose of drawing up commercial treaties intensified in 1822. However, German fears of offending the former colonial powers, principally Spain but also the Holy Alliance and Austrian Chancellor Prince Clemens von Metternich, delayed the process of establishing official diplomatic and economic relations. The newly independent Latin American states, above all Mexico, attempted adroitly to exploit German wishes for trade by requiring in exchange diplomatic recognition and support against the former colonial masters. Prompt U.S. and British recognition of the newly independent American states, and the Monroe Doctrine (December 2, 1823), gave the

Mexican government leverage it was to use to good effect in its relations with the German states.

The contest for domination of commerce with the independent states in Latin America proceeded, with Britain at first in the lead. However, German trade with them expanded rapidly, even though none of the German states ventured to initiate formal commercial relations until 1825. The economic crisis of 1825–1826 led Prussia to approve the exchange of commercial representatives with Mexico. Commerce with Mexico provided an outlet for the surplus production of the Prussian linen industry. Although Prussia and other German states, including the Hanseatic League, concluded treaties of commerce and friendship with Mexico in 1827, these treaties were not signed by Mexico, which continued to maneuver for assistance against Spain. The German states, however, remained chary of risking the wrath of Spain and Austria. Among the Hanseatic cities, where interest in trade with Latin America was particularly strong, Hamburg's sizable investments in Spain inclined it to greater caution than Bremen exercised.[2]

Despite the lack of executed treaties, the volume of goods imported from Mexico by the Hanseatic cities was substantial. In 1826 Bremen's imports from Mexico were valued at 600,000 Reichstaler. The following year Mexico imported German wares valued at $200,000 through one major port alone, Matamoros. In 1829 the value of Mexican imports through Matamoros reached almost a million dollars. The primary German export to Mexico was linens — a commodity that was particularly important to Bremen and constituted 80 percent of the total value of its trade with Mexico. In 1825 eight ships from Hamburg and four from Bremen called at Mexican ports. The number of vessels involved increased during the next few years, but the general ratio of ships from the two German ports persisted. In 1827 there were fifteen ships from Hamburg to six from Bremen. Mexico remained the only state among Spain's former American colonies with which the Hanseatic towns had a treaty, even if unratified, before 1830.[3]

Representatives of the Hanseatic cities and Mexico drafted a second treaty in 1831, and both parties signed it. Once again Mexico ratified neither the treaty with the Hanse nor those with other German states, including Hannover. Not until 1841 did Mexico finally accept treaties with the Hanseatic cities and other German states.[4]

During the 1820s a substantial portion of the still modest German emigration went to Latin America. Thirty percent of all German emigrants arrived there in 1826. In 1830 the declining proportion was still 20 percent. Thereafter the fall was precipitous as the numbers of Germans going to the United States swelled.[5] Most of the German settlers bound for Latin America in the 1820s went to South America, not Mexico. Germans founded farming settlements during the mid-1820s in Brazil, Chile, and Argentina. From the beginning of this substantial movement the Brazilian state promoted and steered emigration.[6]

Texas, then simply one large part of the Republic of Mexico, received initially little of the attention Germans accorded much of Latin America.[7] However, commercial relations with Mexico developed more rapidly than with the South American countries. German exports to Mexico were far greater than German exports to the United States and Brazil combined.[8] In 1820, shortly before Mexico's Declaration of Independence from Spain on February 24, 1821, and prior to the enunciation of the Monroe Doctrine in 1823, a Prussian reserve officer returning from a trip to North America publicly proposed the purchase of Texas by his government. He predicted that when settled with Germans this acquisition would supply an enormous market for German goods in the face of the growing competition of British manufacturers throughout much of the world.[9] Most German merchants in Mexico were located not in Texas, but rather in other parts of the country, principally Mexico City. Largely from Bremen, these merchants played a critical economic role in Mexico. German merchants conducted one-third of the entire wholesale trade of Mexico in 1830. Thirty-nine German firms maintained branches there.[10] Of course, most of these offices were small. They consisted of little more than a merchant and a clerk, but this was true of virtually all branch offices of the world's commercial houses until the late nineteenth century. In 1840, four years after the Texan War of Independence, one-third of Mexican imports and exports still went through German hands.[11] According to one estimate, by 1841 about a thousand Germans resided in Mexico.[12] Many were merchants or employees of merchants; others were miners and engineers involved in the extraction of raw materials. By 1844–1845 the number of German firms in Mexico increased to more than forty-eight, of which forty were headquartered in one or the other of the Hanseatic cities.[13] The larger German firms had sixty-six principals and 133 clerks. By that time there were in the young Republic of Texas representatives of at least three Hanseatic houses with four principals and eight clerks. In addition, more than eleven small German firms were active in Texas. Despite the growth of commerce between Texas and Germany, business with Mexico, the rest of Latin America, and the United States remained far more important to the Hanseatic cities. One hundred thirty-four German firms had branches in the United States in 1844–1845; throughout the States there were some 343 German firms with a total of 465 principals and 774 clerks.

In 1820 Texas was a thinly settled region of Mexico, but already non-Spanish-speaking settlers from Europe and settlers of European origins from the United States had begun to arrive. The ranks of these settlers swelled following Mexico's independence in 1821; Mexico pursued a policy of encouraging the settlement of sparsely populated regions in order not to leave them to the Indians. It was primarily Irishmen and Americans who obtained permission to settle in Texas; members of both groups enjoyed many advantages. The so-called *empresarios*, among them Stephen F. Austin, who had been born in Virginia, received from the Mexican authorities patents authorizing them to find settlers for enormous land grants. The resulting settlements remained very small until well into the 1830s. Almost all were located on a narrow strip along the coast, not more than ten to fifty miles inland. The exceptions were in the south of the region near the great rivers of south and east Texas that flow into the Gulf of Mexico. The small indigenous population of at most a few thousand spoke either Indian languages or Spanish.[14] Few of these people took part directly in the economic and social development that the *empresarios* and the foreign settlers initiated.

The emerging ruling class of Texas was divided into unstable opposing cliques. The principal issues leading to conflicts were how the inhabitants, natural resources, and favorable geographical position of the region were to be exploited. Large plantations employing black slaves had been established. Harbors that could serve as centers for commerce with Latin America were developing. Speculators had appeared and were dealing in both town lots and large tracts of land. The objects of speculation included entire communities that existed only on the drawing board; each speculator tried to win settlers and investors for "his" town, and thereby increase the value of his holdings. Revolving around the large undertakings were many smaller agricultural and urban businesses. Merchants attempted to wring gains from loans and from the sale of supplies to the government. The Mexican government sought to restrict or prevent some enterprises. The introduction of slaves was forbidden in all of Mexico, which had become a republic in 1824, but many settlers did not feel bound to obey these laws and circumvented them.[15]

Although long an advocate of slavery, Austin tried to avoid strife with the Mexican government.[16] His large patent, known as "Austin's Colony," included many of the agriculturally most promising areas of Texas, among them the municipality of Brazoria on the Brazos River, where the Gieseckes were to settle. Austin valued the growth of his colony's commerce with other parts of Mexico during the late 1820s, but he placed his greatest hopes in the export of cotton to Europe. He could cite the enormous U.S. cotton exports, which had mounted from virtually nothing in the short space of thirty years. The extension of slavery in the United States was linked to this success, and many a Texan expected a similar course of events in Texas. The future of Texas was at stake. Mexican laws prohibiting the expansion of slavery were easier to circumvent than were the regulations that prevented the official designation of a port on the Brazos River. Austin and some of the factions among the settlers long endeavored to avoid conflict with the Mexican authorities,[17] but when settlers provoked war with Mexico, Austin had to choose sides. The Republic of Texas was proclaimed, war ensued, the Texans won, and the stream of settlers coming to Texas from Europe and the United States became even larger.

The Lone Star Republic remained independent despite a plebiscite in Texas overwhelmingly in favor of joining the United States. Independence was favored by powerful forces in the United States and Europe as well as Texas. Entry into the Union would upset the balance between the free and the slave states. The claim that Texans were conspiring with others to create a vast slaveholders' realm uniting Texas, the southern United States, Cuba, and other areas of Latin America was among the rumors of the day.[18] The last versions of this bold dream would not be discredited until the defeat of the South in the Civil War. The maintenance of a separate Republic of Texas was useful for British policy, because Texas provided London with a club against American tariff policy. Both Britain and the Continental powers weighed the advantages of a protectorate, whether formal or informal, over Texas. In the meantime, some countries joined Britain in recognizing the fledgling republic: France in 1839, Belgium and the Netherlands in 1840. In the latter year Britain concluded a commercial treaty with Texas that was ratified in 1842. In order to comprehend the prospective extent of European intervention in an independent North American state, it may help to recall that little more than a decade later France under Napoleon III attempted by force of arms to create a Mexican imperial throne for Maximilian, the brother of the Hapsburg Emperor. This endeavor was not finally quashed until after the Civil War in the United States.

Germans began to settle in Texas during the 1820s. Most of the earliest were people who had been living in North America. Among them were some with German or German-sounding names from the German districts of Pennsylvania and other parts of the United States. We have no evidence indicating that the German origins or roots of these people had any particular significance for their activities in Texas.[19] In 1823 a German associate of Austin's, Philipp Bögel, who went under the name Baron de Bastrop in America, founded a community that he gave the last name of his alias. His town was located far into what was then regarded as the interior of Texas: 120 miles up the Colorado River. Some of the settlers of Bastrop were from the Duchy of Oldenburg. Austin took a special interest in encouraging German settlers during the early 1830s,[20] but this effort resulted at best in very modest numbers of Germans coming to Texas.

In 1831 a man from Oldenburg known to the world until recently only by his pseudonym "Friedrich Ernst," obtained land for a settlement in a remote part of Austin's colony. His real name was Christian Friedrich Ernst Dirks. A postal clerk accused of embezzling funds from the Duchy of Oldenburg's postal service, Friedrich Ernst, as we shall continue to call him in these pages, managed to flee with his family to America.[21] Arriving from Europe in New York in 1829, he intended to go to the Missouri Territory. Like many Germans he was acting under the influence of Gottfried Duden's glowing report of his trip to Missouri. Duden's book about the Middle West and his three-year stay in Missouri was one of the earliest German handbooks for emigrants to concern itself with Texas.[22] Although Duden advised Germans to go there under certain conditions, he refused to be diverted from his dream of founding a new German Fatherland in Missouri. Ernst, while in New Orleans en route to Missouri, changed his mind and went to Texas. It was typical of early German immigrants in Texas that before going to Texas Ernst had, if only briefly, been in the United States. In Texas his farm was located south of Bastrop between the Colorado and Brazos Rivers. His endeavor to publicize his settlement achieved much success when an open letter of his was published in North German newspapers. In 1838 he founded his own town, which he named "Industry." In the meantime a sprinkling of other Germans had arrived in Texas, and some of them had started settlements of their own.[23]

In 1834 another North German using a pseudonym published the first influential German book focused on Texas as an attractive land for German immigrants. Detlev Jordt, who later adopted the pen name Detlef Dunt, was born near Kiel in Holstein, but his wife's family lived in the Duchy of Oldenburg, where he unsuccessfully attempted to establish residence.[24]

Having sailed from Bremen to America in 1832, he returned to Oldenburg in connection with the publication of his book and to lead his family to Texas. He noted at the end of his Foreword: "Written at the settlement of Friedrich Ernst on the Mill Creek in Austin's Colony in the state of Texas in New Mexico."[25]

A few other small German settlements in the area between the Colorado and Brazos rivers broadened these modest beginnings during the 1830s. An organization of Germans with the name "Germania" was founded in New York in 1838 following the economic crash of 1837. The organizers of Germania wanted to plant a colony of Germans in the new Republic of Texas. More than 125 people boarded the first ship of German settlers from New York. Arriving in Galveston on Christmas Eve Day 1839, they learned of a horrible epidemic of yellow fever in Houston, which lay on their planned route to the interior. Only a few of the boldest or most foolhardy of them remained in Texas. These people set out for the "German area" north of the town of Austin.[26] Other Germans had early settled in a small area along Coleto Creek northeast of Goliad and northwest of the harbor at Indianola. By 1840 an American emigrant to Texas remarked on the substantial number of Germans in Texas.[27]

German immigrants became more numerous during the last years of the Lone Star Republic. They were welcomed for various reasons. Some saw them as counterweights to the numerous advocates of the incorporation of Texas by the United States. Others found in them sturdy farmers who would stand by Texas loyally in the event of the resumption of war with Mexico. To still others they were greenhorns to exploit. The Congress of Texas passed a law in 1843 requiring the publication of the Republic's laws in German. A rapidly increasing number of handbooks for German emigrants during the 1840s praised, often at the expense of the United States, the virtues of Texas as a place to which to emigrate: immigrants could become citizens in a short time, the Republic gave settlers free land, and additional land could be purchased for ridiculously small sums. A number of handbooks even contended that the propitious time to emigrate to the United States had passed — that Texas had far more to offer Germans.[28]

However, the laws of Texas and their enforcement were not as favorable to Germans and other immigrants as such handbooks made out. According to the Constitution of Texas, each head-of-household in Texas at the time of the declaration of independence of 1836 received a league (4,428 acres) of land from the Republic's own holdings.[29] Unmarried seventeen-year-old males obtained a third of a league. Subsequent immigrants received smaller, but still substantial, tracts: a head of household, 1200 acres from 1836 to 1837, and half of that thereafter. Even 600 acres was of course a considerable amount of land, but most land in Texas at the time had virtually no value until surveyed, cleared, and plowed or settled. Only then did its value rise. The recipient of a land grant generally needed some capital to get to this point, and only in an exceptional case could he do much with a grant of undeveloped land. During the 1840s many settlers sought to obtain better-situated acres that could be developed immediately.

A system similar to that of the former Mexican settlement policy utilizing *empresarios* was in operation in Texas from 1841 to 1844. Settlers with resources obtained land from the government if they convinced other immigrants to settle in a certain area. But the land laws of Texas were executed in such a way that the choicest plots were reserved for settlers from the United States, and even few of these settlers could establish themselves on this free land. They, too, almost always had to purchase well-situated, surveyed land if they wanted to farm.

The projects of the Association for the Protection of German Immigrants in Texas surpassed beyond all measure those of other endeavors to direct Germans to Texas.[30] The association is generally known in English as well as German by the term *Adelsverein,* which refers not to its German title (*Verein zum Schutze deutscher Einwanderer in Texas*), but, sarcastically, to the heavy participation of noblemen, including members of ruling houses, in the venture. It was founded in 1842, following a meeting in Biebrich in the Duchy of Hessen-Nassau, and was converted into a joint stock company two years later. Ruling princes and high nobles from the states of Nassau, Hannover, Hessen-Darmstadt, Hessen-Kassel, Brunswick, Waldeck, Württemberg, Coburg, and Meiningen were among the founders of the *Adelsverein.* King Frederick William III of Prussia supported it discreetly without financing it publicly. Among its announced purposes were the alleviation of pauperism and the creation of new markets for goods. Eighty percent of the profits were to be divided among the shareholders, 10 percent to be set aside in a reserve fund, 5 percent to be used for wages, 3 percent to be used for charitable activities, and 2 percent to be used for scholarly or scientific purposes. Many of its founders expected healthy profits from the organization, as well as the alleviation of overpopulation in their lands. The entire undertaking resulted from speculation based upon inadequate information. The *Adelsverein* obtained a gigantic territory, a land grant of two million acres, but the German princes and their economic partners were not as clever as the North American speculators in Texas when it came to securing choice lands. The large grant was poorly situated, but the association nevertheless sought to settle thousands of Germans there. The colonist would pay a fixed sum and receive in exchange passage to America and the journey through Texas to the association's territory. According to the bylaws of the *Adelsverein*, every unmarried male settler should have capital in the amount of 300 *Gulden* (about 200 Reichstaler), and every head of a large family 600 *Gulden* (about 400 Reichstaler). This attempt to create a new Germany abroad was similar to numerous other projects undertaken prior to the American Civil War.[31] Many similar colonies, such as Hermann in Missouri, were planted in the United States, and a good many of these settlements were directly or indirectly supported by German rulers.

Among the numerous concessions made by the Republic of Texas to Germans and the *Adelsverein* was the provision in 1843 for the publication of laws in German, but the primary interest of the government of Texas was not the success of its German immigrants, but having more land settled and more white inhabitants of non-Mexican, non-Spanish origins. The *Adelsverein* was ultimately defeated by its origins in a mixture of speculation, romantic colonizing impulses, and profit-seeking schemes by noblemen who otherwise continued to favor most of the values of a status society similar to that destroyed by the French Revolution. Prince Carl von Solms-Braunfels, the organization's commissar in the republic from 1844 to 1845, spent many months in Texas, where his aristocratic proclivities jeopardized the entire undertaking. After several catastrophes he was followed by a far more astute nobleman, Otfried Hans von Meusebach, who modestly referred to himself in Texas simply as John O. Meusebach.

The existence and activities of the *Adelsverein* remained for a brief period of great use to the government of Texas. The association provided a counterweight to the force exerted on the one side by Mexico and on the other by the United States. Support from Europe was welcome. The British government was interested in the development of the *Adelsverein*: the German settlers could create a new balance of forces in Texas that would help the British to keep Texas neutral in the event that Great Britain and the United States went to war, an event that remained a distinct possibility.[32]

In 1841, before the beginning of mass immigration, a German traveler estimated the number of Germans in Texas at 10,000 within a total population of 250,000. He claimed that this latter figure included 45,000 Negroes (that is, slaves) and 8,000 "Spaniards" (that is, Spanish-speaking people).[33] He overestimated the total population by half, but his calculation of the proportion of Germans did not miss the mark badly if many of the settlers who came from German areas of the United States are reckoned as Germans. Among the 125,000 inhabitants of the Lone Star Republic in 1841 were approximately 5,000 Germans.[34] Then the numbers of Germans increased rapidly. From 1844 to 1846 some 10,000 German emigrants were shipped to Texas by the *Adelsverein* alone. They came mainly from western and northern Germany: from the Duchy of Nassau, from Hessen, and from Hannover. People from southern Hannover, from the Harz and the cities of Hannover and Hildesheim, were strongly represented among the Hannoverians. Smaller, but still substantial, numbers of emigrants came from other districts of northern and western Germany: from Brunswick, Thuringia, the Münsterland, Mecklenburg, Sachsen-Anhalt, and the Lausitz, as well as from Württemberg in the southwest.[35] Numerous books and articles subsidized by the *Adelsverein* presented an enticing image of Texas. Without following literally the association's slogan "Come with us to Texas," many other Germans made their way there by other means.

Reliable figures are available for the number of passengers who traveled from Bremen to Galveston and New Orleans from 1842 to 1845.[36] The data for New Orleans are relevant because many emigrants sailed from Germany or New York to New Orleans and then booked passage from New Orleans to Galveston or another Texas port. The Bremen firm D. H. Wätjen & Co. began scheduled service between Bremen and New Orleans in 1842.[37] Direct service between Bremen and Texas began soon thereafter when a large supply of potential customers had developed. Paying passengers substituted for freight on the outgoing trip from Germany, and soon the frequency of service between Bremen and Galveston increased. During the 1840s Baltimore, New York, and New Orleans remained the most important U.S. ports for traveling between Germany and America.[38] However, during the period 1843 to 1846 when the *Adelsverein* arranged for much of the emigration to Texas, a total of 7,515 passengers sailed directly from Bremen to Galveston.[39] Table 2 shows the dramatic expansion and then sudden decline of travel between the Weser and Galveston.

As Table 2 shows, the number of ships sailing from the Weser to Galveston was increasing in 1843 before the *Adelsverein* sent its first settlers to Texas. The organization's plans and publicity were already making Texas better known in Germany. The first emigrants under the protection of the *Adelsverein* reached Galveston in July 1844; in 1846, the last arrived. The largest proportional increase in the number of ships from the Weser bound

TABLE 2

Ships from Bremen and Other Weser Ports
Arriving at Selected U.S. Ports, 1841–1847*

Port	1841	1842	1843	1844	1845	1846	1847
New York	38	41	39	56	75	79	107
Baltimore	36	35	37	36	52	50	48
New Orleans	16	28	29	36	56	45	35
Galveston	0	3	8	7	19**	33	4
Total	90	107	113	135	202	207	194

* Source: Pitsch, *Die wirtschaftlichen Beziehungen Bremens zu den Vereinigten Staaten*, p. 219.
** Engelsing, *Bremen als Auswandererhafen*, p. 182, gives instead the figure 32.

for Galveston occurred in 1845, and in the following year the largest absolute increase occurred. From 1844 to 1847 some 60 ships brought Germans to Texas,[40] many of them departing from a Weser port but others from Antwerp or Amsterdam.

Estimates of the numbers of German emigrants bound for Texas during the 1840s are frequently higher than available statistics on the number of Germans landing in Texas. Some of these inconsistencies can be explained by the elevated death rate of emigrants. Mortality was especially high among small children and the elderly, occasionally due to plagues, hardships, and bad provisions on vessels,[41] but more often due to poor and dangerous circumstances during the initial months and years of settlement. Miserable conditions on the long voyage — three to six weeks from Europe to New York if one were lucky, and frequently as long as eight weeks[42] — left many people weak upon arrival. According to a clear-sighted and well-informed contemporary, one-third of all adult immigrants in America died within three years. They fell victim to "the rigors of the climate, . . . unexpected hardships and . . . unaccustomed methods of living."[43]

This apparent exaggeration of mortality rates came closer to realization among Germans in Texas during the mid-1840s than among most other nineteenth-century immigrants. Early deaths of *Adelsverein* immigrants were unusually high. One source estimates that of 5,200 *Adelsverein* immigrants in Texas from 1844 to 1846, more than 350 died during the first

The Lure of Mexico, Texas, and the U.S.

months after arrival.[44] Inadequate planning by the association was the basic cause of these and other deaths. The catastrophe was brought about by the speculative nature of the vast undertaking, the aristocratic attitude of Prince Solms, and the unrestrained greed of some businessmen. Too few supplies and inadequate quarters in Galveston awaited the immigrants. One estimate, perhaps on the conservative side, speaks of a thousand deaths preceding the long trek into the Hill Country.[45]

The U.S. census of 1850 found only 8,300 people in Texas who had been born in Germany, although Germans constituted by far the largest foreign-born segment of the population. The other most common countries of birth (the numbers are in parentheses) were Ireland (1403), England (1002), France (647), Scotland (261), Switzerland (134), and Norway (105).[46] Terry Jordan estimates the size of the "German element" — people born in Germany as well as all inhabitants with one or more parents born in Germany — in Texas in 1850 at 11,621. These 11,621 residents of Texas formed 7.5 percent of the white population and 5.4 percent of the entire population.[47] According to the 1850 census, the population of Texas had reached 212,592, including 58,558 "colored" and slaves.[48] However, the low counts of Germans should not lead us to conclude that fewer than 10,000 German-speaking people had come to Texas by the middle of the century, or that fewer than 10,000 lived there. Even taking into consideration the high death rate and the possibility that a number of Germans left Texas and went to other parts of America, Germans were apparently undercounted in Texas by the 1850 census. Furthermore, the ranks of German-speaking Texans were increased by a sprinkling of people from Switzerland, Alsace, and the Hapsburg Empire, in addition to some German-Americans from the United States.

The Germans concentrated in certain parts of Texas. During the 1840s these localities included not only the districts in the Hill Country and elsewhere in the interior but also Galveston and, after 1845, the section northeast of Houston. By the mid-1850s reliable estimates of the size of the German population of Galveston ran as high as one-third or even one-half of the inhabitants,[49] but during the period of the republic many travelers commented on the omnipresence of Germans in Galveston. In 1843 a newly landed German went to a Catholic mass in that port town and was astonished to hear a sermon in German.[50] Three years later estimates of the size of the city's German population ran as high as one-half.[51] As was true of other people in Galveston, many of the Germans were not permanent residents. However, the Germans had an especially high turnover rate because of the number of *Adelsverein* settlers awaiting the journey to the interior. In 1846 a candidate for the U.S Congress deemed the city's German population significant enough to merit the printing and distribution of leaflets in German.[52] The same year an early, perhaps the first, German newspaper in Galveston began to appear.[53]

The founding of the *Adelsverein*, the frequent reassertion of the independence of Texas, and expectations of a frenzied expansion of trade between Germany and Texas strengthened intercourse between the two countries. Negotiations for a commercial treaty between Texas and the Hanseatic cities began in 1841. The government of the republic was interested not only for commercial reasons, but also because a commercial treaty with the Hanseatic cities could serve as a means of pressuring the United States. If Texas remained independent, such agreements were essential. If, on the other hand, Texas entered the Union, a commercial treaty could serve as a bargaining chip with Washington. Negotiations between the Hanseatic cities and Texas became more intense when in June 1843 William Henry Daingerfield of Texas arrived in Le Havre. Daingerfield was a former member of the Texas Senate and the current secretary of the treasury of the Lone Star Republic when he embarked for France. He was also named *chargé d'affaires* in the Netherlands and empowered to deal with the representatives of the Hanseatic cities.[54] When his negotiations with Belgium stalled, Daingerfield departed for Paris, where he established direct contact with the plenipotentiary of the Hanse, Victor Rumpff. A treaty of friendship as well as commercial and navigation treaties between Texas and the Hanseatic cities of Bremen, Hamburg, and Lübeck were signed on April 17, 1844. The pacts included a most-favored-nation clause. The commercial treaty stipulated that its terms would apply also to the other states of the German Federation if these states so decided. Any such extension of the agreement would automatically go into effect twelve months after simple declarations by both sides. The treaty had a life of twelve years. It required only ratification by the senates of Texas and the Hanseatic cities to be in force. On August 9, 1844 Bremen's Senate approved a resolution granting all Texan vessels the same rights in Bremen's harbors as those possessed by ships from Bremen if the Republic of Texas favored similarly ships from Bremen. On December 13, 1844, Bremen ratified the entire pact. But that was as far as the agreements got. Neither the Texas Senate nor the senates of the other Hanseatic cities ratified it. President Houston of Texas sent it without comment to the Senate, thereby making clear that he was not interested in its ratification. Apparently, he wanted to avoid any step

The Lure of Mexico, Texas, and the U.S.

TABLE 3

Value of Imports and Exports of the Republic of Texas,
1842–1845 (in Dollars)*

	1 Aug 1842– 31 July 1843	1 Aug 1843– 31 July 1844	1 Aug 1844– 31 Oct 1845†
Imports from:			
USA	412,983	593,225	1,151,733
Great Britain	32,475	51,060	9,467
Hanseatic Cities**		27,495	5,114
Germany (incl. Hanseatic Cities)**	12,593		
France	7,425	5,525	2,048
Spanish West Indies	5,730	149	11,185
British West Indies	3,624	3,722	
Belgium		3,516	20,634
Austria's Adriatic Possessions (i.e., Trieste)		1,186	
Yucatán		664	
Sardinia			468
Totals	471,205	86,443	1,204,370
Exports To:			
USA	281,343	249,152	486,327
Great Britain	76,029	205,345	103,484
Hanseatic Cities**		112,095	85,585
Germany (incl. Hanseatic Cities)**	41,711		
France	260	15,435	8,650
Spanish W. Indies	16,427	1,031	23,262
British W. Indies			1,455
Belgium			49,434
Austria's Adriatic Possessions (i.e., Trieste)		29,014	13,469

TABLE 3

(*continued*)

	1 Aug 1842– 31 July 1843	1 Aug 1843– 31 July 1844	1 Aug 1844– 31 Oct 1845
Exports To:			
Yucatán		3,047	
Sardinia			57,552
Totals	415,769	615,119	829,215

*Source: William M. Gouge, *The Fiscal History of Texas* (Philadelphia, 1852), p. 277.
**The terms "Germany" and "Hanseatic Cities" are virtually interchangeable; beginning in August 1843 the commercial statistics of the Republic of Texas used only the latter term.
†The last 15 months before entry of Texas into the USA.

that would complicate the entry of Texas into the United States. Action on the treaty was deferred by the Texas Senate. This came as a surprise in Bremen, where businessmen had already begun to expand trade with Texas. They found to their chagrin that the Lone Star Republic continued to apply the highest tariff instead of the most-favored-nation clause to imports from Bremen.[55]

As can be seen from Table 3, which includes data on foreign trade through mid-1844, the reported value of German exports to Texas more than doubled from 1843 to 1844, while exports from Texas to Germany almost tripled during the same period. The data in the table are useful indicators, but, for several reasons, understate the value of both exports and imports. Although most Lone Star duties remained low, smuggling into Texas, as well as from Texas into the United States, occurred on a large scale along the Texas-U.S. border.[56] Also, despite the rise of Galveston as a port, New Orleans remained, for all practical purposes, the republic's second port. Many goods bound to and from Galveston or another Texas port were shipped via New Orleans. The value of these goods appears under the heading "USA," not that of "Germany" or "Hanseatic Cities." Thus commerce between Texas and Germany was greater than is indicated by the chart.

5

GALVESTON AND ITS HINTERLAND

THE DEVELOPMENT OF GALVESTON into a modern harbor began late but proceeded rapidly.[1] Its continuous development dates only to 1837, although various parts of Galveston Island had served as harbors long before that time. In the early nineteenth century pirates and smugglers there evaded the Mexican authorities with much success.[2] Compared with other major ports, Galveston had several disadvantages. Unlike Manhattan Island, for example, Galveston does not rest on solid rock, nor does much of Galveston rise above sea level. It is little more than a large, vulnerable sandbar. Sooner or later, every early settlement on Galveston Island was destroyed by waves during bad weather. Nevertheless, the Mexican authorities designated it a harbor in 1825. Named both a port of entry and the headquarters of the Texas Navy in 1836, Galveston assumed great potential importance. Then in 1837 a devastating storm, the most destructive that Galveston experienced during the period of the republic, leveled almost every structure on the island. This disaster was followed by a decade of rapid building and expansion.[3] Not long after the storm of 1837 steamboat service, for a trip lasting some 48 hours, was initiated between New Orleans and Galveston.[4] Soon Galveston was well on its way to becoming the Lone Star Republic's greatest commercial center. This success was obtained only because the town's merchants, in cooperation with merchants in Houston, had gained control of the cotton trade on the Brazos River.

During the 1830s, before the ascent of Galveston, many steamers navigated the Brazos, often traveling from New Orleans along the coast of Texas and then up the Brazos to Brazoria and Columbia.[5] The omnibus designation "Brazos Ports" was given on passenger lists and bills of lading as the port of origin for many passengers and cargoes arriving in New Orleans. This designation included not only ports along the Brazos River, but also Quintana at its mouth and Velasco on the Bay of Galveston. The lucrative steamers carried mainly cotton bound for New Orleans and passengers traveling from one Brazos port to another. Under the lead of the firm McKinney & Williams, which had played a major role in financing the revolt against Mexico, the merchants of Galveston battled with other Texas harbors, including the Brazos ports. Facing this hostile alliance Robert Mills, the great opponent of McKinney & Williams, abandoned in the course of the 1840s his efforts to make one of the Brazos towns the principal transshipping point for cotton and other products of the Brazos region.[6] Mills, who nevertheless became very rich and was known before the Civil War as the richest man in Texas,[7] had many ties to the Gieseckes. These associations are reflected in Charles Giesecke's letters. A sandbar and a mudbank at the river's mouth were among the serious natural impediments to the development of the Brazos ports. Only a few feet of water flowed over this obstacle. By 1839 Galveston was winning the struggle for ascendancy. Some 228 ships arrived in Galveston that year; three years earlier scarcely a ship had called there.[8]

The cooperation between Houston and Galveston began at the end of the 1830s.[9] Galveston remained very vulnerable to bad weather at sea; the settlements there were not adequately protected against the waves. Houston was situated forty miles to the northwest on a wide portion of Buffalo Bayou, not far from the area where it flowed into Galveston Bay.[10] Although secure from storms, Houston was unsuited to serve as a mooring area for seagoing vessels. Even though everything had to be transshipped, Houston's hinterland expanded rapidly. Large lorries not unlike those traveling from Bremen to the interior brought goods to and from Houston.[11] One of the advantages of Houston's geographical position was that Buffalo Bayou stretched almost twenty miles to the plantations of the Brazos area. The hinterland of Houston included an area extending some eighty miles westward and northwestward to Bastrop, La Grange, Navasota, Caldwell, and other, smaller settlements.[12]

Not founded until 1836, Houston became that same year the capital of the Republic of Texas, an honor it retained until 1839. During the war with Mexico, Houston benefited from the destruction of Harrisburg, an older town on Buffalo Bayou. Due to the many shallows and banks on the route from Houston to Galveston, navigators had to reckon with little draft. Nevertheless, flatbottomed steamers and other suitable craft soon plied the waters between the two ports. In the mid-1840s Houston began to dominate the alliance with Galveston. At the end of the decade Galveston interests working together with merchants on the Brazos and Trinity rivers attempted to bypass Houston, but this endeavor failed.[13] The terrible hurricane of 1900 flooded Galveston Island and confirmed the predominance of Houston over its former partner city. The building of a great seawall in Galveston came too late. Today Galveston has for all practical purposes long been part of Greater Houston.

During the early 1840s the development of both communities still went forward rapidly. In 1840 the French authorities selected Galveston as a link in a chain of mailship ports serving postal intercourse between France and North and South America. This decision of commercial policy favored the Lone Star Republic.[14] Two primary mail lines were to be serviced by a 450-horsepower steamer. These lines linked Brazil, Cuba, and the West Indies. A subsidiary line employing a 220-horsepower steamer included Vera Cruz, Tampico, Galveston, and New Orleans. Until 1845, however, Galveston had no other regular service with foreign ports except New York and New Orleans.[15] A description of Galveston published in a German periodical in 1844 estimated its permanent population at 3,000.[16] This estimate is valuable because few reliable contemporary estimates of the size of Texas towns are available prior to the late 1840s. Many estimates were made by men who were promoting or denigrating one or more towns. The 1844 German estimate does not appear to be too high, since in 1839 an Englishman with experience in Galveston mentioned the same figure.[17] The U.S. Census of 1850 put the population at 4,177, making Galveston the largest city in Texas.[18] According to the same census, Houston had only 2,396 inhabitants, although earlier claims by travelers, well-wishers, and boosters had long ago arrived at sums twice as large.[19] In 1840 an American claimed Houston had 3,000 and Galveston 4,000 inhabitants.[20] Even given the possibility of great fluctuations in population size — when, for example, the numbers were swollen temporarily by immigrants waiting to move inland — high estimates are suspect. Also, some estimates, both high and low, failed to include slaves or Mexicans.

When the Lone Star Republic sought admission to the Union in 1845, many Galvestonians feared that the foreign trade of Texas would fall into the hands of merchants and shippers from the North. It was complained that foreign vessels would no longer call at Texas ports and that the door to the world would be closed. Texas's carefully constructed relations with Europe and South and Middle America were not yet solid. Galveston's Achilles' heel remained the paucity of routine ties to foreign ports, with the exception of New Orleans and New York. It should come as no surprise that the representatives of Galveston in the Texas Congress opposed statehood.[21]

World of Destination:

MERCHANTS AND IMMIGRANTS IN THE
REPUBLIC OF TEXAS

6

NORTH GERMAN ARRIVALS

THE PRECISE DATE of the Giesecke brothers' arrivals in Texas remains uncertain. One of them, Charles A. Giesecke, was in Texas by 1834.[1] Family traditions on both sides of the Atlantic place a Giesecke in Texas while it was still under Mexican rule.[2] In January 1836, as the Texas War for Independence was getting underway, a shipment of linens for Charles arrived in New Orleans aboard a ship from Bremen.[3] Presumably the linens were forwarded to him in Texas. A "Charles Giesecke" has been listed among the participants in the war, but the evidence that he is our Charles A. Giesecke is inconclusive.[4]

By 1840 Charles A. Giesecke, well established in Texas, was shipping cotton to Germany,[5] and both of his brothers had in all likelihood spent time in Texas. Charles is listed in the Texas census of 1840 as residing in Brazoria, owning six town lots, and having paid the poll tax imposed on all men twenty-two or older.[6] In view of the condition of surviving Texas records, the failure to find among them the names of any other Giesecke in Brazoria or Galveston does not rule out the possibility that Edward or Friedrich Giesecke was living there. The census-taking in 1840 began during the first half of the year, and most of it had been completed by July.[7] Someone arriving during the second half of the year would not be included.

Official ship-passenger lists furnish important information about the comings and goings of the Gieseckes and many other Germans who disembarked in Texas and U.S. ports during the 1830s and 1840s. Unfortunately, there are many gaps in these lists. Until 1873 more Germans traveling to America from a German port sailed from Bremen than Hamburg, and the disproportion between the two ports was enormous in most years before that date.[8] Although Bremen's laws required the submission of passenger lists to the authorities, limited storage space led to the systematic destruction of these lists beginning in the last decades of the nineteenth century;[9] most of the relevant German lists no longer exist. However, U.S. passenger lists in the National Archives provide an alternative source for ports in the United States. Indeed, data entered on these lists are in many, perhaps most, cases virtually identical to the data recorded on the destroyed Bremen lists. The passenger lists of German ships generally provided information not required by U.S. law: occupation, age, and even locality of birth or origin. Mostly Germans, the clerks in the United States responsible for preparing the lists did not bother to omit data not mandated by American law.

The situation with regard to passenger lists for the Republic of Texas is less favorable. The Lone Star Republic enacted legislation similar to the U.S. law of 1819 requiring the submission of passenger lists by the captains of arriving vessels. A Galveston municipal ordinance of 1839 established virtually identical provisions for ships calling there.[10] Regrettably little evidence of the execution of the Texas laws survives,[11] but the passenger lists of ships used by the *Adelsverein*, including those bound for Galveston, have survived. These lists can be made to serve as a partial replacement for another segment of Bremen's destroyed lists. Since a number of the *Adelsverein* ships sailed from other European ports, principally in the Low Countries, the *Adelsverein* lists also furnish records for some ships carrying German emigrants from non-German ports.[12] U.S. passenger lists for Galveston during the early years of Texas statehood are disappointing because so many of them are lost. However, a large proportion of European passengers bound for Texas continued to travel by way of another American port, most often New York, Baltimore, or New Orleans. Nevertheless, the passenger lists cannot be depended on to furnish final destinations, nor can it automatically be assumed that passengers traveled farther than these destinations. Not infrequently, the passengers went on, at the time or soon thereafter, to final destinations not indicated on the lists from Europe. Few of the passenger lists from the first half of the nineteenth century can be relied upon to provide accurate answers in the column headed "Country of Origin." Ship personnel all too often made their own task easier by simply recording the country or state of embarkation. Thus Germans departing Europe via Le Havre became French. Even the usually careful compilers of the Bremen lists frequently took the easy way out and indicated "Bremen" in this column.

The place of the Gieseckes in the flow of Germans to the Americas can be assayed by consulting U.S. passenger lists and supplementing information obtained from them with data from sources pertaining to *Adelsverein* immigrants. A perusal of U.S. passenger lists for New Orleans, New York, Baltimore, and, later, Galveston reveals important patterns in German and other migration to America after the establishment of the lists in 1820. Eventually, the lists become by far most voluminous for New York. This is a consequence of New York's development into the world's largest immigrant port, but into the 1830s Baltimore and New Orleans surpassed or rivaled New York in volume of immigrants. The decisive impetus to New York's predominance was the opening of the Erie Canal in 1825. This new waterway enabled passengers who sailed or steamed up the Hudson River to Albany to gain access easily to the Great Lakes as well as the Midwestern river system in which the Mississippi and its tributaries played the most important roles. Settlers bound for much of the Midwest and part of the Upper South favored the northern routes. These routes were of course not the usual way of reaching Texas, but during the 1830s and 1840s, indeed throughout the nineteenth century, New York remained a commonly used point of transfer to New Orleans for connections to Texas, or even for direct passage to Texas. By the mid-1830s — more precisely, by 1836 — the number of passengers from Bremen and Bremerhaven arriving at American ports had swelled enormously. Beginning in mid-1836, many of the emigrants sailing from Bremen were from the Kingdom of Hannover.

Emigration from Bremen via New Orleans followed a pattern similar to that via New York except that the volume was less. By 1836, however, large numbers of passengers were traveling from Bremen to New Orleans. That same year brought a noticeable increase in the number of people from the Hildesheim district embarking from Bremen. The large-scale arrival of immigrants from Bremen had begun earlier in Baltimore than in other U.S. harbors. In the early 1830s, when Baltimore was the most important U.S. port for commerce between Bremen and the United States, substantial numbers of German emigrants were arriving in the Maryland metropolis. The passenger lists for Baltimore contain until the 1830s numerous entries in the column "Destination" to the effect that individual passengers were sailing on farther to New Orleans or New York. A few years later, when direct voyages between Bremen and New Orleans, New York, and, eventually, Galveston had become common, such annotations became rare.

The problems in interpreting the passenger lists caused by gaps[13] are compounded by the handwriting. Lists for ships sailing from Bremen, for example, often contain confusing mixtures of old German script with Latin script. Nor do these compounds make for the most perplexing lists to decipher or transcribe. Americans, or English-speaking people, are apparently to blame for much of the worst handwriting. German scribes, even when writing in English, usually seem to have had a clearer, more consistent hand.

Despite the manifold difficulties in obtaining accurate surnames and place-names, especially if the towns were small, we find numerous instances of people from the Gieseckes' region of Germany, the southern part of the Kingdom of Hannover. Many of the ships transporting emigrants were of U.S. registry. The lists generally give Bremen as the port of embarkation, making no distinction between Bremen and its new harbor, Bremerhaven. Records from ships arriving in Baltimore and New Orleans from 1834 to 1840 are among the most pertinent to this study, and they contain much valuable data. The adults described in these records were predominantly craftsmen or the wives of craftsmen, but there were also numerous farmers, hired hands (*Knechte*), and maids or hired women (*Mägde*) among them. In the summer of 1834 twenty-four-year-old Wilhelm Dübel from Elze landed in Baltimore. According to the passenger list, he was a miller intending to go to Ohio.[14] Seven days later, at the beginning of August, another ship brought an eighteen-year-old tailor, Frederick Rock [?], to the same port.[15] He came from Alfeld not far from Elze — or perhaps from Alsfeld farther south in Hessen. Alfeld and Alsfeld were often confused on the passenger lists. Since several passengers on the same ship came from southern Hannover, and passengers from the same area often traveled together to ports of embarkation, the possibility is good that the tailor came from Alfeld. Some four weeks later a family of six — Philipp Hess, his wife, and their four children — arrived in Baltimore from Gronau, located also in the Elze area.[16]

Ships sailed to America for the most part during the spring and summer. Thus there are no records of emigrants from the Gieseckes' area for several months following the arrival of the Hess family in Baltimore. In July 1835 a twenty-four-year-old shoemaker named Godfried Dyel [?] from "Allsfeld" [possibly Alfeld?] disembarked with several other members of his family.[17] On December 1 there arrived in Baltimore the first passenger who can be said with reasonable certainty to have come from Alfeld. Although his age was not noted, the passenger, basket-maker Georg Uhrlaub, was listed as an adult.[18]

Only eight days later a merchant, J. F. Kaufman, arrived in New Orleans.[19] We shall often encounter him, under the name Julius Kauffman,[20] in connection with the Gieseckes. On the passenger list of 1835 his country of origin is given as Bremen, but he may well have come from the Kingdom of Hannover, and even from the Hildesheim district.[21] The passenger list, in the column for "country of which intends to become an inhabitant," indicates New Orleans. Only 19 years old when he arrived in New Orleans in 1835, Kauffman had established himself in business in Galveston by 1842,[22] and he soon became one of the best-known merchants in Texas. A relative (brother?), Eduard Kauffman, was in Galveston even earlier, at least by 1840.[23] Charles Giesecke mentioned the Kauffmans repeatedly in his letters, and their names crop up often in German travel literature of the era.[24]

Small clusters of emigrants from Elze and nearby areas of southern Hannover continued to reach America in 1837 and 1838. The Baltimore passenger lists show that two young men — Johann Gerlach, a twenty-six-year-old farmer from Elze, and Heinrich Meyer, a twenty-two-year-old shoemaker from Gronau — disembarked two days apart in July 1837.[25] That fall two passengers from Bockenem arrived in New Orleans a day apart: Gerhard Schulte, a farmer aged seventeen, and Christine Wussken [?], a "servant" aged thirty-five. Their final destinations were not indicated clearly, but presumably the woman intended to reside in New Orleans.[26] In the spring of 1838 an artisan, a goldsmith named H. Schmidt from Alfeld, arrived in New Orleans. His age was given as twenty-seven.[27] That October a miller, J. P. Kallehem [?], from Gronau arrived in Baltimore.[28] The next month a farmer from Elze, eighteen-year-old Carl Adolph Vinze [?], reached New Orleans, apparently giving Missouri as his final destination.[29]

The instances of travelers from the Giesecke's area of Germany illustrate a thesis often advanced about European emigration since the eighteenth century: the areas of a country or region supplying large numbers of emigrants tend to broaden, sometimes slowly, sometimes rapidly; but once emigration has become frequent from an area or region it generally continues until there is a major alteration in conditions in the sending or receiving land. Varying in volume, emigration seldom ceases altogether.[30] Once it has become an established pattern of behavior in a region, only changes such as the erection of legal barriers, the blockage of transportation, or the emptying of entire villages terminates the flow of emigrants. A later instance of this process of "chain migration" is the mass emigration of Eastern European Jews that began in the 1880s and was halted only by the arrival of World War I. In the short space of little more than thirty years, one-third or more of the Jews of Eastern Europe left their homelands.[31] This provides an extreme example of migration with low rates of return during the industrial era. Some 95 percent of the Eastern European Jews in America during the period 1908 to 1924 remained there, although the proportion of return migrants rose to as much as a third among other American immigrants.[32] Some returnees went back to Europe forever while others remained only briefly, but both types of remigrants played an important role in further migration. Through advice, assistance, and example they influenced others to venture the journey to America.

Although Charles Giesecke had come to Texas by 1834, no records have been found for the arrivals and departures of any of the Gieseckes or the development of their business until 1836. The earliest reference to a Giesecke on the passenger lists is an arrival on a ship from Bremen in New Orleans on June 9, 1836. This is some six weeks after the Battle of San Jacinto, the final, decisive battle of the Texas War for Independence. The scrawled name appears to be "Gierke" or "Gieske," and the entry under "country of origin" is "Bremen." The occupation is not specifically indicated but, if the clerk compiling the list employed a consistent system, the designation "merchant" is intended. The age of the young man is given as 26. This is almost correct for Charles A. Giesecke, who was then 25. It must be kept in mind that few of the lists were kept rigorously.[33] If we did not know that a shipment of linens from Germany for Charles had arrived in New Orleans almost six months earlier, we would have to question seriously whether the young merchant named in this entry is really he.

In July the following year a twenty-five-year-old merchant disembarked in New Orleans from a sloop from Galveston. Two spellings of his name are given: on the Quarterly Abstract it is most likely "A. Giesecke,"[34] but on the passenger list itself the name is not as clearly written and appears to be "A. K. Guild."[35] The letters "A. K." probably refer to Charles A. Giesecke's baptismal name "Anton Carl" with the latter spelled with a "K." Using a routine formula, the passenger list describes all of the passengers but one as merchants who "belong to U.S. and [are] going to become inhabitants of New Orleans." The likelihood that Charles A. Giesecke traveled among these merchants is strengthened by the fact that the data in the Quarterly Abstracts frequently are more accurate than those furnished by the passenger lists.[36] The Quarterly Abstracts were supposed to provide summaries that the highest customs official of each port was required to submit every three months to the secretary of state in Washington.

Both of the older Giesecke brothers sailed from Galveston to New Orleans in the winter of 1838. This is a reasonable conclusion to draw from the passenger lists. Entries for "H. W. [?] Gaisicke, Merchant, 27, male" and for "C. Gaisicke, Farmer, 26, male" appear in the Quarterly Abstract under the entries for a brig from Galveston. It is possible, but unlikely, that the first initial of the latter name was intended to be an "F." The age is correct for Charles A. Giesecke and two years off for Friedrich Giesecke. The misspelling of the family name fits the pattern common at the time in Texas and the United States. The entries on the passenger lists for the same two passengers differ from those on the Quarterly Abstract. They are listed — if the unusually sloppy handwriting is correctly interpreted — as "H. Geiske" and "C. Geiske." The occupation of the second passenger is listed as "Planter," the designation Charles A. Giesecke favored for himself. The ages of the two men are given as 28 for the first and 30 for the second.[37] These are almost correct if the ages of the two men are reversed. The apparent "H." preceding the first name on both sets of lists could indicate that Friedrich Giesecke had been given, and actually used, the forename or first initial of his father, Heinrich. On the Quarterly Abstract "country of origin" and "destination" entries both give the United States. On the passenger list, however, the "place of residence" is recorded as New Orleans.[38] This might suggest that at least one of the Gieseckes had not yet taken up residence in Texas, but more likely the reference to residence pertains, as often on passenger lists, merely to the vessel's destination. This last possibility appears all the more probable because there is a notation indicating no baggage. If the Gieseckes were living or staying in Texas, they might well have been visiting New Orleans without baggage. There is inconclusive evidence pointing to business conducted there by Friedrich.[39]

Clear-cut documentation of the Gieseckes occurs in the passenger lists for 1839. An unproblematic entry pertains to Eduard, the youngest of the three brothers, whose first name is anglicized to "Edward." In view of the circumstantial evidence provided by Charles Giesecke's letters, which suggests that Edward was the last of the brothers to reach America, this journey is in all likelihood Edward's first visit. He sailed with a brig from Bremen and arrived in New Orleans on November 23, 1839.[40] His last residence is listed as Elze. The occupation of the passenger whose name precedes his is given as tanner, and a dash in the same position in Edward's entry presumably signifies either ditto or unknown. A notation adds that he has three crates on board.

A year later a Quarterly Abstract refers to another Giesecke, almost certainly Friedrich Giesecke. The passenger sailed with a bark from Bremen and arrived in New Orleans on November 30, 1840. The entry is unambiguous: "F. Giesecke — Merchant — Male — 31."[41] The age is correct.

"Germany" has been entered into the column "country of origin" and "U.S." into the column "destination."

On the basis of the ship lists and other sources we can conclude that at least one of the Gieseckes was active in Texas as early as 1834 and that they were soon, if not from the beginning, importing and exporting goods there. Charles Giesecke probably preceded his older brother, Friedrich, and certainly his younger brother, Edward, in arriving in Texas. Friedrich came at least twice to Texas — in 1838 and again in 1840 — and Edward is unlikely to have preceded him. In any event, Edward was in Texas by the end of 1839 or the beginning of 1840. Friedrich, unlike his younger brothers, did not settle permanently in Texas. In all probability one of the three returned to Germany in 1842. The passenger lists for New Orleans for January 1842 have an entry for a merchant "H." or "F." "Giesike" or "Giisike." This merchant sailed with a sloop from the mouth of the Brazos River in Texas to New Orleans, and "Germany" is entered in the passenger list's column "country to which belongs." This same entry stands in the column headed "country of which intends to become inhabitant." [42] The indicated age, 26, would have been correct for Edward, but is six years off for Friedrich. Did Edward book a place for his brother, or did Friedrich take over a booking for Edward? Perhaps the age was confused in some other way. During the same month at least two shipments of cotton from Galveston bearing Friedrich's mark arrived in New Orleans. [43] We know from Charles's letters that in March 1844 he had returned a few weeks or months previously from Germany. [44] By this date the Gieseckes had been active in Brazoria for some years.

7

BRAZORIA

RISE AND FALL OF A TOWN

Brazoria was one of the oldest Anglo-American settlements in Texas. The past tense is appropriate, for present-day Brazoria is located on a different site. Founded in the mid-1820s to serve as a port on the Brazos River and as a commercial center for Stephen F. Austin's colony,[1] the original town was situated on the left bank of the river some twenty-five to thirty miles upstream from the river's mouth. Almost all of the early descriptions of Brazoria mention either one or the other of these two distances. The discrepancy is to be explained by variations in determining how to take into account the many curves in the Brazos and precisely where the river's broad mouth meets Galveston Bay. The water at the mouth reached a depth of a mere seven to ten feet because of sandbanks, and they continued to pose obstacles to traffic as the port developed. Stephen F. Austin fluctuated in his assessment of the potential importance of the town and other Brazos ports,[2] but Brazoria's development received a fillip once he and other colonists rejected Galveston Island as a port. They decided in favor of the development of ports on the Brazos and the placement of a customs house at the river's mouth.

Austin in the early 1830s wrote optimistically that Brazoria would become the commercial hub of the Brazos region and the adjacent San Bernard River: "It [Brazoria] is improving and flourishing very rapidly and must become a large and very important place in a few years."[3] Although restrained in comparison with many other early descriptions of the town, this portrayal still smacks of the boosterism common to many references to Texas towns in the nineteenth century. Austin's prediction rested more upon wish than sober analysis.

About the same time that Austin penned his expectations for Brazoria the great Bohemian German writer Charles Sealsfield, some of whose most famous works are set in Texas at the time of the Texan Revolution, sailed up the Brazos to Brazoria. Sealsfield reported that the town had over thirty houses, among them three of brick and three with wooden siding; the remainder of the structures were log houses.[4] Detlef Dunt, the early advocate of German emigration to Texas, visited Brazoria about the same time, or perhaps a bit earlier than Sealsfield. Jordt found only a few wooden houses. He was disappointed — doubtless because he had already heard so much about Brazoria.[5] A cynic might remark that to the everlasting bewilderment of German tourists most American houses are even today built of wood. In April of 1833 a young Viennese adventurer, George Bernard Erath, passed through Brazoria and left a more positive assessment than Jordt. Whether this evaluation resulted from much construction in the interim, or merely from a different perspective, is not clear. Erath found forty to fifty houses, about half of which were completed. He reported that the houses were made of pine brought from New Orleans or Mobile, Alabama.[6]

The fortunes of Brazoria continued to fluctuate, but in the 1830s its prospects seemed mostly favorable. In 1831 and 1832 a dispute between the Mexican government and the colonists along the Brazos over the levying of duties heated up, and Brazoria became the center of resistance to the Mexican authorities.[7] When in 1832 Brazoria became a municipality separate from the San Felipe administrative area, the town had already become the seat of a court. Although the court was transferred to neighboring Columbia in 1834, Brazoria was to have the honor of being the temporary capital of the new republic for three months in 1836.[8] That same year the court returned to Brazoria when the town became the seat of newly created Brazoria County. If, as two secondary works claim, Brazoria was burned to the ground by the Mexican Army in April 1836,[9] the event made no great impression on the inhabitants and was not cited by contemporaries as a reason for the later faltering development of the town. At most, a few houses burned. In 1836 more ships arriving in New Orleans from Texas sailed from Brazoria than any other Texan port.[10] Judged by the surviving passenger lists, the years 1829 to 1837–1838 were the great period of ship travel between Brazoria and New Orleans.[11]

The stagnating development of Brazoria was overcome in the mid-1830s, if contemporary reports are to be believed.[12] However, a pessimistic voice from 1836 was prophetic, even though the justification provided was not fully appropriate. D. B. Edward was the principal of a school in New Orleans and had formerly been a teacher in Texas. His *History of Texas* (1836) probably antedated the heady events of the Texas Revolution: "[Brazoria] has heretofore been, and is yet, of considerable consequence; but cannot long remain so, by reason of its proximity to Columbia, and the lowness of its situation; being subject to overflows in a particularly wet season; although the clearing away, and improving of its widely spread timber bottoms, will support its continuance in some measure, as a carrying place."[13] This astute but flawed prediction assumed that commerce and shipping on the Brazos would continue, at least "in some measure," as Principal Edward put it. Understandably, he had no inkling of the meteoric rise of Galveston and Houston.

Many a description in the next years was not so restrained. For example, a Protestant minister who traveled around Texas in 1837 and rapidly penned a history of the Texan Revolution found much to praise in Brazoria:

> [Brazoria] is one of the oldest American towns in Texas, and, in point of trade, a place of importance. The soil of the surrounding country, except a small tract bordering the coast, is very rich and productive, consisting of a deep black mould, resting upon a substratum of red loam; this substratum is in many places 30 or 40 feet deep, and entirely free from stones. . . . Cotton and corn are extensively cultivated and yield abundant crops with but little labor. Almost all kinds of culinary vegetables thrive well. Horned cattle increase in a wonderful manner, and are an immense source of wealth, as they require hardly any attention, and continue pasturing in the extensive and fertile prairies and woodlands during the whole year. Here are many of the wealthiest farmers of Texas.[14]

Another visitor from the United States, the splenetic "Colonel" Stiff who came to Texas in 1838, made many biting remarks in his book on his journey, but he found nothing to complain about in Brazoria: "This is a country town on the West bank of the river, . . . and it is at this time one of the most important towns in point of trade in the country—situated in a fine cotton county that is well cultivated."[15]

A standard reference work on the history of Texas claims that the population of Brazoria fluctuated between three and five thousand in the period 1836 to 1860.[16] Even the lower of these figures is unlikely as the peak, and impossible as the lowest point, during these years. The writers of travel accounts and other authors in the 1830s and 1840s, many of whom gave greatly exaggerated population estimates, made no such extreme claims.

Only a few people, who confused data for the entire county with those for the town of Brazoria, arrived at figures approaching the range of three to five thousand.[17] The estimates of an unknown traveler in 1837 who writes of three to four hundred inhabitants,[18] and of a Briton who visited Texas in 1840 and provided the figure five to six hundred,[19] are more likely to be on the mark for the town. A sober reference to eight hundred for the period 1840 to 1844 in a county history published in 1975 is still a bit high.[20] All of these figures must be questioned as including inhabitants of the surrounding area. A question that must be raised about all population data for Texas during this period — even the more reliable data that do not include the surrounding area — is whether slaves and Mexicans are included. For the period before the Civil War, the number of Mexican inhabitants is of importance only for San Antonio among the larger towns in Texas. The entire county of Brazoria had virtually no Mexicans, and most of the slaves lived on the countryside. Nevertheless, an adequate estimate of the urban population must take African Americans into account. It is uncertain whether most of the estimates cited do so.

How could a town as small as Brazoria have been so important to the early development of Texas? We must discard twentieth-century notions of size to begin to understand the role played during the period of the Republic of Texas by a community with less than a thousand inhabitants. Indicative of its importance, and of its fluctuating fortunes, is the finding that by 1840 at least six different newspapers had been published in Brazoria — and all had gone out of business.[21] The town's uneven development was determined by its varying importance as a port and commercial center. The letters of Charles A. Giesecke from 1844–1845 contain many hints of Brazoria's incipient stagnation.[22] He sees in them mere consequences of a temporary business crisis triggered by poor harvests. However, in 1840 an anonymous traveler offered an analysis that is the product of much riper reflection:

> As long since as the year 1831, Brazoria was regarded as being one of the most growing and important towns in Texas. And for many years since it was considered the door through which emigrants to Texas must find their way to the country. For some cause, probably the difficulty of passing the bar at the mouth of the Brazos, it has not succeeded according to the expectation of its friends. It is, however, a pleasant town beautifully situated upon a handsome elevation. . . . It is . . . surrounded by a fertile and beautiful section of country.

It will probably never be a commercial city, but an interesting and pleasant country town. One reason why this and other such towns are slow in growth is that land [in Texas] is so easily obtained, and its culture so profitable, that mechanics and professional men often prefer residing upon farms at a little distance, to remaining in town.[23]

This balanced assessment of a town or area is a rarity in the literature on Texas at the time.

Francis Moore, the editor of a Houston newspaper, was still bullish on Brazoria's future in 1844. He predicted that the town "will undoubtedly become a place of great importance, as it is situated in a remarkably fertile section of country, the resources of which only require to be developed in order to concentrate at this point an extensive carrying trade." He admired the "beautiful courthouse," several large stores, and many well-kept homes. His description of Houston, which he inaccurately praised as the "first city of the Republic with regard to population and wealth," is illuminating for the purposes of comparison. He wrote that Houston had about fifty stores and several "large and commodious hotels." [24]

Brazoria failed to retain its place of importance as a harbor through the 1840s, but traffic on the Brazos remained intermittently heavy until the middle of the decade, that is, until the time of Charles A. Giesecke's surviving letters of 1844–1845. Although schooners could sail only some sixty to seventy miles up the 800-mile length of the Brazos, small steamboats reached Washington-on-the-Brazos, about 200 miles from the coast.[25] However, the steamer traffic was dangerous and destined ultimately to fail in sustaining the success of Brazoria. The flatbottomed boats often tipped over or ran aground on obstructions. Extensive flooding in 1843 induced planters and merchants along the Brazos to avoid taking great risks; insurance for freight on the river had become prohibitively expensive or impossible to obtain. Overland routes to Houston, located on Buffalo Bayou off Galveston Bay, continued to increase in importance, especially for the middle and upper Brazos region. From Houston wares were shipped to Galveston or New Orleans. By 1845 steamboats were becoming a rarity on the rivers of Texas.[26] The improved business climate induced by the entry of Texas into the Union in 1846 altered the situation. Steamers appeared again in large numbers on the rivers, but Brazoria's days as a major port were gone. New attempts to remove hazards to traffic on the Brazos and improve its navigability failed, as they had before. The necessary capital could not be raised. A short canal was finally constructed through the mouth of the river in 1850, but the often-discussed canal to connect the Brazos to Galveston Bay was not built. Later in the 1850s, railroad lines linked the lower Brazos area with Houston and replaced most of the wagon traffic to that city and Galveston.[27]

Although Brazoria never acquired a large permanent German population, as did Galveston, Houston, and communities in the Hill Country, many Germans in addition to the travelers who wrote about Brazoria found their way there during the 1830s and 1840s. Some arrived because one route to the interior passed through Brazoria.[28] Still others were attracted by the town's reputation as a commercial center, but few remained there permanently. A group of German Catholics arrived in 1839–1840 with a priest, Father Jacob Weiser. They erected a wooden church dedicated as Saint Joseph on-the-Brazos.[29] Apparently neither Father Weiser nor most of his parishioners remained long in Brazoria. The surviving records of the parish go only to 1848. Father James A. Miller, the first pastor whose records have been handed down, baptized many people with German names from 1848 to 1857.[30]

The signs of German transients, and even of some residents, did not indicate a large permanent population of Germans. This segment of the area's inhabitants grew slowly. In all of Brazoria County there lived in 1840 a mere handful of Germans. Evidence in the poll-tax records indicates that, of the county's some three hundred households, at most fifteen — and more likely only three or four — were headed by Germans. Every white male age twenty or older had to pay a poll tax. With the exception of Charles Giesecke, only one other poll-taxpayer of a total of approximately 295 in the county had a surname clearly of German origin. Twelve other poll-taxpayers had names that may well have belonged to Germans.[31]

The size of the German population as indicated by family names increased both relatively and absolutely by the time of the U.S. Census of 1850 but remained small in comparison with the German population of Galveston County. Among the 1,329 whites in Brazoria County, there were now about 100 German-speaking people born in Europe. The census did not distinguish between urban and rural residents. At least 71 adults had been born in Germany: 45 men and 26 women. Twenty-five children had also been born in Germany. In addition to these 96 German-born residents, two Swiss-born adults had German names. Many of the German men were young and single. Three of the German-born women were married to men with non-German names or settled in households headed by men with such names. The inhabitants of Brazoria County included also many people with German names who had come from elsewhere in the United States. A few of these people belonged to the same households as residents who had been born in Germany. This may indicate that some of the Americans still spoke German. Several Swedes and Danes lived in German households.[32]

The brother of the famous German Eighteen-Forty-Eighter Friedrich Kapp lived in the neighboring town of Columbia. Both had fled Europe following the defeat of the Revolution of 1848. Friedrich Kapp passed through Brazoria on his way to visit this brother in 1852. He found everywhere signs of decline and decay, some of them similar to those mentioned by Charles Giesecke in 1845,[33] but Kapp's description seven years later offers slimmer grounds for hope: "The place is on the Brazos and is completely hewn into the woods. The trees extend into the yards and streets of the so-called town. It consists of a few wooden stores [hölzerne Kramläden], a few taverns, a courthouse, and about twenty to thirty private homes, all of which have that same provisional look I had found already in Velasco."[34] Perhaps Kapp was still not fully accustomed to the American habit of building mostly wooden buildings, but the German term he uses for "wooden" often implies "dull" or "styleless." One of the shops he mentioned still belonged to Edward Giesecke.

Today Old Brazoria is overgrown by nature. The county seat was moved in 1897 to Angleton. At the beginning of the twentieth century a new settlement named "Brazoria" was founded. It is situated more than half a mile from the old town.

AGRICULTURE AND SLAVERY IN BRAZORIA COUNTY

Brazoria was an overwhelmingly Anglo-American town in the midst of a county with an almost exclusively Anglo-American and African American population. Most of the county's inhabitants were slaves. According to the Texas census of 1847, Brazoria County had a total of 4,641 residents. This figure includes 3,013 slaves and a mere 604 white females.[35] Almost 68 percent of the county's residents were slaves, the highest proportion of slaves in all of the counties in Texas. Slaves then constituted some 27 percent of the total inhabitants of Texas. Twelve years earlier, in 1835, this proportion had reached only 12 percent.[36] Slavery was expanding rapidly in certain areas of the Lone Star Republic, and Brazoria County was among the foremost.[37]

The labor of hundreds of slaves forged the links that during the 1820s and 1830s bound Texas, and above all the Lower Brazos region, to the world market. Large, profitable exports of agricultural products propelled the Texan economy toward expanding these links. The cultivation of cotton and the raising of cattle for meat and hides fueled the initial drive for exports. Later the impetus came also from the cultivation of sugar cane and tobacco. The expansion of the institution of slavery was tied to larger and larger crops of cotton and sugar cane.[38] An ever increasing number of slaves was introduced legally into Texas under the Lone Star Republic. Although large plantations with over one hundred slaves never gained the importance in Texas that they had in some parts of the American "Old South,"[39] slavery formed the bedrock on which Brazoria County and its economy rested.

Many handbooks and travel guides for German emigrants to Texas sought to downplay the importance of slavery there. German objections to slavery and fears of having to compete with slave plantations and unfree labor were dismissed as groundless. Germans writing on Texas during the 1830s and 1840s offered assurances that there were dim prospects for the continuation and extension of slavery in Texas. Moritz Beyer, the author of a guide for emigrants to North America and Texas published in 1846, wrote reassuringly that slavery was forbidden in German colonies in Texas. He added optimistically that slavery would vanish with the increase in the German population of Texas.[40] On the other hand, there were more pessimistic — or more realistic — warnings to Germans about Texas.[41] Johann G. Büttner, a Calvinist theologian, sought to deter German workers and day laborers from emigrating to Texas. He believed that the existence of slavery depressed wages and viewed Texas as the last choice in the world for German workers. Büttner accurately depicted Texas as a country where slavery was growing swiftly.[42]

The liberal German writer Friedrich Armand Strubberg, who adopted the pen name "Armand," lived for extended periods during the 1830s and 1840s in Texas. He wrote bitter novels depicting life in a slave society, but his viewpoint was one of disdain from a high social position rather than sympathy for the enslaved. Strubberg's father was a rich tobacco merchant from Amsterdam, and his mother came from a French émigré family. Her father had served in the chancellery of Landgrave Frederick II of Hesse-Kassel. Armand was born in Kassel in 1806 and went at age sixteen to Bremen to become a clerk in a large firm. Soon he sailed as a merchant to America, and subsequently he traveled several times back and forth between the Americas.[43] His novel *Saat und Ernte* (Sowing and Harvest) tells of slaves imported illegally into Texas in the mid-1830s and abused by the slave trader Harry Williams.[44] The greedy, self-seeking Williams does not participate in the Texan War for Independence. He leaves the fighting and dying to others while he exploits the opportunity to smuggle another two hundred slaves into Texas. Although Strubberg despised slave traders, other slaveowners are portrayed more sympathetically as enlightened aristocrats. Williams's opposite, the son of a small plantation owner from the northern United States, fights heroically from start to finish in the Texan war against Mexico.

The position on slavery taken by Friedrich Schlecht is a rarity in the German literature on Texas. The cultivated, cosmopolitan Schlecht visited Texas in 1848. He became an apologist for slavery: "As for the treatment of slaves here, it is by far not as harsh as people in Europe usually think. Many a day laborer in Germany would be delighted to exchange his position with that of a slave here and would certainly be quite satisfied with it."[45]

We delude ourselves if we infer a person's position on slavery from his nationality or national origins. It has often been incorrectly asserted that the Germans in America opposed slavery.[46] Equally mistaken is the contention that the position of immigrants on slavery corresponded to the views prevailing in the section of America in which they lived. Too often we hear that the Germans and other European immigrants in the South favored slavery and that those in the North rejected it.[47] Reality was less tidy. The major dividing lines, coupled with the region of residence, were those of occupation, social class, and sources of income. Germans living in the Anglo-American areas of Texas and active as farmers or merchants were not inclined to oppose slavery.[48]

Although Charles A. Giesecke did not have much of a plantation, he allied himself in many ways with the large slaveholders. There is no sign in his letters of hostility to the institution of slavery. It is unclear what practicable alternative he himself had to the use of slave labor on his farm. We should not overlook the ways in which his attitude toward slavery may also have been influenced by his upbringing. Like some of the German writers sympathetic toward American slavery, he was accustomed from birth to the division of the population engaged in agriculture into a few substantial leaseholders or lords (*Gutsherren*), peasants of varying status, and a mass of rural laborers and servants (*Knechte*). If he found slavery shocking and was repulsed by what he saw in Texas, these experiences are in no way reflected in his letters of 1844–1845. A rare indication of possible reservations is a remark he made in his letter of February 10, 1845. Complaining about low cotton prices, he remarks: "Hardly enough to buy shoes for the Negroes. Well, it's a free county, thank God! He who has no shoes can go barefoot." But there is no certainty that this comment was intended to be ironic. There is no conclusive evidence that the sight of slavery in any way alienated him. Rather, a few hints in his letters indicate that he likely shared the then widespread belief that slaves were inferior beings. He took advantage of slavery for his business. Once a European had thrown down roots in America, his position on slavery was influenced more by class, trade, place of residence, and other practical considerations, than by national origins.

The old legend of the enmity toward slavery of virtually all Germans in Texas has much to do with a few passages in Frederick Olmsted's often-cited *Journey through Texas*. The issue of slavery in the United States was becoming acute when Olmsted journeyed through Texas in 1854. He found most Germans poor, but hardworking and rapidly improving themselves materially. He tried at one point in his book to show how the wages of the Germans suffered from the exploitation of slaves by the planters. In another passage he claimed that most Germans were enemies of slavery but added the qualification that "as fast as they acquired property, they followed the customs of the country and purchased slaves."[49] This limitation has often been disregarded by readers of Olmsted's influential work.

A tragic incident in Gillespie County in a German area in the interior of Texas during the Civil War contributed greatly to the subsequent image of Texas Germans. In 1862 more than fifty people, settlers from Germany and their children, were massacred, some in cold blood, because they preferred to fight for the Union rather than the Confederacy.[50] This episode has often been misinterpreted as a sign of general German hostility to slavery.

The belief that the German Texans opposed slavery was seriously challenged during the early twentieth century. A newly forming consensus of American historians regarded slavery and the Old South in a mellow light, while viewing abolitionists hostilely as fanatics who had disrupted the Union.[51] The tendency was to depict Germans and other whites in the South — with the exception of a few traitors — as loyal adherents of the Confederacy. Industrious historians downplayed or even denied indications of antislavery sentiment among Southern whites. This was the position taken by two of the best-known historians of the Texas Germans, Rudolph Biesele and Gilbert Benjamin. Biesele's work was more distorted by these tendencies than was Benjamin's. Biesele suggested that Germans had acquired the false reputation of being hostile to slavery because of the sensational activity of a few radicals, most notably the socialist journalist Dr. Adolf Douai in San Antonio.[52] Benjamin's approach was somewhat different. He acknowledged the widespread animosity of German farmers and artisans toward slavery but downplayed this attitude by interpreting it as a mere economic reflex. He noted that German farmers received a one to two cent premium for their cotton due to its superiority to cotton raised and harvested by slaves.[53] Even Terry Jordan's superb monograph on German Texan agriculture, published during the 1960s, stands under the shadow of the tendency to belittle the significance of German opposition to slavery.[54] More generally, Jordan's innovative work suffers from the tendency to minimize differences between Germans and other whites in nineteenth-century Texas.

To do justice to the issue of attitudes toward slavery during the 1830s and 1840s, we must bear in mind the precarious internal and external circumstances of the Lone Star Republic. Nowhere in Texas were conditions more propitious for a slave revolt than in Brazoria County, with its two-thirds majority population of slaves. The history of actual slave revolts is still spottily researched, but at least one large uprising in the Brazoria area, in 1835, has been reported. According to one account, a hundred slaves were severely punished and several others executed.[55] The slaves evidently had rebelled when news circulated that the Mexican Army was approaching. Many slaves regarded themselves as liberated in 1835–1836 and sought to take advantage of the proximity of Mexican forces. Although Mexican policy failed to exploit this situation, Mexican soldiers frequently treated the slaves as emancipated.[56] Despite the expansion of the slave system facilitated by the Texan victory over Santa Anna's army, the threat of a renewal of hostilities with Mexico served to keep alive the dread of slave uprisings. Much slave unrest was reported in 1841.[57] Free blacks were not permitted to live in Texas under the Lone Star Republic. Although legally the importation of slaves was — with the important exception of slaves from the United States — prohibited, direct imports from other countries were often tolerated.[58]

An export-oriented market economy had emerged in the Lower Brazos area and the region around Galveston and Houston by the 1830s. Capitalist relations had thoroughly penetrated this society, whose very existence depended upon the world market. The intensity of economic development in this section of Texas far exceeded that in Bremen's hinterland. A perusal of the census returns of 1850 confirms the impression of the economic structure of Brazoria County and the Galveston Bay area obtained from other sources. The inhabitants of the region consisted of slaves, craftsmen, and businessmen — whether large or small, whether rural or urban — and little else except children and wives.[59] Often the distinction between rural and urban business had little significance, as we shall see in the case of the Gieseckes. The line between small and wealthy businessmen was more important.

Southern Hannover had fewer business people regardless of the size of the undertaking. Remnants of guilds and feudal agrarian relationships persisted. The business of Brazoria County was business, although the social life of some of the county's wealthier planters was already in the 1840s characterized by an abandon that was sustained by slavery and rich soil, and responded only indirectly to cotton prices on the world market.[60] All in all, the planter in Brazoria County had little in common with the penniless decaying gentility of the North German aristocrat satirized in Karl Immermann's *Baron Münchhausen* (1838). Immermann's character with the ridiculous name Count Schnuck-Puckelig-Erbsenscheucher has only a crumbling castle, petty privileges, and illusions of grandeur. The planter-businessmen and merchant-farmers of Brazoria County are more reminiscent of sober Bremen merchants or, in a number of cases, untitled versions of another of Immermann's unforgettable characters, the great Baron Münchhausen himself: master of deceit, promoter of industry, and booster of get-rich-quick schemes.

8

THE MANY WORLDS OF THE
GIESECKES IN TEXAS

ALTHOUGH THE GIESECKES did not reside in those areas of Texas that acquired large German populations, their lives displayed many of the characteristics of typical German immigrants in Texas, especially the early arrivals. As early as the period of Mexican rule, a few Germans were scattered in coastal areas; more settled along the coast during the rapid development of Galveston in the late 1830s and the 1840s. Some of the Germans eventually moved to the interior when they saw new opportunities there. Many of these opportunities resulted from the arrival of large numbers of Germans under the auspices of the *Adelsverein*. One of those who went to the interior was Francis (Franz) Dietrich. Born in Kassel in 1815, he arrived in Texas in 1834, the same year as Charles Giesecke's probable arrival. Settling first in the coastal town of Refugio not far from Corpus Christi, Dietrich married an Irish woman. He fought in the Texas War for Independence, and then operated a store for many years, first in Washington-on-the-Brazos and later in Austin.[1] Dietrich's social origins in Germany were a step below those of the Gieseckes. In Texas his social standing, lower than Charles Giesecke's, approximated that to which Edward Giesecke's declined.

EXPORT, IMPORT, AGRICULTURE,
AND RETAIL BUSINESS

Some contemporary descriptions of the Gieseckes' store in Brazoria, dating to the period when Edward Giesecke operated the business, have survived. One description is by Hermann Seele, who visited Brazoria in 1844 some four weeks after the date of the first of the surviving letters of Charles A. Giesecke.[2] Seele was the son of a master baker in Hildesheim; his geographical origins were thus close to those of the Gieseckes. Educated at an academy in Hildesheim, he obtained a position as a tutor in the southern Hessen household of Prince Solms of Braunfels, the aristocrat who later briefly represented the *Adelsverein* in Texas. In mid-December 1843 Seele, then twenty years old, arrived in Galveston.[3] If he did not know about the Gieseckes before his arrival, he learned of them shortly thereafter. (One possible intermediary is the German firm Kauffman in Galveston, which had many dealings with the Gieseckes and also did business with the *Adelsverein*.[4]) In April 1844 Seele walked from Galveston to Brazoria:

> On the third day of my walk [*Fußwanderung*] from Dickinson Bayou to Brazoria I reached the left bank of the Brazos River. On the opposite side . . . stood the town of Brazoria. Transportation between the two riverbanks was provided by an old flat-bottomed ferry. . . . Although laid out scarcely ten years earlier in one of the most fertile regions of the Republic, the town had a run-down look in the spring of 1844. Many of the wooden houses stood empty and in disrepair, as did the fences and the wooden sidewalks that were only here and there completed. Weeds flourished in the streets, as well as the neglected gardens. The spacious courthouse might once have been attractive; now it stood out among the trees, gray with age, hostile and unfriendly.
>
> A pleasanter impression was made by the one-story but carefully maintained building in which Mr. Eduard Giesecke has his well-arranged store. It was here that I went and received a friendly reception from my fellow countrymen from my own area [*bei meinen speziellen Landsleuten*]. I spent the evening with them in the sociable [*gemütlich*] German way. The good conversation, accentuated by music, violin, and piano recitals, made me forget that I was in a foreign land and made me feel at home. Among the company was a young man named Ahlers, who makes cigars for them [the Gieseckes].
>
> I spent the night in the store. The Giesecke farm is rather large, has rich soil, and is located near town farther down the river. One of the brothers operates it with the help of negroes. They raise mainly tobacco there. In the winter they also distill brandy. They had no employment for me, and all [other] inquiries about a suitable place for me were unsuccessful.[5]

Seele traveled on to the newly founded town of New Braunfels, and in 1845 opened the first school there.[6]

Seele's depiction of decay in Brazoria in 1844 fits well with the impressions of the town provided by the letters of Charles Giesecke. The main difference is one of style. Where Seele employs somber tones, Charles resorts to dramatic metaphors.[7] One theme is developed antithetically by the two men. Everything that has to do with Edward Giesecke appears in a favorable light in Seele's account, and only in a negative light in Charles's letters. Whether the store was already housed in the former warehouse of Robert Mills, as Charles mentions in his first surviving letter,[8] is likely, but the location cannot be established with certainty from either the letters or Seele's account.

Shortly after Seele's visit, Charles and Edward Giesecke separated their business affairs. Edward retained the general store, for which he already had the main responsibility.[9] Charles's dealings were more complicated. In his letters he often complained that Edward was a lazy spendthrift. Charles faulted Edward for lacking both initiative and business sense. Nor did Charles spare his criticism of his sister-in-law, Liesette Doby (?), a German girl whom Edward married in October 1844. Charles belittled her as a mere serving girl from Mecklenburg. She may have been as young as fifteen at the time of the marriage.[10] That was a bit young even by the Texan standards of the day, and much more so by those of the German bourgeoisie. The severe disproportion between the numbers of men and women in Texas and the very small number of white women in Brazoria County explain early marriages for white females. The number of eligible females was restricted by the general pattern of emigration whereby women were less mobile than men. During the period 1841 to 1845 only 40 percent of the German emigrants were females, and this proportion had increased since the years 1836 to 1840, when it was little more than a third.[11] As late as 1854, a female German passenger arriving in Galveston found to her astonishment that women received offers of marriage even as they disembarked.[12]

Charles manifested no sympathy for his younger brother. The relationship between the two had become so poor that when writing to his older brother in Germany Charles could not do justice to Edward. Charles did not recognize Edward's young bride as a social equal. Both by the social standards the Gieseckes had grown up with and those of the Texas planters, with whom Charles now identified, Edward's wife was unacceptable. Charles's distaste for Edward is evident in his contemptuous reference, in his letter of April 28, 1845, to Edward's store as a "crummy shop" (*Scheißboutik*).[13] Based on other evidence, it did not merit this appellation. Aside from the view of Edward's business activities provided by Charles and Seele, we have three other major contemporary types of information about the store, Edward's finances, and his business practices: material collected by a New York agency that evaluated the credit-worthiness of firms, data from the U.S. Census of 1850, and Edward's will.

The first major source, one long neglected by American historians, is the voluminous archive of a predecessor of today's multinational corporation Dun & Bradstreet. In 1841 Lewis Tappan founded Lewis Tappan & Co., The Mercantile Agency, in New York. This service furnished confidential information about the capitalization of North American firms and their reliability in paying their debts to suppliers and other creditors. Tappan's clients included potential partners as well as wholesalers. Other firms and businessmen supplied most of the data.[14] Tappan's records often contain several entries under the same firm. Next to each entry is a coded reference to the source. The key to the code was, of course, not supplied to his clients. Some entries contradict each other, as is only to be expected. The initial entry on Edward Giesecke dates to early 1848. From then to 1856, the year of his death, there are a dozen entries. The very first is one of the shortest and also one of the most favorable: "Number 1 standing beyond doubt."[15] Other entries make clear that Edward's business remained modest. The misspelling of his name in the ledger as "Giescke" is never corrected, as would no doubt have been done were his firm large. His business is estimated as worth two thousand dollars. The correspondents indicate variously that Edward can be trusted with somewhere between one and four thousand dollars of credit. Only once, in 1851, does a correspondent recommend denying him credit. Charles Giesecke's criticisms of his brother are echoed also in some of the other entries. A few times the correspondents suggest that Edward lacks capital and initiative. Yet, even when he is explicitly faulted in 1849 for having little "enterprise," he is described as "economical, fundamentally of good habits." Once he is said to be worthy of as much credit as he asks for. This entry of 1853 concludes: "Very industrious, prudential, and saving." Another entry of the same year is very loquacious: "Is a Dutchman [that is, a German]. About 40 years old. Married and has a family here. Has lived in this place some years. Does not enjoy 1st rate health. Rather weak. Is perfectly good for all his contracts. Does a lot of cash business. Don't seem to want to extend his business. Purchases his supplies principally at Galveston in small lots. I regard him as a real practical German merchant, safe and honest." His reliability is underscored again in this last statement, as is his lack of ambition. The reference to purchasing goods in small quantities in Galveston is still another allusion to the small scale of his activities. Mention of his poor health was appropriate. Within three years of the date of this entry Edward died, at age 50. The last two entries before the one noting his death strike mostly the same notes already heard. However, the entry of June 1855 — before adding the familiar, "A sound, good man" — asserts that his business is improving. The entry of December 1855 is terse: "[Edward Giesecke is] doing a small safe business for cash. Is Dutchman keeping a regular Country Store." In July 1856 it was reported following his demise that his wife was closing his business.

The repeated references to Edward's German origins were intended to convey the impression that he was cautious and conservative in his financial affairs. German merchants were generally not as inclined as Americans to take big risks. The authors of many handbooks for German emigrants sought to disabuse German merchants of the idea that they were more knowledgeable and cleverer businessmen than their American colleagues.[16] Among those critical of this image of German superiority was C. L. Fleischmann, who was intimately acquainted with business on both sides of the Atlantic. He nevertheless suggested that a German arriving in America with few financial resources might become a big businessman.[17]

Charles Giesecke was still hoping for great success when he wrote his letters in 1844–1845, and his own ambition fueled his criticisms of his younger brother's conduct. Two American historians write of America in the first half of the nineteenth century as the land in which people could still begin life anew, where bankruptcy might be an educational experience rather than a catastrophe.[18] Despite the hyperbole, this assertion conveys something of the differences between the business climate in America and Europe a century and a half ago, but it would have been more accurate if distinctions were made between different parts of North America. Failing in the settled environments of Baltimore, Philadelphia, Hartford, or Boston was much worse than failing in Galveston.

The second major source of information to balance Charles Giesecke's view of his brother is U.S. census records. The impression of Edward Giesecke and his family furnished by the census entries is neither as detailed nor as colorful as that provided by the ledgers of Lewis Tappan & Co., but the two sources are compatible. Described as a "merchant," Edward is reported to own real estate worth a thousand dollars in 1850.[19] How successful his wife was in liquidating his business following his death in April 1856 is uncertain, but she remained a property owner. According to the census of 1860, she owned real estate valued at five hundred dollars.[20] Presumably the store had been sold in the interim, but in 1870 her real estate was reported as worth a thousand dollars.[21] Neither Edward nor his wife owned slaves,[22] as is only to be expected of a small shopkeeping family. None of the existing records indicate what happened to the warehouse which, Charles Giesecke reported in 1844, Edward had recently purchased from the Mills firm.[23]

Edward's will is the third major source of information on his business standing and practices. The list of Edward's assets presented to the county court immediately following his death may underestimate his possessions, but not seriously. According to this inventory he owned a house worth $1200, goods valued at $1000, a horse ($40), and three cows and five calves ($60). In addition, his customers owed him over $500 in cash and over $850 in promissory notes.[24] A better sense of the meaning of these sums can be obtained by comparing them with the information on prices in Texas published by Olmsted after his trip in 1854 to ascertain the prospects for farming and ranching in Texas. Olmsted gave the value of a furnished house in the interior of Texas as about $750. He estimated the price of a cotton plantation of a thousand acres with six slaves (two "prime hands" and four "half hands" or "breeding women") at $9,000.[25] That was far more capital than Edward had at his disposal.

Edward's country store was similar to numerous others in North America at the time. A clear separation between a store and a commission business had not yet developed in many places, especially rural areas and small towns. Even where the two types of businesses could be distinguished, as in Galveston and much of Brazoria County, shopkeepers had to extend long-term credit to farmers, planters, and others to enable the purchase of wares, seeds, and tools. Cash advances were also often made. If the farmer's yield at harvest time was adequate, he made the deliveries he had promised to the store owner or "factor."[26] Before the dissolution of the partnership between Edward and Charles, the two men had to work in tandem in order to achieve success. In addition to running the farm, Charles had the primary responsibility for importing goods from abroad, particularly Germany, and acting as a factor by arranging for the purchase, often in advance, of crops and other products. Yet Charles complained repeatedly that Edward was uncooperative.[27]

Even after the partners took leave of one another, Charles ordered an astonishing variety of wares from their brother Friedrich in Elze. The assorted shoes, hats, violin strings, flutes, hoes, knives, stockings, carpenter's planes, harnesses, linen cloth, hardware, and numerous other goods that Charles requested were not necessarily to be sold in a store. Most if not all of them were to be used in bartering with farmers and planters for agricultural products. Many wares remained very expensive near the frontier. When Charles or Edward ordered goods in Germany instead of New York or New Orleans, they expected to increase their profits by taking advantage of their German connections and their knowledge of German products. To be sure, most handbooks for German emigrants cautioned the emigrants against taking goods with them except for their own use, even if they intended to settle on the frontier.[28] However, what Detlef Dunt had reported about Texas in 1834[29] still held true throughout the decade of the 1830s and during the early 1840s. Merchandise was very dear in Texas. A pair of shoes selling for $1.50 in New Orleans or New York cost $2.50. An American who visited Texas in 1838 ascertained that "house rent, board, labor, and every-thing which a new settler is in want of, is about five to one compared to most places in the United States."[30] From another source, we learn that fabric, which during the same period and even later cost five to six dollars in the United States, cost fifteen to twenty dollars in Texas.[31] The rapid inflation of the currency of the Lone Star Republic and the lack of craftsmen and manufacturing kept prices high.

It is clear from the experiences reported by many Germans, including merchants, that German handbooks and guides for emigrants tended to be much more cautious than similar primers for Americans. In 1834 Dunt recommended bringing very little from Germany. He suggested that articles lacking or expensive in Texas could be purchased from a German merchant in New Orleans. The few items Dunt considered worth bringing from Germany included: iron teeth for harrows, small chains for horse harnesses, stirrups, horse bits, an ordinary flintlock, flax twine, darning needles, a pick hammer for masonry work, iron animal bells, fishing hooks, good horse blankets, and "some of the most common medications such as emetics, rhubarb, Glauber's salt."[32] At the same time Dunt cautioned against the assumption that many of the other items needed by a settler in Texas were truly cheaper in Germany: generally the quality was poorer in Germany. In other instances, he explained, the items sought were unavailable or even unknown in Germany. Years after the publication of Dunt's book, similar passages appeared in other works. Without checking the changing situation, the authors often copied the same old information or composed similar lists.

The American "Colonel" Stiff was more realistic than most of the authors of German guidebooks. He suggested in 1840 that substantial gains could be made by shipping many articles to Texas. The objects he found to be in greatest demand included gunpowder, lead, rifles, Bowie knives, alcoholic drinks, playing cards, violins, pipes, drums, and Jews' harps. He recommended taking blankets since they could be used for clothing as well as bedding. He also mentioned furniture, tools, fruit trees, clothing, medications, books, and boots. Yet he warned his readers to beware of high tariffs.[33]

It is easy to understand why Charles Giesecke expected the importation of many objects directly from Germany to bring substantial profits. The increase in traffic between Bremen and Galveston in the mid-1840s offered the hope of frequent shipments with low freight charges.

COTTON AND BREMEN

Throughout most of the existence of the Lone Star Republic, intense competition for the cotton production of the Brazos area existed. For five years during the later part of this period, Morgan L. Smith, a New Yorker who came to Texas in 1838, maintained a partnership in Columbia with John Adriance, an early settler. The relationship between the two — a rising factor and the shopkeeper with whom he worked in Brazoria County from the late 1830s to the mid-1840s[34] — demonstrates again the dependence of the county's agricultural production upon the world market. Adriance and Smith bought goods, supplies, and provisions on credit and sold them to planters, farmers, and small stores in exchange for cotton, other crops, and cash. Smith often sent orders to New York, where his wealthy father acted as an intermediary for him. There the younger Smith received credit from the large firm John H. Brower & Co.[35] On his many trips he always had a want list of wares and supplies, and he wrote often to his partner in Texas. The historian Abigail Curlee Holbrook explains:

Adriance must have dreaded to open a letter from Smith. Every letter beseeched him to get the cotton; to urge the cotton forward; to keep prices well up; to collect what was due; to get notes for old debts; to touch accounts from customers at a distance with caution;

to scan closely any new names; to watch the old accounts; to sell sugar, coffee, and tobacco in very small quantities until more came; or to sell for cash, cotton, or payment that fall.[36]

Smith knew the planters and their habits and plans. He was in a position to evaluate their cotton and their financial resources. The general store that he and Adriance maintained had over sixty customers whose cotton was marketed in New Orleans, New York, and England. Smith and Adriance sought to keep on hand a broader selection of wares than that offered by other shops in the area. The partners had the facilities to store large quantities of cotton, and they could keep this cotton off the market until the price was satisfactory. They also owned a cotton press and a plantation. The latter provided a suitable place for animals and agricultural implements received from customers unable to pay their debts. Often encountering difficulties in shipping cotton and finding markets, Smith searched for measures to increase foreign trade. Toward the end of 1843 he wrote to Anson Jones, the president of Texas, to plead for the conclusion of a commercial treaty with the United States. Smith feared that direct commerce between Texas and Europe would long remain slight.[37]

Robert Mills and his brothers conducted a business similar to that of Adriance and Smith except that the Mills were even more successful. Robert Mills (1809–1888) became reputedly the richest man in Texas before the Civil War. His business affairs are of importance to us because of his ties to Bremen and his relationship with the Gieseckes.[38] He came from Kentucky, where his father was a well-known, wealthy planter. Following studies at the University of Tennessee and an unsuccessful attempt to develop a plantation in Louisiana, Robert went to Texas in the late 1820s. He and his brother Andrew formed a partnership; their primary place of business until the late 1840s was the town of Brazoria. They were active as merchants, factors, and as owners of a plantation. After the early death of Andrew in the 1830s, a third brother, David G. Mills, arrived in Texas. He assumed primary responsibility for the plantation, while Robert conducted most of the other business. Riding often from farm to farm and plantation to plantation, Robert exchanged hides and furs for provisions and supplies, and he came to know the farmers and planters well. He made himself thoroughly conversant with the standards for cotton established by cotton merchants in Liverpool in 1841. He soon developed into one of the most astute cotton experts in early Texas. Intimately familiar with the cotton of the Brazos and Colorado regions of Texas, he acquired a seventh sense enabling him to predict the cotton crop of a given plantation every year. As a trader in large quantities of cotton, he was annoyed by the many fees, duties, and other charges he had to pay in New Orleans and New York. He attempted to deal directly with European merchants and therefore traveled often to Europe to gather information and make contacts. During the early 1840s he supplied mostly English clients; his cotton was often already sold to the spinning mills before he departed Texas for Europe.

Like many others in Texas, Robert Mills speculated in land, and he prospered in this activity, as in his other endeavors. The success of Mills and his great rival, the firm of McKinney & Williams in Galveston, developed along several parallel lines. As provisioners of the army of the Lone Star Republic, both received in payment widely scattered lands from the holdings of the republic. However, McKinney & Williams apparently owned no large plantations, and from the beginning specialized primarily in the commission business.[39] Robert Mills did not formally move his headquarters from Brazoria to Galveston until 1849, although his offices on the Brazos and at its mouth had long been overshadowed by his operations in Galveston.

In 1839 or 1840 Robert Mills, already shipping some 5,000 bales of cotton annually, set up the first cotton press in Texas. In 1840 the Mills brothers had clear title to over four thousand acres of land, while another fifteen hundred acres awaited merely the final recognition of ownership; this enormous parcel of their holdings was "under survey based on a grant." They also owned in Brazoria County 525 head of cattle and 77 slaves.[40] By 1850 the number of slaves had risen to 235, and by 1860 there were almost 300 slaves merely on three of the Mills' largest plantations in the county.[41] Simply in terms of these numbers of slaves, the Mills were among the very richest people in Texas.[42] According to one source, Robert Mills still owned a total of more than eight hundred slaves in Texas at the end of the Civil War.[43] Already in the 1840s the Mills owned and operated several large plantations in Brazoria County. David G. Mills lived on their plantation Lowood in 1844; it became the county's largest sugar-producing plantation.[44] The Census of 1860 records for him alone real estate worth $364,000 and personal property of $250,000.[45]

By 1850, at the latest, Robert Mills began to acquire a financial interest in firms in big cities. For example, he became a partner in a firm in New York as well as one in New Orleans in 1850. From that year until 1863 one of his partners in Texas was J. W. Jockusch, the Prussian consul in Galveston. Jockusch was a member of the Bremen firm of the Kauffmans, who had many links with the Gieseckes in the 1840s.[46] Another tie was to be formed in the future, when Thomas Giesecke, Charles Giesecke's oldest son, became as a young man a plantation overseer for the Mills.[47]

During the 1840s, while the Mills and others in Texas were making fortunes selling cotton to Europe, Bremen was still considerably behind its great Hanseatic rival, Hamburg, as a cotton port.[48] Bremen did not overtake Hamburg in this respect until the 1850s and 1860s, but the foundations for Bremen's phenomenal later development in the cotton trade were laid in the 1840s. The firm of C. L. Brauer & Son, which was heavily involved in the Texas trade and had many dealings with the Gieseckes, was during this decade the largest importer of cotton in Bremen, but the quantity was still moderate; in 1844 Brauer imported altogether 2,065 bales.[49]

Cotton from Texas played a more strategic role in the development of Bremen's commerce with the United States than has been assumed. Even Curlee Holbrook, who in researching plantation records uncovered many details of the expansion of Texas's world trade, underestimates the significance of cotton in the intercourse between Bremen and Texas.[50] She reports that Henry H. Williams, a partner in the big Galveston firm McKinney & Williams, was requested by A. Schumacher & Co. of Baltimore to have cotton delivered directly to the firm Kulenkampff Brothers in Bremen because inadequate warehouse space had made the importation of cotton by Britons difficult. The British resolved this problem by selling their surplus cotton in Germany. As a result, only one shipload of cotton was delivered in 1847 to the Kulenkampffs in Bremen.[51] This report and others might easily lead one to conclude that as late as 1846–1847 little Texas cotton was reaching Bremen. However, another American historian finds that in the winter of 1845 Robert Mills sold part of the cotton harvested from "Peachpoint," one of his great plantations in Brazoria County, to merchants from Bremen. The best cotton was presumably sold to New York merchants. The poorer quality cotton was dispatched on the bark *Neptun* to Bremen.[52] The *Neptun* arrived on the Weser on April 29, 1845, with 41 bales of this shipment.[53] Data reflecting the development of Bremen's cotton trade and its relationship to Texas from 1840 to 1846 can be seen in Table 4.

In 1842 direct deliveries from Galveston accounted for 9 percent of Bremen's cotton imports. That same year Bremen's merchants and shippers acquired directly some 3 to 7 percent of the Texas cotton harvest. In 1844 shipments of cotton from Galveston constituted 24 percent of the cotton imported by Bremen's merchants; this quantity made up 5 to 12 percent of

Table 4

Cotton (in Bales), 1840–1846 *

	Texas Est. Harvest	Galveston Exports	New Orleans Imports from Texas	Bremen Imports	Bremen Imports from Galveston	Bremen Imports from New Orleans	Bremen Imports from USA
1840	7,900–15,700	?		9,268		1,081	6,161
1841	13,300–37,700	?		8,804		1,704	5,727
1842	15,300–37,700	?		12,935	1,115	6,370	12,310
1843	18,200–37,000	?		20,197	2,232	13,188	20,056
1844	25,900–60,000	?	18,170	13,165	3,098	2,388	12,085
1845	27,000–90,000	?		18,498	4,024	8,825	18,119
1846	18,300–60,000	?		11,895	1,004	4,347	10,348

* Source: Texas Department of Agriculture, *Year Book, 1909*, Texas Department of Agriculture Bulletin, 13, p. 47; Olmsted, *Journey through Texas*, p. 479; Dewitt T. Tarlton, "The History of the Cotton Industry in Texas, 1820–1850," Master's thesis, University of Texas, Austin (1923), pp. 40–49; Webb et al., *Handbook of Texas* 1: 420; Pitsch, *Die wirtschaftlichen Beziehungen Bremens zu den Vereinigten Staaten*, pp. 162–63, 241. The lowest estimates of the Texas cotton corp are taken from the data on commercial cotton crops in the Texas Department of Agriculture, *Year Book, 1909*. Most of the highest estimates are Tarlton's.

the Texas cotton crop. The amount of cotton going directly from Texas to Bremen increased fourfold from 1842 to 1845. Much Texas cotton was finding its way to the Hanseatic town. As early as 1844, the purchase of cotton by Bremen interests was facilitated by the presence of German ships bringing large numbers of emigrants to Texas. Merchants and sea captains preferred to load paying cargo for the return trip to Germany rather than merely taking on ballast. It should also be emphasized that a portion of the cotton shipped from New Orleans to Bremen originated in Texas. Contemporary sources mention the transportation of Texas cotton on the Red River to New Orleans; the provenance of the cotton was deliberately omitted from labels and records.[54] Other Texas cotton — not quite as difficult to trace, and including some from Brazoria County — reached New Orleans legally for transshipment to Bremen or was sold after arrival in New Orleans and dispatched to Bremen.[55] Of less significance is the amount of Texas cotton reaching Bremen by way of other ports. As can be seen in Table 4, direct shipments of Texas cotton from Galveston to Bremen increased every year from 1841 through 1845; then in 1846 the number of bales declined precipitously. This fall was related to the entry of Texas into the United States. From records of ship arrivals in Bremen in 1845 we know that many ships came directly from Galveston with cotton, although the actual loads must have been small, and some continued to arrive in Germany simply in ballast.[56]

The role of the Gieseckes in the cotton trade with Bremen did not approach that played by large cotton merchants such as McKinney & Williams or Robert Mills. The Gieseckes' part is modest, but the fragmentary records document its significance. As we have seen, the earliest evidence of the Gieseckes' shipping cotton from Texas dates to 1840. In July of that year Charles A. Giesecke sent ten bales of cotton from Velasco to New Orleans. These bales were consigned to a merchant with a German name, J. W. Freudenthal.[57] The next recorded cotton shipments by a Giesecke consisted of two lots totaling 42 bales with Friedrich Giesecke's mark. This cotton arrived in New Orleans from Galveston in January 1842.[58] From Charles's letter of March 16, 1844, we know that in 1844 he was responsible at least for a small shipment of five bales of cotton directly from Galveston to Bremen.[59] Five bales are approximately the amount of cotton that a slave on a plantation could pick in a good year.[60] It is improbable that this was Charles's first shipment of cotton directly from Texas to Bremen. If that were so, he would have been likely to comment on the matter in his letter as was his habit. He mentions in this same letter having dispatched with another ship, the *Weser*, hides, deer and calf skins, and tobacco to his brother in Elze about the same time as he sent the cotton. The Gieseckes had been shipping skins, hides, and, presumably, cotton to New Orleans for some years.[61] Charles's letter of June 30, 1845, informs his brother Friedrich in Elze that he is dispatching a chest with "samples of various local cotton wares."[62] Responding to poor cotton prices, many planters were considering raising sugar cane in place of cotton. This was a logical time to promote the cotton trade between Texas and Germany.

Charles never became a big cotton merchant. The successful cotton factors in early Texas were, like the Mills brothers, planters and large slaveholders. In any event, a factor needed much capital. Charles had more success with other undertakings that required less capital. The role of the Gieseckes in the cotton business never became more than modest and did not extend beyond the late 1840s.

It is misleading to characterize either the Old South or Texas as a precapitalist, aristocratic society, as has often been done.[63] The present work offers much evidence for the thesis that even in the South in the vicinity of the Texas frontier a bourgeois society emerged during the 1820s and 1830s. During these decades the cotton trade in Texas reached such gigantic dimensions that entry into it became difficult and held forth little prospect of success unless the entrant were very affluent. The author of the basic study of the American cotton business in the nineteenth century attempts to demonstrate that in small ports even the large planters and factors were dependent upon a few great firms in New York and Liverpool.[64] This well-grounded conclusion suggests that during the 1830s and 1840s entry into the international cotton trade was still promising for merchants with few material resources but with knowledge of and links to Germany. Commerce with Bremen offered an alternative to dealing with the big cotton firms in Liverpool and New York. The undeveloped state of Bremen's cotton trade thus presented opportunities for the small merchant, opportunities that the Gieseckes did not succeed in exploiting on a large scale.

From Charles Giesecke's letters and from other sources we know that he often sent skins and hides, mostly those of cattle, oxen, and sheep, to Germany for sale there. He mentions diverse articles he hopes to sell or trade in Texas. Charles must often have taken hides and skins in exchange for these articles. The earliest documentation of these aspects of the Gieseckes' business activities dates to 1842 and is provided by a cargo manifest that has been preserved among ship passenger lists because the names of passengers are also listed on it.[65] The manifest enumerates three bales of hides and 129 skins. This freight was designated "FG [Friedrich Giesecke]" 1, 2, 3, and 129. It was dispatched by Charles Giesecke to the German firm Hagedorn and Prusner [Prüsener?] in New Orleans. It is likely that this firm forwarded the shipment to Bremen and Elze or perhaps took the goods in exchange for wares. The letters "FG" signify that the freight was to be sold and credited to Friedrich Giesecke's account. It is uncertain how the goods had been acquired. They may have been gained in barter by Friedrich during his stay in Texas, or they may have been taken in trade by Charles Giesecke from farmers, planters, or other customers for his brother's account.

"Plantation," Slavery, and the Tobacco Trade

Charles Giesecke's "plantation," which Hermann Seele described in 1844 as a "rather large farm with rich soil,"[66] was situated on a stream named Varner's Creek, not far from the town of Brazoria. (Martin Varner, for whom the creek was named, had received a Mexican land grant in 1824. Although he came apparently from the United States,[67] his name is almost certainly German in origin. "Werner" was often anglicized to "Varner" or "Warner.") Charles Giesecke raised mainly tobacco in 1844. According to the U.S. Census of 1850 he owned 320 acres, of which only 15 were under cultivation.[68] It is logical to assume that this last figure had increased since 1844. That was the tendency at the time in Texas; as soon as the land was cleared, the cultivated area was expanded.

Although "farmer" was a more appropriate designation for Charles Giesecke than "planter," there was never a legal basis in the American South for the use of one term or the other.[69] Neither expression was employed systematically; the difference between the two was more social than economic or statistical. The "planter" owned more slaves and more land than a mere farmer. Even more important, planters were reckoned as people who exercised authority over other adults. The planter belonged to the upper class, and neither he nor any member of his family worked the land alongside the slaves. "Planter" conveyed an air of gentility. The U.S. Census of 1860 attempted to restrict the use of the term to a person with at least twenty slaves. Owners of that many slaves constituted a tiny prestigious minority of the white populace; Charles Giesecke and many other farmers of moderate means were flattered to be addressed as "planters."

Charles never owned anything approaching twenty slaves. In his letter of October 22, 1845, he tells his brother Friedrich that he is letting his "plantation" lie fallow for a year and therefore has only one old slave to maintain the property. Charles often had more slaves on his property, even during this early period, but they were rented from other slaveowners. According to the U.S. Census of 1850, he owned two slaves. One was a nineteen-year-old female,[70] the other a man of the prime age of thirty-one. In 1860 Charles had only one slave, a male, seemingly the same person he had owned in 1850.[71] Charles's father-in-law eventually owned several slaves, but it is not clear how much more than reflected prestige Charles derived from the social status this gave the older man.

It is not surprising that Charles described himself as a planter and identified enthusiastically with the planter aristocracy. There were good reasons why his agricultural endeavors remained small in proportion to those of the large planters. The precondition for a larger agricultural enterprise was considerable capital, mainly for the purchase of slaves. The large planters specialized in cotton until the mid-1840s, and even beyond. Curlee describes, for example, tobacco as a "minor product" of James F. Perry's large

Peach Point Plantation in Brazoria County. In 1846 Perry delivered some 2500 pounds of tobacco to Robert Mills for Mills to sell.[72] Charles had at the time decided to specialize in growing tobacco.

It was symptomatic of developments in commerce and agriculture in both Texas and Germany that Charles concerned himself with tobacco. Germans in Texas played an important part in its cultivation.[73] He tried to promote the tobacco trade between Bremen and Texas and frequently sent tobacco samples and tobacco for sale to Bremen and Elze in 1844–1845.[74] His gains from this trade were apparently slight. As can be seen in his letters of 1844–1845, he lacked the capital necessary to plant as much tobacco as he thought profitable and to make commitments to other farmers to purchase more tobacco from them than he had previously. He sought to overcome these obstacles. He could improve his business prospects greatly if he procured from his brother in Elze, or through this brother's intervention, German goods to sell advantageously in Texas. Then, too, he might find a merchant in Bremen who would purchase tobacco from him at a satisfactory price. Although the tobacco harvest of 1845 was good in Texas, Charles still had no purchasers in Bremen, and, if we credit his complaints, his brother Friedrich in Elze had neglected — from ignorance, incompetence, laziness, or sloppiness — to assist him with the matter in Bremen. Charles had urgently asked him to find an alternative to the Bremen firm Richter to buy tobacco from Texas.[75] The Bremen firm C. L. Brauer & Son, with which the Gieseckes had many dealings, was perhaps too large to provide an appropriate outlet for Charles's tobacco. The Brauer firm, which had already existed in Bremen in Napoleon's day, was to become not only one of the largest European importers of cotton but also of tobacco. This ascent was already far advanced during the 1840s. At the beginning of the 1850s Brauer overtook its two largest competitors in Bremen, the firms F. and E. Delius and D. Wätjen.[76]

A related undertaking of Charles Giesecke, the making and marketing of cigars, depended on his agricultural activities. Both from his letters, and from Hermann Seele's report on the journey from Galveston to Brazoria in 1845,[77] we know that the Gieseckes in Texas made cigars, or had them made. Charles writes of the thousand cigars that he delivered weekly to Galveston.[78] A contemporary expert on the cigar industry stated that an experienced cigarmaker could roll 500 to 1000 cigars of good quality per day.[79] The young German named Ahlers, whom Charles mentions briefly and whom Seele describes as a cigarmaker for the Gieseckes, is unlikely to have spent most of his time rolling cigars.[80] Charles was very familiar with various types of tobacco and cigars, although presumably he had learned the fabric trade in Germany. In the light of the rapid increase in the consumption of cigars in the United States and Germany during the 1830s and 1840s, his advice to his brother Friedrich to start a cigar factory in Germany had much to recommend it.

The numerous shortcuts and fraudulent tricks that Charles suggests to his brother for handling tobacco are not simply the discoveries of a ripe and fanciful imagination spurred on by the pursuit of profit. From other sources we know much about unethical practices in his section of Texas. The Columbia merchant John Adriance related that during the 1840s he purchased tobacco in Washington County, Texas, to be used for cigars. Adriance had these cigars packed in boxes with a pretty label reading "Havana Cigars." Havanas already occupied an envied place among cigars.[81] He sold the falsely labeled cigars in New York, where no one seems to have detected the swindle.[82] Of course this tale of provincial guile besting the city slickers should be viewed with almost as much skepticism as the most recent offer to sell the Brooklyn Bridge. Although the demand for cigars was rising during the 1840s, New York did not become a big center of the cigar industry until after the Civil War. By levying only a small duty on foreign-made cigars, the U.S. customs regulations of 1846 enabled inexpensive German cigars to drive American-made ones from the New York market. During the next twenty years the demand for cheap tobacco goods was met by German exports, while fine cigars were imported from Cuba.[83]

The U.S. Census of 1850 classifies Charles Giesecke as a "farmer" and estimates the value of his real estate at a mere $200.[84] The agriculture schedule of the census presents a clearer picture: Charles had become a "stockraiser." Like many other small farmers, he specialized in livestock. There is no mention in the census of his involvement with tobacco. The monetary value of his farm is listed at $150, the value of his slaughtered animals during the past year at $110. His farm in 1850 included, as we have seen, 14 acres of cultivated, and 306 of uncultivated, land. Ten years later the number of improved acres had increased to 24, and the number of unimproved acres to 1300.[85] The value of his farm had risen to $990, whereas the value of the agricultural implements and machinery remained unchanged at $100. In 1850 he had owned no sheep; in 1860 he had 225. The value of his livestock, $1455 in 1860, had quadrupled.

Charles must be reckoned among the smaller farmers in Texas in 1860. A number of suggestive comparisons supporting this conclusion can be made on the basis of a statistical inquiry into the distribution of wealth in

The Gieseckes in Texas

the state from 1850 to 1860.[86] Real estate, personal property, and slaves were very unequally distributed among the whites of Texas. In 1850 almost one-third of the households owned no real estate, and in Brazoria County the proportion of nonowners was considerably larger. On the other hand, a mere 0.3 percent of the white population in Texas owned real estate valued at $50,000 or more.[87] This tendency toward inequality of wealth became more pronounced between 1850 and 1860. The inquiry into the distribution of wealth in Texas divides the nonslave population into four groups. Statistically, Charles Giesecke belonged to one of two groups between virtually propertyless whites, on the one side, and wealthy planters and merchants, on the other side. In 1860 this group of modest means constituted 35.1 percent of the households and held 12.5 percent of the total wealth. A small, very rich group composed of 2.2 percent of the households held 32.2 percent of the wealth, while a much larger group of 38.8 percent of the households held only 2.2 percent. Between the group of modest means to which Charles Giesecke belonged and the small group of the very rich stood a fourth group that accounted for 23.9 percent of the households, but possessed 53.2 percent of the wealth.[88]

Although Charles Giesecke did not belong to the most affluent groups, he stood out from the generally poor European segment of the population. The heads of households in 1860 born outside Texas and the United States had, on the average, only half the wealth of other Texans. Although Charles belonged to a segment of the white population that had more wealth than the average,[89] he was not well-to-do by the standards set by the slaveholding population to which he belonged. The mean value of slaveholders' wealth in 1860 was $18,370, far more than he possessed, and yet by virtue of his ownership of one slave he belonged to the group of slaveholders. Moreover, in Brazoria County the mean was certainly much higher than elsewhere in Texas.[90]

The census of 1860 classifies Charles Giesecke as a planter,[91] a designation contrary to the official instructions to census takers, for he lacked the requisite twenty slaves. This misclassification may reflect the social prestige of his family and his in-laws, but we should note that many other farmers in Brazoria County were similarly misclassified as planters by the enumerators. The value of his real estate was given as a modest $1100 and the value of his personal property at $1000.[92]

Charles Giesecke's letters document his long-standing desire for acceptance as an equal by the planters. With the breakup of his partnership with his brother Edward and the consequent ebbing of his activities as a merchant, it was only to be expected that he would be drawn to seek the social prestige accorded planters in the slave state of Texas. He achieved his goal. His marriage provides evidence of his ability to identify himself with the planters. Although the number of white women in Brazoria County was very limited, Charles Giesecke married the daughter of a well-regarded American family. On July 26, 1845, three months before the date of his last surviving letter, he and Sarah Mary Davis were wed.[93] She was born in Missouri in 1825,[94] of parents originally from Kentucky. Her father, Thomas Kincheloe Davis, presumably arrived with his dependents in Brazoria County in 1830,[95] but his family had prior ties to Texas. His uncle William Kincheloe was among the first settlers in Austin's Colony[96] and, along with other relatives, was one of the colony's prominent members.[97] According to the Texas Census of 1840, Thomas Kincheloe Davis owned fifty head of cattle and much land: 4,428 acres "under survey."[98] Presumably he obtained the final official recognition of his title to this land on September 1, 1846. The land was probably that granted, upon application, to every head of household who was in Texas when its independence from Mexico was proclaimed on March 2, 1836.[99]

The U.S. Census of 1850 describes Davis as a farmer with real estate worth $2000 — ten times that of his son-in-law Charles Giesecke.[100] According to the agricultural schedule of the census, Davis owned thirty acres of cultivated land[101] — almost twice as much as that possessed by the younger man. The sales value of Davis's butter, $1500, was four times as high.[102] Due to an oversight, or because Davis later owned no slaves, there is no entry for him on the Slave Schedules for 1850. The Census of 1860 enumerates five slaves for Davis: two young women and three small children.[103] Apparently he had already divided his land with his son; the elder Davis's will of 1872 left his children 1750 acres of land.[104] A logical inference from several of the sources cited is that Davis, like his son and son-in-law, had become primarily a stock raiser.

It was desirable for Charles Giesecke as an immigrant in a land of immigrants to establish good relations with the predominant English-speaking group in Texas. He accomplished this in his business as well as his personal relationships. These relationships can be charted not only on the basis of his letters and other written sources, but also — with caution — through family traditions. Some of these traditions have found their way into print during the past century; others have been related only orally.[105] It is claimed that he came to Texas in 1824.[106] Insisting upon his arrival early in the history of Austin's Colony, this legend is perhaps one of several instances whereby his history was commingled with that of his wife's family, for his wife's great uncle was among the earliest colonists, "Austin's Old Three Hundred," and it is even claimed that his father-in-law had lived with this relative in Texas long before Giesecke's own documented arrival in 1834. In other tales, information about the two families is so fused that none is readily extractable. One story relates that when Charles's wife returned from his burial toward the end of the Civil War she freed the family's slaves. Since at the time of the Census of 1860 he had only one slave, this tale pertains more likely to his father-in-law, who outlived him by a decade. The Giesecke family says of his wife that she came from well-known families of the Old South: President of the Confederacy Jefferson Davis is said to have been her cousin; President James Monroe her uncle; William Barret Travis, the hero of the Alamo, another of her cousins. And an uncle from the Davis family is said to have participated in the decisive battle of the Texan War of Independence, the Battle of San Jacinto.[107]

Of greater significance for us here are tales of Charles Giesecke's arrival in Texas and his first years there. These yarns manifest a marked tendency to obscure his German origins. This tendency resulted not only from his and the family's wish to display strong Anglo-American roots, but also from the family's desire to dissociate the Gieseckes from the enemy of the United States in two world wars. Like other U.S. states harboring large numbers of Germans and their descendants, Texas was the site of vicious anti-German campaigns during World War I. One story evasively depicts Charles Giesecke as the accomplished scion of an eminent European or Alsatian family.[108] According to a variant of this yarn, he had studied at a famous European university and was a chemist or an apothecary. Clearly, this variant legend confuses Charles with his great grandfather Bodo Christoph Sander, court apothecary to the Duke of Brunswick.[109] Other stories maintain that Charles Giesecke was a piano teacher, performed on the concert stage in New York, and tuned pianos. A closely related claim is replete with the Romantic depiction of an outsider who became socially acceptable: he traveled to Texas as a stowaway after fleeing Europe to avoid military service; landing in Velasco, he was summoned to the plantation of his future father-in-law to tune the piano.[110]

Additional insights into the lives of German immigrants in the world of nineteenth-century planters can be gained from the novel *Konrad Bäumlers weiter Weg. Ein Texas-Deutscher Roman* (Konrad Bäumler's Long Journey: A Texas German Novel), published in 1938.[111] A comparison of

Charles Giesecke with the hero of this well-researched historical novel about a German in Texas is useful because the author, Heinrich Meyer, a former instructor of German at Rice University, draws on wide reading in both scholarly and imaginative literature about Texas Germans. The novel's protagonist, Konrad Bäumler, comes from a somewhat more mobile society than Charles Giesecke, but his first world also is that of a small German town. Located in South Germany, in Franconia, this community has been treated shabbily by the royal Bavarian authorities. Bäumler's father is a successful apothecary and chemist. After the father's death Konrad, who has followed in his father's footsteps and studied pharmacology and chemistry, decides to do what he can in America with his inheritance. Traveling by way of New York, he meets a young gentleman whose father owns a plantation with 300 (!) slaves in Georgia. Bäumler works there for a while to gain experience. The plantation owner has been adversely affected by the economic crash of 1837, and Bäumler acquires cheaply several of his slaves. The proceeds enable the Georgia planter to pay his debts. Bäumler travels to Texas via New Orleans in 1842 with $20,000 and the slaves whom he has purchased. His German bride has joined him in America. Bäumler purchases a plantation south of San Felipe on the upper Brazos near the homestead of a German friend. The action of the novel continues through the Civil War, but the early years of the story are those that are useful for comparison with the situation of Charles Giesecke.

Meyer deliberately contravenes the stereotypical German identified with opposition to slavery.[112] Although both Konrad Bäumler and Charles Giesecke are burgher sons from small towns, Bäumler has never been a merchant. He comes directly from the ranks of the university-educated bourgeoisie to which many of Giesecke's ancestors belonged. Bäumler's specific motivations for going to America are better known to us than Giesecke's. The two are similar with regard to their farming activities, although the capital that Bäumler brings is a fortune in comparison with Giesecke's wealth. Indeed, Bäumler's inheritance is an enormous sum for the era. He is so wealthy that he immediately becomes a big planter. Giesecke lives among the overwhelmingly English-speaking populace, while Bäumler has settled in the predominantly German area some distance to the north and west of the Brazos. Yet both men associate mainly with Anglo-Americans, and Giesecke's young wife is an American. Bäumler's German spouse is soon alienated from him, as happens all too easily when the man lives and works largely in the world of the Anglo-Americans while his spouse remains shut off in the household. Bäumler falls in love with the wife of his Texan friend Roger. All in all, the historical truth of the Gieseckes is more engaging and more believable than the wooden characters in Meyer's scholarly novel.

DISTILLING IN TEXAS

The distillery on the Giesecke farm had many advantages during the mid-1840s. Charles Giesecke relates breathlessly in his letters that he is compelled to distill (*brennen*). The colloquial German expression for distilling has the basic meaning of "to burn," with many of the same rich associations that "burn" has in English. These associations contribute to the frantic tone of these passages in his letters.

Like other distilleries of that period in Texas, Charles's was a small operation, making whiskey from corn or potatoes brought by local farmers. As late as 1834 Detlef Dunt had stated categorically that there were no distilleries in Texas.[113] His complaint was exaggerated, for farmers produced some whiskey. Moreover, a small distillery was already to be found in 1829 on Martin Varner's farm in the immediate area where the Giesecke farm was later located.[114] To be sure, there were no large distilleries in Texas, and a German craftsman unsuccessfully seeking work in a distillery in Texas in 1840 concluded ruefully that most of the liquor came from the United States.[115] However, Texas levied a high duty on all imported liquor except French cognac.[116] The high duties on liquor provided the bulk of the Lone Star Republic's revenues.[117] Thus, to meet the demand for less expensive drink, there was much incentive to distilling in Texas.

During the mid-1840s, the period of the surviving letters of Charles Giesecke, agriculture in the rich Brazos area was being transformed. Although improved cotton harvests had followed the bad harvests of the early 1840s, cotton prices were low. Farmers in search of other cash crops soon were relying on sugar cane. An early, optimistic report on this shift appears in Charles Giesecke's letter of February 10, 1845. A new U.S. duty on imported cotton reinforced the trend.[118] By the 1850s sugar cane had displaced cotton as the most important agricultural product of Brazoria County.[119] A planter had to invest much capital in order to switch and make a sugar plantation profitable. A successful operation required the construction of a small sugar factory outfitted with the necessary sugar-processing equipment.

The great increase in planting sugar cane in the middle and lower

Brazos area led Charles Giesecke to write enthusiastically about making rum. Merchants and newspaper articles urged farmers to make sugar and molasses, and by 1846 the planters were sending large quantities of sugar to Galveston. The deliveries that year amounted to 213 hogsheads of sugar and 327 barrels of molasses. That was not the total production, for some sugar and molasses was sold directly to neighbors or local merchants. The next year, 1847, sugar production soared to 3,000 hogsheads.[120] Much sugar cane in Brazoria County was converted to molasses, a large part of which was, in turn, utilized in making rum. Like many other optimistic residents of the county who hoped to make a rapid switch from cotton planting to sugar cane, Charles greatly underestimated the time required for the changeover. Above all, he ignored one great retardative force — the shortage of capital.[121] But the population of Texas was, as many travelers pointed out in their publications, quite thirsty. It was logical to assume that Texans would soon drink more rum.

Entry into the Union in 1846 undermined prospects for building sizable distilleries in Texas. The disappearance of the republic's duties on alcoholic beverages opened the new U.S. state's market to the products of the enormous distilleries that had developed in the Ohio and Mississippi valleys.[122] These smoking, steam-driven behemoths produced the whiskey that Americans, including Texans, generally preferred over all other alcoholic drinks; distilling in Texas became unprofitable. Although neglecting to mention the special danger from this competition, Charles Giesecke's surviving letters provide ample evidence that he was aware of the economic consequences of the incorporation of Texas into the United States and that he assessed cogently these consequences for his business affairs.

The information about distilling methods that he requested from his brother in Germany was less important than issues of commercial policy. Technology was not by itself the key to solving the difficulties of distilling in Texas. The Kingdom of Hannover provided a more favorable business climate for distilleries. Although Hannover levied a heavy tax on distilleries, improved technology led to important advances in the industry there during the 1830s.[123]

CRAFTSMEN AND EMIGRATION

Another aspect of distilling is central to the dynamics of German emigration throughout much of the nineteenth century — the departure of large numbers of craftsmen from Germany. Charles Giesecke requests from his brother in Elze not only information about the latest distilling techniques, but also additional craftsmen. Like so many other occupations in Germany, most of those connected with distilling were still embedded in the guild system. Coopers, coppersmiths, and other artisans necessary to construct, operate, and maintain a distillery were organized into guilds along medieval lines.[124] To be sure, the Kingdom of Hannover had no distillers' guild — although it did have a brewers' guild — but a distillery, like any other business, could be opened only with government permission.

The systematic promotion of the emigration of German craftsmen to America has been neglected in the scholarly literature, not simply in the literature on Texas.[125] Guild restrictions on access to artisan occupations remained in place in most of Germany until 1869. Throughout much of the nineteenth century Germany had an even larger surplus of craftsmen than of merchants. Artisans were displaced by the advance of industrialization, the mechanization of production, the decay of the guild system, and the relative decline in the number of masters. German tailors, bakers, cabinetmakers, carpenters, butchers, wheelwrights, millers, turners, shoemakers, saddlers, and practitioners of many other crafts roamed Europe in search of employment.[126] Paris was the mecca of German artisans in the 1830s and 1840s, but, while its numerous small shops engaged many of the 80,000 or more Germans living in this famed metropolis,[127] other craftsmen went overseas. Artisans constituted a disproportionate segment of German emigrants in the 1840s and 1850s. Although forming a mere 6 percent of the population of Hesse-Darmstadt in 1846, artisans furnished nearly 40 percent of the emigrants.[128] Guidebooks for German emigrants touted the opportunities for craftsmen in America. For example, Nicholas Hesse, a sanguine German visitor in the mid-1830s, approved of the emigration of "all craftsmen whose trade is connected with practical life and who have no chance to support themselves and their families in Germany."[129] He went on to distinguish carefully which artisans should consider going to America, to recommend localities where specific trades were in demand, and to detail who should banish any thought of emigrating. In this last category of people who would be unable to find suitable employment in America, Hesse emphatically included state officials, gentlemen farmers, artists, and military officers.[130] By the middle of the nineteenth century, Germans made up a large proportion of the craftsmen in American cities such as Boston, New York, Buffalo, Poughkeepsie, Jersey City, Philadelphia, Chicago, Milwaukee, Detroit, South Bend, and St. Louis.[131] Van Ravenswaay's great work on German crafts and architecture in Missouri documents the presence of numerous German artisans there at midcentury.[132]

Although studies such as van Ravenswaay's are lacking for artisans in Texas,[133] it is known that many a nineteenth-century guidebook pointed artisans toward Texas. Attempting to justify the subtitle of his guide to Texas, "Primarily for Peasants and Craftsmen," Ottomar von Behr claimed that he had come into contact in America "almost solely with peasants and craftsmen."[134] Traugott Bromme's *Handbuch für Auswanderer* (Handbook for Emigrants) singled out Texas as a desirable place for members of two "estates" to settle: farmers (*Landwirte*) and craftsmen.[135] Attracted by descriptions of Texas and by the demand for craftsmen near the frontier, and encouraged by merchants such as the Gieseckes, German craftsmen arrived in large numbers in Texas during the 1840s. For the time being, many of them escaped the mechanization and industrialization that had menaced them in Germany.

In letters dated February 10, February 18, and April 28, 1845, Charles Giesecke asks his brother Friedrich to arrange that a cooper and a distiller be sent to him from Germany. Charles assumes that Friedrich will be able to fulfill this request easily. Lacking critical information, we can only speculate as to whether young Ahlers, the Giesecke's cigar maker, arrived in Texas through a similar process.[136] Charles carefully specifies that he requires properly trained, competent artisans. In his letter of April 24, 1845, he admonishes his brother not to send "another depraved student." We do not know for certain whether the "Adolph" he mentions in this connection is identical to the Adolph Pohlmann whose name turns up several times in the surviving letters. Adolph Pohlmann arrived at age twenty in Texas in 1844. According to a standard work on Germans in Texas during that year, he came from "Launau [Lauenau?] near Elze, Hannover."[137] Although located in the then Kingdom of Hannover, Lauenau is not as "near" the Elze we have looked at — nor for that matter another, smaller Elze — as this statement implies. The reference to Elze in the records raises for us the question of a link between Friedrich Giesecke and Pohlmann.[138]

During the mid-1840s, and continuing beyond those years, Friedrich Giesecke served as an emigration agent. Emigration agents arranged for transportation and assumed responsibility for the formalities necessary for the emigrant to reach his goal. Like Friedrich, most of these agents took up the emigrant trade alongside other business, particularly innkeeping or insurance sales. Until very recently emigration agents have been sadly neglected by researchers into nineteenth-century history; even now there is no study of them in Lower Saxony.[139] That Friedrich advertised in a regional newspaper to offer his services is evident from a July 1846 advertisement in which he provided a list of three-masted ships with copper-clad bottoms that he represented.[140] This advertisement—the earliest yet located for Friedrich—as well as later ones specify departure dates for ships. Many of the same vessels are referred to in Charles Giesecke's letters. In advertisements placed by Friedrich during the next three months, trips from Bremen to New York, Baltimore, New Orleans, and Galveston are announced, and these notices indicate a sailing every other week to Galveston. Using a standard formula repeated in each advertisement, Friedrich assures the reader: "I know the following ships as well as their captains and can recommend them as experienced seamen. The prices have been greatly reduced."[141] For several years he ran notices frequently. After the bad harvest of 1847 in Germany, there were almost a dozen emigration agencies in the small city of Hildesheim alone.[142] Agencies in addition to Friedrich's operated also in Elze and other small towns in the Hildesheim district, including Alfeld, Bockenem, Eldagsen, and Sack. As late as 1850 Galveston appeared often as a destination in Friedrich's advertisements. Other emigration agents advertising in the same newspaper frequently listed New Orleans but seldom Galveston.

One advertisement of this period, placed by an ignorant or unscrupulous emigration agent, asserted that fifteen to twenty dollars per day could be earned in America.[143] This claim was preposterous. The shortage of craftsmen and laborers in America had driven up wages there, but not to such dizzying heights. More modest claims of higher wages came closer to reality. Artisans were rare near the frontier and in recently settled regions of America. Until 1840 people in the United States or in Europe who came to Texas were usually those attracted by agrarian, rather than nonagrarian, pursuits. The great demand for artisans in Texas made the republic attractive to many a German craftsman after 1840. Artisans formed a substantial part of the stream of Germans who went to Texas.

Attempts by the Gieseckes to induce German craftsmen to go to Texas have to be understood as part of this broad movement. During the past few decades some revisionist scholars have approached skeptically the common image of poverty-stricken artisans in Germany during the 1830s and 1840s,[144] but these reservations pertain mainly to secondary issues. It has been claimed that the number of masters actually increased, although it declined in relationship to the number of apprentices and journeymen;

certain artisan trades were not in the poor shape that others were after 1825; commercial freedom had advantages as well as disadvantages for many an artisan. Despite these and other qualifications, the basic tendency of the period is clear. Older skills were downgraded and rendered obsolete by encroaching industrialization and the competition of new industries, above all those of Britain. The fabric of traditional work relationships was rent asunder.[145] Many people whose skills had lost their value were motivated to migrate. The departure of craftsmen from Germany was aided by merchants like the Gieseckes, who profited both from the transatlantic traffic and from the labor of these new arrivals in America. While thousands of German artisans went to Paris and other European cities, others extended their search for employment across the Atlantic.

Ira Berlin and Herbert Gutman have shown that contrary to common belief many European immigrants made their homes in the antebellum South. Berlin and Gutman indicate that the numbers of Europeans have seemed small in proportion to the total population, but that in southern cities immigrants constituted a large proportion of the white population. Concentrated in the Lower South, these Europeans made up half to two-thirds of the population in many cities, and large numbers of these immigrants were artisans. They often displaced remaining black craftsmen as well as many native-born white craftsmen. Except for Irish immigrants, the great majority of Europeans in Southern cities were artisans.[146]

Even a rural slave district in Texas such as Brazoria County drew a large number of European artisans during, and probably beyond, the period of heavy migration from both the United States and Germany during the middle decades of the nineteenth century. Of the forty-five German men in Brazoria County in 1850, 85 percent were craftsmen — thirty-six in all. In addition, four of the Germans listed as without occupation were probably craftsmen too. The leading trade was carpentry (seventeen men), followed by seven barrel makers and a scattering of other craftsmen: a bricklayer, two wheelwrights, two tailors, two butchers, a shoemaker, a ropemaker, and three gardeners.[147] We have in Brazoria County a striking instance of the disproportionate occupational distribution of German immigrants. German farmers were deterred by the predominance of slave plantations. German professionals were discouraged by the relatively small potential German clientele and its dispersal. Yet certain artisans were powerfully drawn to Brazoria County.

Artisans were attracted in far larger numbers to Galveston, and there they began arriving early. A young Irish diplomat located in Galveston from

1839 to 1840 praised in his diary the expertise of German craftsmen there.[148] According to the census of 1850, Galveston County had a free population of 3500, of which almost half, 48 percent, were foreign born. Fourteen percent of the foreign-born inhabitants were artisans, and over half of all artisans were Germans. As late as 1860, 45 percent of Galveston's artisans had been born in Germany.[149] Many of the artisans contributed vitally to the rise of Galveston by producing the substitutes for imports that at least one scholar has found crucial to the success of ports.[150] As might be expected in a seaport, the German population was much more diverse than in Brazoria County. Although many craftsmen resided in Galveston, there were also many Germans at the extremes of the social structure: on the one hand, laborers; on the other, merchants and a scattering of professionals. Five physicians and eleven merchants were among the nonartisan Germans in 1850. Nearly half (43 percent) of the German men aged 18 and over were identified in that same year as craftsmen. The distribution of artisan occupations in Galveston differed substantially from that in Brazoria County. For example, although carpenters (32) were by far the most common German artisans in Galveston, there were many shoemakers (22) and many cabinetmakers (12), but only two coopers. The luxury trades in Galveston were well represented by Germans: two goldsmiths, a silversmith, a watchmaker, a confectioner, an upholsterer, and a piano-maker. Other artisans were engaged in occupations not represented in largely rural Brazoria County: four printers, a bookbinder, ten painters, three bricklayers, and a brickmason.[151] There were artisans in Galveston in occupations that Germans did not fill or scarcely filled in the older city of New Orleans, where American-born craftsmen held down many of the best artisan jobs. As we know from Charles Giesecke's letters as well as other sources,[152] numerous German artisans in America returned to Germany after a short period. One of these, a coppersmith named Höhne, has told his story, and presumably many of the returnees departed for the same reason as he — they found no suitable work.[153]

Good records for the debarkation of artisans in Texas during the period of the republic are lacking,[154] but an indication of the proportions of artisans among German emigrants to Texas can be found in figures for the arrival of artisans in Galveston from Europe in 1846–1850. In 1846, 8 percent of the Germans arriving in Galveston from foreign ports were artisans. A peak of 19 percent was reached in 1849, and the proportion remained high in 1850 at 16 percent.[155] Other statistics help us to comprehend the dimensions of this flow of artisans and their overrepresentation among German emigrants: it has been estimated that in the late 1840s the population of Germany consisted of a low of 4 percent artisans in one area, and a high of 8 percent in another.[156] The proportion of artisans among emigrants to Galveston far exceeded both of these figures.

A preliminary study of Galveston's immigrants finds that the city received vastly disproportionate numbers of artisans in certain occupations. For example, although in 1850 a mere 0.25 percent of the passengers from foreign ports entering the United States came through Galveston, 7 percent of the butchers, 8 percent of the bakers, and 12.5 percent of the millers landed in Galveston.[157] Guidebooks and merchants helped to draw some types of artisans to Texas in large numbers, at least for a few years. Additional studies of U.S. ports, drawing on the rich resources of the passenger lists, are necessary for the formulation of more detailed conclusions.

Surviving government records for the early stages of emigration from the Gieseckes' homeland, the Hildesheim district, to America mention 240 people emigrating in 1834. Eleven years later, in 1845, the number had increased sixfold to 1437 — and this the first half of the year.[158] In 1834 few people emigrated officially, and the number who left surreptitiously was probably not much larger. Of course the names of merchants or would-be merchants such as Charles Giesecke, who probably left Germany in the early 1830s, are unlikely to appear in emigration records, since many merchants departed on business, not as emigrants. Unfortunately, the fragmentary surviving records for the Hildesheim district do not list the occupations of emigrants; only the numbers for each locality are given, beginning in 1834. However, a published account describes six males, all young, who left that same year for America from one town and its environs in the Hildesheim district. As is characteristic of the early stages of emigration from an area, most of the men were petty bourgeois of the sort described by Michael Piore in a later era as "initial middle class migrants."[159] Only one was an artisan, a journeyman cabinetmaker. The others were shop assistants and candidates, or potential candidates, for public positions in the Church or schools: a student of theology, a candidate for a teaching position, two shop assistants or merchant helpers, and a man who had been a clerk in an apothecary.[160] Although these callings, like many other occupations, were overcrowded in Germany, the emigrants were unlikely to obtain in America similar positions utilizing their education and training unless large numbers of other Germans followed them.

According to the census of 1850 a German ropemaker named Conrad Lehnhoff, probably from the Hildesheim district, lived in the house of Edward Giesecke.[161] Many Texas Germans who owned small businesses acted as unofficial emigration agents. Edward Giesecke may also have been among those so engaged.

EPILOGUE: REFLECTIONS ON MIGRATION

OUR ACQUAINTANCESHIP WITH THE GIESECKES in the Hildesheim district and in Texas should lead us to discard persistent stereotypes that for two centuries have formed both the German and the American conception of German emigration to the United States. Both the Germany the Gieseckes left and the Texas that became their second homeland were developing bourgeois societies. When Charles Giesecke wrote his letters to his brother in the mid-1840s, Texas was almost as much an outpost of German as of North American capitalism.

The social and economic development of areas that joined the circle of rising bourgeois societies late, as occurred with Texas after 1820, has been explored unevenly.[1] We know more about the beginnings of these processes than about many subsequent stages in their development. More has been written on the voyages of discovery, on the earliest European settlements of the Americas, on Jamestown and Plymouth, than on the later processes leading to the establishment of African American slavery. The situation in the colonized land after the founding of the first settlements has been of less interest than the adventurous years of exploration and conquest. This research gap is less obvious but often wider when an area is neglected by later developments, as is the case with Brazoria County and the town of Brazoria. Due to the attraction of patriotic interest in the role of the Brazos area in the War of Independence against Mexico, we know more, if still remarkably little, about the early and mid-1830s than we do about the 1840s. To understand the history of commerce and the role of firms, as well as the impact of urbanization, immigration, and emigration on society, we must examine more than the great successes of John Jacob Astor, Carl Schurz, or August Belmont; more than the enterprises that prosper and develop into well-known firms and big businesses; more than the small settlements that one day become world cities; more than the poor immigrants who become enormously wealthy. We must examine also the businesses, the towns, and the people who do not fare as well, including those who, under the pressure of events, fail, or simply disappear.

The Gieseckes fit neither the stereotype of the nineteenth-century immigrant in America nor that of the German in Texas. They did not arrive virtually penniless; they did not become millionaires; nor did they fail or become impoverished. They did not all stay in America. They did not settle among other Germans in Texas and preserve German culture or speech. Although Charles Giesecke became a farmer, and thus fits one stereotype of the nineteenth-century German immigrant, he had aspired to something more — to be a real planter or a large merchant. The Gieseckes would gladly have been wealthier, happier, and more successful in both Germany and Texas. These aspirations can be inferred from Charles Giesecke's letters and from the social situation of the Gieseckes on both continents.

In Texas they found a commercial civilization similar in many respects to the one they had known at home in Germany. The same laws of capitalism were at work in both societies, if under different circumstances. The business practices, the bookkeeping methods, and often even the scale of business were similar. The primary difference was the existence of commercial freedom in Texas. Such freedom had already been established in the United States, where it was encouraged by the hostility to mercantilist practices expressed by the American Revolution. Every white person in Texas and the United States with the means to buy and sell could deal in virtually any commodity. In reality, of course, only a small minority of the white population of an area such as Brazoria County exercised this freedom of commerce. In the Kingdom of Hannover, in Bremen, and, more generally, in Germany prior to the Revolution of 1848 and the subsequent reforms culminating in Bismarck's unification, a series of restrictions constrained commerce and prohibited altogether many business activities. The widow Giesecke had to battle for months before she obtained permission from the authorities to open a yard-goods store in Elze. She finally succeeded, not so much because she was persistent, or even lucky, but because she belonged to a locally prominent family. Another difference between Texas and Germany was that business in Germany was more specialized. We could counterpose the Gieseckes' yard-goods store in Elze to their general store in Brazoria. The greater specialization of business in Germany was linked to the restriction of freedom of commerce there, not to the nature of capitalism.

The institution of slavery in Texas did not set the Lone Star Republic apart from Germany. Much of the land in both Texas and Germany was held by the masters of large estates — mostly aristocrats in Germany, and planters in Texas. The similarities in the countryside are most striking when, on the German side, we focus on Prussia east of the Elbe, or on parts of the Habsburg Empire. An instructive recent comparison bringing out the similarities between the Prussian Junkers and American slaveholders can easily be extended, on the one side, to other areas of Germany, including Hannover, and to Texas on the other side.[2] Indeed, some of the areas in which large aristocratic estates existed were to be found in the Gieseckes' region of southern Hannover. Neither slavery nor the remnants of serfdom were incompatible with a developed capitalist economy in Germany and Texas.

It was not a sign of complete failure when Charles Giesecke became mainly a stock raiser and Edward Giesecke a storekeeper. Yet, neither were these attainments the great success that Charles had dreamed of. We are now in a position to understand the external grounds for his shift from merchant with a "plantation" to farmer. We have traced the forces in Texas, and in the world at large, that favored this shift, even though many aspects of his personal life both before and after 1845 remain hidden from scrutiny.

The problems that he as a businessman had to confront and master were already clear at the time of his letters in 1844–1845. One important consideration was whether Texas would become part of the Union. He knew that the high U.S. duties on imported textiles and certain other goods would compel him to reconsider importing many wares. The precipitous decline in direct commercial traffic between Germany and Galveston for several years after 1845 made his situation more difficult. This change was not as disadvantageous to larger merchants in Galveston, such as Eduard and Julius Kauffman, because that port experienced a great expansion despite the changeover of the mid-1840s and the collapse of direct shipping between Germany and Texas. The Kauffmans succeeded on a large scale. Eduard Kauffman was one of the founders of the Galveston Chamber of Commerce in 1845.[3] Julius Kauffman became both director of the National Bank of Texas and U.S. consul in Bremen.[4] The Kauffmans and their heirs, together with several partners, founded a succession of firms. The most famous of these was known from 1872 onward as Kauffman & Runge. Long Galveston's leading importer of coffee, spirits, and provisions, this firm also played a major role in the cotton trade.[5]

The decline of the Brazos ports destroyed one of the potential underpinnings of the Gieseckes' business. Brazoria was no longer an up-and-coming commercial center, as it had been during the 1830s and the early 1840s. The Kauffmans had the advantage of having established themselves in the rising port of Galveston at a propitious moment.

Yet all of the factors thus far adduced to explain the fate of the Gieseckes are matters of the sort that a successful merchant has to contend with. More basic to the limitation of the Gieseckes' business activities was their shortage of capital. This deficiency can be seen repeatedly in Charles Giesecke's letters. We have no indication that he or Edward ever overcame, however briefly, this obstacle. Ironically, the partnership between the brothers in Texas limited rather than expanded their resources. In a letter of March 16, 1844, Charles reports that Edward wants his share of his inheritance from their mother, whom all three sons would predecease. Whether Edward obtained anything from her in the mid-1840s is unknown. We do know that after her death in 1871 her children or their heirs received shares of her long-deceased husband's property and that for most of them this distribution amounted to little.[6] Of her four children, only her daughter, Riecke, was still alive. Fortunately Riecke's quarter share did not have to be further divided among her heirs, as did the shares of Charles and Friedrich. Nor was her share devastated by fees for transmission to Texas and for distribution there, as happened to the share of Edward's daughter. Had the shares that passed on to the heirs of the sons been left intact, instead of being divided among the grandchildren, the portions would have been larger, but still quite modest. The shares of each of the two sons who died in Texas amounted to 850 Gold Marks in 1879, when the case was finally closed.[7] If in 1844–1845 Edward and Charles Giesecke had been in possession of this money, they could have better financed their business affairs, and their market chances would have been more favorable. Although Charles often expressed himself vigorously and conveyed the impression that he would soon succeed in a big way in business, it appears that he was in the end too cautious. Despite his rhetoric, he lacked boldness. He feared the big risks that might have brought him great success despite his small capital.

Since an important part of Charles's business dealings required the cooperation of his brother Friedrich in Elze, we must consider the consequences of communications difficulties between the continents. The extent to which Charles relied upon Friedrich for news about markets, prices, and firms is unclear. Friedrich's failure to respond to his brother's frequent questions, or the delay of the answers, made Charles's task considerably more difficult. Clearly he hoped to obtain dependable reports from Friedrich. Charles's impressive familiarity with merchants, wares, and business conditions in Bremen and the Hildesheim district was of little use in the end if he could not obtain prompt and reliable information from trustworthy sources in Germany. Charles had a highly developed sense for detail. It was precisely this sort of sense that C. L. Fleischmann, his clever and well-informed German-American contemporary, maintained was essential if one were to be in a position to anticipate fluctuations in prices and make substantial profits.[8] As we have seen, opportunities for buying cheap and selling dear abounded in the vicinity of the frontier in Texas.[9]

The "failure" of the Gieseckes must be relativized and seen in its historical dimensions. Few of their contemporaries gained more success than Charles or Edward Giesecke. In America, as in Germany, many businessmen went bankrupt, while others simply vanished without formalities. Most merchants began under even less favorable circumstances and did not do as well as the Gieseckes. The German surfeit of merchants was squandered in the "land of unlimited possibilities." Many made their contribution to the economic development of North Germany and Texas and then disappeared virtually without a trace. The Gieseckes distinguished themselves by leaving a clear trail. Edward died in 1856, Charles in 1864 or 1865, and Friedrich in 1865. They were among the fortunate who had progeny, progeny who survived and learned something about them.

In Germany, the Gieseckes remained merchants for another generation, until the male line died out. Carl Giesecke, the only son of Friedrich, left Elze at age sixteen or seventeen, served an apprenticeship in a Bremen export-import house, and never again lived in his home town. He later worked in New York and Stockholm, as well as Bremen, and eventually had his own firm, but it remained small.

From the perspective of the late twentieth century, we can see clearly how the small businessmen with their modest capital were swallowed up by the big capitalists, as began to occur with the Gieseckes in the 1840s and 1850s. The Mills brothers in Texas, the Kauffmans in Galveston and Bremen, the firm Brauer & Son in Bremen proved victorious. However, a look at a slightly later era reveals the transiency of even those firms, as well as the decline or failure of individual capitalists. View, for example, the case of Robert Mills. Arguably the richest man in Texas at the time of the demise of Edward Giesecke in 1856, Mills died impoverished in 1888 after he had twice gained and twice lost a fortune.[10] During many of the same years when the Mills and the Gieseckes sought fortunes, Karl Marx was seeking to comprehend the dynamics of the historical processes that led to riches for the few and misery for the many.

The neglect of small merchants by students of immigration has led to many an overgeneralization. Similarly, the neglect of immigrant craftsmen until recently has distorted our view of the immigrant. The understandable preoccupation of research with mass immigration and, to a lesser extent, with a few highly educated and very visible immigrants, has left us unprepared to deal with many a nineteenth-century arrival. A suggestive recent scholarly exchange on the application of the concepts of acculturation and assimilation to the history of immigrants reflects this neglect.[11] Nevertheless, some recent studies of German immigrants are more inclined to weigh the factor of social class in both the sending and the receiving countries.[12] This provides, as I have shown in the present work, one of the keys to understanding the immigrant. Of course the explanatory power of class has its limits, even when applied to merchants. A good reminder of these limits can be found in the family history of the journalist Hermann Hagedorn. At age nineteen, his father left the small town of Nienburg on the Weser in the Kingdom of Hannover, bound for America. In Brooklyn he resumed his career as an apprentice merchant. The Hagedorn family in America was to split into those like Hermann, who assimilated, and those like his father and brother, who refused to take this final step and returned to Germany during World War I.[13]

Many of us hesitate to leave the rich table the past offers us unless we gain some comfort, however humble. Some reassurance lies in the consolation of a world unified, not divided, by culture, despite its separation into political entities increasingly organized along national and nationality lines. The culture of ascending capitalism during the first two-thirds of the nineteenth century was as unified, and almost as homogeneous, as was once the world of the medieval Christian clergy. The Gieseckes could move without evident unease among three worlds: their *Heimat*, the home of the people the Pied Piper of Hamelin on the Weser left behind; the environment of the newly ascending Hanseatic city of Bremen; and the beyond-the-seas realm of Stephen F. Austin and Sam Houston. Even the leisure activities of the bourgeoisie were international and often unified, depending more upon social position than nationality or native tongue. Charles Giesecke's letter of October 22, 1845, describes the young American woman whom he had married three months earlier. His initial reference to her makes her virtually interchangeable with the mail-order bride selected by his brother in Elze, a woman whose name arrived, in Charles's words, "a mail day" too late. But Charles assures Friedrich that he has not forsaken bachelorhood for naught. As Charles pens his last surviving letter to his brother, his wife is seated before the piano, that international symbol of nineteenth-century bourgeois culture,[14] and is playing the venerable "Life Let Us Cherish." Lest any doubt about the familiarity of the music arise, Charles adds the German in parentheses: "Freut Euch des Lebens." He writes further that he foresees much happiness and is entirely satisfied with his young mate. Perhaps this happiness was not as modest as his career as a merchant.

Letters from Texas

1844–1845

The Merchant and Farmer Charles A. Giesecke in Brazoria, Republic of Texas, to His Brother, the Merchant Friedrich Giesecke in Elze, Amt (Subdistrict) Gronau-Poppenburg, Kingdom of Hannover

Among my father's papers I found a small packet of old letters he had shown me briefly two or three times at most. On these rare occasions he spoke about his ancestors and relatives who had been merchants in Mexico. They were, he said, in the export-import business, as if they had been big merchants. He had little more to relate about them, for his romantic attitude toward this aspect of the family past was restrained by his prosaic approach to life. He lacked any hint of the gift for story-telling. At least equally inhibiting were his experiences growing up during World War I.[1] Like many others of his generation born in the late nineteenth or early twentieth centuries, he had been intimidated, indeed terrorized, by peer pressure and the nationwide campaign of anti-German propaganda into not wanting to be associated publicly — or, for that matter, in most private situations — with anything German. This fear effectively throttled much of his interest in his antecedents.

The recipient of the letters, Friedrich (Fritz) Giesecke (1809–1865), was the great grandfather of my father on his mother's side of the family. Since Friedrich Giesecke lived most of his life in Germany and died in Elze, then less than an hour's southerly train ride from Hannover, I assume the letters remained in Germany until either Friedrich's son, Carl Giesecke (1845–1926), who was a merchant principally in Bremen, New York, and Stockholm, or Friedrich's son-in-law, my grandfather Walter Struve (1871–1929), returned them to America. Although Carl Giesecke became a citizen of the United States as a young man and resided there for two periods of his life, he lived out the final years of his long life in Kirchrode, a community not yet incorporated into the city of Hannover. It is possible that my grandfather Walter Struve, originally from Osterode am Harz, a town two hours southeast of Hannover by rail, brought the letters back with him on one of his last trips to Germany in the 1920s. My grandfather and his British partner founded a stocking factory on the edge of Philadelphia shortly before the turn of the century. In 1901 this Walter Struve married Marie Giesecke, the daughter of Carl Giesecke. The two families were already linked by ties of friendship and business. Carl Giesecke had gone to boarding school in Germany with the father of Walter Struve. Marie's children never learned anything from her about relatives in Texas; shortly after the birth of her last child in 1905 she disappeared forever into the Philadelphia Institute, a progressive center for the mentally ill. Her children were told their mother had died.

We have no way of ascertaining who first bundled the letters together. Doubtless they were preserved because they pertained to vital matters of inheritances and troubled personal relationships. They remained of interest to succeeding generations because they shed light on kin and the activities of the Giesecke family in America. No other letters from the correspondence of the Giesecke brothers have turned up. We have no reason to assume that during the period of the surviving letters, from March 16, 1844 to October 22, 1845, Charles Giesecke (1811–1864/65) wrote other letters to his brother Friedrich. It would be nice to have at least one letter from Friedrich to Charles. A theme running through Charles's letters is his often-repeated complaint that he had heard nothing from Friedrich. Finally, on October 30, 1845, Charles mentions a reply from Friedrich. Preserved with the letters was a note to Friedrich from C. L. Brauer & Son, the Bremen firm with which the Gieseckes often did business.[2] Almost all of the notations from Brauer that occasionally appear on the outside of the letters have been omitted from the abridged translation of the letters in this appendix.

I have shortened the text of the letters by a fifth. Most of the excisions consist of repetitions or lists of wares. My object was to increase the readability of the letters without compromising seriously their historical value. I have retained two samples of the long lists. Many of the repetitions came about because of the method of composition. Charles was not always certain which letter would arrive first. Letters often acquired multiple postscripts while he awaited suitable means of getting his correspondence to Germany. Each letter consists of one or more sheets of paper folded, and ordinarily sealed with wax, in the once customary way so that no envelope is necessary. Three of the letters, that of February 10, 1845, that of March 7, 1845, and that of June 30, 1845, were enclosed in other letters or in freight shipments. The address segments of these letters bear no trace of postage, the full address is not given, and in one instance, the letter of March 7, 1845, the entire address portion of the letter is written over. Seeking to limit the consequences of the loss or delay of a letter in transit, Charles usually sent his orders to Elze by way of different ships and routes.

A few repetitions have been retained because they are typical of Charles's penchant for entreating, criticizing, and chastising his brothers. In our own day the products of this sort of proclivity are condemned as "verbal abuse," and there is little reason to believe that Charles's outbursts were taken in good spirit by their objects. In particular the youngest of the brothers, Edward Giesecke (1815–1846), was in Texas and making many problems for Charles.

Charles wrote his often embittered missives in a good hand. His punctuation and spelling were a bit idiosyncratic and outdated; inconsistencies are characteristic of much German manuscript material before the middle of the nineteenth century. He expressed himself in a racy German displaying few if any of the ponderous Teutonisms that Mark Twain and other Americans have mocked in German prose. Although he used High German, his diction betrays certain North German regionalisms in usage and construction. In the middle of the nineteenth century, and still today, the speech patterns of Germans of the same social class and status but in different areas, often even localities, vary greatly. The range of the variations in the spoken language, most of them reflecting the persistence and influence of dialects, far exceeds the differences found in English as spoken in all of North America and the British Isles. In several places he uses American words. He translates some of these into German, but usually assumes his brother will have no difficulty understanding them.

In translating the letters I have made no effort to concoct an antiquated English that might appear to the reader characteristic of the period when Charles wrote. I have sought to tap the full resources of today's American vernacular and at the same time convey the flavor of his spicy diction. Evident omissions have been supplied, obvious slips rectified, and other small changes made to improve clarity. The conventions to which Charles adhered favored well-nigh endless run-on sentences. These have been altered, as has the whimsical paragraphing.

Galveston
March 16, 1844

Dear Brother,

I have been here for three days and am awaiting the lighter. The Brig *Weser*[3] departs tomorrow. On the lighter I have an additional five bales of cotton[4] and 800 pounds of tobacco, both of which I shall now send with the Brig *Antoinette*.[5] [An itemized, annotated list of the shipment on the *Weser* follows: 84 hides, 8 deerskins, 8 calfskins, and two boxes of leaf tobacco weighing a total of 350 pounds.]

You are to receive these things via Messrs. C. L. Brauer & Son in Bremen. There are all together 2712 pounds. You are to pay in accordance with the bill of lading only one cent per pound for freight, and not a bit more. There are nine ships out of Bremen here, and they cannot get any cargo. . . .

Sell everything as advantageously as possible and write what happens.

We have had a north wind for three days. I have a toothache again. My face [is] swollen. Send me some fresh elderberry blossoms. They have cured me time and again.

Ed. [Edward Giesecke] did not buy the Stuart house,[6] but instead bought [Robert and/or D. G.] Mills's[7] old warehouse. [Edward] also wasted another $300. When I came home,[8] he didn't have a dollar in the house! A fine partner. We had to borrow RSS[9] from Mills to pay for passage, taxes, and Ahlers.[10] Enough to drive one crazy. He [Edward] has written to you. He wants his inheritance. I can't bear to write any more because of the pain.

CAG [Charles A. Giesecke]

Brazoria
January 24, 1845

Dear Brother,

We received the crate of merchandise from September 1 in good condition. Instead of 22 linen trousers we found only 20. We shall have to return the socks. Everyone laughs at them. They say those folks forgot to knit the legs on the socks: "You most [sic] send them back and get the legs." [The preceding sentence is in English in the original]. There are only five dozen anyway. Otherwise, everything was correct and in the best condition.

We have no use for linens like this sample at that price. We can pay at most four *Mariengroschen*[11] per ell.[12] In Bremen Chr. Meyer[13] offered me Alfelder *Stiege* linen[14] at about eight *Groten*[15] per ell. I bought some of the same Meyer linen bleached at 13 *Reichstaler*[16] per 100 double ell[17] at four feet.[18] In this case the ell at two feet was about 4 5/8 *Groten*. The following article goes well here: gray Bodenwerder linen,[19] *Halbladen* [*Halblacken?*][20] No. 2. . . . I received over 1,000 yards of it from Captain Haesloop,[21] and in Bremen it costs 7 1/2 *Groten* per yard, or about 5 *Reichstaler* per ell. It is 5/4 wide; the Bodenwerder and Meyer linens are one ell wide. In the course of the year we have sold 1,500 [?] yards of this. Enclosed are samples of them. Alfelder *Stiege* linen would go nicely here. I wanted to buy 50 *Stiegen* from Meyer, but he would not sell me less than 100 *Stiegen*. The next time you get to Bremen go to him and look it over. Judging from your sample, linen is more expensive in Alfeld than in Bremen.

Wait until I write before you send anything. Perhaps I shall come over. I am still waiting for an answer from Basse.[22]

Greetings to Mother and Riecke[23] and your Wife.[24]

Your Brother,
Chas. A. Giesecke

Make out this bill properly and send it back to me.

P.S. If you cannot sell my tobacco for 10 *Mariengroschen* per pound, then let it sit. Surely there are people other than Richter[25] in Germany who buy tobacco.

Brazoria
Feb. 10, 1845

Dear Fritz,

The 10th of February, and still no answer to my letters! Riecke doesn't write, nor does Basse. It is now a full year since I wrote. A[dolph] Pohlmann[26] thinks you must have received the crate in the middle of October. Last week I received a letter from C. L. Brauer & Son dated Dec. 14. What's the explanation? Has all hell broken out there as well as here?

In all my life I've never seen business as wretched as now. Just think, there are now seven shops here, and not a one has a thing to do. This place is as if dead. The people have for the most part made good harvests, but now cotton goes for nothing. Think of this: 4 to 4 1/2 cents per pound, and even at these prices the planters can't sell it. There are too few ships in

Galveston, and the merchants themselves have no money. Still worse, they [the planters] get at most an advance of 3 1/2 [per pound] in gold. Hardly enough to buy shoes for the Negroes. Well, it's a free county, thank God! He who has no shoes can go barefoot.

Nothing except a fusel oil[27] distillery will go here now. People keep running to me with potatoes to sell. When I go to Galveston, everybody wants whiskey. I can sell 100 barrels of whiskey more easily than 100 bales of cotton. I've got to distill whether I want to or not. Come what may. Send me two hard workers, a cooper and a distiller. I'll give them a wage they'll be satisfied with.

When I was there,[28] you said something to me about artificial fermentation. Can you get me the information? I can do very well if I make only a cent [per gallon?] more. That would be a hell of a lot in a year. Tomorrow I'm going to pack a barrel full of tobacco scraps. If you send me the information and it works, you'll have the tobacco in exchange. If it doesn't work, I'll charge you 11 *Groschen*[29] per pound for it. If equipment I don't have here is necessary, you'll of course have to send it along. Otherwise the formula won't help me. Send me also an *Ancker*[30] of cherry syrup. More is not advisable; it might sour in the extreme heat of the summer.

Everything has changed here. People don't know what to do. They can't exist any more with these cotton prices. Write me promptly everything about tobacco. There is much tobacco being grown here this year. Don't depend simply on Richter. You must try all of Hannover and Brunswick, as well as Hildesheim.[31] There's nothing to be done with tobacco in Bremen. They think there that we're simpletons in Texas. A lot of sugar plantations have been laid out here already. Everyone wants to give up cotton. Here in the neighborhood this year 150 barrels of sugar at 1000 pounds each and about 300 barrels of molasses have been made. I can now buy molasses here at 25 cents per gallon. Don't be surprised if within three years we're exporting rum from Texas. Even Mills is planting sugar instead of cotton. You can scarcely imagine how much everything here has changed, and changes daily. In three years you won't be able to recognize the country. More tomorrow.

Your brother,
CAG [Charles A. Giesecke]

You must have your tobacco scraps cut and mixed with Puerto Rican rum. The tobacco has to be chopped up as finely as possible. Otherwise it won't burn well. Ad[olph] P[ohlmann] says you want to start a tobacco factory. That would be very practical, but do it right. In the first place, you know you don't understand how to make cigars. And if you start with your apprentices, you all will just ruin the tobacco without making any cigars. And if anyone buys some from you, he'll do it only once. Have a cigar maker sent to you from Bremen who has learned the craft so that he makes each cigar like the one before. Make sure he doesn't roll in the filler wet.[32] Then something will come of it. Such a business has to be run the right way.

Give my regards to your wife.

Your brother,
Chas. A. Giesecke

I don't know what else to write until I finally get letters from you. I don't have to bother writing to you anything about shipping me goods. You certainly won't be too weighed down by it. I wish you would come over and get the brat [Edward Giesecke] to cough up [*klopftest den Bengel*] the $600 dollars from his blunder with Mills. Send me both of his [Edward Giesecke's] letters as soon as possible. If he writes you about shipping anything, tell him he should turn to Mills.

The Above [Charles A. Giesecke]

Brazoria
February 18, 1845

Dear Brother,

At last I have reached a decision. It is impossible to come over there. I am writing with today's mail so that you can send me some things this spring if possible.

You should have in your hands already the tobacco that was sent on the *Ferdinand*.[33] The remaining five pieces of the shipment you will receive via the *Neptune*.[34] I am sending to you with the latter in addition a barrel and a box of my own product with letters, samples, etc.

Send the following. . . . [35][At one point on the list Charles, obviously alluding to shoes he or Friedrich had ordered from Germany, perhaps from Elze, remarks: "There's no form to the shoes and boots. The boys there don't do decent work. In three days the soles were hanging off the boots."]

Yesterday I had to go to a plantation four miles from here. This year Dr. Gautier[36] wants to send 10,000 bushels of sweet potatoes and 2,000 bushels of corn,[37] half of which is to be distilled, and he wants to give me two Negroes for the job. Send me in any event a distiller and a cooper with the next ship. Write me immediately *everything* [Charles's emphasis] about tobacco. It looks as if 40,000 pounds of tobacco will be raised [in the "neighborhood?"] this year. If I can depend on the price, there's something to be made with tobacco, but pay attention so that you don't get us both into a mess, as you did with the hides and cotton.

In the crate you'll find letters that are as detailed and clear as possible about each item. Send everything to me at my own address. Otherwise I'll never get it.

Now I have written enough to you. You certainly can't complain that you didn't know.[38]

Greetings to Mother, Riecke, and your wife.

Your brother,
Chas. A. Giesecke

Ask Uncle Basse[39] if he has forgotten me.

Brazoria
March 7, 1845

Dear Brother,

Today I am sending you again from my plantation through the good offices of Messrs. E[duard] Kaufmann & Co.,[40] Galveston. . . . [The reference is to G(iesecke) shipments 25, 26, and 27. Included were a barrel of tobacco weighing 395 pounds net and a "barrel of scraps of the best leaf tobacco. Sell the former for my account as advantageously as possible and credit me with the proceeds. The scraps are yours gratis."]

Send me the following items:
1 dozen fine black felt hats like the ones I always used to buy in Bremen — at about 14–15 *Reichstaler* per dozen.
2 dozen large padlocks.
2,000 large Schwabacher[41] needles.
Linen twist, but good quality.
1 dozen horse bridles.
1 dozen cotton saddle blankets.
Some violin strings of all sorts.
2 pounds of common pins.
Some of the same on cardboard.

Some fishing line.

[A hand in the margin directs the reader to "See new sample" for one or more of the next few items.]

8 pieces of calico at 8 *Schillinge.*

8 pieces of ditto at 10 *Schillinge.*

8 pieces of ditto at 11 *Schillinge.*

4 pieces of ditto at 13 *Schillinge.* But all colorfast.

8 pieces of ordinary calico at 4 *Schillinge.*

4 pieces of genuine white half-linen.

4 pieces of ditto imitation (all cotton).

6 pieces of fine white shirting.

6 pieces of medium quality ditto. I bought this last article cheaply in Bremen.

2 pieces of gray Nankeen [42]

1 or 2 pieces of Irish or Bielefelder [43] linen for blouses.

2 dozen cotton suspenders.

4 dozen ditto reinforced.

1 dozen shaving mugs.

1 dozen Nürnberg shaving cases with mirrors.

4,000 lighters.

4 bits with square butt ends to fit the old brace.

2 dozen polished English [44] table knives with white handles at 2 *Reichstaler.*

1 dozen pair of white English polished patent table knives at 5 *Reichstaler.*

2 cards of fine one- and two-blade sturdy pocket knives.

1 dozen pruning knives.

6 dozen ordinary linen socks, but with legs. [45]

4 dozen cotton mole stockings.

1 gross of mother-of-pearl shirt buttons.

3 dozen pocket combs.

1 dozen dressing ditto (but otherwise none).

12 dozen [rolls] of white cotton twist on wooden spindles, very coarse and strong (not fine).

1 good D-flute with 4 keys.

4–6 dozen ordinary cotton cloths.

4 pieces of fringe.

1 dozen vests.

2 pieces of brown calfskin.

2 gross of steel pens like the last ones (without styles).

2 dozen pairs of cotton gloves.

1 dozen black very large silk cravats, perhaps 6/4 [46] twist.

12 pieces of muslin. It is in great demand now.

Some ladies' gloves.

2 pounds of snuff.

25 pounds of saltpeter.

5 pounds of green vitriol.

6 pounds of cream of tartar.

2 pounds of camphor.

2 pounds of rhubarb.[47]

To try out, 1 piece of strong gray Manchester.[48]

3 pieces of mousseline de laine[49] cloth.

1 piece 8/4[50] cotton material for skirts. There's a cloth here that's called jersey; it's half wool, half cotton. Just like your buckskin,[51] but cheaper and yet strong. It goes very well here.

1 piece of blue striped material for beds and mattresses.

1/2 dozen black silk vests.

1 piece of black merino [wool] for inner linings.

For me, 1 Friesian coat.[52]

1 pound of fine sealing wax.

1/2 dozen boxes of seals.

From Schürhof in Gevelsberg,[53] to try out, 2 dozen English hoes at 8 inches.[54]

1 dozen ditto at 7 inches.

1 dozen ditto at 10 inches.

1/2 dozen shingling hammers.

1/2 dozen fine English claw hammers with handles.

1/2 dozen ordinary polished stonemasons' trowels with handles at 8 inches.

1/2 dozen trunk hinges at 6 inches.

1/2 dozen ditto at 8 inches.

1/2 dozen ditto at 12 inches.

1/2 dozen ditto at 18 inches.

1 dozen black currycombs with 6 rows of teeth.

6 pounds of white tapioca.

1 box of ca. 25 pounds of small dried plums [*Zwetschen*].

1 piece of gros de Naples.[55]

1 piece of brightly colored silk twill handkerchief material 5/4 to 6/4 wide.

12 pieces of netting for mosquitoes.

To try out, 1 box of about 25 pounds of sterol lights; 6 per pound. Ad[olph] P[ohlmann] tells me that these are as good as those here, but cheaper.

3 demijohns at 5 *Stübchen*.[56]

6 ditto at 2 *Stübchen*.

6 ditto at 1 *Stübchen*. [The demijohns] to be bought in Bremen and filled with medium coarse barley grits.

360 [57] Silesian linen like that Ad[olph] P[ohlmann] got from you.

2 good sun bonnets.

1 hatchet and 1 pitchfork for my own use.

1 alcohol meter and thermometer. Mine are still good, but since we need to use them constantly, I am worried about them.

Send everything to my own address.[58] What you do with him [Edward Giesecke] is no longer of any concern to me.

Chas. A. Giesecke

[Four postscripts, two dated and two undated, follow.]

Regarding crate G [Giesecke Shipment] No. 28: there are 16 1/2 pounds of wax in addition to samples of my tobacco. The latter still goes on my old account.

CAG [Charles A. Giesecke]

Galveston
April 25, 1845

4 dozen white women's stockings like those we used to buy in Brunswick. If you dispatch these articles to me toward fall, then send me 1/2 piece of good finely woven blue woolen cloth with camphor to protect against moths.

Galveston
April 28 [1845]

I wrote this letter at home to send with the *Neptun*, but I was too late. Today I sold a barrel of cognac and a barrel of rum here for $60. Just the beginning. Can't cognac be given a scent? I'm going to try it with small roasted plums when you send me some.

At Mr. Kaufman's today I saw that the freight charges for tobacco are climbing beyond all measure. [The next sentence is an apparent *non sequitur*. The two sentences in this paragraph are linked only by the ideas of business problems and the association of rising prices with the hoisting of goods.] The windlass can't do the job anymore. I must use some other device.

I haven't received a letter from there [Elze] since I left (with the exception of what was in the crate and [what was brought by] Ad[olph] P[ohlmann]. Did the courting turn your head?[59] I must know *everything precisely* [Charles Giesecke's emphasis] about tobacco. Otherwise there'll be losses again. What am I supposed to make of your sending along Richter's letter? He writes that he has enough tobacco. Should we have none for anyone else? Write me briefly about everything. There's a lot of tobacco being raised here this year, but if you can't give a price, then you must write me immediately so that the people here don't think me a fool. This year I must give the people what I promise them, and if I can't do that any more, the planting will cease.

Send me a distillery hand, but not another depraved student. When I left, Ed. [Edward Giesecke] had rented a Negress for his wife. Can't you send Riecke over? She could tell Edward's wife a thing or two. That would work out just famously. After all, Riecke can speak Low German.[60]

Greet your wife and tell her I answered her letter six weeks ago. My letter will come with the next opportunity. I am very punctual with my correspondence.

CAG [Charles A. Giesecke]

This letter and the goods [for shipment] were, as you can see, ready for two months, but I couldn't get it [sic] on the ship *Neptun*. I had to keep crate No. 25 here. I can't sell any more tobacco, and I have no more cigars.

When I come home, I'll move into the Pilsbury house.[61] I have it free for two years. And if I lay out about $50 for repairs, I'll get it for three years. That's how cheap houses here are now!!! And that filthy beast[62] [Edward Giesecke] pays $700 for a crummy shop,[63] from which Mills gets $300 in cash alone. All this if you still wonder why you get nothing, where it all is. Who let him get the authority for this??? The time is long past when I should have extricated myself. Now he wants to make a lady out of his Mecklenburg servant girl.[64] He buys what he wants without saying a word to me. You must come here[65] so you can meet your nice kin.

Texas is probably going to the United States next year.[66] Then everything will change.

[Charles A. Giesecke]

Brazoria
June 30, 1845[67]

Dear Fritz,

This morning I set out to ride to Galveston when I met [Adolph?] Pohl-mann's brother.[68] The Brig *Ferdinand* was in Galveston already on the 19th of this month, and still no letter. I didn't know what to think. What am I to make of your letter? As I have been thinking to myself, I have written you at least five times asking you to write me everything and in detail about the prospects for tobacco, but I hear not a word. With your last crate you sent me Richter's letter in which he writes that he is well supplied with cigar tobacco for this year. What am I to make of that? Is there no one else in all of Germany who sells tobacco except Richter?

On the 21st inst., two days after the arrival of the *Ferdinand*, E. Kauf-man made a special trip up here from Galveston and said to me: "Have you heard yet? Have you heard yet? Your tobacco fetched 15 *Reichstaler* in gold." I acted quite indifferent. He told me that this price is something entirely new there. He wanted to buy tobacco immediately, but none is ripe yet. He had the samples of my tobacco in his pocket. Didn't I write you that you shouldn't let go of tobacco in Bremen?

I don't know what to do now. I have so few wares at present that I can't think of buying any for you. Here in the neighborhood 40,000 pounds [of tobacco] are being raised this year. Everything is closed now. What non-sense to have had the tobacco cut! Richter didn't want it. In Bremen they wanted it for nothing. So you lose your head as usual and have it cut up. With that you ruin up there [in Bremen?] your 6-*Groschen* tobacco. If you had stuck your nose in, you would have smelled at once that it was West Indian tobacco. All the nicer that the leaves were so big. Any clever cigar maker would have seen immediately that he could cut away the outer leaves between the stems without cutting directly across the stems — or do you all in Germany want to teach me how to make cigars? This tobacco burned to ashes like fleece and had an aroma better than ordinary Havana, but in a pipe it burns black and takes on a sickening odor from the juice. Even the finest genuine Havana leaf tobacco is no good in a pipe. As soon as the pipe is a quarter smoked, it begins to stink.

Well, tell me whether you don't want to come to your senses in your lifetime. You're no Swabian so that you have to be 40 before you wise up.[69] All good things come in threes.[70] You've made three blunders now,

Appendix 1

131

and I hope you've learned from them. Think first of your speculation in *Kümmel* [brandy]. Second, think of your own stupidity here. Third, think of my nice partnership [with Edward Giesecke]. Well really, who made it — you or I?

Now I'm going to propose a speculative venture to you. If you follow my directions literally and to the letter, I'll vouch for its success. But if you let your fancy get the better of you, your hearing is defective. First, have a good cigar maker sent to you from Bremen. He'll understand craftsmanship. In other words, you lay a handful of cigars in front of him. He's to work from them and make each like the last. Then have a quarter case of good cigars made — on trial — in Bremen. You must take pains to find out what type is most popular. Cigars are like women's hats — every year a new fashion. Regalia is the best here,[71] but they are difficult to make. If you don't make them especially well, they look wretched. Every week now I make my thousand cigars and send them off to Galveston, where I get $10 per thousand.[72]

Now I know whom I'm working for. We [Charles and Edward Giesecke] didn't have any cigars the last two months we were together [in partnership]. I was supposed to take care of the tobacco, and he [Edward] played cards with his wife and brother-in-law or went for a stroll. I had to have a stomach that could digest fish hooks.

Ad[olph] P[ohlmann] says you want to begin making cigars with your apprentices. That would be a mistake even if you wanted to lose your money. You all would shred up the tobacco, and anyone stupid enough to buy cigars from you, would certainly not do it again. Of course you can get a thousand already made for 24 to 30 *Mariengroschen*. From my tobacco you can surely make 3,500 to 4,000 per hundred pounds and still have scraps of ca. 40 pounds left over. If you have the scraps cut up, try our method. Have them sliced as fine as hair. Use a good sharp knife and move the blade only the slightest bit forward with each stroke. Let the tobacco dry in the air and pack it loosely in packets. If Havana tobacco is cut coarsely, it burns straight through the leaf, something it cannot in the least tolerate. [The City of] Hannover must be a good place for cigars. If you pack them in a box, take a bottle of genuine rum, some vanilla, muscadine, carnation, and laurel. Let this stand six to eight days, and then with a feather flick some of it into the box. The cigars will take on a pleasant aroma.

If you still haven't sent me a cooper, then don't bother. Texas will probably go to the United States next January. Then it will be all over for whiskey, and by the time I can get enough molasses here to make it worth my while [to make rum], two years may well elapse.

This year an enormous amount of tobacco and sugar was planted here. Nothing was to be done with cotton last year, but this year there was. The cotton from '44 was very nice and was paid at 4 to 4 1/2 cents [per pound]. If E[dward] hadn't been such a slovenly beast,[73] we could make good in cotton this year all our losses.

I hear that the ship *Neptun* is supposed to be sailing from there [Germany] in the middle of October.[74] Don't pass up the opportunity [to send wares to me]. First, so I can get into the harness again. Second, so the merchandise arrives here before January, for as soon as we become part of the United States, we'll get an entirely different and monstrously high tariff. You already know what you have to send. I need not repeat it. Don't have any more fabrics or shoes made up until I write. There is an awful tax on textiles in the United States. I also don't want any more of the Circassian[75] that you have been sending. Don't send woolens either. Of course send the fabric that you've already had made up. But under no circumstances send something I haven't noted. Follow my instructions to the letter. As for calico, send me a good selection, but you must try to buy it tax-free. We are selling terribly cheaply now. Calico, for which we were getting 3 to 4 bits[76] per yard, now goes for 18 to 20 cents, but mostly cash.[77] And now one does steadier and better business.

I think I'll send you a bill of exchange for Brauer via E[duard] Kaufmann. I can sell cotton and hides in Galveston more advantageously in exchange for American goods than if I send them [cotton and hides] there [to Germany]. Write me exactly what you can give for tobacco. I can't ship it cheaper than 6 *Mariengroschen* [per pound] f. o. b. Galveston. If you hadn't gotten cold feet in Bremen, we could have kept on smuggling for a couple of years.

I hear that a German [tobacco] cutter[78] in Galveston can be had cheaply. I'll buy it if possible. Otherwise, I must have one from over there [Germany]. I can't make do any more without one. When I have one, I'll discard the poor tobacco, cut it up, and send you only the best cigar leaf. Then we can outwit the others. Cut tobacco can be sold here as well as in Galveston at very good prices.

Can't you get a hold of about 6 dozen large pieces of cotton cloth? A square yard each. The others are always "to[o] little"[79] for the Negroes. Madras cloth. Send me also, if possible from Bremen, a ton of Swedish iron. [There follows a detailed list of various sizes. Some of the iron is to be "suitable for plows."] I have written to Brauer & Son about this iron. You can find out whether they are sending me some. In case you want to send me the iron yourself, you must first reach an agreement on the freight. (At most 8 to 10 dollars per ton. Kaufmann doesn't pay more than that.) For crockery 8 cents per cubic foot. For dry-goods 15 cents.

Also from Bremen: two quarter cases of fine yellow candies. About 6 dozen wool socks, put camphor and tobacco in them.

Also: 30 cheap narrow cotton bands. I use them now to tie up my cigars when I send them to Galveston.

Also from Bremen: 100 pounds of chalk.

As before, send me one letter via New Orleans, and another with the ship. There is nothing more maddening than when one doesn't know what's inside. Just don't send me any more people to get on my back.

I still haven't completely settled up with Ed[ward Giesecke]. Just think, since my departure he's laid out $800 for himself. That way one can't get anywhere. He will owe me $300 to $400. As soon as I have settled up with him, I'll send you a complete and detailed account of what he owes me. You must deduct this debt from my old account and enter it against his account. There's no other way to do it. If I bring suit against him, the lawyers will take a share. Then too, you have enough power over him. You can speak to Mother about the matter. You got him here, and I don't want to take the bread out of his mouth. If he can make a go of it, he has my best wishes! He'll gradually earn enough to live on.

In crate G[iesecke] [An empty space remains for the number.] you'll find samples of various local cotton wares. Take account of them as much as possible so that I can compete with the others. As soon as you sell the tobacco (in 14 containers marked "G"[80]) weighing 2,194 pounds, send me the detailed invoice so that I can get straightened out with Ed[ward].

Again, don't pass up the next opportunity to send me something. Greet your wife and son.[81]

Your brother,
Chas. A. Giesecke

The crate contains 16 1/2 pounds of wax. You can give it to Riecke.[82] I had to open the crate again. . . . The letters in it have been ready for three months.

Brazoria
October 22, 1845

Dear Brother,

Your letter of June 30 of this year reached me today. I don't know whether you cannot or will not understand me. I want an itemized invoice for the things you have sold, not for those I have gotten from you. I have written you more than once that CAG [Charles A. Giesecke] containers Number 1 through 9 are my own. Further, [mine are the things I sent] via the *Johann Dethard*:[83] a barrel[84] [of tobacco samples], No. 26; a barrel[85] of tobacco cuttings (gratis), No. 27; and 960 ox horns.

Do you think I want to pay Edward rental for Negroes, and later pay for his debts with my tobacco? (If you had written me how much [containers Number] 15 and 18 were sold for, I could have computed it [my share], but in this form I can only take a guess.) As for the costs of your *Kümmel*[*wasser*],[86] I have already lost more from the affair than you, and you can't ask that I pay for all your stupid deals. As for the interest since my departure [from Germany], I'll have to accept it, but I do want to send you Mills's original receipt for $800. Then you can see for whom and why I have to pay this interest. I shall then send you also both our joint, and my new separate, account statements. Further, you have to divide in half with Eduard your last invoice [for goods sent] via the *Apollo*, for he has had a half since July 1844. I think the matter won't be settled unless you finally come over here.[87] But don't come as did [the biblical] Jacob when he returned and had forgotten to ask his master[88] what he should do. If you come here at my request and fail, I'll pay for the mess.

In case you will and must come, couldn't you do something with rum? If one were, for example, to pack a small keg of rum in every barrel of tobacco, that would be about 30 gallons. You could smuggle the rum into [the Kingdom of] Hannover, thereby paying for your trip. You should know and understand this better than I. But don't think that our rum is as good as the best Jamaican. It's better though than the usual West Indian rum. E. Kaufman[n] wondered about that. He thought it would bring about 54 to 60 *Groten* [per gallon] in Bremen.

I've really got a problem with tobacco. Kaufman[n] offered me an advance and [proposed] purchasing with him on a joint account. But since my means were very limited, and since you didn't answer me, and I really don't want to let trading in tobacco get out of my hands, I had to agree [to buy jointly with Kaufmann]. I have in this way bought almost 3,000 pounds.

Appendix 1

135

I have also bought already a barrel[89] of approximately 400 pounds of ordinary [tobacco] cuttings for you and billed you at five cents [per pound]. You can make good use of it at that price. A lot of cigar tobacco is mixed in. At what price can you send me cigar boxes? I would like 250 one by fours, i. e., with the sides assembled.

Fräulein Nieman comes a mail day [*einen Posttag*] too late.[90] Tomorrow I shall have been married for three months. My wife's name is Sarah Maria, née Davis. . . . [91]

Congratulations on the baptism.[92] Tell Riecke I have sent her wax. She can get money or gold for it. Eduard sold two pairs of suspenders. He kept three, and I kept three. I wore one for my wedding (but I can't give much [for it]. You'll have to let me have it cheaper). If I sell the other two, I'll send [the] money. (People fear to pay much for such things now — hard times.)

Edward owes me $350. What should I do about it? I have already written you people about it. In the next crate I'll send you our invoices. Then you can convince yourself. I had wanted you to work it out with Mother. I know Mother is bequeathing him KLSS[93] except the 300. If I sue him, what do I gain? I would be offered at most $150 for the house in its present condition. I would have to give the lawyer $100 if I sued him, and I'd have to put an attachment on what he's to get in the future. What would I have then? $100 for the lawyer, $100 for my trip, and I'd be out perhaps $200. That's damned poor arithmetic. I wish you and Mother could take care of the matter together.

This year I have had to let my plantation lie fallow, for I saw the storm coming. But now it's passed. I must plant tobacco assiduously next year. This year I have only an old Negro who keeps everything in order and makes repairs. I now have twenty acres fenced in.

My wife is drying okra for you. (Even I didn't know that was possible.) Then you all can eat beef stew with okra or French gumbo [soup or stew]. Next year she wants to send you figs preserved in sugar. It's too late [in the season] for that now.

While I am writing, my wife is playing the piano and singing "Life Let Us Cherish" (*Freut Euch des Lebens*).[94] Now at least I have some happiness in my life. At least I have joy to my complete satisfaction in this matter.[95] Who knows? Perhaps my fortunes have turned. There's an American saying that "Fortune can not be always against one."[96]

I have got the hell rid of Adolph [Pohlmann?].[97] I have never been bothered by a worse pest in all my life. When I last saw him, he looked as sweet as a kiss. I guess he is now civilized. I hope the fellow you're sending me is accustomed to working.

I have been in good health the entire summer. (So much for my marriage.)

What's the explanation for the enormous difference in weight? [Charles goes on to complain in detail about a missing 276 pounds of goods sent to Germany by himself and his brother Edward.]

The crates and barrels[98] still cost $30. You should charge people for them. I have to pay dearly for hogsheads here — $1.50 [each]. For a crate, from $.75 to $2 each. I heard today that two ships out of Bremen have arrived [in Galveston].

Your brother,
Charles A. Giesecke

Regards to Mother, Riecke, your wife, and Carl [Friedrich's infant son]. [Regards also to Uncle] Basse and Aunt [Sophie Friederike Christine Basse] and Horns.[99]

[The next two lines are in English in the original.]

12 o'clock good night,

go to bed. My wife is waiting

P.S. The coffee we brought with us from Bremen weighed out exactly to our weight — 10.00 [pounds].[100]

[Charles A. Giesecke]

Chart of the Giesecke Family:

SOME RELATIONSHIPS AMONG THE GIESECKE, SANDER, BASSE, AND STRUVE FAMILIES

Hans Giesecke (1657–1714)
Blacksmith in Gittelde
m. Gittelde 1689
Anna Dorothea Timme, widowed Just
d. Gittelde 1718
|
Hans Jürgen Giesecke (1690–1749)
Burgher with Brewing Rights [*Brauer*]
and Farmer in Gittelde
m. Anna Orthia Mügge
|
Johannes Zacharias Giesecke (1729–1796)
Farmer and Trader in Gittelde
m. Windhausen 1766
Johanne Christiane Böhlke (1742–1824)
|
Heinrich Friedrich Giesecke
b. Gittelde 1776
d. Bockenem 1831
Merchant in Bockenem

Daniel Sander of Elze
Documented 1640
|
Brun Sander the Elder of Elze
Documented 1654–1692
Treasurer [*Kämmerer*] of Elze
|
Ludolf Sander, Sr. d. ca. 1713
Princely Court Smithy to the Celle Line
m. Anna Maria Haarstick d. 1721
(His brother Heinrich Daniel Sander
was mayor of Elze.)
|
Ernst Friedrich Sander d. 1766
Innkeeper of the "Güldener Stern" in Elze
(now Hauptstraße 47)
2d m. Elze 1744

m. Elze 1808

Friedrich Giesecke (1809–1865)
Merchant and Cottager [*Kötner*] in Elze
m. Bremen 1844 Marie Basse (1821–1904)
(See next spread, lower right corner.)
Four children, among them
|
Christoph Carl Giesecke (1845–1926)
Merchant in Bremen, New York, and
Stockholm. 1st m. Bremen 1877
Meta (Anna Margarete) Meyer b. Bremen 1858
|
Marie Sophie Henriette Giesecke (1878–1927)
m. Philadelphia 1901 Wilhelm Hermann *Walter*
Struve b. Osterode am Harz 1871
d. Philadelphia 1929 (Grandfather of the Author)

Anton Carl (Charles A.) Giesecke
(1811–1864/65) Merchant and Farmer in
Brazoria County m. Brazoria County 1845
Sarah May (Mary) Davis (1825?–1895)
Six children

Thomas Davis Giesecke
(1847/48–1931)

Frederika Giesecke
(1850/51–after 1920)

Johannes Sander, Sr.
b. Wernigerode 1579
d. Bornum near Bockenem 1644
Pastor in Bornum 1610–1644
|
Philipp Petrus Sander
(1628–1690) Pastor in Elze

Johann Wilhelm Sander
(1657?–1732)
Captain and Notary
Judicial Administrator of
the Bock von Wülfingen
Family

Philipp Joachim Sander
(1661–1725) Pastor in Elze
|
Sophia Sander (1694–1759)
m. Anton Heinrich Falcke
(1683–1745) Mayor of Elze
|
Johann Philipp Konrad Falcke
(1724–1805) Dr. Jurisprudence
Director Electoral Hannoverian
Chancery of Justice
|
Ernst Friedrich Hektor Falcke
(1751–1809) Dr. Jurisprudence
Mayor of Hannover, 1783–1809
|
Georg Friedrich Baron von Falcke
(1783–1850) 1845 Royal
Hannoverian Privy Councillor

Peter Konrad Sander
(1662?–1758) Treasurer of Elze
|
Henriette Amalie Sander
(1724–1771) m. Elze 1744

Sophia Dorothea Sander
(1755–1813)   m. Elze 1779 Anton Christian Sander. See middle of next page.

Henriette Sophie Sander
(1780–1858) m. Elze 1801
Johann Alhardt Horn
(1767–1851) District Surgeon
[*Landchirurg*] in Gronau
Five children

Johann Friedrich Bodo Sander
(1782–1803)

Luise Amalie Sander
(1785–1871)

Ernst Eduard (Edward) Giesecke
(1815–1856) Merchant and Shopkeeper in
Brazoria m. Brazoria 1844
Liesette Doby (1829?–1874)
|
Lisette Giesecke (1852/54– ?)
m. Brazoria County ca. 1871?
William Korner

Sophie Dorothea Friederike Giesecke
(1819 ?) m. Elze 1852
Johann Georg Adolf Ludecke (1803– ?)
Royal Hannoverian Tax Collector

Cornelius Giesecke
(1852–1934)

Jane Giesecke
(ca. 1855– ?)

Henrietta Giesecke
(ca. 1858–after 1930)

Charles Edward Giesecke
(1863–1946)

Johannes Sander, Sr.
b. Wernigerode 1579
d. Bornum near Bockenem 1644
Pastor in Bornum 1610–1644

Philipp Petrus Sander
(1628–1690) Pastor in Elze

Friedrich Sander
(1669–1760)
Mayor of Stralsund

Georg Dietrich Sander
(1671?–1736)
Pastor in Oberg

Daniel Otto Sander
(1675– ?) District
Physician in Alfeld

Bodo Christoph Sander
b. Oberg ca. 1709
d. Wolfenbüttel 1763
Princely Apothecary in Wolfenbüttel
2d m. Elisabeth Henriette Lauterbach (1726– ?)

Anton Christian Sander
b. Wolfenbüttel 1752
d. Elze 1820
Merchant [*Kauf- und Handelsherr*]
Mayor of Elze

Sophie Friederike Christine Sander
(1788–1869)

m. Elze 1808

no issue

Hinrich Basse d. after 1696
Provider of a Full Team of Draft Animals [*Vollspänner*] to lands of
the Cloister Wittenburg in Elze (now Enge Straße 2)
2d m. Margarete Koch, Stepmother of Tönnies Basse
|
Tönnies Basse (1660–1720)
Member of the Municipal Council in Elze m. before 1697
His wife's maiden name was Starke; her father was
Hinrich Starke (now Hauptstr. 27)
|
Johann Basse (1689–1741)
Burgher with Brewing Rights and municipal
officeholder in Elze (now Hauptstr. 35)
m. Elze 1722 Ilse Maria Hagemann (1700–1773),
daughter of Mayor Arend Erich Hagemann d. 1734

Johann Friedrich Basse (1723–1777)
Burgher with Brewing Rights, Surgeon
[*Wundarzt*], and Municipal Treasurer in Elze
(now Hauptstr. 35) m. 1748 Sophia Elisabeth
Meyer (1727–1769), daughter of Mayor Johann
Philipp Meyer. 2d m. 1770 Beata Sophia
Domann (d. 1813), daughter of a burgher
and merchant in Höxter. Children
from both marriages

Johann *Konrad* Basse (1753–1800)
Burgher with Brewing Rights and Farmer
with Half Team of Draft Animals
in Elze (now Hauptstr. 24)
m. 1781 Sophia Dorothea Mundt d. 1807
|
Christian Ludwig Basse (1755–1829)
Burgher with Brewing Rights, Merchant
[*Kauf- und Handelsherr*], and Mayor of Elze
(1799–1807) (Now Hauptstr. 53) m. 1782
Johanne Christiane Meyer
(from Kirchbrak?) d. after 1828

Christoph *Carl* Basse (1776–1851)
Burgher with Brewing Rights, Cottager with
Draft Animals [*bespannter Kötner*], Municipal
Officeholder (1808, 1815–1820), and Treasurer
(1821–1850) in Elze (now Hauptstr. 35) m. 1808
Sophie Friederike Sander (1788–1869)

Friedrich Heinrich Basse (1775–1844/after 1854?)
Merchant and White-Lead Manufacturer in
Bremen m. Bremen 1820
Rebekka Antoinette Achelis (1791–1854)
|
Marie Basse (1821–1904)
m. Friedrich Giesecke (1809–1865)
(See previous spread, lower left corner.)

NOTES

Full bibliographical data are given routinely only at first mention in these notes; the most detailed data are generally to be found in the Bibliography.

PREFACE

1. Walter Struve, *Die Republik Texas, Bremen und das Hildesheimische. Ein Beitrag zur Geschichte von Auswanderung, Handel und gesellschaftlichem Wandel im 19. Jahrhundert. Mit den Briefen eines deutschen Kaufmanns und Landwirts in Texas 1844-1845,* Quellen und Darstellungen zur Geschichte Niedersachsens, 96 (Hildesheim: Verlag August Lax, 1983).

2. Walter Struve, "German Merchants, German Artisans, and Texas during the 1830's and 1840's," *Yearbook of German-American Studies,* 23 (1988): 91–103.

3. Terry G. Jordan, *German Seed in Texas Soil. Immigrant Farmers in Nineteenth-Century Texas* (Austin, 1966).

INTRODUCTION

1. For a good study of this inheritance see Donald E. Chipman, *Spanish Texas, 1519–1821* (Austin, 1992).

2. The founding in the late 1970s of the German Texan Heritage Society was indicative of renewed interest in Texas in German immigrants and their descendants. This organization publishes a periodical now known as the *Journal of the German-Texan Heritage Society.* Papers from the conference that led to the founding of the society are collected in Glen E. Lich and Dona Reeves, eds., *German Culture in Texas: A Free Earth. Essays from the 1978 Southwest Symposium* (Boston, 1980). For other signs of contemporary interest in Texas Germans see Theodore Gish and Richard Spuler, eds., *Eagle in the New World: German Immigration to Texas and America* (College Station, Tex., 1986).

3. James A. Michener, *Texas* (New York, 1985).

4. Robert A. Caro, *The Years of Lyndon Johnson: The Path to Power* (New York, 1984), pp. 69, 100; Art Kowert, "LBJ's Boyhood among the German Americans in Texas," *Newsletter of the German-Texan Heritage Society* 9 (1987): 210–212. John-

son's mother, whose maiden name, Huffman, betrays German ancestors on one side of her family, taught English informally for years to many German-speaking children. Caro, *Years of Lyndon Johnson*, pp. 60–61.

5. See, for example, Frank Thistlethwaite, "Migration from Europe Overseas in the Nineteenth and Twentieth Centuries," in *XI Congrès International des Sciences Historiques*, vol. 5, *Histoire Contemporaine* (Stockholm, 1960), p. 33.

6. For some of the recent exceptions to this generalization see Walter D. Kamphoefner, *The Westfalians: From Germany to Missouri* (Princeton, 1987) or the German edition of this work, *Westfalen in der Neuen Welt. Eine Sozialgeschichte der Auswanderung im 19. Jahrhundert* (Münster, 1982); Bruce C. Levine, *The Spirit of 1848: German Immigration, Labor Conflict, and the Coming of the Civil War* (Urbana, 1992).

7. An outstanding exception to this generalization is an important study focused on agriculture by the historical geographer Terry G. Jordan, *German Seed in Texas Soil: Immigrant Farmers in Nineteenth-Century Texas* (Austin, 1966).

8. Among the studies during the past quarter century that stress the ease of migration for Germans are Thomas Sowell, *Ethnic America: A History* (New York, 1981), pp. 65–68; Joachim Reppmann, *"Freiheit, Bildung und Wohlstand für Alle!" Schleswig-Holsteinische "Achtundvierziger" in den USA 1847–1860*, (Wyk auf Föhr, 1994). For a classic presentation of the opposing, pessimistic point of view, focusing on Eastern and Southern Europeans from 1880 to 1930, see Oscar Handlin, *The Uprooted: The Epic Story of the Great Migrations That Made the American People* (Boston, 1973). For another example of the "pessimistic" view, see Michael Novak, *The Rise of the Unmeltable Ethnics* (New York, 1973). In addition to Kamphoefner's *Westfalians* and Levine's *Spirit of 1848*, recent interpretations challenging both the pessimists and the optimists include John Bodnar, *The Transplanted: A History of Immigrants in Urban America* (Bloomington, 1987); and, generally, the publications resulting from the Chicago Project to study German workers: e.g., Hartmut Keil and John Jentz, eds., *German Workers in Industrial Chicago, 1850–1910: A Comparative Perspective* (DeKalb, Ill., 1983); Hartmut Keil, ed., *German Workers' Culture in the United States, 1850–1920* (Washington, 1988). One of the characteristics of many of the works breaking with both the "optimistic" and the "pessimistic" views is careful attention to the role of social class in structuring the outcome of migration.

9. Again, Kamphoefner's *Westfalians* might be cited as an excellent example of such studies. For other examples see some of the essays in two symposia: Paul G. Buchloh, Brigitte Dix, and Eitel Timm, eds., *Die vergessenen Deutschen: Schleswig-Holsteiner in Nordamerika* (Kiel, 1983); Frank Trommler and Joseph McVeigh, eds., *America and the Germans: An Assessment of a Three-Hundred-Year History*, 2 vols. (Philadelphia, 1985).

10. Stanley Nadel, *Little Germany: Ethnicity, Religion, and Class in New York City, 1845–1880* (Urbana, 1990), p. 1. Kamphoefner's *Westfalians* provides another recent instance of emphasis upon regional identities of Germans. So too does the collection of emigrants' letters that he helped to edit: see either the English edition, Walter D. Kamphoefner, Wolfgang Helbich, and Ulrike Sommer, eds., *News from*

the Land of Freedom: German Immigrants Write Home, trans. Susan C. Vogel (Ithaca, 1991), or the German edition (which lists Helbich first among the editors), *Briefe aus Amerika: Deutsche Auswanderer schreiben aus der Neuen Welt 1830– 1930* (Munich, 1988). Nadel's contention that "German dialects formed the basis of German particularism" (p. 14) is surely an instance of putting the cart before the horse.

11. Of the vast literature on Sealsfield, see especially Franz Schüppen, *Charles Sealsfield. Karl Postl: Ein österreichischer Erzähler der Biedermeierzeit im Spannungsfeld von Alter und Neuer Welt* (Frankfurt am Main, 1981); Glen Lich, "Sealsfield's Texas: Metaphor, Experience, and History," *Yearbook of German-American Studies* 22 (1987): 71–79; Walter Grünzweig, *Das demokratische Kanaan: Charles Sealsfields Amerika im Kontext amerikanischer Literatur und Ideologie* (Munich, 1987); Jerry Schuchalter, "*Geld* and *Geist* in the Writings of Gottfried Duden, Nikolaus Lenau, and Charles Sealsfield: A Study of Competing America-Paradigms," *Yearbook of German-American Studies* 27 (1992): 49–73.

12. See, for example, long articles in two of Germany's leading newspapers: David Eisermann, "Als der Baron zu den Komantschen ging: Seit 150 Jahren siedeln deutsche Auswanderer in Texas," *Frankfurter Allglemeine Zeitung,* November 8, 1986; Marc Surminski, "Traum von einem freien 'Neu-Deutschland' unter der Sonne von Texas endete vor anderthalb Jahrhunderten mit einer Auswanderer-Katastrophe: 'Dunkle Geschäfte mit deutschem Blute,'" *Die Zeit* (North American ed.), November 20, 1992.

13. Its proper name was the *Verein zum Schutze deutscher Auswanderer in Texas.* The newspapers cited in the previous note as well as several other publications testify to this intermittent interest. Among the more engaging or probing are Fritz Scheffel, *Deutsche suchen den Garten der Welt: Das Schicksal deutscher Auswanderer in Texas vor 100 Jahren* (Stuttgart, 1937); Georg Smolka, "Auswanderung und Kolonisationsprojekte im Vormärz," in *Staat und Gesellschaft: Festschrift für Günther Küchenhoff,* ed. Franz Mayer (Göttingen, 1967), pp. 229–246; Harald Winkel, "Der Texasverein. Ein Beitrag zur Geschichte der deutschen Auswanderung im 19. Jahrhundert," *Vierteljahrschrift für Sozial- und Wirtschaftsgeschichte* 55 (1968): 348–372. Smolka's essay is better researched than Winkel's despite Smolka's false assumption that Stephen F. Austin (1793–1836) was still alive during the 1840s. Among the rare exceptions to the German preoccupation with the *Adelsverein* in works dealing with Texas are Fr[iedrich?] Hertneck, *Kampf um Texas* (Leipzig, [1941?]) and Dagmar Auspurg, "Deutsche Einwanderung nach Texas im 19. Jahrhundert," Staatsexamensarbeit, Bochum University (1977).

14. See Dirk Hoerder, ed., *Labor Migration in the Atlantic Economies: The European and North American Working Classes during the Period of Industrialization* (Westport, Conn., 1985); Imre Ferenczi, "Proletarian Mass Migration," in *International Migrations,* ed. Walter F. Willcox, vol. 1 of 2 vols. (New York, 1929–1931).

15. A classic exposition is Harry Jerome, *Migration and Business Cycles* (New York, 1926). Jerome deals mainly with the period after 1870. A penetrating consideration of aspects of the relationship between migration and economic conditions

can be found in Klaus J. Bade, "Massenwanderung und Arbeitsmarkt im deutschen Nordosten von 1880 his zum 1. Weltkrieg: Überseeische Auswanderung, interne Abwanderung und kontinentale Zuwanderung," *Archiv für Sozialgeschichte* 20 (1980): 265–323. For an analysis of the extent of German return migration see Walter D. Kamphoefner, "Umfang und Zusammensetzung der deutsch-amerikanischen Rückwanderung," *Amerikastudien* 33 (1988): 291–307. More fragmentary discussions of German return migration are to be found in two other works: Andreas Grether and Sabine Scheuermann, "Rückwanderung aus Amerika. Zum Problem der Rückkehr aus der Fremde," in *Der große Aufbruch: Studien zur Amerikaauswanderung,* ed. Peter Assion, (Marburg, 1985), pp. 215–220; Alfred Vagts, *Deutschamerikanische Rückwanderung: Probleme, Phänomene, Statistik, Politik, Soziologie, Biographie* (Heidelberg, 1960). Partly for technical reasons Vitranen's pioneering study of Finns has not served as a model for research on Germans: Keijo Virtanen, *Settlement or Return: Finnish Emigrants, 1860–1930, in the International Overseas Return Migration Movement* (Helsinki, 1979).

16. Dudley Baines, *Emigration from Europe, 1815–1930* (Houndsmills and London, 1991), p. 39.

17. Handlin, *The Uprooted.* For the concepts "acculturation" and "assimilation," see: Milton Gordon, *Assimilation in American Life: The Role of Race, Religion, and National Origins* (New York, 1964); Russell Kazal, "Revisiting Assimilation: The Rise, Fall, and Reappraisal of a Concept in American History," *American Historical Review* 100 (1995): 437–471.

18. O. E. Rølvaag, *Giants in the Earth: A Saga of the Prairie* (1st American ed. 1927, New York, 1973).

19. Johannes Gillhoff, *Jürnjakob Swehn, der Amerikafahrer* (1917, Berlin, 1920). The new edition published by DTV (Munich, 1978) is actually an abridged edition, although the publisher gives no indication of this. Since the sections on Jürnjakob's return to Germany are omitted, the intensity of his growing distaste for the United States is substantially diminished. Johannes and Theodor Gillhoff, *Mine Markow, der neue Amerikafahrer* (Berlin, [1957?]) is a poor attempt to exploit the popularity of the earlier novel.

20. Walter P. Webb, *The Texas Rangers: A Century of Frontier Defense,* 2d ed. (Austin, 1965); *The Great Frontier* (Boston, 1952).

21. Herbert G. Gutman, "Work, Culture, and Society in Industrializing America," in his *Work, Culture, and Society in Industrializing America: Essays in American Working-Class History* (New York, 1976).

1

1. Gustav von Gülich, *Über den gegenwärtigen Zustand des Ackerbaus, des Handels und der Gewerbe im Königreiche Hannover* (Hannover, 1827), p. 81.

2. Jörg Jeschke, *Gewerberecht und Handwerkswirtschaft des Königreichs Hannover im Übergang 1815–1866: Eine Quellenstudie* (Göttingen, 1977), pp. 28, 35–36.

3. For general discussions of German emigration in the nineteenth century

see: Mack Walker, *Germany and the Emigration, 1816–1885* (Cambridge, Mass., 1964); Peter Marschalck, *Deutsche Überseewanderung im 19. Jahrhundert: Ein Beitrag zur soziologischen Theorie der Bevölkerung* (Stuttgart, 1973); Wolfgang Köllmann and Peter Marschalck, "German Emigration to the United States," *Perspectives in American History* 7 (1973): 499–554; Klaus J. Bade, ed., *Deutsche im Ausland. Fremde in Deutschland: Migration in Geschichte und Gegenwart* (Munich, 1992), pp. 135–230.

4. Nicholas Hesse, "Nicholas Hesse, German Visitor to Missouri, 1835–1837," ed. and trans. William G. Bek, *Missouri Historical Review* 43 (1948): 145.

5. Martha Scale, *Geschichte der Stadt Alfeld (Leine) in neuer Sicht* (Alfeld, 1973), p. 92.

6. Dietrich Saalfeld, "Handwerkereinkommen in Deutschland vom ausgehenden 18. Jahrhundert bis zur Mitte des 19. Jahrhunderts" in *Handwerksgeschichte in neuer Sicht*, ed. Wilhelm Abel (Göttingen, 1970), p. 74.

7. SAE IV C., Kämmereiregister 1817 and 1824. I am indebted to Jürgen Huck for this reference.

8. Fritz Peters, "Über bremische Firmengründungen in der 1. Hälfte des 19. Jahrhunderts," *Bremisches Jahrbuch* 36 (1936): 308.

9. Fictional literature is not reality, but it often reflects reality. See, for example, Juliane Mikoletzky, *Die deutsche Amerika-Auswanderung des 19. Jahrhunderts in der zeitgenössischen fiktionalen Literatur* (Tübingen, 1988), p. 352. Mikoletzky examined over 150 nineteenth-century German-language novels dealing with emigration to the United States. Thirty-eight of these novels were published between 1835 and 1857. About 9 percent of the emigrants depicted in the novels of this period were involved in commerce.

10. Ibid.; Ludwig Beutin, "Bremisches Bank- und Börsenwesen seit dem 17. Jahrhundert," in his *Gesammelte Schriften zur Wirtschafts- und Sozialgeschichte*, ed. Hermann Kellenbenz (Cologne, 1963), p. 195. See also the excellent examination of the question of founding new firms during the first half of the nineteenth century in Rolf Engelsing, "Die wirtschaftliche und soziale Differenzierung der deutschen kaufmännischen Angestellten im In- und Ausland 1690–1900," in *Zur Sozialgeschichte deutscher Mittel- und Unterschichten*, ed. Rolf Engelsing (Göttingen, 1973), pp. 81–87. Cf. Percy Ernst Schramm, "Die deutschen Überseekaufleute in Rahmen der Sozialgeschichte," *Bremisches Jahrbuch* 49 (1964): 31–54. Schramm's argument that the 1820s, and even beyond, were favorable times for founding new firms is unconvincing. Karl Löbe emphasizes that the climate of opinion in Bremen during the 1820s and beyond was so pessimistic that many young merchants went overseas. Karl Löbe, *Das Weserbuch* (Hameln, [1968?]), p. 58.

11. Peter Marschalck, "Der Erwerb des bremischen Bürgerrechts und die Zuwanderung nach Bremen um die Mitte des 19. Jahrhunderts," *Bremer Jahrbuch* 66 (1988): 298.

12. Ernst Hieke, *Zur Geschichte des deutschen Handels mit Ostafrika*, 1. Teil: *Das hamburgische Handelshaus Wm. O'Swald & Co. 1831–1870* (Hamburg, [1939]), p. 240.

13. *Die Weser-Zeitung* (Bremen), February 10, 1846. The data are taken from a table entitled "Übersicht der deutschen Handels-Etablissements auf überseeischen Märkten im Jahre 1844–45." This table is the second part of an article on "Deutschlands überseeischer Handel." My data on overseas firms are derived from the same source.

14. Ludwig Beutin, *Bremen und Amerika: Zur Geschichte der Weltwirtschaft und der Beziehungen Deutschlands zu den Vereinigten Staaten* (Bremen, 1953), p. 69.

15. Hesse, "Nicholas Hesse," pp. 378–379. My recalculation of Hesse's table.

2

1. Heinrich Friedrich's father was Johann Zacharias Giesecke. The description of the father as an "Acker- und Handelsmann" comes from church records. I have utilized genealogies prepared by two genealogists. The first is the deceased former *Oberstudienrat* Fritz Plathner of Hannover, who in 1938 enclosed the genealogy in a letter to Dr. Friedrich Kruse in Halle. I am grateful to Dr. Kruse's nephew, retired *Bankdirektor* Klaus Nötzel of Bad Godesberg, for a copy of this letter and the accompanying genealogy. The second genealogist is retired *Studienrat* Adolf Giesecke of Salzgitter Bad, whose material is discussed below. At the christening of Heinrich Friedrich his father was referred to as an "Ackermann und Brauherr," that is, a farmer and townsman entitled to brew his own beer or have it brewed for him. Lower Saxon State Archive (Niedersächsisches Staatsarchiv) Wolfenbüttel. 102 N Gittelde. Bd. 3, S. 122. Hereafter this archive will be cited as Staatsarchiv Wolfenbüttel. In the marriage record of Heinrich Friedrich his father is described as a "businessman in Gittelde [*Kaufmann zu Gittelde*]" (NHH. Hann. 74 Gronau VI B8, Nr. 1. Heiratsliste des Kirchspiels Elze im Canton Elze vom Jahre 1808). In the Protestant church records in Elze he is referred to simply as a "citizen [*Bürger*]" of Gittelde. Superintendency of the Evangelical Lutheran Church (Superintendentur der evangelisch-lutherischen Kirche), Elze. Church and parish records (*Kirchenbücher*). Hereafter cited as "Church Records, Elze."

Other sources of information on Heinrich Friedrich's ancestors include data from Adolf Giesecke, who during the 1930s pursued the history of his family in the Staatsarchiv Wolfenbüttel. A direct descendant of the grandfather of Heinrich Friedrich, Adolf Giesecke was born and grew up in Gittelde. He was kind enough to place at my disposal his notes on the official "Beschreibung des Fleckens Gittelde" of 1757, which he located in the Staatsarchiv Wolfenbüttel during the 1930s but I failed to find some four decades later; presumably it was misplaced or destroyed. This document describes the property of the widow of the grandfather of Heinrich Friedrich, Johann Jürgen Giesecke. She had over 30 *Morgen* of farmland, 5 *Morgen* of meadows, and 8 *Morgen* of ponds. A *Morgen* was somewhat less than an acre.

2. In SB there is a record of "the carter Gieseke of Gittelde" in 1845. (This is one of several variant spellings of the family name. This particular variant was often used into the nineteenth century by the Giesecke family we are following.) A young

tutor had returned to Germany after a stay in Baltimore. He engaged the carter Gieseke to transport his belongings from Bremen to Osterode am Harz. A copy of this letter of February 23, 1845, is in SB. 2 — P.8.B.b., Bd. 1 (1839–1847). Maßregeln dagegen, daß Auswanderer aus Binnenländern, welche ursprünglich sich für überseeische Länder bestimmt hatten, nicht im Bremischen verbleiben und polizeiliche Maßregeln in Rücksicht auf solche Auswanderer überhaupt.

3. Erich Keyser, *Niedersächsisches Städtebuch* (Stuttgart, 1952), p. 34.

4. See Friedrich Buchholz, *Geschichte von Bockenem* (Hildesheim, 1843); Friedrich Günther, *Der Ambergau* (Hannover, 1887), pp. 79, 362–363; *Die Kunstdenkmale der Provinz Hannover, 10, 2: Der Kreis Marienburg* (Hannover, 1910), pp. 22–23; Ludolf Nord, *Die Stadt Bockenem 1131–1931. Mit einer Betrachtung über die geschichtliche Entstehung des Ambergaus* (Hildesheim, 1931), pp. 9–11; Manfred Klaube, *Der Ambergau im 19. Jahrhundert und in der Gegenwart* (Bockenem, 1973), pp. 36–38.

5. NHH. Hann. 52 Nr. 2720.

6. Ibid.

7. In the old cemetery in Bockenem three imposing weathered monuments for Senator Giesecke and his sisters were still standing in 1978. On the tobacco factory see Günther, *Der Ambergau*, p. 79; Friedrich Freitag, *Rund um Bockenem. Geschichtsbilder aus dem Ambergau*, 2. Teil. (n.p., [1978?]), pp. 184–185.

8. NHH. Hann. 52 Nr. 2485. Beschwerde des Friedrich Giesecke und Consorten zu Bockenem über den Canton-Maire 1809-1810.

9. Advertisement in Bockenem's *District-Zeitung*, 1813, No. 47. Cited in *Ostfälische Heimat*, 1939, No. 12. I am indebted to the late Professor Georg Haeseler of Bockenem for calling my attention to this last reference.

10. Freitag, *Rund um Bockenem*, p. 178.

11. Ibid.; Reinhard Oberschelp, *Niedersachsen 1760–1820. Wirtschaft, Gesellschaft, Kultur im Land Hannover und Nachbargebieten*, 2 vols., (Hildesheim, 1982), 1: 153. The complaint by Friedrich Giesecke and his four colleagues proved unsuccessful in the immediate future since the authorities in Hannover protected peddling. Freitag, *Rund um Bockenem*, p. 178.

12. The bourgeois honorific *"Demoiselle"* appears in the civil marriage records. NHH. Hann. 74 Gronau VI B 8, Nr. 1. Heiratsliste des Kirchspiels Elze im Canton Elze vom Jahre 1808.

13. Keyser, *Niedersächsisches Städtebuch*, p.121.

14. SAE. XIII, Nr. 2. Steuerliste von 1803; XVI B Nr. 2. My description of the Sander family rests mainly on material in SAE and on genealogical charts that Jürgen Huck generously prepared, placed at my disposal, and has continued to update. I have been able to develop some of these charts farther. Other material is to be found in Peter Bardehle, ed., *Die Kopfsteuerbeschreibung des Hochstifts Hildesheim von 1664. Ergänzt durch die Landschaftsbeschreibung von 1665* (Hildesheim 1976), pp. 439, 442; *Deutsches Geschlechterbuch (Genealogisches Handbuch bürgerlicher Familien)* 158 (Limburg, 1971), pp. 375–379; Georg Seebaß and F.-W. Freist, *Die Pastoren der braunschweigischen evangelisch-lutherischen Landeskirche*, 2 vols. (Wolfenbüttel, 1969–1974), 1: 36; Philipp Meyer, ed., *Die Pastoren*

der Landeskirche Hannovers und Schaumburg-Lippes seit der Reformation, 3 vols. (Göttingen, 1941–1953); Friedrich Conze, *Die Familie Conze aus Elze* (Berlin, 1941), pp. 22–24, 32–33. The Conzes are related to the Sanders. Friedrich Conze's book confuses the Sander line of pastors with that of the Sander line of postal administrators. Beginning in 1793 the "postal line" served as representatives of the Prussian posts. I am indebted to the late Werner Conze, a prominent German historian, for a copy of this privately printed book by his uncle and for further material on their ancestors. For the "postal Sanders" see Jürgen Huck, "Das Post- und Fernmeldewesen in der Stadt Elze, "*Archiv für deutsche Postgeschichte*, 1972, Heft 2, 131. Examination of guides to students enrolled at the universities of Helmstedt and Göttingen turned up little positive evidence.

15. Information on the Horn family is derived from the *Deutsches Geschlechterbuch (Genealogisches Handbuch bürgerlicher Familien)* 17 (Görlitz, 1910), p. 56. I am also indebted to retired *Bankdirektor* Klaus Nötzel of Bad Godesberg for a copy of the unpublished genealogical chart prepared by himself and his uncle, Dr. Friedrich Kruse: "Die Nachkommen des Apothekers Anton Friedrich Horn aus Gronau/Hannover." This chart begins only with Anton Friedrich Horn, son of Johann Alhardt Horn and Henriette Sophie Horn, née Sander.

16. NHH. Hann. 74 Gronau VI B8, Nr. 1. Heiratsliste des Kirchspiels Elze im Canton Elze vom Jahre 1808.

17. NHH. Hann 72 Elze III B. Stadt Elze. Kontrakte, Meierdingsprotokolle, Ehestiftungen 1831–1840.

18. SAE. III 12. Kämmerei-Sachen im Allgemeinen betr. Anstellung von Kämmerei-Rechnungsführer 1820/21–1840; XVI B, Nr. 5. Prozeß-Sachen. Stadt Elze gegen Kämmerer Basse Erben 1852-1855. See also NHH. Hann. 72. Elze II A. Stadtgericht Elze. Kontrakte, Meierdingsprotokolle, Ehestiftungen 1831–1840. According to this last file, Basse had to pledge his entire personal resources in 1832 because of a legal dispute in an inheritance case.

19. SAE. IV C, Nr. 23. Kämmereiregister 1824.

20. On the fires of the 1830s see Günther, *Der Ambergau*, p. 360; Klaube, *Der Ambergau*, p. 37. Later, the catastrophe of 1847 left most of the town in ashes. Günther remarks that following the great fire of 1847 many families emigrated to America. Unfortunately, he does not pursue the matter. Günther, *Der Ambergau*, p. 362.

21. Jürgen Huck, "Elze, die Stadt der Brände," *Niedersachsen. Zeitschrift für Heimat und Kultur*, 1949, Heft 4, 133–135.

22. NHH. Hann. 74 Gronau VIII B 2 Nr. 13. Handelsbefugnisse Elzer Bürger 1826–1855.

23. See the Glossary for a discussion of the *Morgen*, based on F. W. O. L. Freiherr von Reden, *Das Königreich Hannover statistisch beschrieben. Zunächst in Beziehung auf Landwirtschaft, Gewerbe und Handel*, 2 vols. (Hannover, 1839), 1: 533.

24. NHH. Hann. 74 Gronau VIII B 2 Nr. 13.

25. NHH. Hann. 74 Gronau II E Nr. 7.

26. NA. Passenger Lists of Vessels Arriving at New Orleans, November 23, 1839. Microcopy 259, Roll 19.

27. NHH. Hann. 74 Gronau I C Nr. 9, Bd. 2. Geschäftsberichte des Magistrats der Stadt Elze 1840–1847. For similar complaints about artisans in nearby villages see Buchholz, *Geschichte von Bockenem*, p. 118.

28. NHH. Hann. 74 Gronau I C, Nr. 9, Bd. 2–3. Geschäftsberichte des Magistrats der Stadt Elze für 1842, 1847, 1848.

29. Stadtarchiv Alfeld. I H 4d Nr. 2. Bekanntmachung der königlichen Landdrostei in Hildesheim wegen Anordnung einer Linnen-Legge in der Stadt Alfeld. Linen weavers are mentioned only in passing in Scale, *Geschichte der Stadt Alfeld*, p. 102. On the institution of linen standard offices see Oberschelp, *Niedersachsen 1760–1820*, 1: 180–181.

30. Information gathered by me in 1978 from an old exhibit in the Heimatmuseum Alfeld.

31. Marcus Lee Hansen, *The Atlantic Migration, 1607–1860: A History of the Continuing Settlement of the United States* (1st ed., 1940, New York, 1961). One of the most effective parts of Hansen's great work is its examination of the relationship between emigration and the decline of the old guild-dominated linen industry from 1815 to 1850. On German and Hannoverian economic development during this period see also Hans Mottek et al., *Wirtschaftsgeschichte Deutschlands*, 3 vols. (Berlin, 1959–1975), 2: 107; Hans Linde, "Das Königreich Hannover an der Schwelle des Industriezeitalters," *Neues Archiv für Niedersachsen* 24 (1951): 413–443.

32. Oberschelp, *Niedersachsen 1760–1820*, 1: 183–184.

33. See Gülich, *Über den gegenwärtigen Zustand des Ackerbaus, des Handels und der Gewerbe im Königreiche Hannover*, pp. 41–49; von Reden, *Das Königreich Hannover*, 1: 354–361.

34. Von Reden, *Das Königreich Hannover*, 1: 360–361.

35. Ibid., 1:, 354, 360–361.

36. Gülich, *Über den gegenwärtigen Zustand des Ackerbaus, des Handels und der Gewerbe im Königreiche Hannover*, pp. 41–49; Linde, "Das Königreich Hannover an der Schwelle des Industriezeitalters," pp. 433–442. Linde finds in the Hannoverian *Domizilordnung* (1827), which restricted the geographical mobility of the populace, a critical factor retarding the development of an industrial proletariat.

37. Although the issue of capital formation in Germany during the first half of the nineteenth century has received inadequate attention, there can be little doubt that agriculture long remained the greatest source of capital. Richard H. Tilly, "Capital Formation in Germany in the Nineteenth Century," in *Cambridge Economic History of Europe*, vol. 7, part 1 (Cambridge, 1978), pp. 425, 428, 698. See also Knut Borchardt, "Zur Frage des Kapitalmangels in der 1. Hälfte des 19. Jahrhunderts in Deutschland," *Jahrbücher für Nationalökonomie und Statistik* 173 (1961): 401–421.

38. See the basic works on northwestern German agriculture during this period: Werner Wittich, *Die Grundherrschaft in Nordwestdeutschland* (Leipzig,

1896), pp. 7, 413–414, 420–451; Werner Conze, *Die liberalen Agrarreformen Hannovers im 19. Jahrhundert* (Hannover, 1947), pp. 3–16; Wilhelm Treue, *Niedersachsens Wirtschaft seit 1760: Von der Agrar- zur Industriegesellschaft* (Hannover, 1964), p. 22. A recent article provides a good survey in English with specific references to the Hildesheim district: Stefan Brakensiek, "Agrarian Individualism in North-Western Germany, 1770–1870," *German History* 12 (1994): 137–179. See also the comments on the development of agriculture in the Elze and Bockenem areas in Käthe Mittelhäußer, ed., *Der Landkreis Alfeld (Regierungsbezirk Hildesheim): Kreisbeschreibung nebst Raumordnungsplan und statistischem Anhang*, (Bremen-Horn, 1957), pp. 172–174; Günther, *Der Ambergau*, p. 9; Klaube, *Der Ambergau*, p. 9; Freitag, *Rund um Bockenem*, p. 135.

39. See Conze, *Die liberalen Agrarreformen Hannovers*, p. 16; Mittelhäußer, *Der Landkreis Alfeld*, p. 174.

3

1. Detlef Dunt [Detlev Thomas Friedrich Jordt], *Reise nach Texas. Nebst Nachrichten von diesem Lande für Deutsche, welche nach Amerika zu gehen beabsichtigen* (Bremen, 1834). For an extended discussion of the significance of Jordt's work see my introduction to the English translation to be published by the University of Texas Press, Austin.

2. Dunt, *Reise nach Texas*, pp. viii, 128. Some later travel guides were more demanding. For example, in 1847 the retired (Prussian?) Captain Sommer recommended bringing "at least a few hundred [*Reichs*]*taler*]." Carl von Sommer, *Bericht über meine Reise nach Texas im Jahre 1846. Die Verhältnisse und den Zustand dieses Landes betreffend* (Bremen, 1847), p. 65.

3. The preceding examples are derived from "Die wirtschaftliche und soziale Differenzierung der deutschen kaufmännischen Angestellten im In- und Ausland 1690–1900" in Rolf Engelsing, ed., *Zur Sozialgeschichte deutscher Mittel- und Unterschichten* (Göttingen, 1973), pp. 73–74, 84–85.

4. A good survey of German immigration can be found in Kathleen Neils Conzen, "Germans," in *Harvard Encyclopedia of American Ethnic Groups*, ed. Stephen Thernstrom (Cambridge, Mass., 1980), pp. 405–425. See also her bibliographical essay in *Immigration History Newsletter* 12, no. 2 (1980): 1–14. For a brief recent treatment see Willi Paul Adams, *The German-Americans: An Ethnic Experience*, trans. L. J. Rippley and Eberhard Reichmann (Bloomington, Ind., 1993).

5. See Agnes Bretting and Hartmut Bickelmann, *Auswanderungsagenturen und Auswanderungsvereine im 19. und 20. Jahrhundert* (Stuttgart, 1991); Peter J. Brenner, *Reisen in die Neue Welt: Die Erfahrung Nordamerikas in deutschen Reise- und Auswandererberichten des 19. Jahrhunderts* (Tübingen, 1991); Stephan Görrisch, "Die gedruckten 'Ratgeber' für Auswanderer. Zur Produktion und Typologie eines literarischen Genres," in Peter Assion, ed., *Der große Aufbruch: Studien zur Amerikaauswanderung* (Marburg, 1985), pp. 51–70.

6. See Hildegard Meyer, *Nordamerika im Urteil des deutschen Schrifttums bis zur Mitte des 19. Jahrhunderts. Eine Untersuchung über Kürnbergers "Amerika-*

Müden" (Hamburg, 1929); Hans Fenske, "Die deutsche Auswanderung in der Mitte des 19. Jahrhunderts: Öffentliche Meinung und amtliche Politik," *Geschichte in Wissenschaft und Unterricht* 25 (1973): esp. 228. Without adequate proof Fenske contends that immediately after 1815 the German states aided rather than hindered emigration.

7. See Mikoletzky, *Die deutsche Amerika-Auswanderung des 19. Jahrhunderts in der zeitgenössischen fiktionalen Literatur.*

8. Hans Mahrenholtz, "Über den Umfang der Auswanderung aus Niedersachsen," *Norddeutsche Familienkunde* 7 (1958): 82. See also Friedrich Rauers, *Geschichte des Bremer Binnenhandels im 19. Jahrhundert: Namentlich unter den alten Verkehrsformen und im Übergang* (Bremen, 1913), p. 45.

9. NHH. Hann. 80 Hildesheim I E 212. General-Polizei. Emigrationen. Generalia.

10. Ibid.

11. Ibid. In 1843–1844 the number of emigrants from Alfeld had already risen greatly. Stadtarchiv Alfeld, I. C. 2. Nr. 1. Gesuche um die Erteilung von Auswanderungs-Bescheinigungen 1831–1858.

12. *Hildesheimer Zeitung*, September 27, 1844. The continuation of the theme with an article on emigration to Texas was announced, but I have been unable to locate this sequel.

13. Walker, *Germany and the Emigration*, p. 43.

14. Ibid., p. 47. Cf. Brinley Thomas, *Migration and the Rhythm of Economic Growth* (Manchester, 1951), pp. 94–95, 224. Thomas sees in the wave of German emigration at the middle of the nineteenth century a reflex of overpopulation.

15. SB. Bürgereidbücher; *Adreßbuch der Freien Hansestadt Bremen*, 1844. It is possible that Sanders from Elze already lived in Bremen. Conze mentions Sanders from Elze in Bremen, but apparently they lived there at the end of the nineteenth century. He does not examine the question whether Sanders were already living there in the early part of the century. Conze, *Die Familie Conze aus Elze*, p. 33.

16. Johann Achelis and Hans Achelis, *Die Familie Achelis in Bremen 1579–1921* (Bremen, 1921), p. 21.

17. Ibid., pp. 19–20; Franz Josef Pitsch, *Die wirtschaftlichen Beziehungen Bremens zu den Vereinigten Staaten von Amerika bis zur Mitte des 19. Jahrhunderts* (Bremen, 1974), p. 201; [Maria Möring], *Joh. Achelis & Söhne Bremen: Export-Import* ([Bremen, 1976?]).

18. Information in this paragraph regarding godparents is derived from Church Records, Elze.

19. [Möring], *Joh. Achelis & Söhne*, p. 20; *Adreßbuch der Freien Hansestadt Bremen*, 1845. It has not been possible to establish any relationship between Tilman Gloystein and the Bremen merchant Nicholas Gloystein. The latter and his family played a major role in the development of Bremen's commerce, including the cotton trade, with America. On the activities of Nicholas Gloystein and his family see Moritz Lindeman, "Zur Geschichte der älteren Handelsbeziehungen Bremens mit den Vereinigten Staaten von Nordamerika," *Bremisches Jahrbuch* 10 (1878): 130; Hermann Wätjen, "Zur Geschichte der bremischen Südseefischerei

in 19. Jahrhundert," *Bremisches Jahrbuch* 25 (1914): 140–142; Hermann Kellenbenz, "Der Bremer Kaufmann. Versuch einer sozialgeschichtlichen Deutung," *Bremisches Jahrbuch* 51 (1969): 43; Beutin, "Von drei Ballen zum Weltmarkt. Kleine Bremer Baumwollchronik 1789–1872" in his *Gesammelte Schriften zur Wirtschafts- und Sozialgeschichte*, p. 120; Otto Höver, *Von der Galiot zum Fünfmaster: Unsere Segelschiffe in der Weltschiffahrt 1780–1930* (Bremen, [1934]), p. 190.

20. The circumstantial evidence consists largely of the familiarity with Bremen manifest in Charles's letters and the Gieseckes' family ties there. During the 1820s and 1830s a few people named Gieseke had firms, including a major cigar factory, in Bremen. *Adreßbuch der Freien Hansestadt Bremen*, 1827 and 1839. We have no evidence that any of these Bremen Giesekes were related to, or had any contact with, the Bockenem Gieseckes.

21. Evidence is to be found in the ship passenger lists in NA cited throughout this work; see especially notes to Ch. 6.

22. M. J. Haller cited in Hermann Wätjen, *Aus der Frühzeit des Nordatlantikverkehrs: Studien zur Geschichte der deutschen Schiffahrt und deutschen Auswanderung nach den Vereinigten Staaten bis zum Ende des amerikanischen Bürgerkriegs* (Leipzig, 1932), p. 9.

23. Ibid., p. 12. Unfortunately Wätjen does not pursue the question whether U.S. merchants played a role in financing Bremen's shipping. It would be helpful if we could be certain that they did not.

24. Hans Szymanski, *Die Anfänge der Dampfschiffahrt in Niedersachsen und den angrenzenden Gebieten von 1817 bis 1867* (Hannover, 1958), pp. 15, 121–132; Beutin, *Bremen und Amerika*, p. 58; Karl H. Schwebel, "Bremer Kaufleute im Auslande," in *Bremen-Bremerhaven: Häfen am Strom* (7. Aufl., Bremen, 1966), p. 134; Löbe, *Das Weserbuch*, pp. 210, 283–284, 287.

25. Among the contemporaries see *Über Auswanderung. Von einem Kaufmanne in Bremen* (Bremen, 1842). This businessman claims that the lack of German colonies necessitates systematic emigration (p. 5), and he seeks to show "how closely the continuation of emigration is tied to our shipping" (p. 8). Among the historians who have examined the problem of the development of the hinterland, see: Wilhelm von Bippen, *Geschichte der Stadt Bremen*, 3 vols. (Bremen, 1892–1904), 2: 492; Rauers, *Geschichte des Bremer Binnenhandels*, pp. 11–14; Ludwig Beutin, "Wirtschaftsraum und Wirtschaftsart der Hansestädte," in his *Gesammelte Schriften zur Wirtschafts- und Sozialgeschichte*, pp. 11–12; Beutin, *Bremen und Amerika*, p. 39.

26. Rauers, *Geschichte des Bremer Binnenhandels*, p. 15.

27. David Eltis, "Free and Coerced Transatlantic Migrations: Some Comparisons," *American Historical Review* 88 (1983): 255.

28. Friedrich Gläbe, *Die Unterweser: Chronik eines Stromes und seiner Landschaft* (Bremen, 1963), p. 105. For the attempt during the early twentieth century to divert many Eastern European Jews from New York to Galveston as a port of entry, see Bernard Marinbach, *Galveston: Ellis Island of the West* (Albany, 1983).

29. *Chamber's Edinburgh Journal*, June 13, 1846, in Oscar Handlin, ed.,

Immigration as a Factor in American History (Englewood Cliffs, N.J., 1959), pp. 24–25.

30. Francis Joseph Grund, *Handbuch und Wegweiser für Auswanderer nach den Vereinigten Staaten von Nordamerika* (Stuttgart, 1843), p. 25.

31. Wätjen, *Aus der Frühzeit des Nordatlantikverkehrs,* p. 22.

32. Rauers, *Geschichte des Bremer Binnenhandels,* p. 17.

33. Keyser, *Niedersächsisches Städtebuch,* p. 56; Hans-Ludwig Schaefer, *Bremens Bevölkerung in der ersten Hälfte des 19. Jahrhunderts* (Bremen, 1957), p. 35.

34. Rauers, *Geschichte des Bremer Binnenhandels,* pp. 13, 20; Hansen, *Atlantic Migration,* p. 190.

35. Eduard Beurmann, *Skizzen aus den Hansestädten* (Hanau, 1836), p. 259.

36. Pitsch, *Die wirtschaftlichen Beziehungen Bremens zu den Vereinigten Staaten,* p. 208.

37. Schaefer, *Bremens Bevölkerung,* p. 115.

38. Rauers, *Geschichte des Bremer Binnenhandels,* p. 20, n. 3.

39. Hansen, *Atlantic Migration,* pp. 190, 192.

40. See ibid., p. 190; Ludwig Beutin, "Drei Jahrhunderte Tabakhandel in Bremen" in his *Gesammelte Schriften zur Wirtschafts- und Sozialgeschichte,* p. 108.

41. Von Reden, *Das Königreich Hannover,* 1: 440, 442.

42. G. C. Bocris, *Beschreibung aller in Handel vorkommenden Tabaksgattungen, deren Produktionsländer, Kultur, Eigenschaften und Gebrauch* (Bremen, 1833), p. 42.

43. Ibid., p. 41. Bocris referred to "Hessentabak." By this he meant tobacco grown along the Werra River from Wanfried to Allendorf (today's Bad Sooden-Allendorf).

44. Willis N. Baer, *The Economic Development of the Cigar Industry in the United States* (Lancaster, Pa., 1933), p. 41.

45. See Letters of February 10 and June 30, 1845. These and other letters in the Appendix to the present work will be cited simply by their dates.

46. Beutin, *Bremen und Amerika,* p. 69.

47. Schaefer, *Bremens Bevölkerung,* p. 219.

48. Beutin, "Drei Jahrhunderte Tabakhandel," pp. 100, 106.

49. Rauers, *Geschichte des Bremer Binnenhandels,* pp. 19–20, n. 3–4; Beutin, "Von drei Ballen zum Weltmarkt," pp. 62, 71; Rolf Engelsing, *Bremen als Auswandererhafen 1683/-1880* (Bremen 1961), p. 73; Pitsch, *Die wirtschaftlichen Beziehungen Bremens zu den Vereinigten Staaten,* pp. 159, 161–162.

4

1. Wilhelm Pferdekamp, *Auf Humboldts Spuren: Deutsche im jungen Mexiko* (Munich, 1958), p. 43; Hendrik Dane, *Die wirtschaftlichen Beziehungen Deutschlands zu Mexiko und Mittelamerika im 19. Jahrhundert* (Cologne, 1971), pp. 57–58, 157. Of the general analyses of German-Mexican commercial relations in the nineteenth century see, in addition to Dane's book, Brígida von Mentz et al., *Los Pioneros del imperialismo alemán en Mexico* (Mexico City, 1982).

2. Manfred Kossok, *Im Schatten der Heiligen Allianz: Deutschland und La-teinamerika 1815–1830. Zur Politik der deutschen Staaten gegenüber der Unabhängigkeitsbewegung Mittel- und Südamerikas* (Berlin, 1964), pp. 138–145, 148–149, 164, 168; Manfred Kossok, "Zur Geschichte der deutsch-lateinamerikanischen Beziehungen (Forschungs- und Periodisierungsprobleme)," *Hansische Geschichtsblätter* 82 (1964): 75; Walther L. Bernecker, *Die Handelskonquistadoren: Europäische Interessen und mexikanischer Staat im 19. Jahrhundert* (Wiesbaden, 1988), pp. 163, 185, 189, 192–197; Jürgen Prüser, *Die Handelsverträge der Hansestädte Lübeck, Bremen und Hamburg mit überseeischen Staaten im 19. Jahrhundert* (Bremen, 1962), p. 42.

3. Kossok, *Im Schatten der Heiligen Allianz*, pp. 151, 158; Dane, *Wirtschaftliche Beziehungen Deutschlands zu Mexico und Mittelamerika*, pp. 57–58.

4. Prüser, *Handelsverträge*, pp. 42–47; Kossok, *Im Schatten der Heiligen Allianz*, pp. 153–154, 179.

5. Bade, *Deutsche im Ausland, Fremde in Deutschland*, p. 199. Frederick Luebke suggests that during the 1820s more Germans may have gone to Brazil than to the United States. Frederick C. Luebke, "Patterns of German Settlement in the United States and Brazil, 1830–1930," in his *Germans in the New World: Essays in the History of Immigration* (Urbana, 1990), pp. 93–109. For German emigrants to Brazil in the 1820s, see also Frederick C. Luebke, *Germans in Brazil: A Comparative History of Cultural Conflict during World War I* (Baton Rouge, 1987), pp. 7–23.

6. Ibid., pp. 200, 206.

7. Central America remained of little attraction to Germans for some decades. Dane, *Wirtschaftliche Beziehungen Deutschlands zu Mexico und Mittelamerika*, pp. 78, 148.

8. Ibid., p. 152.

9. J. Valentin Hecke, *Reise durch die Vereinigten Staaten in den Jahren 1818 und 1819*, 2 vols. (Berlin 1820–1821), 1: 199.

10. Hermann Kellenbenz, "Verkehrs- und Nachrichtenwesen, Handel, Geld-, Kredit- und Versicherungswesen 1800–1850," in *Handbuch der deutschen Wirtschafts- und Sozialgeschichte*, ed. Hermann Aubin and Wolfgang Zorn, 2 vols. (Stuttgart, 1971–1976), 2: 403; Dane, *Wirtschaftliche Beziehungen Deutschlands zu Mexico und Mittelamerika*, p. 65.

11. Manfred Kossok, "Preußen, Bremen und die 'Texas-Frage' 1835–1845," *Bremisches Jahrbuch* 49 (1964): 84.

12. Dane, *Wirtschaftliche Beziehungen Deutschlands zu Mexiko und Mittelamerika*, p. 18.

13. The data on German firms is derived from "Übersicht der deutschen Handelsetablissements auf überseeischen Märkten im Jahre 1844–45," *Weser-Zeitung*, February 8 and 10, 1846.

14. Neither Donald Chipman nor David Weber accepts an estimate much above 3,600 for the period of Spanish rule; Chipman, *Spanish Texas*, pp. 206, 216, 241; David J. Weber, *The Spanish Frontier in North America* (New Haven, 1992), pp. 194–195.

15. An excellent introduction to the early history of Texas is still William R.

Hogan, *The Texas Republic: A Social and Economic History* (Norman, Okla., 1946). Two other studies are particularly useful for their analyses of the interplay of social and economic interests during the period prior to the entry of Texas into the Union in 1846: Elgin Williams, *The Animating Pursuits of Speculation: Land Traffic in the Annexation of Texas* (New York, 1949); Andreas Reichstein, *Der texanische Unabhängigkeitskrieg: Ursachen und Wirkung* (Berlin, 1984), also available in an English edition: *Rise of the Lone Star: The Making of Texas*, trans. Jeanne R. Willson (College Station, Tex., 1989). Reichstein's preoccupation with land speculation at the expense of other economic activities is less convincing than Williams's analysis. Neither work succeeds in unraveling the intricate web of land dealings spun by the Galveston Bay and Texas Land Company, Samuel M. Williams, David G. Burnet, Sam Houston, Stephen F. Austin, Lorenzo de Zavala, José Antonio Mexía, and others. For a good statement of the role of slavery in the Texas War for Independence, see Paul D. Lack, "Slavery and the Texas Revolution," *Southwestern Historical Quarterly* 89 (1985): 181–202.

16. Eugene C. Barker, *The Life of Stephen F. Austin, Founder of Texas, 1793– 1836: A Chapter in the Westward Movement of the Anglo-American People* (2d ed., Austin, 1949), pp. 201–202.

17. Ibid., pp. 180–181.

18. See for example, N. Doran Maillard, *The History of the Republic of Texas . . . and the Cause of Her Separation from the Republic of Mexico* (London, 1842), pp. 150–151; Marquis James, *The Raven: A Biography of Sam Houston* (Indianapolis, 1929), p. 342. On the issue of annexation see Williams, *Animating Pursuits*, 19–20; Reichstein, *Der texanische Unabhängigkeitskrieg*, pp. 170–206; Joseph W. Schmitz, *Texan Statecraft, 1836–1845* (San Antonio, 1941); Eugene C. Barker, "The Annexation of Texas," *Southwestern Historical Quarterly* 50 (1946): 49–74; John H. Schroeder, "Annexation or Independence: The Texas Issue in American Politics, 1836–1845," *Southwestern Historical Quarterly* 89 (1985): 137–164.

19. Dagmar Auspurg, "Deutsche Einwanderung nach Texas im 19. Jahrhundert," However, without adequate documentation, Auspurg ascribes too much significance to the "Germandom" of settlers from the United States.

20. See Eugene C. Barker, ed., *The Austin Papers*, 3 vols. (Washington, 1924– 1928), 2: 402, 415, 453, 477, 559, 577, 705.

21. On Dirks and his activity, see Miriam Corff York, *Friedrich Ernst of Industry* (Giddings, Tex., 1989); Ann Lindemann, James Lindemann, and William Richter, eds., *Historical Accounts of Industry, Texas, 1831–1986* (New Ulm, Tex., 1986). For the older literature on Dirks and early German settlements, see Gilbert G. Benjamin, *The Germans of Texas* (Philadelphia, 1909), pp. 16–21; Moritz Tiling, *History of the German Element in Texas from 1820 to 1850. And Historical Sketches of the German Texas Singers' League and Houston Turnverein from 1853 to 1913* (Houston, 1913), pp. 15, 18; Rudolph L. Biesele, *The History of the German Settlements in Texas, 1831–1861* (Austin, 1930), p. 43; Jordan, *German Seed in Texas Soil*, p. 41; Terry G. Jordan, "The German Element," in Joseph Wilson, ed., *Texas and Germany: Crosscurrents* (Houston, 1977), p. 3.

22. Gottfried Duden, *Bericht über eine Reise nach den westlichen Staaten*

Nordamerikas und einen mehrjährigen Aufenthalt am Missouri in den Jahren 1824, 25, 26 und 27. In Bezug auf Auswanderung und Überbevölkerung (1. Aufl., 1829, St. Gallen, 1832). On Duden see William G. Bek, "The Followers of Duden," Missouri Historical Review 14–19 (1919–1925) [18 articles]. For the place of Duden's work in German travel and emigrant literature, see Brenner, Reisen in die Neue Welt; Theresa Ann Mayer Hammond, "American Paradise: German Travel Literature from Duden to Kisch," Ph.D. diss., University of California Berkeley (1977).

23. Glen Lich, The German Texans (San Antonio, 1981), pp. 45–46.

24. Dunt, Reise nach Texas. On Dunt see my introduction to the American translation of his book to be published by the University of Texas Press.

25. Dunt, Reise nach Texas, p. viii.

26. Tiling, History of the German Element in Texas, pp. 44–45; Don H. Biggers, German Pioneers in Texas: A Brief History of Their Hardships, Struggles, and Achievements (Fredericksburg, Tex., 1925), pp. 20–21; Robert W. Shook, "German Migration to Texas, 1830–1850: Causes and Consequences," Texana 10 (1972): 230.

27. Texas in 1840. Or the Emigrant's Guide to the New Republic . . . By an Emigrant Late of the U.S., introd. Rev. A. B. Lawrence, New Orleans (New York, 1840), p. 228.

28. See, for example, Friedrich W. von Wrede, Lebensbilder aus den Vereinigten Staaten von Nordamerika und Texas (Kassel, 1844), p. 3. According to the book's title page, Wrede was a "retired royal Hannoverian captain and a citizen of the Republic of Texas."

29. On the republic's land-grant policy and its significance for Germans see Hogan, Texas Republic, pp. 10–12; Tiling, History of the German Element in Texas, pp. 54–55. See also the level-headed contemporary summary in Friedrich Höhne, Wahn und Überzeugung. Reise des Kupferschmiede-Meisters Friedrich Höhne in Weimar über Bremen nach Nordamerika und Texas in den Jahren 1839, 1840 und 1841 (Weimar, 1844), pp. 186–187.

30. The best short description of the Adelsverein is in Shook, "German Migration to Texas," p. 231 ff. Also worth consulting are: Georg Smolka, "Auswanderung und Kolonisationsprojekte im Vormärz" in Franz Mayer, ed., Staat und Gesellschaft: Festschrift für Günther Küchenhoff (Göttingen, 1967), pp. 229–246; Harald Winkel, "Der Texasverein: Ein Beitrag zur Geschichte der deutschen Auswanderung im 19. Jahrhundert," Vierteljahrschrift für Sozial- und Wirtschaftsgeschichte 55 (1968): 348–372. Despite Smolka's false assumption that Stephen F. Austin (1793–1836) was still alive during the 1840s, his essay is better researched and more penetrating than Winkel's. Klaus Gröpner, Im Winter brach der Regenbogen: Der deutsche Treck nach Texas (Vienna, 1978), is an unreliable, sensationalistic study.

31. See esp. the great suggestive work of the British historian John A. Hawgood, The Tragedy of German-America: The Germans in the United States of America during the Nineteenth Century and After (New York, 1940). The bylaws of the Adelsverein are available in English translation in Benjamin, The Germans of Texas.

32. See, for example, Arthur Ikin, *Texas. Its History, Topography, Agriculture, Commerce, and General Statistics . . . Designed for the Use of the British Merchant, and as a Guide to Emigrants* (1841; reprint, Austin, 1964), pp. 62–63; William Kennedy, *Texas: The Rise, Progress, and Prospects of the Republic of Texas,* 2 vols. (London 1841), 1: xxii–xxix, xl–xliii; 2: 310, 416–419. Gröpner advances the old thesis that the entire undertaking was initiated by the British. His crucial documentation consists of a few vague allusions to British sources. Gröpner, *Im Winter brach der Regenbogen,* p. 68.

33. A. Kordül, *Der sichere Führer nach und in Texas* (Rottweil am Neckar, 1846), p. 80 (cited in Benjamin, *The Germans of Texas,* p. 56). Figures almost as high are supplied by Traugott Bromme, *Neuestes vollständigstes Hand- und Reisebuch für Auswanderer aus allen Klassen und jedem Stande nach den Vereinigten Staaten von Nordamerika* (Bayreuth, 1846), p. 264. In 1845 the population of Texas totaled perhaps 125,000. Walter P. Webb et al., eds., *The Handbook of Texas,* 3 vols. (Austin 1952–1976), 1: 321.

34. Compare the estimates in Jordan, *German Seed in Texas Soil,* pp. 47–50.

35. Glen Lich, "German Emigration Contracts in the General Land Office," *Texas Library* 38 (1976): 19; Ethel Hander Geue, *New Homes in a New Land: German Immigration to Texas, 1846–1861* (Waco, Tex., 1970), p. v; Chester William Geue and Ethel Hander Geue, *A New Land Beckoned: German Immigration to Texas, 1844–1847* (Waco, Tex., 1966); Terry G. Jordan, "The Pattern of Origins of the *Adelsverein* German Colonists," *Texana* 6 (1968): 245–257; Jordan, *German Seed in Texas Soil,* p. 47. The names of the German places of origin of many of the settlers listed in the works by the Geues are mutilated, often beyond recognition. The names of many of the ships and passengers are included in *Neu-Braunfelser Zeitung, Jahrbuch für 1936* and in the newspaper's hundredth anniversary issue, *Neu-Braunsfelser Zeitung* (New Braunfels, Texas), August 8, 1952.

36. Benjamin, *The Germans of Texas,* pp. 104–105; Engelsing, *Bremen als Auswandererhafen,* p. 181.

37. Pitsch, *Die wirtschaftlichen Beziehungen Bremens zu den Vereinigten Staaten,* p. 95.

38. On Baltimore and New Orleans as immigrant ports, see Dean R. Esslinger, "Immigration through the Port of Baltimore" and Joseph Logsdon, "Immigration through the Port of New Orleans," in M. Mark Stolarik, ed., *Forgotten Doors: The Other Ports of Entry to the United States* (Philadelphia, 1988), pp. 61–74, 105–124. The importance of New Orleans as an immigrant port for Germans is reflected in German fiction dealing with emigration to America. Of 281 immigrants depicted in a selection of novels appearing during the period 1835 to 1857, seventy arrived in New Orleans and fifty-six in New York. Mikoletzky, *Die deutsche Amerika-Auswanderung des 19. Jahrhunderts in der zeitgenössischen fiktionalen Literatur,* p. 346.

39. Engelsing, *Bremen als Auswandererhafen,* p.181. See also Benjamin, *The Germans of Texas,* pp. 104–105; Tiling, *History of the German Element in Texas,* p. 53. The source of all such references remains the *Weser-Zeitung* of the 1840s.

40. Geue and Geue, *A New Land Beckoned,* p.5.

41. It has been calculated that the mortality rate on the voyage from Europe to New York was 1.4 percent during the period 1836–1853. However, the same study finds a rise to 3.1 percent in 1849. R. L. Cohn, "Mortality on Immigrant Voyages to New York, 1836–1853," *Journal of Economic History* 54 (1984): 297, 299–300. See also the more general treatment of the problems of emigrants' journeys by sea in Günter Moltmann, "Das Risiko der Seereise: Auswanderungsbedingungen im Europa-Amerika-Verkehr um die Mitte des 19. Jahrhunderts," in *Festschrift für Eberhard Kessel zum 75. Geburtstag*, ed. Heinz Duchardt and Manfred Schlenke (Munich, 1982).

42. See, for example, von Wrede, *Lebensbilder*, p. 12; Bromme, *Neuestes vollständigstes Hand- und Reisebuch*, p. 334; Ottomar von Behr, *Guter Rath für Auswanderer nach den Vereinigten Staaten von Nordamerika mit besonderer Berücksichtigung von Texas. Vorzüglich für Landleute und Handwerker nach eigener Erfahrung geschrieben* (Leipzig, 1847), pp. 30–31; von Sommer, *Bericht über meine Reise nach Texas*, p. 11; Heinrich Ostermayer, *Tagebuch meiner Reise nach Texas in Jahre 1848–1849* (Biberach, 1850), p. 14; Friedrich Schlecht, *Mein Ausflug nach Texas* (Bunzlau, 1851), p. 7.

43. Marcus Lee Hansen, *The Immigrant in American History*, ed. Arthur M. Schlesinger (New York, 1964), p. 52. Hansen invokes the authority of J. S. Buckingham, *America. Historical, Statistic, and Descriptive*, 3 vols. (New York, 1841), 2: 93, for the claim that such a high proportion of immigrants failed to survive more than three years in America, but there is no reference to the matter on the indicated page or nearby in Buckingham's work. Similar assertions persist in the literature on immigration. A recent work by an historian who regards himself as an optimist remarks: "The totality of disillusionment and calamities was probably at least a third of the immigration flow." Franklin D. Scott, *The Peopling of America: Perspectives on Immigration*, American Historical Association Pamphlet, 241 (Washington, 1984), p. 7. See also Friedrich Burgdörfer, "Die Wanderungen über die deutschen Reichsgrenzen im letzten Jahrhundert," *Allgemeines Statistisches Archiv* 20 (1930): 161–196, 383–419, 537–551.

44. Benjamin, *The Germans of Texas*, p. 9.

45. Shook, "German Migration to Texas," p. 235. See also Geue and Geue, *A New Land Beckoned*, p. 17.

46. U.S. Census Bureau, *The Seventh Census of the United States, 1850* (Washington, 1953), p. xxxvii.

47. Jordan, "The German Element in Texas," p. 2.

48. *Seventh Census of the U.S.*, p. 506.

49. Earl W. Fornell, *The Galveston Era: The Texas Crescent on the Eve of Secession* (Austin, 1961), p. 129.

50. Hermann Seele, *Die Zypresse und Gesammelte Schriften: Eine Legende aus der Zeit der ersten deutschen Ansiedlungen in West-Texas* (New Braunfels, Tex., 1936), p. 36. According to a history of the Catholic Church in Texas, mass had been celebrated in Galveston since December 28, 1838. James Talmadge Moore, *Through Fire and Flood, The Catholic Church in Frontier Texas, 1836–1900* (College Station, Tex., 1992), p. 17.

51. Von Sommer, *Bericht über meine Reise nach Texas*, p. 20; von Behr, *Guter Rat für Auswanderer*, p. 88.

52. Margaret Swett Henson, *Samuel May Williams: Early Texas Entrepreneur* (College Station, Tex., [1976?]), p. 136.

53. T. Herbert Etzler, "German-American Newspapers in Texas: With Special Reference to the Texas *Volksblatt*, 1877–1879," *Southwestern Historical Quarterly* 51 (1954): 423

54. See Schmitz, *Texan Statecraft*, pp. 217–223; Manfred Kossok, "Prussia, Bremen, and the 'Texas Question,'" *Texana* 3 (1965): 242, 245–246.

55. Schmitz, *Texan Statecraft*, pp. 217–223.

56. See, e.g., Ikin, *Texas*, p. 68.

5

1. Still essential is Charles W. Hayes, *Galveston: History of the Island and the City*, 2 vols. (1879; reprint, Austin, 1974). See also Andrew F. Muir, "The Destiny of Buffalo Bayou," *Southwestern Historical Quarterly* 47 (1943): 91–106; Joseph Lynn, *The Texas Gulf Coast: Its History and Development*, 4 vols. (New York, 1955); Fornell, *Galveston Era* (Austin, 1961); Kenneth W. Wheeler, *To Wear a City's Crown: The Beginnings of Urban Growth in Texas, 1836–1865* (Cambridge, Mass., 1968); David G. McComb, *Galveston: A History* (Austin, 1986). Muir's article remains indispensable on the relationship between Galveston and Houston in the nineteenth century.

2. J. O. Dyer, *The Early History of Galveston*, Part 1 (Galveston, 1916).

3. Hayes, *Galveston*, 1: 320.

4. James E. Winston, "Notes on Commercial Relations between New Orleans and Texan Ports, 1838–1839," *Southwestern Historical Quarterly* 34 (1930): 92–94; Clark, *Texas Gulf Coast*, 1: 379.

5. Travis L. Smith, *Steamboats on the Brazos*, in Travis L. Smith et al., *History of Brazoria County* [and two other works] (Houston, 1958), pp. 65–66; Pamela Ashworth Puryear and Nath Winfield, *Sandbars and Sternwheelers: Steam Navigation on the Brazos* (College Station, Tex., [1976?]), pp. 37–58.

6. Hayes, *Galveston*, 1: 377–378; 2: 926.

7. Fornell, *Galveston Era*, p. 45.

8. Hayes, *Galveston*, 1: 268, 375.

9. Muir, "Destiny of Buffalo Bayou," pp. 101–102; Hogan, *Texas Republic*, p. 74; Marilyn McAdams Sibley, *The Port of Houston: A History* (Austin, [1968]), pp. 57–58.

10. Ikin, *Texas*; von Behr, *Guter Rath für Auswanderer*, p. 48. See also Louis J. Wortham, *A History of Texas: From Wilderness to Commonwealth*, 5 vols. (Fort Worth, 1924), 5: 232.

11. Francis Richard Lubbock, *Six Decades in Texas: Or Memoirs of Francis Richard Lubbock*, ed. C. W. Raines (Austin, 1910), p. 102; Muir, "Destiny of Buffalo Bayou," p. 102.

12. McComb, *Houston*, p. 24.

13. In addition to the German- and English-language travel literature of the era, much of which has been cited in the notes above, see Muir, "Destiny of Buffalo Bayou," pp. 95, 101; James E. Winston, "Notes on Commercial Relations between New Orleans and Texan Ports, 1838–1839," *Southwestern Historical Quarterly* 34 (1930): 95–96; T. L. Smith, *Steamboats on the Brazos*, pp. 65–66; Sibley, *Port of Houston*, p. 65; Wheeler, *To Wear a City's Crown*.

14. Hayes, *Galveston*, 1: 467–468. About 1840 G. A. Scherpf, the German author of a study of development of the Texan Republic, had complained of the lack of direct passenger lines between Europe and Texas: Europeans wishing to travel there had to go by way of the United States. Scherpf mentioned recent attempts to develop links between Marseilles and Liverpool. G. A. Scherpf, *Entstehungsgeschichte und gegenwärtiger Zustand des neuen, unabhängigen, amerikanischen Staates Texas* (Augsburg, 1841), p. 55.

15. Hayes, *Galveston*, 1: 467–468.

16. [Moritz Tiling?], "Die Deutschen in Texas vor der Massen-Einwanderung im Jahre 1844," *Deutsch-Texanische Monatshefte* 11 (1907): 90. The estimate is ascribed simply to an essay "Aus dem Wanderbuche einer Dame. Texas und der Golf von Mexiko," in the periodical *Ausland*.

17. Francis C. Sheridan, *Galveston Island, Or a Few Months Off the Coast of Texas: The Journal of Francis C. Sheridan, 1839–1840*, ed. Willis W. Pratt (Austin, 1954), p. 43.

18. U.S. Census Bureau. *The Seventh Census of the U.S. 1850* (Washington, 1853), p. 504.

19. Ibid. There were also more sober estimates. In 1840 the young German businessman Gustav Dresel put the population at 1,500 to 2,000. Gustav Dresel, "Tagebuch von Gustav Dresel über seinen Aufenthalt in Texas 1837–41," ed. Julius Goebel, *Jahrbuch der Deutsch-Amerikanischen Historischen Gesellschaft von Illinois* 20–21 (1920–1921): 368. Maillard mentions a census of 1839 according to which Houston had 2,073 inhabitants. Maillard, *History of the Republic of Texas*, p. 363.

20. Orceneth Fisher, *Sketches: Texas in 1840* (1840; reprint Waco, Tex., 1964), p. 35.

21. Hayes, *Galveston*, 1: 463–464, 467–468.

6

1. Austin Colony records list Charles A. Giesecke as arriving on an unspecified date that year. Villamae Williams, ed., *Stephen F. Austin's Register of Families* (reprint, Baltimore, 1989), p. 85. He is listed simply as "Charles Gieske [*sic*] 23 years of age, native of Germany. Single man." The misspelling of his surname is one of several versions of "Giesecke" appearing in American records and in ship passenger lists.

2. According to a persistent family tradition in Texas, Charles Giesecke arrived in Texas in 1824 from Germany, New York, or Georgia. Both of the following sources mentioning 1824 derive ultimately from this same oral tradition: James A.

Creighton, A *Narrative History of Brazoria County* ([Angleton, Texas], 1975), p. 25; Brazoria County Library, Angleton, Texas. Brazoria County Survey Committee. File 29. The same date, arising from the same tradition, is given in letters to me from the following: Brazoria County Library, February 4, 1976; Asa A. Giesecke (grandson of Charles A. Giesecke), Angleton, May 12, 1976; Jack P. Giesecke (great grandson of Charles A. Giesecke), West Columbia, February 6, 1976. The year 1824 is also given in several twentieth-century obituaries of members of the Giesecke family in Texas. However, an arrival this early is improbable. In 1825 Charles A. Giesecke, then still known as Anton Carl Giesecke, was confirmed in Bockenem as recorded in the church records there. Letter from Professor Dr. G. Haeseler (Bockenem) to me, March 31, 1976. Charles's brothers Friedrich and Edward were confirmed in 1823 and 1829. It is doubtful that any of the Gieseckes arrived until the 1830s. In 1824 Charles was 13 years old, Friedrich 15, and Edward a mere 9.

Family tradition in Germany is less specific than that in Texas but correctly indicates the arrival in Texas of a Giesecke prior to 1836. A letter written by a family genealogist invokes the authority of Friedrich Giesecke's daughter, then still alive in Elze, as describing her father as having been a merchant in Bockenem, Elze, and Mexico. Letter of Oberstudienrat i.R. Fritz Plathner (Hannover) to Dr. Friedrich Kruse (Halle), April 29, 1938. I am indebted to a nephew of Dr. Kruse, retired Bankdirektor Klaus Nötzel (Bonn-Bad Godesberg), for a copy of this letter. The assertion in the letter is compatible with a brief, often repeated statement by my father that his ancestors on his mother's side had been merchants in Mexico. As best I know, he had no knowledge of Plathner's letter. My father was conversant with relevant data such as the date of Texas independence, and he had apparently looked up the location of Brazoria. He may have been drawing upon what he had heard while growing up in Philadelphia. In any event, his family had, to my knowledge and that of my father's older brother, no contact with the Gieseckes in Texas. However, despite the absence of my father's mother in the home, my grandfather remained in touch with his father-in-law, Christoph *Carl* Giesecke, the son of Friedrich Giesecke. Christoph Carl Giesecke spent many years of his life in America. Since matters of inheritance involving the Texas and German Gieseckes were resolved only after the death of his grandmother in 1871, he had reason and opportunity to keep up with his relatives in the Lone Star State. Coming to New York as a young man, Christoph Carl Giesecke worked for the New York branch of a Bremen export-import firm during the 1860s and became a naturalized U.S. citizen, but did not remain permanently in the United States. Based mostly in Bremen and Stockholm, he later worked for his father-in-law's merchant firm in Sweden and eventually went into business for himself in Germany. Following his divorce in the 1890s, he lived part of his later years in the New York area and the Hanseatic cities, and his last years in the Hannover area. (Documentation, including his U.S. naturalization certificate and his resumé, is in my possession.)

3. NA. Record Group 36. Cargo Manifests. New Orleans, 1836/1850. The ship arrived January 5, 1836. No quantity is specified on either the manifest or the passenger list, although the latter also lists the shipment.

4. For the references, see William von Rosenberg, *Kritik der Geschichte des Vereins zum Schutze der deutschen Auswanderer nach Texas* (Austin, 1894), p. 7; Moritz Tiling, *History of the German Element in Texas*, p. 34. Rosenberg cites simply the "Texas State Archives"; Tiling, simply the "muster rolls" of the participants in the Texas War for Independence. These references could not be confirmed in Austin. There is no conclusive evidence that anyone named Giesecke fought for Texas in 1835–1836. The originals of the lists of participants were destroyed in a fire in the office of the Adjutant General of Texas in 1855. Prior to this fire much of the data on these lists had been transcribed, since veterans of the war were rewarded principally with land grants. I am indebted to then archivist of the Texas State Archives, Dr. Michael J. Dabrishus, for extensive searches for material and for a detailed letter of February 18, 1981. If a Carl or Charles Giesecke served in the war, he may be another man of that name. Geue and Geue mention a Charles Giesecke who settled in Washington County in 1836. Geue, *New Homes in a New Land*, p. 3. Records first published in 1841 indicate that a Charles Giesecke had received a "first-class headright," a grant of a third of a league of land (1476 acres), in Colorado County. The recipient of such a grant had to have been a "resident citizen" in Texas in 1836 at the time of the Declaration of Independence. Carolyn R. Erickson and Frances T. Ingmire, eds., *First Settlers of the Republic of Texas: Headright Land Grants Which Were Reported as Genuine and Legal by the Traveling Commissioners, January 1840*, 2 vols. (Nacogdoches, 1982), 1: 74. This may have been Charles A. Giesecke, but according to the U.S. Census of 1850, two men named Charles Giesecke from Germany lived in Colorado County. One was recorded as aged 50, the other 40 — about the same age as Charles. V. K. Carpenter, ed., *The State of Texas: Federal Population Schedules, Seventh Census of the United States*, 4 vols. (Huntsville, Ark., 1969), 2: 543, 547. The family data indicate clearly that neither of these two men was Charles A. Giesecke, who is recorded by both the Texas Census of 1840 and the U.S. Census of 1850 as living in Brazoria County. Although his name is entered under 1834 in Williams, *Stephen F. Austin's Register of Families*, the name Giesecke does not appear at all in two of the other most important biographical finding aids for early Texas: the Biographical Index of Texas in the Barker History Center at the University of Texas at Austin; and Marion D. Mullins, ed., *The First Census of Texas, 1829–1836: To Which Are Added Texas Citizenship Lists, 1821–1845 and Other Early Records of the Republic of Texas* (Washington, 1959).

5. On July 16, 1840, a schooner from Velasco, Texas, arrived in New Orleans with ten bales of cotton shipped by Charles A. Giesecke. NA. Record Group 36, Box 141.

6. His last name is misspelled "Gisicke." Gifford White, ed., *The 1840 Census of the Republic of Texas* (Austin, 1966), pp. 19–20.

7. Ibid., Preface.

8. See esp. the chart in Konrad Fuchs, "Zur Auswanderungsproblematik in Deutschland im 19. Jahrhundert" in *Festschrift für Eberhard Kessel zum 75. Geburtstag*, ed. Heinz Duchardt and Manfred Schlenke (Munich, 1982), p. 172.

9. Later, most of the surviving lists, presumably the more recent ones, not

those in which we are interested here, were destroyed in the course of the Allied bombing of Germany during World War II. Rolf Engelsing, *Bremen als Auswandererhafen*, p. 161; Karl Werner Klüber, "Wiedergefundene Bremer und Hamburger Auswandererlisten," *Genealogie* 15 (1966): 329–332.

10. Hayes, *Galveston* 1: 355.

11. The surviving fragments, from the years 1838, 1840, and 1841, are in the Texas State Archives in Austin among the records of the Bureau of Customs of the Republic of Texas. I am indebted to Dr. Michael Dabrishus of the Texas State Archives for a search of these records. Letters of Dr. Dabrishus to me, October 27 and November 23, 1977.

12. The *Adelsverein* lists are in the Texas State Archives among the Colonization Papers of the Secretary of State. Some of the material from these lists was published in New Braunfels, Texas, in the *Neu-Braunfelser Zeitung, Jahrbuch*, 1936, and the *Neu-Braunfelser Zeitung*, August 21, 1952. A larger and more convenient collection of data from the passenger lists of Germans arriving in Texas can be found in the works of the Geues: Geue and Geue, *A New Land Beckoned*; Geue, *New Homes in a New Land*. These two volumes are marred by obvious mistakes in transcribing information from the lists. Another way of identifying German immigrants in Texas is provided by the contracts that *Adelsverein* emigrants concluded with that organization. The surviving contracts are located in the General Land Office in Austin. See Glen Lich, "German Emigration Contracts in the General Land Office," *Texas Library* 38 (1976): 19–21. Ira A. Glazier and P. William Filby are the editors of a very ambitious data collection from U.S. passenger lists of tremendous potential value to the study of German immigrants that is badly compromised by massive transcription errors; see Antonius Holtmann, "Snares for the Genealogist and the Historian: A Critique," *Newsletter of the Society for German-American Studies* 14 (1993): 17–24, for a review of the first twenty-two volumes of Ira A. Glazier and P. William Filby, eds. *Germans to America: Lists of Passengers Arriving at U.S. Ports* (Wilmington, Del., 1988–). A useful survey of passenger lists from ships arriving in the United States is provided by Robert P. Swierenga, "List upon Lists: The Ship Passenger Records and Immigration Research," *Journal of American Ethnic History* 10 (1991): 42–53.

13. Some of the gaps in the passenger lists are filled or partly filled by microfilms available from the U.S. National Archives. For example, many U.S. lists for Baltimore are lost, but under the terms of a Maryland law lists had to be submitted also to state authorities. Damaged or missing U.S. lists are often replaced by copies of the state lists.

14. NA. Microcopy 255, Roll 1. Passenger Lists of Vessels Arriving at Baltimore, 1820–1891. July 21, 1834. I am indebted to Fräulein E. Ding of the Superintendency of the Evangelical Lutheran Church in Elze for her search of records confirming Dübel's origins in Elze.

15. NA. Microcopy 255, Roll 1. Passenger Lists of Vessels Arriving at Baltimore, 1820–1891. August 2, 1834.

16. Ibid., ca. September 1, 1834.

17. Ibid., July 6, 1835.

18. Ibid., December 1, 1835.

19. NA. Microcopy 259, Roll 13. Passenger Lists of Vessels Arriving at New Orleans, 1820–1902. December 9, 1935.

20. In the 1830s there were several merchants named Kaufmann and Kauffmann in Bremen. The earliest apparent entry for Julius Kauffmann in the surviving passenger lists for Galveston is in 1848. A "J. Kauffmann" arrived on December 15 of that year on the bark *Neptun* from Bremen. His age is not given. NA. Microcopy 575, Roll 3. Lists of Passengers Arriving at Miscellaneous Ports on the Atlantic and Gulf Coasts and at Ports on the Great Lakes, 1820–1873. The U.S. manuscript census returns for 1850 contain an entry under Galveston for Julius Kaufman. He is listed as a merchant thirty-five years old with real estate worth $4500. Carpenter, *Seventh Census of the United States*, 2: 766. Julius Kauf[f]man[n] later entered into partnership with Julius Runge of Bremen, who had been born in Westphalia. Although leaving Germany only a year after Kauffman, Runge spent five years in Baltimore and four in New Orleans before coming to Indianola, Texas in 1845. Apparently Runge entered Kauffman's business in 1866. On the firm Kauffman & Runge, see esp. Andrew Morrison, ed., *The Industries of Galveston* (Galveston, 1883). The Rosenberg Library in Galveston houses many of the firm's papers, primarily those of the Runges. Although containing many photocopies of material pertaining to Runge, a recent book is of little use: Henry J. Hauschild, *The Runge Chronicle: A German Saga of Success* (Austin, 1990), see esp. p. 7.

21. This statement is based upon the absence in Bremen of data indicating he was born there, and from circumstantial evidence derived from Charles A. Giesecke's letters. See Appendix.

22. This dating of the firm Julius Kauffman & Co. is that given in the finding guides of the Rosenberg Library.

23. S. C. Griffin, *History of Galveston, Texas: Narrative and Biographical* (Galveston, 1931), p. 36; Wheeler, *To Wear a City's Crown*, pp. 71–72.

24. See, for example, von Sommer, *Bericht über meine Reise nach Texas*, pp. 25, 28; Victor Bracht, *Texas in Jahre 1848: Nach mehrjärigen Beobachtungen dargestellt. Mit verschiedenartigen Zugaben, Auszügen aus Briefen* (Elberfeld and Iserlohn, 1849), pp. 253, 283; Schlecht, *Mein Ausflug nach Texas*, p. 48. D. H. Klaener, one of Julius Kauffman's earliest partners, spent most of his time beginning in 1840 in Galveston. In 1842 he was named consul for the Republic of Texas by Bremen, and by 1844 he had business dealings with the *Adelsverein*. See Geue and Geue, *A New Land Beckoned*, p. 52; Pitsch, *Die wirtschaftlichen Beziehungen Bremens zu den Vereinigten Staaten*, p. 86.

25. NA. Microcopy 255, Roll 2. July 26 and 28, 1837. Gerlach's name could not be located in the Church Records, Elze.

26. NA. Microcopy 259, Roll 15. November 27 and 29, 1837.

27. Ibid., Roll 16. May 21, 1838.

28. NA. Microcopy 255, Roll 2. October 25, 1838.

29. NA. Microcopy 259, Roll 19. November 26, 1839. The parish records mention a Friedrich August Hinze. Church Records, Elze.

30. See, for example, Walker, *Germany and the Emigration*, pp. 46–47; Philip

Taylor, *The Distant Magnet: European Emigration to the U.S.A.* (New York, 1971), pp. 89–90; Walter D. Kamphoefner, *Westfalen in der Neuen Welt: Eine Sozialgeschichte der Auswanderung im 19. Jahrhundert* (Münster, 1982). The U.S. ed. of the last work differs from the German version: *The Westfalians. From Germany to Missouri* (Princeton, 1987). On the general issue of geographical concentration, see the exemplary study of Danes, based on massive statistical evidence, by Kristian Kvidt, *Flight to America: The Social Background of 300,000 Danish Emigrants* (New York, [1975?]), esp. pp. 103–104.

31. Moses Rischin, *The Promised City: New York's Jews, 1870–1914* (New York, 1970), p. 20; Arthur A. Goren, "Jews," in *Harvard Encyclopedia of American Ethnic Groups*, ed. Stephan Thernstrom (Cambridge, Mass., 1980), p. 579.

32. Leonard Dinnerstein and David M. Reimers, *Ethnic Americans: A History of Immigration and Assimilation* (New York, 1975), p, 39; Goren, "Jews," p. 581.

33. NA. Microcopy 259, Roll 14. June 9, 1836. Much the same data are given in the Quarterly Abstract except no age is indicated.

34. NA. Microcopy 272, Roll 1. Passenger Lists of Vessels Arriving at New Orleans. Quarterly Abstract, 1820–1875. July 26, 1837.

35. NA. Microcopy 259, Roll 15. July 26, 1837.

36. The cause is not obvious. Perhaps the original lists were frequently used for the "Quarterly Abstract," while the passenger lists were in this case mere copies. Unfortunately, the principal use of the Quarterly Abstracts has been simply to fill gaps in the passenger lists.

37. NA. Microcopy 259, Roll 16, February 5, 1838.

38. NA. Microcopy 272, Roll 2, February 5, 1838.

39. A New Orleans cargo manifest from 1839 refers to a shipment of molasses from Galveston for "FG." These initials appear in later records as Friedrich Giesecke's mark, but in this instance the initials are not enclosed in an up-ended square. Hence the identity of the consignee cannot be established with certainty as Friedrich Giesecke. NA. Record Group 36, Box 121. January 14, 1839.

40. NA. Microcopy 259, Roll 19. November 23, 1839.

41. NA. Microcopy 272, Roll 2. November 30, 1840. There is no corresponding entry on the passenger lists themselves — a not uncommon discrepancy in these sources.

42. NA. Microcopy 259, Roll 2. January 22, 1842. Again, there is no corresponding entry in the Quarterly Abstract.

43. NA. Record Group 36, Box 94. The steamboat *New York* arrived in New Orleans from Galveston on January 10, 1842. On board were fifteen bales of cotton belonging or consigned to Friedrich Giesecke. On January 21 the same steamer brought seventeen more bales displaying his mark.

44. Letter of March 16, 1844.

7

1. In the absence of substantial scholarly literature on Brazoria, an anonymous contribution in a standard reference work remains important: "Brazoria" in

Webb et al., *Handbook of Texas*, 1: 207–208. For the period prior to the Texas Revolution an older standard work must be consulted: Hubert Howe Bancroft, *History of the North Mexican States and Texas*, 2 vols. (San Francisco, 1884–1889), 2: 114, 117–121. References to Brazoria in German travel literature and in handbooks for emigrants are of great value. Some of these references are cited below. An article in the sesquicentennial edition of a local newspaper is useful mainly for its description of the town's recent past: Raul Castillo, Jr., "Brazoria: Past, Present, and Future," *Brazoria Banner*, April 9, 1986. Although neither scholarly nor well documented, Creighton's county history is essential: Creighton, *Narrative History of Brazoria County*. Also worth mentioning is a very weak unpublished source: Elizabeth Lane, "History of Brazoria County," master's thesis, Texas College of Arts and Industries, Kingsville (1948).

2. See Stephen F. Austin, "Description of Texas in 1831," in Eugene C. Barker, ed., *Readings in Texas History* (Dallas, 1929), p. 123; Barker, *Life of Stephen F. Austin*, p. 180.

3. Austin, "Description of Texas in 1831," p. 123.

4. Charles Sealsfield [Karl Postl], *Das Kajuetenbuch. Oder nationale Charakteristiken* (1st ed., 1841, Halle, [1887]), p. 13. See the superb English-language edition in John Q. Anderson, ed., *Tales of Frontier Texas* (Dallas, 1966). An English version first appeared in 1843 in *Blackwood's Magazine* (Edinburgh).

5. Dunt, *Reise nach Texas*, p. 75.

6. George Bernard Erath, *Memoirs of Major George Bernard Erath*, ed. Lucy A. Erath (Austin, 1923), p. 15.

7. Bancroft, *History of the North Mexican States and Texas*, 2: 114, 117–121.

8. Forrest E., Ward, "Pre-Revolutionary Activity in Brazoria County," *Southwestern Historical Quarterly*, 64 (1960): 212.

9. Joseph Lynn Clark, *The Texas Gulf Coast: Its History and Development*, 4 vols. (New York, 1955), 1: 355; Webb et al., *Handbook of Texas*, 1: 207.

10. This statement is based on the numerous surviving passenger lists. NA. Microcopy 259, Rolls 13–14; Microcopy 272, Roll 1.

11. Ibid.

12. See Puryear and Nath, *Sandbars and Sternwheelers*, p. 6.

13. David B. Edward, *History of Texas* (Cincinnati, 1836), p. 30.

14. Chester Newell, *History of the Revolution in Texas. Particularly of the War of 1835–1836. Together with the Latest Geographical, Topographical, and Statistical Accounts of the Country* (New York, 1838), p. 141. It is typical of the bookish German Scherpf, who claimed to have been in Texas, that he translated almost word for word Newell's passage on Brazoria and quoted it without acknowledgment in his comprehensive book on Texas. Scherpf, *Entstehungsgeschichte und gegenwärtiger Zustand des neuen, unabhängigen, amerikanischen Staates Texas*, p. 92.

15. Edward Stiff, *The Texan Emigrant. Being a Narration of the Adventures of the Author in Texas and a Description of the Soils, Climate, Productions . . . of That Country* (Cincinnati, 1840), p. 64.

16. "Brazoria," in Webb et al., *Handbook of Texas*, 1: 207. Another improbable claim is that the town had five thousand inhabitants on the eve of the Civil War.

Clark, *Texas Gulf Coast*, 1: 356. The estimates are so extravagant that they cannot result simply from confusion of the town with the county.

17. See Brazoria County Federation of Women's Clubs, ed., *History of Brazoria County* ([Angleton, Tex.?], 1940), p. 11; Ward, "Pre-Revolutionary Activity in Brazoria County," p. 213.

18. Andrew F. Muir, ed., *Texas in 1837: An Anonymous Contemporary Narrative* (Austin, 1958), p. 123.

19. N. Doran Maillard, *History of the Republic of Texas*, p. 363.

20. Creighton, *Narrative History of Brazoria County*, p. 162. Creighton accepts the estimate provided by Francis Moore, *Description of Texas* (2d ed., New York, 1844), p. 53. Moore was the editor of the *Telegraph and Texas Register*, which moved to Houston in May 1837. The estimates for Texas towns on an otherwise excellent map of 1844 prepared for the U.S. Department of State are unreliable. The figure of 200 for Brazoria comes apparently from an earlier time. On the other hand, the estimates for Galveston (5,000) and Houston (4,500) are on the high side. The data given for other towns includes 200 for Austin and 350 for Columbia. *Map of Texas and Countries Adjacent. Compiled in the Bureau of Topographical Engineers from the Best Authorities for the State Department. Under the Direction of Col. J. J. Albert, Chief of Corps. By W. H. Emory, First Lieutenant, War Department. Published by Order of the U.S. Senate* (Washington, 1844). A copy of this map is in the Map Division of the New York Public Library.

21. "Brazoria" in Webb et al., *Handbook of Texas*, 1: 207.

22. See Appendix.

23. *Texas in 1840. Or the Emigrant's Guide to the New Republic*, p. 213. The author of this work was in Texas in 1840.

24. F. Moore, *Description of Texas*, pp. 53, 80. According to the Census of 1850, Galveston had 4,177 and Houston 2,396 inhabitants. U.S. Census Bureau, *The Seventh Census of the United States 1850. . . . A Statistical View of Each of the States* (Washington, 1853), pp. 504. Presumably each of these figures includes slaves.

25. Orceneth Fisher, *Sketches: Texas in 1840*, p. 24.

26. Travis L. Smith, *Steamboats on the Brazos*, pp. 65–66; Puryear and Nath, *Sandbars and Sternwheelers*, pp. 37–59.

27. See Creighton, *Narrative History of Brazoria County*, pp. 211–212; Puryear and Winfield, *Sandbars and Sternwheelers*, pp. xvii–xviii; Muir, "Destiny of Buffalo Bayou," pp. 102–105.

28. See, for example, the "Remarks on Texas" on a map dated 1836 in J. H. Young, *New Map of Texas with the Contiguous American and Mexican States* (Philadelphia, 1836). A copy of this map is in the Map Division of the New York Public Library.

29. See Creighton, *Narrative History of Brazoria County*, p. 170.

30. Father Weiser's name does not appear in the tax lists of 1840. See White, *1840 Census of the Republic of Texas*. The surviving parish records, written in English, are in St. Mary's Church in Freeport. The German surname Müller is often anglicized to "Miller," but this practice by itself provides no evidence that he was

German. Father Miller was succeeded in 1857 by a priest with an unmistakably German name, J. G. Beerschneider, and with German handwriting in English. I am indebted to Father Patrick J. Cummings of St. Joseph's Catholic Church in Brazoria for copies of these records. Based largely on material in the Catholic Archives of Texas in Austin and on printed sources, James Talmadge Moore's history of the early Catholic Church in Texas makes no mention of these early German Catholics in the Brazoria area, nor does Moore devote much attention to the subject of Germans in Texas. J. T. Moore, *Through Fire and Flood*.

31. See White, *1840 Census of the Republic of Texas*.

32. NA. Microcopy 432, Roll 908. Seventh Census of the U.S. 1850. Population Schedules. Texas. See also Carpenter, *Seventh Census of the United States*, vol. 1.

33. See Letter of February 10, 1845.

34. Friedrich Kapp, "Amerikanische Reiseskizzen II [on Texas]," *Atlantische Studien von Deutschen in Amerika* 2 (1853): 180.

35. Creighton, *Narrative History of Brazoria County*, p. 194.

36. Fornell, *Galveston Era*, pp. ix–x; Hogan, *Texas Republic*, pp. 21, 75.

37. The county's slave population expanded from some 1,316 in 1840 to 3219 in 1848. White, *1840 Census of the Republic of Texas*, Foreword; Allen A. Platter, "Educational, Social, and Economic Characteristics of the Plantation Culture of Brazoria County, Texas," Ph.D. diss., University of Houston (1961), p. 11. In 1834 the slave population of the entire Department of the Brazos, which included not only the future Brazoria County, but also much other territory, was estimated at a mere 1,000. Abigail Curlee, "The History of a Texas Slave Plantation, 1831–1863," *Southwestern Historical Quarterly* 27 (1922): 86.

38. Fornell, *Galveston Era*, pp. viii–ix.

39. Curlee, "History of a Texas Slave Plantation," p. 88.

40. Moritz Beyer, *Das Auswanderungsbuch. Oder Führer und Ratgeber bei der Auswanderung nach Nordamerika und Texas* (Leipzig, 1846), p. 169.

41. See, for example, the preoccupation with slavery in the lively book by W. Steinert, *Nordamerika, vorzüglich Texas im Jahre 1849. Reisebericht. Ein Buch für Auswanderer, besonders für Auswanderungslustige* (Berlin, 1850). Steinert is very critical of Victor Bracht's widely circulated book with its paens of praise for Texas: Bracht, *Texas in Jahre 1848*. Bracht's book is also available in translation: *Texas in 1848*, trans. Frank Schmidt (San Antonio, 1931).

42. Johann G. Büttner, *Briefe aus und über Nordamerika. Oder Beiträge zu einer richtigen Kenntnis der Vereinigten Staaten und ihrer Bewohner, besonders der deutschen Bevölkerung* 2, wohlfeilere Ausgabe, 2 vols. (Dresden and Leipzig, 1847), 2: 213–214. Büttner was for a short time professor at the Theological Seminary of the High German Reformed Synod of Ohio. See his *Die Vereinigten Staaten von Nordamerika. Mein Aufenthalt und meine Reisen in denselben vom Jahre 1834 bis 1841*, 2 vols. (Hamburg, 1844).

43. See Preston A. Barba, *The Life and Works of Friedrich Armand Strubberg*, ([Philadelphia], 1913), pp. 28–32; Leroy H. Woodson, *American Negro Slavery in the Works of Friedrich Strubberg, Friedrich Gerstäcker, and Otto Ruppius* (Washing-

ton, 1949), p. 42; Armin O. Huber, "Frederic Armand Strubberg, Alias Dr. Shubbert: Townbuilder, Physician, and Adventurer, 1806–1889," *West Texas Historical Association Yearbook* 38 (1962): 37.

44. F. A. Strubberg, *Saat und Ernte*, 5 vols. (Leipzig, 1866). One scene is set in Brazoria.

45. Schlecht, *Mein Ausflug nach Texas*, p. 49.

46. An interesting example is provided by the popularly written work of a German chauvinist whom Hitler took seriously as an authority on the United States: Colin Ross, *Unser Amerika: Der deutsche Anteil an den Vereinigten Staaten* (Leipzig, 1936), pp. 215–219.

47. See, for example, Maldwyn Allen Jones, *American Immigration* (Chicago, 1960), p. 165; Max I. Dimont, *The Jews in America: The Roots, History, and Destiny of American Jews* (New York, 1980), p. 129. Even a recent work on slavery in Texas suggests tentatively the generalization that Germans there were not especially antislavery in their attitudes. Randolf B. Campbell, *An Empire for Slavery: The Peculiar Institution in Texas, 1861–1865* (Baton Rouge, 1989), pp. 215–217.

48. Even in the "German" areas of Texas some people were slaveholders. For a survey of this situation see Jordan, *German Seed in Texas Soil*, pp. 106–110.

49. Frederick Law Olmsted, *A Journey through Texas: A Saddletrip on the Southwest Frontier* (New York, 1860), pp. 133, 432–433.

50. See Robert W. Shook, "The Battle of the Nueces, August 10, 1862," *Southwestern Historical Quarterly* 66 (1962): 31–42; Claude Elliott, "Union Sentiment in Texas, 1861–65," *Southwestern Historical Quarterly* 50 (1947): 453, 457, 465. See also the eyewitness accounts in Guido E. Ransleben, *A Hundred Years of Comfort in Texas: A Centennial History* (San Antonio, 1954), pp. 86–123.

51. Perhaps the most enduring works of these revisionists are Ulrich B. Phillips's studies of slavery, *American Negro Slavery* (New York, 1918) and *Life and Labor in the Old South* (1929, reprint, Boston and Toronto, 1963).

52. Biesele, *History of the German Settlements in Texas*, pp. 197–207.

53. Benjamin, *The Germans of Texas*, p. 119; see also pp. 208–232. Another important monograph on Texas Germans did not follow these trends. Moritz Tiling emphasized union sentiment among the inhabitants of West and North Texas and took a clear position against racism. Tiling, *History of the German Element in Texas* (1913), pp. 130–131. A similar emphasis on the freedom-loving traditions of much of the German population can be found in the contributions to Lich and Reeves, *German Culture in Texas*, esp. pp. 211–213.

54. Jordan, *German Seed in Texas Soil*, pp. 106–110. Recent literature is far from conclusive on these issues. While Hubert Heinen finds no particular pattern in German sentiments during the Civil War, Walter Kamphoefner stresses the extent of pro-Union, antislavery views. Hubert Heinen, "German-Texan Attitudes toward the Civil War," *Yearbook of German-American Studies* 20 (1985): 19–32; Walter D. Kamphoefner, "Texas Germans and Civil War Issues: The Evidence from Immigrant Letters," *Journal of the German-Texan Heritage Society* 13, no. 1 (1991): 16–23.

55. Wendell G. Addington, "Slave Insurrections in Texas," *Journal of Negro*

History 35 (1950): 412; Herbert Aptheker, *American Negro Slave Revolts* (New York 1963), p. 93; Paul D. Lack, "Slavery and the Texas Revolution," *Southwestern Historical Quarterly* 89 (1985): 182, 190–193.

56. Lack, "Slavery and the Texas Revolution," pp. 193–196; Aptheker, *American Negro Slave Revolts*, pp. 32, 82.

57. Addington, "Slave Insurrections in Texas," p. 415.

58. Many contemporaries remark on this anomaly. See, for example, Sheridan, *Galveston Island*, p. 89.

59. NA. Microcopy 432, Roll 908. Seventh Census of the U.S., 1850. Population Schedules of Some Texas Counties; Roll 917. Texas Slave Schedules. See also Carpenter, *Seventh Census of the United States*. For an analysis of the wealthy from 1850 to 1860, see Randolf B. Campbell and Richard G. Lowe, *Wealth and Power in Antebellum Texas* (College Station, Tex., 1977), pp. 33, 51.

60. See the suggestive remarks made in 1848 in the diary of a visitor to a Brazoria County plantation, future U.S. president Rutherford B. Hayes, in Curlee, "History of a Slave Plantation," pp. 113–114.

8

1. Dora Dietrich Bonham, *Merchant to the Republic* (San Antonio, [1958?]). Bonham, who is Dietrich's granddaughter, explicitly dissociates her work from history, but despite her naiveté and mysticism, the book has merit as a poetic attempt to confront the past.

2. Hermann Seele, *Die Zypresse und Gesammelte Schriften: Eine Legende aus der Zeit der ersten deutschen Ansiedlungen in West-Texas* (New Braunfels, Tex., 1936). The translation will also be cited below: *The Cypress and Other Writings of a German Pioneer in Texas*, trans. Edward C. Breitenkamp (Austin, 1979). This posthumously published book consists of excerpts from Seele's diary that were first published in the *Neu-Braunfelser Zeitung* in New Braunfels in 1889–1890.

3. [Edward C. Breitenkamp?], "Introduction," in Seele, *The Cypress*, p. xi; Geue and Geue, *A New Land Beckoned*, p. 17.

4. Geue and Geue, *A New Land Beckoned*, pp. 52, 61.

5. Seele, *The Cypress*, pp. 57–58. I have made numerous small changes in the translation.

6. Seele died in Texas in 1902. Geue and Geue, *A New Land Beckoned*, pp. 17–18, 147.

7. See letter of February 10, 1845.

8. Letter of March 16, 1844.

9. Some of their undertakings had probably never been joint. For example, early in 1843 Edward placed an advertisement in a Galveston newspaper for wares he had imported from New York. *Civilian and Galveston City Gazette*, February 18, 1843. SAB. 2 — C. 26. Verhältnisse der Hansestädte zu Texas 1840–1846.

10. Edward Giesecke married on October 21, 1844. Marriage License and Certificate, Brazoria County Courthouse, Angleton, Texas. His wife died in Texas in 1874. On her tombstone her date of birth was given as June 16, 1829, and her

place of birth simply as "Germany." Cradle of Texas Chapter of the Daughters of the Republic of Texas, comp., "A List of Old Brazoria County, Texas, Cemeteries during or before 1900," (Freeport, Tex., n.d.), copy in Brazoria County Library, Angleton. The tombstone, which disappeared about twenty years ago, was viewed on March 3, 1971, by Charles A. Giesecke's great grandson Jack Giesecke, who kindly provided me with a copy of the inscription. Jack Giesecke, letter to the author, February 6, 1976. The data given for Lisette Doby Giesecke in the U.S. Censuses of 1850, 1860, and 1870 are inconsistent and also at variance with other evidence. On the basis of these censuses, her birth year must have been between 1821 and 1827. That would make her two to eight years older, and aged 17 to 23 at marriage. Her first name is spelled various ways in the census records. NA. Microcopy 432, Roll 908. Seventh Census of the U.S., 1850. Population Schedules of Some Texas Counties; Microcopy 653, Roll 1289, Eighth Census of the U.S., 1860. Population Schedules of Some Texas Counties; Microcopy 593, Roll 1576. Ninth Census of the U.S., 1870. Population Schedules of Some Texas Counties.

11. The precise figure for females among German immigrants is 36.5 percent. Marschalck, *Deutsche Überseewanderung im 19. Jahrhundert*, p. 72.

12. Henry B. Dielmann, "Emma Altgelt's Sketches of Life in Texas," *Southwestern Historical Quarterly* 63 (1959–1960): 365.

13. My translation is deliberately euphemistic. Today, as in 1845, German usage permits expressions that Americans and Britons still regard as street talk.

14. After several name changes Tappan's firm was known from 1859 to 1933 as R.G. Dun & Company, and its records are stored under this name. These "Handwritten Credit Ledgers" of R.G. Dun & Company are in Historical Collections, Baker Library, Harvard University Graduate School of Business Administration, Boston. Hereafter cited as R.G. Dun, Handwritten Credit Ledgers. The surviving registers have no entries for Charles Giesecke — most likely because after 1845 he was active mainly as a farmer, not as a merchant. For a discussion of Lewis Tappan & Co. see Dun & Bradstreet, *Dun & Bradstreet: The Story of an Idea* ([New York?], 1968).

15. This and all other quotations in this paragraph are from R.G. Dun, Handwritten Credit Ledgers. I have replaced the many abbreviations with words.

16. See, for example, Duden, *Bericht über eine Reise nach den westlichen Staaten Nordamerikas*, pp. 321–322; Hesse, "Nicholas Hesse," p. 145; Traugott Bromme, *Neuestes vollständigstes Hand- und Reisebuch für Auswanderer aus allen Klassen und jedem Stande nach den Vereinigten Staaten von Nordamerika* (Bayreuth, 1846), pp. 316–318; C. L. Fleischmann, *Erwerbszweige, Fabrikwesen und Handel der Vereinigten Staaten von Nordamerika* (Stuttgart, 1850), pp. 534–536.

17. Fleischmann, *Erwerbszweige, Fabrikwesen und Handel der Vereinigten Staaten*, p. 537. Fleischmann worked for many years in the U.S. Patent Office in Washington. Later he served as an American consul in Germany.

18. John A. Krout and Dixon Ryan Fox, *The Completion of Independence, 1790–1830* (New York, [1944]), p. 3.

19. NA. Microcopy 432, Roll 908. Seventh Census of the U.S., 1850. Population Schedules. The data can also be found in Carpenter, *Seventh Census of the*

United States, 1: 211. The expression "merchant" was often used instead of "store-keeper," but "merchant" had a more genteel ring. See Lewis E. Atherton, *The Pioneer Merchant in Mid-America* (Columbia, Mo., 1939), pp. 29–30. According to the Census of 1850 the German merchant Julius Kauffman, whom we met earlier, owned real estate in Galveston with a value of $4,500. Another German merchant there, J. W. Jockusch, had $5,000 worth of real estate. Carpenter, *Seventh Census of the United States*, 2: 761, 766.

20. NA. Microcopy 633, Roll 1289. Eighth Census of the U.S., 1860. Population Schedules.

21. NA. Microcopy 593, Roll 1576. Ninth Census of the U.S., 1870. Population Schedules.

22. NA. Microcopy 432, Roll 917. Seventh Census of the U.S., 1850. Texas Slave Schedules; Microcopy 653, Roll 1309. Eighth Census of the U.S., 1850. Texas Slave Schedules.

23. Letter of March 16, 1844.

24. Brazoria County Courthouse. Angleton, Texas. Estate No. 642. "Last Will and Testament of Ernest Eduard Giesecke" and the "Inventory of Estate."

25. Olmsted, *Journey through Texas*, p. 206.

26. Lewis E. Atherton, *The Southern Country Store 1800–1860* (Baton Rouge, La., [1949]), pp. 14–15, 18, 46–47, 49–54, 145–146; Abigail Curlee Holbrook, "Cotton Marketing in Antebellum Texas," *Southwestern Historical Quarterly* 71 (1970): 431–455; Harold D. Woodman, *King Cotton and His Retainers: Financing and Marketing the Cotton Crop of the South, 1800–1925* (Lexington, Ky., 1968); pp. 47, 77, 129; Fleischmann, *Erwerbszweige, Fabrikwesen und Handel der Vereinigten Staaten*, p. 536; N. S. B. Gras, *Businessmen and Capitalism: An Introduction to Business History* (New York, 1939), p. 165.

27. See Appendix.

28. See, for example, Duden, *Bericht über eine Reise nach den westlichen Staaten Nordamerikas*, pp. 321, 330; Bromme, *Neuestes vollständigstes Hand- und Reisebuch für Auswanderer*, pp. 317–318.

29. Dunt, *Reise nach Texas*, p. 30.

30. Stiff, *The Texan Emigrant*, p. 187.

31. Wheeler, *To Wear a City's Crown*, p. 67.

32. Dunt, *Reise nach Texas*, p. 30.

33. Stiff, *The Texan Emigrant*, pp. 188–190.

34. Curlee Holbrook, "Cotton Marketing in Antebellum Texas," pp. 442–447.

35. Apparently this firm was not connected with the major Bremen firm C. L Brauer & Co., which was of great significance for the Gieseckes, the development of Bremen's tobacco trade, and, generally, German commerce with the Americas. See below.

36. Ibid., p. 442.

37. Ibid., p. 445. For a contemporary German literary portrait of a man in Texas en route to becoming a successful big businessman see Strubberg, *Saat und Ernte*, 1: 167. Although this figure has much in common with Morgan L. Smith

(as well as with Robert Mills), he settles on the perimeter of Buffalo Bayou in the vicinity of Houston.

38. On the Mills brothers see, above all, the well-informed sketches by Abigail Curlee Holbrook in Webb et al., *Handbook of Texas,* 2: 200; and in her "Cotton Marketing in Antebellum Texas," esp. 451–455. See also Platter, "Educational, Social, and Economic Characteristics of the Plantation Culture of Brazoria County," pp. 133–136; Hayes, *Galveston,* 2: 924–926; Gouge, *Fiscal History of Texas,* pp. 235–236; Williams, *Animating Pursuits of Speculation,* pp. 131, 134; Hogan, *Texas Republic,* pp. 101–103; Fornell, *Galveston Era,* pp. 45–46. Part of the ledgers of R.G. Dun & Company on the Mills brothers, notably that on their firm in Galveston, is apparently lost. The surviving portions are of little use for our purposes. There are a few entries on the firm in Brazoria from 1847 into the 1850s; the next entries are on Robert Mills after the Civil War. R.G. Dun & Company, Handwritten Credit Ledgers.

39. Hayes, *Galveston,* 2: 817, 820–821; A. L. Carlson, *A Monetary and Banking History of Texas: From the Mexican Regime to the Present Day, 1821–1929* (Fort Worth, 1930), pp. 1–4, 8; Joe B. Frantz, "The Mercantile House of McKinney & Williams, Underwriters of the Texas Revolution," *Bulletin of the Business Historical Society,* 26 (1952): 2, 5; Margaret Swett Henson, *Samuel May Williams: Early Texas Entrepreneur* (College Station, Tex., [1976?]), pp. 24, 112.

40. White, *1840 Census of the Republic of Texas,* p. 22.

41. NA. Microcopy 432, Roll 917. Seventh Census of the U.S., 1850. Texas Slave Schedules; Microcopy 653, Roll 1309. Eighth Census of the U.S., 1860. Texas Slave Schedules.

42. For comparative measures of the Mills' enormous wealth see Campbell and Lowe, *Wealth and Power in Antebellum Texas,* esp. pp. 138–149.

43. Fornell, *Galveston Era,* pp. 45–46.

44. Platter, "Educational, Social, and Economic Characteristics of the Plantation Culture of Brazoria County," pp. 133, 135–136; Curlee Holbrook, "Cotton Marketing in Antebellum Texas," p. 452; Creighton, *Narrative History of Brazoria County,* pp. 204, 480, 485, 487, 490–491.

45. NA. Microcopy 653, Roll 1289. Eighth Census of the U.S., 1860. Population Schedules.

46. Platter, "Educational, Social, and Economic Characteristics of the Plantation Culture of Brazoria County," p. 136; Webb et al., *Handbook of Texas,* 2: 200; Griffin, *History of Galveston,* p. 35.

47. Abigail Curlee [Holbrook], "A Study of Texas Slave Plantations, 1822–1865," Ph.D. diss., University of Texas, Austin (1932), p. 93. Curlee interviewed Thomas Giesecke during the 1920s.

48. Rauers, *Geschichte des Bremer Binnenhandels,* p. 19; Beutin, "Von drei Ballen zum Weltmarkt," p. 71; Engelsing, *Bremen als Auswandererhafen,* p. 73; Pitsch, *Die wirtschaftlichen Beziehungen Bremens zu den Vereinigten Staaten,* pp. 161–162.

49. Pitsch, *Die wirtschaftlichen Beziehungen Bremens zu den Vereinigten Staa-*

ten, p. 204. The head of the firm in 1844 was the Royal Hannoverian Vice Consul in Bremen, August Wilhelm Ludolph Brauer. *Adreßbuch der Freien Hansestadt Bremen* (Bremen, 1844). C. L. Brauer & Son was conducting trade between New Orleans and Bremen as early as 1835–1836. NA. Record Group 36. Cargo Manifests. New Orleans, 1836–1850. On April 17, 1843, the 25-year-old merchant J. A. Brauer, presumably a member of the firm, arrived in New Orleans from Havana aboard the steamer *Habanna*. Many Germans, mostly merchants, were traveling on this same vessel. NA. Microcopy 259, Roll 122. Passenger Lists of Vessels Arriving at New Orleans. In 1863 Carl Ludwig Brauer applied for reinstatement of his *Bürgerrecht* "after an extended absence overseas." Peter Marschalck, ed., *Inventar der Quellen zur Geschichte der Wanderungen, besonders der Auswanderung, in Bremer Archiven*, p. 91. A good reminder of the limitations of archival documentation is provided by a list (apparently from ca. 1810 into the 1840s) of Bremen firms with commercial relations with the Americas. Brauer & Son is listed as doing business simply with Rio de Janeiro, Havana, and Philadelphia. Library of Congress, Washington. Manuscript Division. Germany, Bremen. Archiv der Handelskammer (microfilms). C. 48. d. Verzeichnis der nach Amerika Handlung treibende Häuser in Bremen n.d. [ca. 1810–1840+]. On C. L. Brauer & Son see also Friedrich Prüser, "Vom Bremer Überseekaufmann," *Abhandlungen und Vorträge [der Bremer Wissenschaftlichen Gesellschaft]*, 14 (1940), 31; Johannes Ültzen-Barckhausen, *Bremische Schiffahrt vor 100–200 Jahren in ihrer Bedeutung für bremische Handels-, Firmen- und Familiengeschichte* (Leipzig, 1933), p. 60; Beutin, *Von drei Ballen zum Weltmarkt*, p. 120; Hermann Kellenbenz, "Der Bremer Kaufmann. Versuch einer sozialgeschichtlichen Deutung," *Bremisches Jahrbuch* 51 (1969): 41; Pitsch, *Die wirtschaftlichen Beziehungen Bremens zu den Vereinigten Staaten*, pp. 94, 204.

50. Curlee Holbrook, "Cotton Marketing in Antebellum Texas," pp. 446–447.

51. Ibid.

52. Platter, "Educational, Social, and Economic Characteristics of the Plantation Culture of Brazoria County," pp. 36–37.

53. SB. 2 – R. 11. e. 3. Verzeichnis der Abfahrten und Ankünfte auf der Weser für 1845.

54. See, for example, Arthur Ikin, *Texas*, p. 68.

55. A promising source for research on international commerce consists of the voluminous uninventoried cargo manifests for the harbor of New Orleans located in the U.S. National Archives. Record Group 36. There are approximately 270 archival boxes simply for the period 1836 to 1850. I sampled them for the purposes of the present study. One dimension of commerce between New Orleans and Germany can be traced through lists of exports on "inward cargo manifests" from German ports (for all practical purposes, Hamburg and Bremen) to New Orleans. A substantial part of these exports consisted of linens that were probably used mainly as clothing for slaves.

56. SB. 2 – R. 11. e. 2, Bd. 3. In 1840 Stiff wrote that Galveston exported only cotton, but had since the supply was inadequate most ships returned from Galveston in ballast. Stiff, *Texan Emigrant*, p. 150.

57. Since the mark on this cargo was "RU," Giesecke had probably purchased

it from someone else, or, less likely, was serving as a factor. NA. Record Group 36, Box 141.

58. The steamer *New York* arrived on January 21, 1842, with ten bales; eleven days later the same steamer brought seventeen bales. NA. Record Group 36, Box 94. Friedrich Giesecke's mark was "FG." Both lots were consigned to F. de Ligardi. Apparently, the great storm of 1900 destroyed almost all of the cargo manifests in Galveston. NA. Civil Archives Division. Judicial and Fiscal Branch. Letter to me, January 6, 1978.

59. See Appendix. Letter of March 16, 1844.

60. Olmsted, *Journey through Texas,* p. 208; Dewitt T. Tarlton, "The History of the Cotton Industry in Texas, 1820–1850," master's thesis, University of Texas (1923), p. 29. If Charles Giesecke succeeded in the plan outlined in the letter, he sent the cotton with the Bremen brig *Antoinette.* Seven months later, at the end of another journey eastward from Galveston, the *Antoinette* anchored on the Weser with a cargo that included 596 bales of cotton for the firm C. L. Brauer & Son. Archive of the Chamber of Commerce (Archiv der Handelskammer), Bremen. Liste der eingekommenen Waren für 1844.

61. On November 25, 1842, a schooner sailing from Velasco reached New Orleans. The cargo included skins and hides sent by the Gieseckes. This shipment will be described in detail below. The same schooner brought 224 bales of cotton sent by the Mills. NA. Microcopy 259, Roll 22. Passenger Lists of Vessels Arriving at New Orleans, November 25, 1842.

62. See letter of June 30, 1845.

63. See Edward Pessen's incisive rejection of the thesis that the antebellum South was precapitalist. Edward Pessen, "How Different from Each Other Were the Antebellum North and South?" *American Historical Review* 85 (1980): 1125, 1146–1147. The thesis that the South was a bourgeois society underlies the recent book by Shearer D. Bowman, *Masters and Lords: Mid-Nineteenth Century U.S. Planters and Prussian Junkers* (New York, 1993). For a study dealing with the question of commerce on the frontier see the regional study by Robert D. Mitchell, *Commercialism and Frontier: Perspectives on the Early Shenandoah Valley* (Charlottesville, Va., 1977).

64. Woodman, *King Cotton,* pp. 129–130.

65. NA. Microcopy 259, Roll 22. Passenger Lists of Vessels Arriving at New Orleans, November 11, 1842.

66. Seele, *Die Cypresse,* p. 47.

67. On Varner see Webb et al., *Handbook of Texas,* 2: 834–835; Platter, "Educational, Social, and Economic Characteristics of the Plantation Culture of Brazoria County," pp. 176, 181. Varner's name appears in the Texas census of 1840, but not in the U.S. Census of 1850. White, *1840 Census of the Republic of Texas,* p. 155; Carpenter, *Seventh Census of the United States.*

68. NA. Microcopy 432, Roll 908. Seventh Census of the U.S., 1850. Population Schedules.

69. For the general concept of a planter in the South, see Shearer D. Bowman, "Antebellum Planters and Vormärz Junkers in Comparative Perspective," *American*

Historical Review 85 (1980): 781–782. For planters in Brazoria County see Curlee [Holbrook], "A Study of Texas Slave Plantations," p. 28, n. 62.

70. NA. Microcopy 432, Roll 917. Seventh Census 1850. Texas Slave Schedules.

71. Ibid.

72. Curlee [Holbrook], "History of a Texas Slave Plantation," p. 103.

73. See esp. Jordan, *German Seed in Texas Soil*, pp. 69–70.

74. See letters of March 3, 1844, February 18, 1845, March 7, 1845 (including postscript), April 28, 1845, June 30, 1845, October 22, 1845.

75. The *Adreßbuch der Freien Hansestadt Bremen* for 1844 and 1846 lists three businesses with the name Richter: (1) Johann Heinrich Richter, a cigarmaker; (2) C. A. Richter, a merchant; and (3) a firm Richter & Krebs. There is also an entry for Carl Friedrich August Richter, a partner in the last firm. For the history of Richter & Krebs see Peters, "Über bremische Firmengründungen," pp. 340, 348.

76. During the 1840s Brauer was importing one thousand to fifteen hundred barrels of tobacco per year. Pitsch, *Die wirtschaftlichen Beziehungen Bremens zu den Vereinigten Staaten*, p. 204.

77. Seele, *Die Cypresse*, p. 47.

78. See Letter of June 30, 1845.

79. Fleisichmann, *Erwerbszweige, Fabrikwesen und Handel der Vereinigten Staaten*, p. 86.

80. See Charles Giesecke's letter of March 26, 1844; Seele, *Die Zypresse*, p. 47. I have been unable to document Ahler's arrival or his activities after leaving the Gieseckes. One of two entries on the ship lists, arrivals in New Orleans from Bremen, may pertain to him. On June 5, 1840, a 37-year-old farmer J. H. Ahlers from "Hannover" arrived with his wife and small daughter. On December 9, 1843, Gerhard Ahlers, 47, and Hermann Ahlers, 17, both farmers and from "Alshausen [*sic*]," landed. This reference may be to one of the communities named "Ahlshausen" in Southern Hannover, or perhaps to Alfhausen near Quakenbrück, northwest of the city of Hannover. NA. Microcopy 259, Rolls 20, 23. Passenger Lists of Vessels Arriving at New Orleans. We have no proof that any of these Ahlers went to Texas.

81. It is noteworthy that Friedrich Ernst in a letter to a Texas newspaper in 1840 stressed that his cigars resembled Cubans. York, *Friedrich Ernst of Industry*, p. 42.

82. Abner J. Strobel, *The Old Plantations and Their Owners of Brazoria County, Texas*, in Travis L. Smith et al., *A History of Brazoria County* [and two other works] (Houston, 1958), p. 55.

83. Willis N. Baer, *The Economic Development of the Cigar Industry in the United States* (Lancaster, Pa., 1933), pp. 41, 44.

84. NA. Microcopy 432, Roll 908. Seventh Census of the U.S., 1850. Population Schedules.

85. The "Agricultural Schedules IV: Agricultural Productions" of the 1850 and 1860 censuses are in the Texas State Archives in Austin, not in the U.S. National Archives.

86. Campbell and Lowe, *Wealth and Power in Antebellum Texas*. This work is based on an evaluation of the censuses of 1850 and 1860.

87. Ibid., pp. 33, 51, 139.

88. My recalculation of the sums in Table 11 in ibid., p. 46. As a result of an obvious error the sum of the wealth percentages in Table 11 is given as 100.0 instead of 100.1 percent.

89. See ibid., pp. 57, 139, 143.

90. Ibid., pp. 58, 144.

91. NA. Microcopy 653, Roll 1289. Eighth Census of the U.S., 1860. Population Schedules.

92. Ibid.

93. Brazoria County Court, Angelton. Marriage Records. A marriage announcement appeared in *The Planter* (Brazoria), August 1, 1845. This announcement is cited in the *Angelton Times*, March 15, 1972. I am indebted to Jack P. Giesecke (Angleton) for this citation of the announcement.

94. The data pertaining to her age given in the various censuses are inconsistent, but her gravestone in the old cemetery in present-day West Columbia, Texas, indicating she was born in 1825 appears to be reliable. Asa A. Giesecke (West Columbia) saw the stone there. Letter of February 2, 1976 from Jack P. Giesecke.

95. Gifford White, ed., *1830 Citizens of Texas* (Austin, 1983), p. 40. However, other important records list him as arriving in Texas in 1834 and applying for a land grant only in October 1835. Williams, *Stephen F. Austin's Register of Families*, p. 154. Creighton, *Narrative History of Brazoria, County*, p. 25, gives the date for the family's arrival in Texas as 1835.

96. Mullins, *First Census of Texas*, p. 47.

97. Webb et al., *Handbook of Texas*, 1: 958; Creighton, *Narrative History of Brazoria County*, pp. 25, 116. Thomas Kincheloe Davis may have spent some time in Austin's Colony earlier. Its Census of 1826 has an entry for Thomas Davis. See Mullins, *First Census of Texas*, p. 44.

98. White, *1840 Census of the Republic of Texas*, p. 20.

99. See Creighton, *Narrative History of Brazoria County*, p. 504.

100. NA. Microcopy 432, Roll 908. Seventh Census of the U.S., 1850. Population Schedules.

101. Texas State Archives. Seventh Census of the U.S., Schedule IV.

102. Ibid. The results of Schedule IV of the Census of 1860 for Davis cannot be located. This is either the result of an oversight, or because they are with the data from another post office. The census of 1850 includes data from the entire county entered on sequential sheets. In 1860, however, the agriculturalists are entered by the post office.

103. NA. Microcopy 653, Roll 1309. Eighth Census of the U.S., 1860. Slave Schedules.

104. Brazoria County Court, Angelton. The will is dated 1872 and was presented to the Probate Court in Brazoria in 1879. I am indebted to Asa A. Giesecke of West Columbia for a copy of the will.

105. The most important family traditions are documented above.

106. The belief of twentieth-century Texas Gieseckes that their ancestor Charles Giesecke arrived in Texas in 1824 may result from confusion with the Martin Varner for whom Varner's Creek is named; at least part of the land received by Varner in 1824 subsequently belonged to Charles Giesecke. On Varner see Webb et al., *Handbook of Texas*, 2: 834–835; Platter, "Educational, Social, and Economic Characteristics of the Plantation Culture of Brazoria County," pp. 176, 181.

107. This last assertion is probably correct. See Creighton, *Narrative History of Brazoria County*, p. 118. The man in question was Jesse Kincheloe Davis, the twin brother of her father, Thomas Kincheloe Davis.

108. This particular classification is reminiscent of assertions during and after World War I that U.S. General John J. Pershing's ancestors, who emigrated in the eighteenth century from a German-speaking district of Western Europe near the Rhine, came originally from Alsace, spoke both French and German, and descended from a Huguenot family. See Edgar J. Pershing, *The Pershing Family in America* (Philadelphia, 1924), pp. vii, 13, 15.

109. See Chart of the Giesecke Family in the present volume.

110. Although I have been unable to establish any nineteenth-century evidential basis for the stories in this paragraph, many aspects of them are plausible. The New York ship passenger lists do not contain Charles Giesecke's name. NA. Microcopy 237, Rolls 1–37. Passenger Lists of Vessels Arriving at New York, 1820–1897. My inquiries to Mexican archives failed to locate passenger lists for the harbors of Velasco, Quintana, Brazoria, and Columbia. His name is absent from the incomplete published guides to matriculants at German universities. See, e.g., Götz von Selle, ed., *Die Matrikel der Georg-August-Universität zu Göttingen 1734–1837* (Hildesheim, 1937).

111. Heinrich Meyer [pseud. H. K. Houston Meyer], *Konrad Bäumlers weiter Weg: Ein Texas-Deutscher Roman* (Stuttgart, 1938).

112. See the autobiography by Heinrich Meyer, *Was bleibt: Bemerkungen über Literatur und Leben, Schein und Wirklichkeit* (Stuttgart, 1966), p. 154.

113. Dunt, *Reise nach Texas*, p. 59.

114. See Barker, *Austin Papers*, 2: 243. See also Webb et al., *Handbook of Texas History*, 2: 834.

115. Friedrich Höhne, *Wahn und Überzeugung. Reise des Kupferschmiede-Meisters Friedrich Höhne in Weimar über Bremen nach Nordamerika und Texas in den Jahren 1839, 1840 und 1841* (Weimar, 1844), p. 195.

116. See the tables in N. Doran Maillard, *The History of the Republic of Texas . . . and the Cause of Her Separation from the Republic of Mexico* (London, 1842), pp. 357, 360; William M. Gouge, *The Fiscal History of Texas* (Philadelphia, 1852), p. 282.

117. Edmund T. Miller, *A Financial History of Texas* (Austin, 1916), p. 31.

118. Curlee [Holbrook], "A Study of Texas Slave Plantations," pp. 177–178, 181, 183–184; William R. Johnson, *A Short History of the Sugar Industry in Texas* (Houston, 1961), p. 13; J. Carlyle Sitterson, *Sugar County: The Cane Sugar Industry in the South, 1753–1950* (Lexington, Ky., [1953?]), pp. 30, 41–43. Johnson and

Sitterson base their accounts of sugar production in antebellum Texas largely on Curlee's work.

119. Curlee [Holbrook], "A Study of Texas Slave Plantations," p. 188; Platter, "Educational, Social, and Economic Characteristics of the Plantation Culture of Brazoria County," p. 48; Creighton, *Narrative History of Brazoria County*, ch. 10.

120. Curlee [Holbrook], "A Study of Texas Slave Plantations," pp. 181–183.

121. See ibid., p. 183. See also Platter, "Educational, Social, and Economic Characteristics of the Plantation Culture of Brazoria County," pp. 46–48. Giesecke may also have realized that the Texans would prefer other alcoholic beverages to rum.

122. For a breathtaking description of these distilleries see Fleischmann, *Erwerbszweige, Fabrikwesen und Handel der Vereinigten Staaten*, pp. 322–324. Texas remained without a significant distillery during the entire antebellum period. See Muir, "Destiny of Buffalo Bayou," p. 93.

123. Von Reden, *Das Königreich Hannover*, 1: 436.

124. See the chart in ibid., 1: 518–521.

125. For an assessment of the state of the research see Walter Struve, "German Merchants, German Artisans, and Texas during the 1830's and 1840's," *Yearbook of German-American Studies* 23 (1988): 91–92, 98.

126. Siegfried Müller, "Gesellenwandern in der ersten Hälfte des 19. Jahrhunderts, dargestellt am Beispiel Hannovers," *Historisches Jahrbuch* 107 (1987): 83–86. Klaus Bade argues in a provocative article that the *Wanderzwang*, the requirement that journeymen seek work in a community other than that where they were trained, was introduced in the eighteenth century as a means of relieving pressure on overcrowded occupations and ensuring adequate work (*Nahrung*) for local artisans. Klaus J. Bade, "Altes Handwerk, Wanderzwang und 'gute Polizey:' Gesellenwanderung zwischen Zunftökonomie und Gewerbereform," *Sozial- und Wirtschaftsgeschichte* 69 (1982): 1–37.

127. Carl Wittke, *The Utopian Communist: A Biography of Wilhelm Weitling* (Baton Rouge, La., 1950), p. 19.

128. Wolf-Heino Struck, "Die Auswanderung aus Hessen und Nassau in die Vereinigten Staaten," *Nassauische Annalen* 89 (1978): 97, n. 139; Bruce C. Levine, "In the Heat of Two Revolutions: The Forging of German-American Radicalism," in *"Struggle a Hard Battle": Essays on Working-Class Immigrants*, ed. Dirk Hoerder (DeKalb, Ill., 1986), p. 21. On the general issue of artisan emigration and its motivation see Dirk Hoerder, "An Introduction to Labor Migration in the Atlantic Economies, 1815–1914" in Hoerder, *Labor Migration in the Atlantic Economies*, p. 6. See also Helbich, Kamphoefner, and Sommer, *Briefe aus Amerika*, pp. 276–277.

129. Hesse, "Nicholas Hesse," p. 140.

130. Ibid., pp. 140–152.

131. Robert Ernst, *Immigrant Life in New York City, 1825–1863* (New York, 1949), pp. 214–217; Theodore Hershberg et al., "Occupation and Ethnicity in Five Nineteenth-Century Cities: A Collaborative Inquiry," *Historical Methods Newsletter* 7 (1974): 197, 214; Dean R. Esslinger, *Immigration and the City: Eth-*

nicity and Mobility in a Nineteenth-Century Midwestern Community (Port Washington, N.Y., 1975), p. 84; Conzen, *Immigrant Milwaukee*, pp. 67, 69, 73, 95–113; Bruce Laurie, Theodore Hershberg, and George Alter, "Immigrants and Industry: The Philadelphia Experience, 1850–1880," in *Philadelphia: Work, Space, Family, and Group Experience in the Nineteenth Century*, ed. Theodore Hershberg (New York, 1981), p. 109; Agnes Bretting, *Soziale Probleme deutscher Einwanderer in New York City 1800–1860* (Wiesbaden, 1981), pp. 192–194; Hartmut Keil, "German Workers in Nineteenth-Century America: Working-Class Culture and Everyday Life in an Urban Industrial Setting," in Trommler and McVeigh, *America and the Germans*, 1: 191; Levine, "In the Heat of Two Revolutions"; Bruce C. Levine, "Free Soil, Free Labor, and *Freimänner*: German Chicago in the Civil War Era," in Keil and Jentz, *German Workers in Industrial Chicago*, p. 164. Conzen (p. 73) provides a table that conveniently brings together the results of several studies of cities. Bretting's statistics are derived from Ernst.

132. Charles van Ravenswaay, *The Arts and Architecture of German Settlements in Missouri: A Survey of a Vanishing Culture* (Columbia, Mo., 1977), esp. pp. 301–309.

133. A study of the New Braunfels area observes that the second largest occupational group among young immigrant Germans consisted of artisans and craftsmen. The largest occupational group was wagoners and laborers. Lauren A. Kattner, "Growing Up and Town Development: Social and Cultural Adaptation in a German-American Town," master's thesis, University of Texas at Dallas (1987), p. 17.

134. Von Behr, *Guter Rath für Auswanderer*, p. iii.

135. Bromme, *Neuestes, vollständigstes Hand- und Reisebuch für Auswanderer*, p. 303.

136. His name appears neither on the surviving ship's lists nor in reference works such as Geue and Geue, *A New Land Beckoned*.

137. Ibid., p. 133.

138. Pohlmann later went to New Braunfels and died there prematurely at age 21 or 22 on November 11, 1846. Ibid., p. 133. See also Ferdinand A. von Schwedler, "Deutsche Einwanderer in Texas (USA) 1844," *Genealogie* 17 (1968): 157.

139. Bretting's work closes a gaping hole in the general literature, but since she made little or no use of the archives in Hannover and Bremen, a pressing need for a study of Lower Saxony still exists. See Agnes Bretting and Hartmut Bickelmann, *Auswanderungsagenturen und Auswanderungsvereine im 19. und 20. Jahrhundert* (Stuttgart, 1991). This is actually two monographs published under one title.

140. *Hildesheimer Zeitung*, July 31, 1846. I am grateful to Jürgen Huck for a newspaper clipping that first directed my attention to this subject: H. Knösel, "Vor 100 Jahren ausgewandert. Auswanderungsagenturen gab es in Alfeld, Elze und Sack," *Alfelder Zeitung*, January 11, 1965. This article mentions advertisements by Friedrich Giesecke starting only in 1848.

141. *Hildesheimer Zeitung*, July 31, 1846.

142. Knösel, "Vor 100 Jahren ausgewandert."

143. Ibid.

144. See, e.g., K. H. Kaufhold, "Handel und Industrie 1800–1850," in Aubin and Zorn, *Handbuch der deutschen Wirtschafts- und Sozialgeschichte*, 2: 323–327.

145. See above all, Werner Conze, "Sozialgeschichte 1800–1850," in Aubin and Zorn, *Handbuch der deutschen Wirtschafts- und Sozialgeschichte*, p. 439. See also Wilhelm Abel, ed., *Handwerksgeschichte in neuer Sicht* (Göttingen, 1970), pp. 114–115; Martha Scale, "Zur Entwicklung von Handwerk und Industrie in einer niedersächsischen Kleinstadt in der ersten Hälfte des 19. Jahrhunderts. Dargestellt am Beispiel der Stadt Alfeld," in Abel, *Handwerksgeschichte in neuer Sicht*, pp. 173–202. On the social conditions encouraging handicraftsmen to emigrate see also Beutin, *Bremen und Amerika*, p. 45; Theodore Hamerow, *Restoration, Revolution, Reaction: Economics and Politics in Germany, 1815–1871* (Princeton, 1958), pp. 75–87; Walker, *Germany and the Emigration*, pp. 47, 51–52; Marschalck, *Deutsche Überseewanderung im 19. Jahrhundert*, p. 12.

146. Ira Berlin and Herbert G. Gutman, "Natives and Immigrants, Free Men and Slaves: Urban Workingmen in the Antebellum American South," *American Historical Review* 88 (1983): 1178–1180, 1187–1188. See also Bruce Laurie, *Artisans into Workers: Labor in Nineteenth-Century Europe* (New York, 1989). Berlin and Gutman neglect to tap the resources of the admittedly difficult to use ship passenger lists.

147. The above figures are derived from Carpenter, *Seventh Census of the United States*, 1: 209–227.

148. Sheridan, *Galveston Island*, p. 46. The diary of a German craftsman in Houston during the 1830s was published posthumously: Gustav Dresel, "Tagebuch von Gustav Dresel über seinen Aufenthalt in Texas 1837–41," ed. Julius Goebel, *Jahrbuch der Deutsch-Amerikanischen Historischen Gesellschaft von Illinois* 20–21 (1920–1921): 338–476.

149. Adam Struve, "Economic Mobility among Foreign-Born Artisans in the Antebellum Lower South: The Case of Galveston, Texas," typescript, 1986, Table 1. As noted below, I am also indebted to my son Adam for other material on immigrant artisans in Texas.

150. Jane Jacobs, *Cities and the Wealth of Nations: Principles of Economic Life* (New York, 1985).

151. Carpenter, *Seventh Census of the United States*, 2: 757–807. My statistics do not include rural Dickinson's Bayou, which, although part of Galveston County, was enumerated separately. In the remainder of the county, which included some rural areas, there were 366 German-born men aged 18 and over. Of these, 207 were non-artisans or had no occupation listed; 159 were artisans. See also the appendix to Struve, "German Merchants, German Artisans, and Texas during the 1830's and 1840's," pp. 99–100.

152. See, for example, Höhne, *Wahn und Überzeugung*.

153. See ibid.

154. Unfortunately two important reference works with lists of German immigrants fail to specify occupations: Geue and Geue, *A New Land Beckoned*; Geue, *New Homes in a New Land*.

155. Adam Struve, "Artisans among Galveston-Bound Immigrants, 1846–1850," typescript, 1985. This essay exploits recently published passenger lists: Galveston County Genealogical Society, *Ships Passenger Lists: Port of Galveston, Texas, 1846–1871* (Easley, S.C., 1984).

156. Aubin and Zorn, *Handbuch der deutschen Wirtschafts- und Sozialgeschichte,* 2: 324, cited in A. Struve, "Artisans among Galveston-Bound Immigrants."

157. A. Struve, "Artisans among Galveston-Bound Immigrants." The statistics for the United States were calculated from William J. Bromwell, *History of Immigration to the United States* (New York, 1856).

158. NHH. Hannover. Hann. 80 Hildesheim I E Nr. 212, Bd. 2.

159. Michael Piore, *Birds of Passage: Migrant Labor and Industrial Societies* (Cambridge, 1980), p. 138.

160. Johann Georg Friedrich Renner, *Aus der Geschichte der Stadt Osterode am Harz* (Osterode am Harz, 1977), p. 74. The first edition appeared in 1833. The six men were "ein Kandidat der Theologie, ein Schulamtskandidat, zwei Kaufmannsdiener, ein Apothekergehilfe, ein Tischlergeselle."

161. The family name Lehnhoff was common in Elze. See NHH. Gronau II E. Nr. 7. Part of the same record group contains a file about the establishment of a ropemaker's guild in Elze in 1844. Hann. 74 Gronau VIII (Polizeisachen und Gewerbe). However, a member of a Lehnhoff family from Elze believes that Conrad Lehnhoff was not from Elze proper. Information from the apothecary Hans Lehnhoff of Hannover.

Epilogue

1. For comparative purposes, see a study of Bavaria by a historical sociologist: Werner von der Ohe, "Bayern im 19. Jahrhundert — ein Entwicklungsland? Möglichkeiten und Grenzen des Beitrags der vergleichenden Sozialforschung," in *Aufbruch ins Industriezeitalter,* edited by Claus Grimm, vol. 1: *Linien der Entwicklungsgeschichte* (Munich, 1985). Von der Ohe is interested mainly in the process of industrialization, but his work has broad implications.

2. Bowman, *Masters and Lords.* For Germany, see also Jerome Blum, *The End of the Old Order in Rural Europe* (Princeton, 1978).

3. Hayes, *Galveston,* 2: 718/-719. See also Schlecht, *Mein Ausflug nach Texas,* p. 48.

4. Hayes, *Galveston,* 2: 953; Morrison, *Industries of Galveston.*

5. R.G. Dun, Handwritten Credit Ledgers, vol. 13, pp. 49, 266; Dun, Barlow & Co., *The Mercantile Agency Reference Book (and Key). Contains Ratings of the Merchants, Manufacturers, and Traders Generally Throughout the United States and Canada. July 1871* (New York, 1871), entry for Kauffman & Runge; Morrison, *Industries of Galveston;* Howard Barnstone, *The Galveston That Was* (New York, 1966), p. 98.

6. Probate Records of the Giesecke minors, 1876–1879, Brazoria County Courthouse. Angleton, Tex.

7. Ibid. The deceased Edward's only child, a daughter, received $213 after the

costs of the intermediaries were deducted. Charles had five living children whose shares were correspondingly less except for the two youngest, who were still minors in 1876 at the time of the distribution. Because of the additional administrative charges, these two found themselves with a mere $15 each.

8. Fleischmann, *Erwerbszweige, Fabrikwesen und Handel der Vereinigten Staaten*, p. 537.

9. For a recent study of the critical role of merchants, many of them immigrants, on another frontier, see Kim M. Gruenwald, "Settling the Old Northwest: Changing Family and Commercial Strategies in the Early Republic," Ph.D. diss., University of Colorado, 1994.

10. Abigail Curlee Holbrook, "Robert Mills" in Webb et al., *Handbook of Texas*, 2: 200.

11. Elliott R. Barkan, "Race, Religion, and Nationality in American Society: A Model of Ethnicity — From Contact to Assimilation," *Journal of American Ethnic History* 14 (1995): 38–75. See also the responses by Rudolph J. Vecoli, Richard D. Alba, and Oliver Zunz, as well as Barkan's rejoinder, in the same issue of the same periodical, pp. 76–101; see also Kazal, "Revisiting Assimilation."

12. Some examples: Nadel, *Little Germany*, esp. pp. 153–154; Keil, *German Workers' Culture in the United States*; Keil and Jentz, *German Workers in Industrial Chicago*; Reinhard R. Doerries, *Iren und Deutsche in der Neuen Welt: Akkulturationsprozesse in der amerikanischen Gesellschaft im späten neunzehnten Jahrhundert* (Stuttgart, 1985).

13. Hermann Hagedorn, *The Hyphenated Family: An American Saga* (New York, 1960).

14. The author of a perceptive work on German-language imaginative literature on the United States comments on the presence of a piano in the novels and stories she examines as "the classical musical instrument of the bourgeoisie of the Biedermeier period." Mikoletzky, *Die deutsche Amerika-Auswanderung des 19. Jahrhunderts in der zeitgenössischen fiktionalen Literatur*, p. 235. Mikoletzky implies misleadingly that the piano was a distinctively German instrument.

APPENDIX — LETTERS

1. See Walter Struve, "Deutsch in Amerika?" *literatur-express* 2 (1989): 12–13.

2. For a discussion of this communication from Brauer see notes below to Charles's letter of October 30, 1845.

3. A schooner brig, the *Weser*, belonged to the Bremen firm C. L. Brauer & Son. It returned to Bremen on May 18, 1844. The vessel sailed frequently (beginning as early as 1843?) between Bremen and Galveston. *Verzeichnis der bremischen Seeschiffe für das Jahr 1844* (Bremen, [1844?]); SAB. 2 — R. 11. e. 3. Bd. 3. Copies of the *Verzeichnis* for 1844 and 1845 are in the University Library in Bremen. See also "Brauer" in Index of the present work.

4. A bale of cotton weighed about 181 kilograms, or 333 pounds. Pitsch, *Die wirtschaftlichen Beziehungen Bremens zu den Vereinigten Staaten*, p. 162.

5. A brig *Antoinette* belonged to the Bremen firm A. Unkraut & Son. *Ver-*

zeichnis der bremischen Seeschiffe für das Jahr 1844. The *Antoinette* arrived from Galveston at a Weser port on October 11, 1844 (for the second time that same year?). Its cargo included tobacco and cotton for the firm C. L. Brauer & Son. Archive of the Chamber of Commerce, Bremen. E. II. a. Liste der eingekommenen Waren 1844.

6. From various censuses, passenger lists, references works, and other sources we know of several people named Stuart, Steward, and/or Steurt in Brazoria before 1845. Most likely, the reference is to J. McNeal Steurt, who in 1840 owned two and a half lots in the town of Brazoria. White, *1840 Census of the Republic of Texas*, p. 23. The next most likely possibility is Charles B. Stewart, who had a pharmacy in Brazoria but moved, perhaps as early as 1835, to San Felipe de Austin. Webb et al., *Handbook of Texas*, 2: 671–672. The third possibility is a Dr. Stewart, who presumably died in a duel about 1837. James, *The Raven*, p. 303. Confusion of this Dr. Stewart with Charles B. Steward has occurred in the historical literature. See, for example, Elizabeth Le Noir Jennett, ed., *Biographical Dictionary of the Texan Conventions and Congresses, 1812–1845* (n.p., [1941?]), p. 176.

7. The Mills brothers were merchants and planters. See Index.

8. Probably from Germany.

9. *Rote solidi?* This jargon means cash, which is clearly the general meaning of the abbreviation. However, the handwriting is unclear. The abbreviation may actually read RLL, which could refer to one of three other possibilities: (1) An encoded sum. (2) *Reales* or *regalia libra*, terms pertaining to the Spanish and Mexican monetary unit and silver coin known to Americans as a "bit" (as in the expression "two bits") and valued eight to a dollar. (3) *Riales*; the *rial* was a gold coin that also circulated in the Republic of Texas and was valued at 10 shillings. See Carlson, *A Monetary and Banking History of Texas*, p. 6. See also Edward W. Neusinger, "The Monetary History of the Republic of Texas," *Southwestern Historical Quarterly* 57 (1953): 82–90; Louis Lenz, "Texas Money," *Southwestern Historical Quarterly* 51 (1953): 175–180.

10. A German who worked for the Gieseckes. See Index.

11. See Glossary.

12. See Glossary.

13. Refers probably to Christ. Meyer, a linen merchant [*Linnenklanderer*] in Bremen. *Adreßbuch der Freien Hansestadt Bremen* (Bremen, 1844 and 1846 editions).

14. Alfelder pertains to the town of Alfeld. *Stiege* is an old German designation for 20, the equivalent of an English "score." *Stiege* linen was cut into lengths of 20 ells. "Alfelder *Stiege* linen" was one of many simple "Osnabrücker linens" often sold in the Caribbean area and in South America. See von Reden, *Das Königreich Hannover*, 1: 344. Such linens were commonly used for slaves' clothes.

15. See Glossary.

16. See Glossary.

17. Fabrics in Germany were sometimes sold in units of double ells.

18. The reference is to the German foot. See Glossary.

19. Bodenwerder is on the Weser some 12 miles southwest of Elze. The little

town is best known as the residence of the notorious "Lying Baron," Hieronymus Münchhausen (died 1797), whom Karl Immermann immortalized in literature in 1838 in the novel *Münchhausen*.

20. *Halbladen* pertains to a fabric width or size. *Halbla[c]ken* designated an inexpensive weave made partly of linen yarn and partly of a coarser fiber such as hemp.

21. Captain of the schooner brig *Weser* and, within a year, of the newly built bark *Neptun*, both owned by C. L. Brauer & Son. For the *Weser* and the *Neptun* see Index.

22. Either Christoph *Carl* Basse, the Giesecke brothers' uncle residing in Elze, or, less likely, Christoph Carl Basse's brother, Friedrich Heinrich Basse, a manufacturer of white lead in Bremen. Inconclusive evidence indicates that the latter Basse died in 1844. Christoph Carl Basse and his wife, Sophie Friederike Christine neé Sander, were childless; she was one of the older sisters of Charles Giesecke's mother. The Basses were a patrician family in Elze. The wife of Charles's brother Friedrich also was a Basse, but from the Bremen branch of the family. Marriages between members of successive generations among German (and other) merchant families of the era were common, occasionally involved cousins, and served to counteract the dispersal of financial resources. When the marriage partners came from different cities or towns, the nuptials created useful geographical ties. The relationship among the Gieseckes, Sanders, and Basses was particularly close, but by no means unusual. As late as the 1890s Friedrich Giesecke's son Carl turned to his cousin Doris Basse of Schwerin in Mecklenburg when he found himself in business and personal difficulties. For the Basse family see also Index. On the role of marriage and family relationships in Germany see a monograph with broader implications than the title suggests: Marion A. Kaplan, *The Making of the Jewish Middle Class: Women, Family, and Identity in Imperial Germany* (Oxford, 1991).

23. The nickname of Friederike Giesecke, the youngest of the Giesecke siblings. Still unmarried, she lived with her mother in Elze.

24. The last two words are in English in the original. In 1844 Friedrich Giesecke had married *Marie* Henriette Sophie Basse of Bremen. She was the daughter of the brother of his uncle by marriage.

25. A firm in Bremen. See Index.

26. From Lauenau in the Kingdom of Hannover, he had recently arrived at age 20 in Texas. See Index.

27. Charles is being humorous. Fusel oil is a poisonous substance often present in rotgut and other improperly distilled liquor.

28. Charles means Elze or Germany and alludes to a recent visit. There is other evidence in his letters that he returned to Texas in late 1843 or early 1844. See, e.g., his letter of March 16, 1844.

29. See Glossary.

30. A small keg. See Glossary.

31. Charles is referring to the entire Kingdom of Hannover, the Duchy of Brunswick, and the Hildesheim district.

32. This and some of Charles Giesecke's other discussions of cigars are remark-

ably similar, even in wording, to those of Friedrich Ernst in a letter in English dated April 14, 1845, to Houston's *Texas Telegraph and Register*. Other communications by Ernst on cigars were published in the same newspaper in 1840 and 1848, but these do not bear the same striking resemblance to Giesecke's remarks to his brother. See the extensive quotations from Ernst's letters in York, *Friedrich Ernst of Industry*, pp. 34–43.

33. A Bremen brig that often sailed between Bremen and Galveston with *Adelsverein* passengers.

34. Another Bremen bark that was owned by C. L Brauer & Son and often sailed with *Adelsverein* passengers.

35. There follows a long list very similar to that in the letter of March 7, 1845. The two lists are apparently different versions of the same order. Both the letter of February 18 and that of March 7 were likely sent some weeks later. They reached Fritz Giesecke by different routes. The letter of March 7, 1845, was probably packed in a shipment of goods, as Charles implies. Part of this same letter was written on what would normally have been its outside, including the address side. Although sealed and fully addressed, it was not franked. See n. 67 below.

36. The physician, Peter W. Gautier, formerly of South Carolina, owned a plantation in Brazoria County. In 1850 he was credited with 20 slaves. NA. Microcopy 432, Rolls 908 and 917. Seventh Census of the U.S., 1850. Population and Slave Schedules. Gautier was a vigorous proponent of U.S. statehood for Texas. Lubbock, *Six Decades in Texas*, p. 167.

37. Both "sweet potatoes" and "corn" are in English.

38. Charles means that their brother Edward is unreliable.

39. See the preceding letters.

40. A German firm with which the Gieseckes had many ties. In Texas the name was usually spelled "Kauffman" in English. See Index.

41. The town of Schwabach in Middle Franconia, Bavaria, was an old needle-making center.

42. A heavy cotton fabric.

43. Located in Westphalia, Bielefeld was an old linen-weaving center some 70 miles west of Elze.

44. The expression "English" here and elsewhere in these letters in connection with merchandise refers to a grade of merchandise, not the place of manufacture.

45. Sarcasm. Charles refers to defective socks from Germany. See his letter of January 24, 1845.

46. Refers to the width.

47. Probably for medicinal purposes.

48. *Haidmanschester*, a coarse cotton fabric.

49. Originally a light French worsted.

50. Refers to width.

51. A heavy woven fabric.

52. A coat of the *Biedermeier* era that was made from a coarse woolen weave similar to sheepskin.

53. Schürhof was the name of a firm. Gevelsberg in the Ruhr was an old metal-industry center producing scythes and other agricultural implements.

54. German: *Zoll*. In most parts of Germany the *Zoll* was somewhat less than a U.S. inch. See also Glossary under "Foot."

55. A heavy silk fabric.

56. An old North German liquid measure equal to four to five quarts depending on the region. In Hannover the *Stübchen* held slightly more than a U.S. gallon — 4.12 quarts.

57. The German is "6 *Schock*." A *Schock* was an old North German term for 60. It continued to be used for some merchandise, especially linen, during much of the nineteenth century.

58. Among the items on the deleted list of February 18, but not on that of March 7, are 1 gross of mother-of-pearl shirt buttons, 6 dozen machine-made buttons, and 12 pieces of muslin, "each piece enough for a dress."

59. Pertains to Friedrich Giesecke's "courtship" leading to his marriage the preceding year.

60. Edward Giesecke had married Lisette Doby from Mecklenburg on October 21, 1844. Charles implies disdainfully that his new sister-in-law is uncultured, cannot speak High German correctly, and uses a Mecklenburg variant of the Low German (*Plattdeutsch*) dialects employed by the lower classes in North Germany. Generalizing about the territory of the Hannoverian state, Reinhard Oberschelp writes that by the early nineteenth century the language normally used by the upper classes was High German. He quotes a contemporary to the effect that Low German formed "an almost impenetrable barrier between" the lower estates, on the one side, and the higher, educated estates, on the other. Oberschelp, *Niedersachsen 1760–1820*, 2: 162; see also p. 159. Wilhelm Wachsmuth provides a suggestive perspective on the use of Low German in Charles's native Hildesheim district after the Reformation: "It [Low German] was also not entirely scorned in higher circles. On the contrary, it was used with pleasure in circumstances of warm familiarity. *Above all, Catholics liked to employ it* [my italics]." Wachsmuth, *Geschichte von Hochstift und Stadt Hildesheim* (Hildesheim, 1863), p. 250. Such attitudes may further explain the aversion of Hildesheim Protestants to Low German. As a descendant of Lutherans, including pastors, Charles had strong local or regional reasons for disliking Low German. Another important exception to the use of Low German is Protestant Bremen. There it continued to have a strong influence on the speech of the entire population. Indeed, the resilience of Low German in nineteenth-century Bremen became almost mythical. See Adam Storck, *Ansichten der Freien Hansestadt Bremen und ihrer Umgebung* (Frankfurt am Main, 1822), p. 372; Schaefer, *Bremens Bevölkerung*, p. 55.

61. Timothy Pilsbury had a farm in the Brazoria area. He was a former representative and senator of the Texas Republic. After serving as chief justice of Brazoria County, he returned in 1844 to the Texas Senate. On April 14, 1845, he was to chair a public meeting in Brazoria calling for the entry of Texas into the United States. Later that same year he was elected to the U.S. Congress from Texas. White,

1840 Census of the Republic of Texas, p. 23; Carpenter, *Seventh Census of the United States*, 1: 212; Jennett, *Biographical Dictionary of the Texan Conventions and Congresses*, p. 154; Platter, "Educational, Social, and Economic Characteristics of the Plantation Culture of Brazoria County, Texas," p. 154; Webb et al., *Handbook of Texas*, 2: 379; Creighton, *Narrative History of Brazoria County*, pp. 185, 187. In 1850 Pilsbury owned 10 slaves. NA. Microcopy 432, Roll 917. Seventh Census of the U.S., 1850. Slave Schedules.

62. *Schweinigel.*

63. *Scheißboutik*, literally "shit shop."

64. Charles's derogatory term for Edward's wife.

65. There is a large rip in the letter at this point. A word or two may be missing, perhaps "again."

66. Although Charles Giesecke was writing amid events that confused many of his contemporaries, his prediction was accurate. In June 1844 the U.S. Senate had rejected a treaty with the Lone Star Republic that would have made Texas a state. The winner of the presidential election of 1844, James K. Polk, had favored statehood for Texas during the campaign. On March 1, 1845, shortly before he assumed office, the U.S. Congress passed a resolution in favor of statehood. President John Tyler, in one of his last actions in office, offered Texas membership in the Union. President Anson Jones of Texas responded by summoning an assembly that would take a position on the offer and draft a new constitution for the State of Texas should the U.S. proposal be accepted. Charles was writing his letter at this point in the chain of events. Next the Congress of Texas voted in June 1845 to accept the proposal and therefore rejected a treaty of recognition and friendship with Mexico. The assembly convened in Texas by Anson Jones accepted the U.S. offer on July 4, 1845. Subsequently, the U.S. Congress approved the new constitution of Texas, and on December 29, 1845, President Polk proclaimed statehood for Texas. Although Texas officially became a member of the Union on this day, an interregnum ensued. The newly elected officeholders of the State of Texas did not replace the officeholders of the Lone Star Republic until February 19, 1846. During this interregnum Texas and the United States bargained over many unresolved issues pertaining to the status of Texas.

67. This letter, although sealed, is addressed simply to "Mr. Fr. Giesecke, Elze." There is no indication that postage was paid. It was enclosed in one of the other letters Charles mentions at the end of this one, or, more likely, in a subsequent letter or shipment.

68. It has not been possible to identify this brother with certainty, but there are two candidates: The first is Heinrich Christoph Conrad Pohlmann from "Horst." Unfortunately there was more than one community of this name in Hannover, and it is unclear which is meant. This Pohlmann arrived from Bremen in 1845 with the Brig *Weser* in Galveston. Geue and Geue, *A New Land Beckoned*, p. 133. The second possibility is H. Pohlmann, a 22-year-old farmer who arrived from Bremen with the ship *Olbers* in New Orleans on June 13, 1845. The name of his home town is not given on the passenger list. NA. Microcopy 259, Roll 24. Passenger Lists

of Vessels Arriving at New Orleans. Quarterly Abstract. As indicated above, lists from the Quarterly Abstracts are occasionally substituted in the microcopies for lists missing from the passenger lists.

69. An allusion to a German saying: "Die Schwaben werden erst im vierzigsten Jahre gescheit." ("The Swabians come to their senses only in their fortieth year.") Friedrich Giesecke still had four years to go before he reached this age of reason.

70. A German saying as well as an English-language one.

71. This description is borne out by an informed contemporary's classification of Regalia as one of the best types of cigars. Fleischmann, *Erwerbszweige, Fabrikwesen und Handel der Vereinigten Staaten*, p. 86. The previously mentioned Galveston firm Ed. Kauffman & Co. advertised on February 18, 1843, in the *Galveston City Gazette* that it had received via the brig *Weser* a shipload of new wares. Among them were 200,000 cigars of various types, including Regalias. SAB. 2 — C. 26. Verhältnisse der Hansestädte zu Texas 1840–1846. Friedrich Ernst's letter of April 14, 1845, to the *Texas Telegraph and Register* discusses at length how to raise tobacco for this same type of cigar. See York, *Friedrich Ernst*, p. 39.

72. Fleischmann estimated that a good worker could not make more than 500 Regalias a day. The same worker could make 1,000 cigars of a "more common sort" and between 1,500 and 2,000 of "the well-known Kentuckies that people have to be satisfied with in the interior sections [of the United States]." Fleischmann, *Erwerbszweige, Fabrikwesen und Handel der Vereinigten Staaten*, p. 86.

73. *Schweinigel.*

74. The *Neptun* sailed from the Weser bound for Galveston with 214 emigrants on October 2, 1845. It did not reach Texas until December 3, 1845. Geue and Geue, *A New Land Beckoned*, p. 168.

75. A diagonally woven fabric originally made entirely of wool, later partly of mohair or cotton, Circassian was suitable in Germany, but not Texas, for summer clothing.

76. A "bit" pertains to a Spanish and Mexican monetary unit and silver coin valued at eight to the dollar. Hence the calico had been selling for the equivalent of 37.5 to 50 cents.

77. "Cash" is in English rather than German.

78. A device with a blade and a box to contain the cuttings.

79. In English in the original.

80. An empty space for the numbers is blank.

81. Friedrich Giesecke's first child, Christoph *Carl* Giesecke, had been born the night of May 1, 1845. The news reached Charles in Texas in less than eight weeks.

82. For preserving food?

83. This brig belonged to Lüdering & Co. of Bremen and made many trips to Galveston with *Adelsverein* emigrants. It left the Weser on April 18, 1845, with 115 emigrants and anchored in Galveston on June 20. On September 12 the same vessel returned to Galveston with more emigrants. It had already set sail from Galveston on September 25. *Verzeichnis der bremischen Seeschiffe für das Jahr 1845* (Bre-

men, [1845?]); Geue and Geue, *A New Land Beckoned*, p. 167. The vessel probably carried the cargo mentioned by Charles on the last-mentioned return journey to Germany.

84. *Faß*. See Glossary.

85. In English in the original.

86. The reference is to an unsuccessful transaction involving a type of brandy. See Charles's letter of June 30, 1845, above.

87. Friedrich may well have seriously contemplated coming. On March 26, 1846, the Bremen firm C. L. Brauer & Son wrote to him about shipments from Texas and went on to inform him: "Our *Neptun* is definitely going to Galveston on April 15. . . . We have only a few cabin accommodations left. . . . Please advise us immediately if you want to travel on it." The letter and a bill for freight from Galveston, also from Brauer, were preserved with Charles Giesecke's letters. Actually, the departure of the *Neptun* may have been delayed. According to official records in Bremen, it did not arrive in port on the Weser until April 29, when it returned with a cargo of cotton from Galveston. SB. 2 — R. 11. e. 3. Bd. 3. However, von Sommer reports that he sailed with the *Neptun* bound for Galveston on April 17. Von Sommer, *Bericht über meine Reise nach Texas*, p. 5. The bill from Brauer included freight for a shipment of tobacco for Friedrich Giesecke labeled "FG No. 30," but not mentioned by Charles in his surviving letters. The freight was for the journey from Galveston on board the bark *Hercules*, a ship owned by C. Melchers & Co. of Bremen. *Verzeichnis der bremischen Seeschiffe für das Jahr 1845*. The *Hercules* had returned on March 7 to the Weser from Galveston with a cargo that included much cotton. SB. 2 — R. 11. e. 3. Bd. 4.

88. Charles is identifying Jacob with Friedrich and the master with their mother.

89. *Faß*. See Glossary.

90. The mail-order bride proposed by Friedrich may have been Theres[i]a Niemann. Aged twenty-two, she arrived by ship from Bremen in New Orleans on October 30, 1845. NA. Microcopy 259, Roll 24. Passenger Lists of Vessels Arriving at New Orleans. Less likely possibilities are two sisters born in Germany, but living together in Galveston in 1850 according to the Census of 1850: Eliza and Frederica Nieman, aged 30 and 32. Carpenter, *Seventh Census of the United States*, 2: 767.

91. Charles and Sarah Ma[r]y Davis were married in Brazoria on July 26, 1845.

92. Friedrich Giesecke's son Christoph *Carl* Giesecke was born on May 2, 1845. News of the christening, which was not held until June 22, was probably contained in Friedrich's letter of June 30, 1845, alluded to by Charles.

93. Rather than representing a coded sum or item, this likely means the equivalent of "not a red cent [*keinerlei Solidi*]."

94. The title is given this way in the original: first in English, then in German.

95. This translation preserves the vagueness of the referent in the German. Charles is alluding to his relationship with his wife.

96. In English, with a translation into German, in the original.

97. For Adolph Pohlmann's fate see Index.

98. *Fässe*. See Glossary under *Faß*.

99. The Giesecke brothers' Aunt Henriette Sophie Horn née Sander and her husband, the surgeon Johann Alhardt Horn. The Horns lived in Gronau.

100. Charles's statement about the coffee implies a much more recent trip by him to Germany than seems likely on the basis of the ship passenger lists and circumstantial evidence elsewhere in the surviving letters. His most recent return from Germany had probably been in late 1843 or early 1844.

GLOSSARY OF WEIGHTS, MEASURES, AND MONETARY UNITS [1]

ANCKER. An old German liquid measure equal to about ten U.S. gallons. As in Charles Giesecke's letters, the term often referred to a keg of this capacity. Taken over from Dutch and German, the term "anker" was once used in English, but probably not much in Texas during the 1840s.

BARREL. When employed as a liquid measure, the English-language term barrel was the equivalent of 32 gallons.

ELL (German, *Elle*). An old measure used especially for textiles. Its length varied widely. In England, it was equal to about 45 inches; in the Low Countries, about 27 inches. In the German states there were over a hundred different ells, varying from less than 20 to over 31 inches.

FOOT (German, *Fuß*). The German foot was divided into twelve *Zoll*. The length of the foot varied in different areas of Central Europe. The Prussian foot was the equivalent of 12.361 English inches, the Hannoverian foot a mere 11.5 inches.

GROSCHEN. A general designation for a small German coin, usually of silver. In the currency systems of most German states the *Thaler* (q. v.) was, by the mid-1840s, divided into 24 *Groschen*, and the latter, in turn, into 12 *Pfennig*. *Groschen* did not constitute part of the currency of Bremen and other German states along the North Sea and Baltic. See also *Grote*.

The standard *Groschen* was also known as a *Gutegroschen* to distinguish it from other types of *Groschen*. A relevant example of the latter is the *Mariengroschen* (q. v.), worth only half as much.

GROTE. A small silver coin that was part of Bremen's currency. Unlike other German states, Bremen had a currency based on a gold standard. A Bremen *Thaler* was divided into 72 *Groten*. Five Bremen *Thaler* had the value of a *Louis d'or*. The smallest of Bremen's coins were *Schwaren*, five of which had the value of a *Grote*. See also *Groschen*.

HOGSHEAD (German, *Oxhoft*). An English and American liquid measure equal to 252 gallons.

MARIENGROSCHEN. Long a type of *Groschen* in some parts of North Germany, including the Kingdom of Hannover and the Duchy of Brunswick. A *Mariengroschen* had half the value of a standard *Groschen*. There were 36 *Mariengroschen* to a *Thaler*. See also *Groschen* and *Grote*.

MORGEN. A land measure: a Prussian *Morgen* was approximately two-thirds of an acre, while a Hannoverian *Morgen* was slightly smaller (0.974 Prussian *Morgen*) and the *Morgen* still in use in the Hildesheim district was even smaller (0.934 Prussian *Morgen*).

REICHSTALER (spelled *"Reichsthaler"* until the twentieth century). A widely used German coin. Commonly referred to simply as a *Thaler*. From 1834 to 1857 it contained 16.704 grams of silver in Hannover.[2] A German work published in 1847 listed a Prussian Thaler as worth 68.5 U.S. cents, and a Bremen Thaler as 78.5 cents.[3]

SCHILLING. Plural: *Schillinge*. (English, shilling). Generally refers to a small German coin unless preceded by some indication that the British shilling is intended. The *Schilling* was more often a part of the monetary systems of the eastern than the western German states.

STIEGE. Plural: *Stiegen*. An old German designation for 20. The English equivalent is a score, but *Stiege* was used especially for linens.

THALER (spelled *Taler* in twentieth-century German). See *Reichstaler*.

GLOSSARY

1. Based primarily on *Der nordamerikanische Freistaat Texas. Ein Führer und Ratgeber für solche, die dahin auswandern wollen* (Heilbronn 1847); Aubin and Zorn, *Handbuch der deutschen Wirtschafts- und Sozialgeschichte*; Fleischmann, *Erwerbszweige, Fabrikwesen und Handel der Vereinigten Staaten*; F. A. Frauendorf, *Der Abbreviator. Hilfsbuch für Schriftsetzer, Korrektoren, Verlagsbuchhändler usw.* (Leipzig, [1888]); Jeschke, *Gewerberecht und Handwerkswirtschaft des Königreichs Hannover*; Friedrich Pauer, *Die Vereinigten Staaten von Nordamerika nach erfolgtem Anschluß der Republik Texas. Mit besonderer Beziehung auf deutsche Auswanderer* (Bremen 1847); von Reden, *Das Königreich Hannover*; Carl von Sommer, *Bericht über meine Reise nach Texas*; Fritz Verdenhalven, ed., *Alte Maße, Münzen und Gewichte aus dem deutschen Sprachgebiet* (Neustadt an der Aisch, 1968).

2. Jeschke, *Gewerberecht und Handwerkswirtschaft des Königreichs Hannover*, p. 508.

3. Pauer, *Die Vereinigten Staaten von Nordamerika nach erfolgtem Anschluß der Republik Texas*, p. 254.

BIBLIOGRAPHICAL ESSAY AND BIBLIOGRAPHY

I.
THE FUTURE OF RESEARCH ON THE ATLANTIC MIGRATION OF GERMANS DURING THE FIRST HALF OF THE NINETEENTH CENTURY

Research on German emigration to the New World and on the closely related topics of commercial and cultural relations between the German-speaking lands and the United States during the antebellum period should seek to bring together the rich sources available on both sides of the Atlantic. Systematic investigations, including statistical studies, can be based on ship passenger lists and census returns in the United States when combined with German sources such as church records, state censuses, and other official data on individuals. The passenger lists form a vast mass of material. Although they have been available on microfilm for some time from the National Archives in Washington, German researchers have neglected them until recently, while Americans have used them primarily for genealogical research. The reputation of the passenger lists as the plaything of family genealogists is unfortunate. The lists provide a wealth of information, all the more revealing because the records are almost complete for most U.S. ports from 1820 onward. These lists can be supplemented with some surviving German passenger lists, mainly from Hamburg, that are located in the State Archives of Hamburg (Staatsarchiv der Freien und Hansestadt Hamburg), as well as with the passenger lists of the principal emigrant ports of France, Britain, Belgium, and the Netherlands. Despite gaps and other problems, the lists are well suited to the statistical analysis of international migration. They contain not only the names of ships and captains, but frequently also the occupations and places of origin of the passengers. The lists could be used, for example, to determine how many persons of a given occupation sailed to America, where they came from, where they intended to go, or how old they were. An ambitious project to publish the American lists in a usable, indexed form began several years ago, under the editorship of Ira A. Glazier and P. William Filby: *Germans to America: Lists of Passengers Arriving at U.S. Ports* (Wilmington, Del., 1988–). Unfortunately, the reliability of this edition is compromised by poor editorial decisions and large-scale transcription errors. See the devastating critique by Antonius Holtmann, "Snares for the Genealogist and the Historian. A Critique," *Newsletter of the Society for German-American Studies* 14 (1993): 17–24.

The letters of German emigrants and those of their correspondents in Europe constitute another underutilized source. Understandably, more has been done with the correspondence of those who departed than with that of those who remained in Europe. A helpful guide to this and much other material in German archives and libraries is offered by *Americana in deutschen Sammlungen: Ein Verzeichnis von Materialien zur Geschichte der Vereinigten Staaten von Amerika in Archiven und Bibliotheken in der BRD und West-Berlin*, Deutsche Gesellschaft für Amerika-Studien (5 vols., mimeo., Cologne, 1967). Unfortunately, this guide is woefully in need of updating and fails to note many of the collections available at the time of its preparation. An instance of an important omitted collection can be found in Porz, in a subsidiary of Cologne's Municipal Archive. That archive has copies of letters sent from Houston during the period 1857–1874 by Balthasar Schmitz, who was born in Porz-Ensen and donated a monument to his native village. (See Heinrich Schneider, "Porzer Wegkreuze," *Unser Porz* 2 [1961]: 20. I am indebted to Jürgen Huck, formerly director of the Porz Archive, for this reference.)

Several published collections of letters about, or sent from, America are available. *Was die Deutschen aus Amerika berichteten 1828–1868*, edited by Maria Wagner (Stuttgart, 1984), contains topically arranged excerpts from a few published works. A collection of Swiss letters skillfully edited by Leo Schelbert and Hedwig Rappolt provides useful glimpses of Swiss German emigrants in America: *Alles ist ganz anders hier: Auswandererschicksale in Briefen aus zwei Jahrhunderten* (Freiburg im Breisgau, 1977). The letters sent from Texas in this Swiss collection date only from the period 1875–1877. The most extensive collection of German letters is *Briefe aus Amerika: Deutsche Auswanderer schreiben aus der Neuen Welt 1830–1930* (Munich, 1988). Wolfgang Helbich, Walter D. Kamphoefner, and Ulrike Sommer, the editors of this volume, go to great lengths to provide helpful information on both the correspondents and the recipients of their letters. An American edition of this last work also is available: *News from the Land of Freedom: German Immigrants Write Home*, translated by Susan C. Vogel (Ithaca, 1991).

II.
BIBLIOGRAPHY

A. Archival and Unpublished Sources

1. Germany

Lower Saxon Central State Archives
(Niedersächsisches Hauptstaatsarchiv) Hannover (NHH).

Hann. 52 Nr. 2485	Beschwerde des Friedr. Giesecke zu Bockenem über den Kanton-maire 1810.
Hann. 52 Nr. 2486	Kommunalpertinenzien der Stadt Bockenem 1810–1812.
Hann. 52 Nr. 2720	Statistische Nachrichten der Stadt Bockenem 1808.
Hann. 72 Elze III A	Stadtgericht Elze. Kontrakte, Meierdingsprotokolle und Ehestif-tungen 1674–1850.
Hann. 72 Elze III B	Stadt Elze. Kontrakte und Ehestif-tungen 1815–1843.
Hann. 72 Elze IX D Nr. 14–18	Amtsgericht Elze. Hypotheken-bücher 1815–1866 und Register.
Hann. 72 Elze IXE Nr. 1	Repertorium der Testamente, Edik-talladungen und Verkäufe des Amtsgerichts Elze. From the eigh-teenth century to the end of the nineteenth century.
Hann. 72 Elze IX E Nr. 2	Testamentenbuch des königlichen Amtsgerichts Elze. From the begin-

	ning to the end of the nineteenth century.
Hann. 74 Gronau IC Nr. 9	Geschäftsberichte des Magistrats zu Elze 1840–1851.
Hann. 74 Gronau IC Nr. 10	Geschäftsberichte des Amts Elze 1852–1858.
Hann. 74 Gronau II D Nr. 1a	Bevölkerungstabellen 1808–1812.
Hann. 74 Gronau II E Nr. 7	Statistik, Volks- u. a. Zählungen in der Stadt Elze in den Jahren 1833, 1836, 1839, 1842, 1848.
Hann. 74 Gronau VI B 8 Nr. 1	Zivilstandsregister der Parochie Elze 1808.
Hann. 74 Gronau VII B 11 Nr. 1	Erbenzinssachen der Stadt Elze 1809–1840.
Hann. 74 Gronau VIII B 2 Nr. 13	Handelsbefugnisse Elzer Bürger 1826–1855.
Hann. 80 Hildesheim I E Nr. 212	Die Auswanderung nach Nord-Amerika und Brasilien 1824–1862.
Hann. 80 Hildesheim Nr. 7272–7275	Die Stadt Bockenem. Register über Einnahmen und Ausgaben 1796–1801.
Hann. 80 Hildesheim Nr. 7819	Amt Wohldenberg. Kopfsteuerregister (auch der Stadt Bockenem) 1758.
Hann. 80 Hildesheim Nr. 8332	Amt Wohldenberg. Kopfsteuerregister (auch der Stadt Bockenem) 1773.
Hann. 80 Hildesheim Nr. 8765	Okular-Landbeschreibung der Stadt Bockenem 1692 (mit einem Einwohnerverzeichnis).

Lower Saxon State Archives
(Niedersächsisches Staatsarchiv) Wolfenbüttel

102 N Gittelde. Bd. 3	Records pertaining to the inhabitants of Gittelde.

Archives of the Free Hanseatic City Bremen
(Staatsarchiv der Freien Hansestadt Bremen [SB]).

2 — B. 13. b. 4.	Hanseatische diplomatische Agenten, Konsuln usw. bei den Vereinigten Staaten von Nordamerika und Korrespondenz mit denselben. New Orleans 1817–1867.
2 — B. 13. b. 12.	Hanseatische diplomatische Agenten, Konsuln usw. bei den Vereinigten Staaten von Nordamerika und Korrespondenz mit denselben. Galveston 1846–1867.
2 — C. 26.	Verhältnisse der Hansestädte zu Texas 1840–1846.
2 — P. 8. b.	Auswanderung 1839–1851.
2 — P. 8. c. 1. a.	Maßregeln dagegen, daß Auswanderer aus den Binnenländern, welche ursprünglich sich für überseeische Länder bestimmt hatten, nicht im Bremischen verbleiben und polizeiliche Maßregeln in Rücksicht auf solche Auswanderer überhaupt 1832 1860.
2 — P. 8. c. 1. b.	Ditto. 1839–1847.
2 — R. 11. e. 1.	Schiffslisten und statistisches Material über Schiffe 1765–1876.
2 — R. 11. e. 2.	Schiffslisten und statistisches Material über Schiffe 1839–1871.

Bibliographical Essay and Bibliography

| 2 — R. 11. e. 3. | Listen der ein- und auslaufenden Schiffe 1837–1850. |

Bürgereidbücher.

Archive of the Chamber of Commerce (Archiv der Handelskammer), Bremen.

| E. II. a. | Listen der eingekommenen Waren 1842, 1844. |

Municipal Archive (Stadtarchiv) Elze (SAE).

III 12.	Kämmerei-Sachen im Allgemeinen betr. Anstellung von Kämmerei-Rechnungsführer 1820/21–1840.
IVC.	Kämmereiregister 1817, 1824.
XIIl Nr. 2	Steuerliste von 1803.
XVl B. Nr. 5	Prozeß-Sachen. Stadt Elze gegen Kämmerer Basse Erben 1825–1855.

Superintendency of the Evangelical Lutheran Church (Superintendentur der evangelisch-lutherischen Kirche), Elze.

Church and parish records (Kirchenbücher).

Municipal Archive (Stadtarchiv) Alfeld.

I. C. 2. Nr. 1	Gesuche um die Erteilung von Auswanderungs-Bescheinigungen 1831–1858.
I. H. 4. d. Nr. 2	Die Errichtung einer Linnen-Legge in Alfeld 1828.
I. H. 4. i. Nr. 83	Erlaubnis zur Übernahme von Agenturen zur Vermittlung von Überfahrtsverträgen nach Überseeischen Häfen im 19. Jahrhundert.

2. United States

U.S. National Archives and Records Service (NA). Washington.

Passenger Lists

Microcopy 237	Passenger Lists of Vessels Arriving at New York, 1820–1897.
Roll 1–37	1820–1839.
Microcopy 255	Passenger Lists of Vessels Arriving at Baltimore, 1820–1891.
Roll 1–2	1820–1840.
Microcopy 259	Passenger Lists of Vessels Arriving at New Orleans, 1820–1902.
Roll 3–25	1823–1846.
Microcopy 272	Passenger Lists of Vessels Arriving at New Orleans. Quarterly Abstract, 1820–1875.
Roll 1–2	1820–1845.
Microcopy 575	Lists of Passengers Arriving at Miscellaneous Ports on the Atlantic and Gulf Coasts, and at Ports on the Great Lakes, 1820–1873.
Roll 3	Galveston, Texas, 1846–1871.
Microcopy 261	New York. Customs Passenger Lists, 1820–1897, in the National Archives. Index.
Roll 35–36	Index for Gas — Gilb and Gilc — Gom, 1820–1846. (Of little use.)
Microcopy 334	Supplemental Index to Passenger Lists of Vessels Arriving at Atlantic and Gulf Ports (Excluding New York), 1820–1874.
Roll 63–64	Index for Gen — Gilc and Gild — Gll.

Ship Cargo Records.

Record Group 36.	Cargo Manifests. New Orleans, 1836–1850.

Census Records.

Microcopy 432	Seventh Census of the U.S., 1850.
Roll 908	Population Schedules of Some Texas Counties.
Roll 917	Texas Slave Schedules.
Microcopy 653	Eighth Census of the U.S., 1860.
Roll 1289	Population Schedules of Some Texas Counties.
Roll 1309	Texas Slave Schedules.
Microcopy 593	Ninth Census of the U.S., 1870.
Roll 1576	Population Schedules of Some Texas Counties.

Library of Congress, Washington. Manuscript Division.

Germany, Bremen. Archiv der Handelskammer (microfilms).
A. I. 1. Auswanderer 1841–1875.
C. 48. d. Verzeichnis der nach Amerika Handlung treibende Häuser in Bremen n. d. [ca. 1810–1840+].

Texas State Archives. Austin, Texas.

Seventh Census of the U.S., 1850. Schedule IV. Agricultural Productions. Brazoria County.
Eighth Census of the U.S., 1860. Schedule IV. Agricultural Productions. Brazoria County.
Ship Lists. Galveston. 1838, 1840, 1841.

Brazoria County Courthouse. Angleton, Texas.

Wills and other documents pertaining to the Gieseckes.

Rosenberg Library, Galveston, Texas.

Kauffman and Runge Records
Galveston Weekly News, scattered issues 1842–1849.

Baker Library, Harvard University, Graduate School of Business Administration, Boston, Mass. Historical Collections.

R.G. Dun & Company (a predecessor of Dun & Bradstreet Corporation). Handwritten Credit Ledgers. 1841–1872.

B. Published Primary Sources and Guides to Primary Sources

Achenbach, Hermann. *Tagebuch meiner Reise nach den nordamerikanischen Freistaaten. Oder das neue Kanaan.* Düsseldorf, 1835. Quotes a short letter from Texas.

"Die Ackerverfassung, die Zwergwirtschaft und die Auswanderung." *Deutsche Vierteljahrsschrift* 20 (1842): 106–191.

Adreßbuch der Freien Hansestadt Bremen. Bremen, 1815–1847.

Allen, Winnie, and Carrie Walker Allen, eds. *Pioneering in Texas: True Stories of the Early Days.* Dallas, 1935.

Anderson, John Q. *Tales of Frontier Texas.* Dallas, 1966.

Über Auswanderung. Von einem Kaufmanne in Bremen. Bremen, 1842.

"Auswanderung im Allgemeinen und nach Nordamerika insbesondere." *Deutsche Vierteljahrsschrift* 21 (1843): 191–215.

Bardehle, Peter, ed. *Die Kopfsteuerbeschreibung des Hochstifts Hildesheim von 1664: Ergänzt durch die Landschaftsbeschreibung von 1665.* Veröffentlichungen der Historischen Kommission für Niedersachsen und Bremen, 27a. Hildesheim 1976.

Barker, Eugene C., ed. *The Austin Papers.* 3 vols. Washington, 1924–1926.

———. *Readings in Texas History.* Dallas, 1929.

Behr, Ottomar von. *Guter Rath für Auswanderer nach den Vereinigten Staaten von Nordamerika mit besonderer Berücksichtigung von Texas. Vorzüglich für Landleute und Handwerker nach eigener Erfahrung geschrieben.* Leipzig, 1847.

Bek, William G. "The Followers of Duden." *Missouri Historical Review* 14–19 (1919–1925). 18 parts.

Bek, William G. SEE Hesse, Nicholas.

Beurmann, Eduard. *Skizzen aus den Hansestädten.* Hanau, 1836.

Beyer, Edward. *Cyclodrama: Malerische Reise von Bremen nach New York und durch die Vereinigten Staaten von Nordamerika zurück nach Hamburg.* 1846. 2 Aufl., Dresden, n.d.

Beyer, Moritz. *Das Auswanderungsbuch. Oder Führer und Ratgeber bei der Auswanderung nach Nordamerika und Texas.* Leipzig, 1846.

Bocris, G. C. *Beschreibung aller in Handel vorkommenden Tabaksgattun-*

gen, deren Produktionsländer, Kultur, Eigenschaften und Gebrauch. Bremen, 1833.

Börnstein, Heinrich. *Fünfundsiebzig Jahre in der Alten und in der Neuen Welt: Memoiren eines Unbedeutenden*. 2 vols. 1881. Reprint. New York, 1986.

Bracht, Victor. *Texas in Jahre 1848. Nach mehrjährigen Beobachtungen dargestellt. Mit verschiedenartigen Zugaben, Auszügen aus Briefen*. Elberfeld, 1849. Translation: *Texas in 1848*. Translated by C. F. Schmidt. San Antonio, 1931.

Brauns, Ernst Ludwig. *Ideen über die Auswanderung nach Amerika*. Göttingen, 1827.

———. *Praktische Belehrungen und Ratschläge für Reisende und Auswanderer nach Amerika*. Braunschweig, 1829.

Bromme, Traugott. *Neuestes vollständigstes Hand- und Reisebuch für Auswanderer aus allen Klassen und jedem Stande nach den Vereinigten Staaten von Nordamerika*. Bayreuth, 1846.

Buckingham, J. S. *America: Historical, Statistic, and Descriptive*. 3 vols. New York, 1841.

Burkart, Joseph. *Aufenthalt und Reisen in Mexiko in den Jahren 1825 bis 1834. Bemerkungen über Land, Produkte, Leben und Sitten der Einwohner und Beobachtungen aus dem Gebiete der Mineralogie, Geognosie, Bergbaukunde, Meteorologie, Geographie*. Stuttgart, 1836.

Büttner, Johann G. *Briefe aus und über Nordamerika. Oder Beiträge zu einer richtigen Kenntnis der Vereinigten Staaten und ihrer Bewohner, besonders der deutschen Bevölkerung*. 2. wohlfeilere Ausgabe. 2 vols. Dresden and Leipzig, 1847.

———. *Die Vereinigten Staaten von Nordamerika. Mein Aufenthalt und meine Reisen in denselben vom Jahre 1834 bis 1841*. 2 vols. Hamburg, 1844.

Carpenter, V. K., ed. *The State of Texas, Federal Population Schedules, Seventh Census of the United States*. 4 vols. Huntsville, Ark., 1969.

Day, James M., ed. *Handbook of Texas Archival and Manuscript Depositories*. Texas Library Monograph, 5. Austin, 1966.

Deutsche Gesellschaft für Amerika-Studien. Köln. "Americana in deutschen Sammlungen. Ein Verzeichnis von Materialien zur Geschichte der Vereinigten Staaten von Amerika in Archiven und Bibliotheken in der BRD und West-Berlin." 5 vols. 1967 Mimeographed. Copy in Library of Congress, Washington.

Dielmann, Henry B. "Emma Altgelt's Sketches of Life in Texas." *Southwestern Historical Quarterly* 63 (1959–1960): 361–84.

Dobie, J. Frank, ed. *Legends of Texas*. Publications of the Texas Folklore Society, 3. Austin, 1924.

————. *Southwestern Lore*. Publications of the Texas Folklore Society, 9. Dallas, 1931.

Dresel, Gustav. "Tagebuch von Gustav Dresel über seinen Aufenthalt in Texas 1837–1841." Edited by Julius Goebel. *Jahrbuch der Deutsch-Amerikanischen Historischen Gesellschaft von Illinois* 20–21 (1920–1921): 338–476.

Dubester, Henry J., ed. *State Censuses: An Annotated Bibliography of Censuses of Population Taken after the Year 1790 by States and Territories of the U.S.* Washington, 1948.

Duckwitz, Richard. *Aufstieg und Blüte einer Hansestadt: Von bremischer Leistung in der Welt*. Bremen, [1951?].

Duden, Gottfried. *Bericht über eine Reise nach den westlichen Staaten Nordamerikas und einen mehrjährigen Aufenthalt am Missouri in den Jahren 1824, 25, 26 und 27. In Bezug auf Auswanderung und Überbevölkerung*. 1. Aufl. 1829, St. Gallen, 1832.

Dun, Barlow & Co. *The Mercantile Agency Reference Book (and Key). Contains Ratings of the Merchants, Manufacturers, and Traders Generally Throughout the United States and Canada. July 1871*. New York, 1871.

Dunt, Detlef. *Reise nach Texas. Nebst Nachrichten von diesem Lande für Deutsche, welche nach Amerika zu gehen beabsichtigen*. Bremen, 1834.

Edward, David B. *History of Texas*. Cincinnati, 1836.

Eggerling, H. W. C. *Beschreibung der Vereinigten Staaten von Nordamerika mit besonderer Berücksichtigung deutscher Ansiedlungen daselbst*. 2. Aufl., Hildesheim [1845?]. An earlier edition (Wiesbaden, 1832) is mentioned in the *Hildesheimer Zeitung*, June 10, 1845, but I could not locate a copy of this edition.

Ehrenberg, Hermann. *Fahrten und Schicksale eines Deutschen in Texas*. Leipzig, 1845.

Engels, Friedrich. *Über die Bremer: Briefe, Aufsätze, Literarisches*. Bremen, 1966.

Erath, George Bernard. *Memoirs of Major George Bernard Erath*. Edited by Lucy A. Erath. Austin, 1923.

Filby, William P., ed. *Passenger and Immigration Lists Index: A Guide to Published Arrival Records of 300,000 Passengers Who Came to the United States and Canada in the Seventeenth, Eighteenth, and Nineteenth Centuries*. Detroit, 1980.

Fisher, Orceneth. *Sketches: Texas in 1840*. 1840. Reprint: Waco, Tex., 1964.

Bibliographical Essay and Bibliography

Fleischmann, C. L. *Erwerbszweige, Fabrikwesen und Handel der Vereinigten Staaten von Nordamerika.* Stuttgart, 1850.

Galveston County Genealogical Society. *Ships Passenger Lists: Port of Galveston, Texas, 1846–1871.* Easley, S.C., 1984.

Geue, Chester William, and Ethel Hander Geue. *A New Land Beckoned: German Immigration to Texas, 1844–1847.* Waco, Tex., 1966.

Geue, Ethel Hander. *New Homes in a New Land: German Immigration to Texas, 1846–1861.* Waco, Tex., 1970.

Glazier, Ira A., and Filby, P. William, eds. *Germans to America: Lists of Passengers Arriving at U.S. Ports.* Wilmington, Del., 1988–.

Gracy, Alice D., Jane Summer, and Emma G. Gentry, eds. *Early Texas Birth Records, 1838–1878.* 2 vols. Austin, 1969–1971.

Gruhne, Fritz. *Auswandererlisten des ehemaligen Herzogtums Braunschweig ohne Stadt Braunschweig und Landkreis Holzminden 1846–1871.* Quellen und Forschungen zur Braunschweigischen Geschichte, 20. Braunschweig, 1971.

Grund, Francis Joseph. *Handbuch und Wegweiser für Auswanderer nach den Vereinigten Staaten von Nordamerika.* Stuttgart, 1843. Includes a section on Texas.

Gudehus, Jonas Heinrich. *Meine Auswanderung nach Amerika in Jahre 1822, und meine Rückkehr in die Heimat im Jahre 1822. Nebst Bemerkungen über den kirchlichen, ökonomischen und moralischen Zustand der dortigen Deutschen und Winke für Auswanderungslustige.* 2 vols. Hildesheim, 1829.

Gülich, Gustav von. *Über den gegenwärtigen Zustand des Ackerbaus, des Handels und der Gewerbe im Königreiche Hannover.* Hannover, 1827.

Haeberlin, Carl Ludwig [pseud. H. R. Belani]. *Die Auswanderer nach Texas. Historisch-romantisches Gemälde aus der neuesten Zeit.* 3 vols. Leipzig, 1841. Not seen.

Hecke, J. Valentin. *Reise durch die Vereinigten Staaten in den Jahren 1818 und 1819.* 2 vols. Berlin, 1820–1821.

Herff, Ferdinand von. *The Regulated Emigration of the German Proletariat. With Special Reference to Texas. Being Also a Guide for German Emigrants.* Translated by Arthur L. Finck. San Antonio, 1978.

Hesse, Nicholas. "Nicholas Hesse, German Visitor to Missouri, 1835–1837." Edited and translated by William G. Bek. *Missouri Historical Review* 41-43 (1946–1948). 7 parts.

Hildesheimer Zeitung, 1844–1850.

Hodgskin, Thomas. *Travels in the North of Germany*. 2 vols. Edinburgh, 1820.

Höhne, Friedrich. *Wahn und Überzeugung. Reise des Kupferschmiede-Meisters Friedrich Höhne in Weimar über Bremen nach Nordamerika und Texas in den Jahren 1839, 1840 und 1841*. Weimar, 1844.

Holley, Mary Austin. *Texas*. Lexington, Ky., 1836.

Ikin, Arthur. *Texas. Its History, Topography, Agriculture, Commerce, and General Statistics. . . . Designed for the Use of the British Merchant, and as a Guide to Emigrants*. London, 1841. Reprint: Austin, 1964.

Jenkins, John Holland. *Recollections of Early Texas*. Edited by John Holmes Jenkins. Austin, 1958.

Kapp, Friedrich. "Amerikanische Reiseskizzen II [on Texas]." *Atlantische Studien von Deutschen in Amerika* 2 (1853): 173–182.

———. *Aus und über Amerika. Tatsachen und Erlebnisse*. 2 vols. Berlin, 1876.

———. "Die Geschichte der deutschen Ansiedlungen des westlichen Texas und deren Bedeutung für die Vereinigten Staaten." *Atlantische Studien von Deutschen in Amerika* 8 (1857): 176–186.

Kennedy, William. *Texas: The Rise, Progress, and Prospects of the Republic of Texas*. 2 vols. London 1841.

Klotzbach, Kurt, ed. *Die Solms-Papiere: Dokumente zur deutschen Kolonisation von Texas*. Wyk, 1990.

Klüber, Karl Werner. "Wiedergefundene Bremer und Hamburger Auswandererlisten." *Genealogie* 15 (1966): 329–332.

Kordül, A. *Der sichere Führer nach und in Texas*. Rottweil am Neckar, 1846.

Körner, Gustav. *Das deutsche Element in den Vereinigten Staaten von Nord-Amerika 1818–1848*. 2d ed. Cincinnati, 1884.

Kürnberger, Ferdinand. *Der Amerika-Müde. Amerikanisches Kulturbild*. Frankfurt am Main, 1857.

Linn, John J. *Reminiscences of Fifty Years in Texas*. 1883. Reprint. Austin, 1935.

Lockhart, John Washington. *Sixty Years on the Brazos: The Life and Letters of Dr. John Washington Lockhart, 1824–1900*. Edited by Jeannie Lockhart Wallis. New York, 1966.

Löher, Franz. *Geschichte und Zustände der Deutschen in Amerika*. Cincinnati and Leipzig, 1847.

Lubbock, Francis Richard. *Six Decades in Texas: Or Memoirs of Francis Richard Lubbock*. Edited by C. W. Raines. Austin, 1910.

Maillard, N. Doran. *The History of the Republic of Texas . . . and the Cause of Her Separation from the Republic of Mexico.* London, 1842.

Maltitz, R. von. *Hand- und Reisebuch für Auswanderer nach den Vereinigten Staaten von Nordamerika.* Bremen, 1843.

Map of Texas and Countries Adjacent. Compiled in the Bureau of Topographical Engineers from the Best Authorities for the State Department. Under the Direction of Col. J. J. Albert, Chief of Corps. By W. H. Emory, First Lieutenant, War Department. Published by Order of the U.S. Senate. [Washington], 1844.

McClintock, William A. "Diary of a Trip Through Texas and Northern Mexico in 1846–47." *Southwestern Historical Quarterly* 34 (1930–1931): 20–37, 141–158, 231–238.

Marschalck, Peter, ed. *Inventar der Quellen zur Geschichte der Wanderungen, besonders der Auswanderung, in Bremer Archiven,* Veröffentlichungen aus dem Staatsarchiv der Freien Hansestadt Bremen, 53. Bremen, 1986.

Meyer, Philipp, ed. *Die Pastoren der Landeskirche Hannovers und Schaumburg-Lippes seit der Reformation.* 3 vols. Göttingen, 1941–1953.

Miller, Thomas Lloyd, ed. *Bounty and Donation Land Grants of Texas, 1835–1888.* Austin, 1967.

Moore, Francis. *Description of Texas.* 2d ed. New York, 1844.

Mullins, Marion D., ed. *The First Census of Texas, 1829–1836: To Which Are Added Texas Citizenship Lists, 1821–1845, and Other Early Records of the Republic of Texas.* Special Publications of the National Genealogical Society, 22. Washington, 1959.

Neu-Braunfelser Zeitung, August 21, 1938, and August 21, 1952. New Braunfels, Tex.

Neu-Braunfelser Zeitung: Jahrbuch für 1936. New Braunfels, Tex. [1936?].

Newell, Chester. *History of the Revolution in Texas. Particularly of the War of 1835–1836. Together with the Latest Geographical, Topographical, and Statistical Accounts of the Country.* New York, 1838.

Der nordamerikanische Freistaat Texas. Ein Führer und Ratgeber für solche, die dahin auswandern wollen. Heilbronn, 1847.

Olmsted, Frederick Law. *A Journey through Texas: A Saddletrip on the Southwest Frontier.* 1857, New York, 1860. Also: James Howard, ed. (Austin, 1962).

Ostermayer, Heinrich. *Tagebuch meiner Reise nach Texas in Jahre 1848–1849.* Biberach, 1850.

Pauer, Friedrich. *Die Vereinigten Staaten von Nordamerika nach erfolgtem Anschluß der Republik Texas. Mit besonderer Beziehung auf deutsche Auswanderer.* Bremen, 1847.

Racknitz, Johann von. *Vorläufer. Als Leitfaden für Auswanderer nach dem Staate Texas, an den Flüßen St. Marco, Colorado, auch Rio de la Canos, im Gebiet Neumexiko in Nordamerika.* Meersburg, 1832. Not seen.

Roemer, Ferdinand von. *Texas. Mit besonderer Rücksicht auf deutsche Auswanderung und die physischen Verhältnisse des Landes nach eigener Beobachtung geschildert.* Bonn, 1849.

Ross, Georg von. *Der nordamerikanische Freistaat Texas. Nach eigner Anschauung und nach den neuesten und besten Quellen für deutsche Auswanderer.* Rudolfstadt, 1851.

Schelbert, Leo, and Hedwig Rappolt, eds. *Alles ist ganz anders hier: Auswandererschicksale in Briefen aus zwei Jahrhunderten.* Freiburg im Breisgau, 1977.

Scherpf, G. A. *Entstehungsgeschichte und gegenwärtiger Zustand des neuen, unabhängigen, amerikanischen Staates Texas.* Augsburg, 1841.

Schlecht, Friedrich. *Mein Ausflug nach Texas.* Bunzlau, 1851.

Schütz, Kuno Damian Freiherr von. *Texas. Ratgeber für Auswanderer nach diesem Lande.* Wiesbaden, 1847.

Sealsfield, Charles [Karl Postl]. *Gesammelte Werke.* 15 vols. Stuttgart, 1845–1847.

———. *Das Kajuetenbuch. Oder nationale Charakteristiken.* Halle, [1887].

Seebaß, Georg, and F.-W. Freist, eds. *Die Pastoren der braunschweigischen evangelisch-lutherischen Landeskirche.* 2 vols. Wolfenbüttel, 1969–1974.

Seele, Hermann. *Die Zypresse und Gesammelte Schriften: Eine Legende aus der Zeit der ersten deutschen Ansiedlungen in West-Texas.* New Braunfels, Tex., 1936. Translation: *The Cypress and Other Writings of a German Pioneer in Texas.* Translated by Edward C. Breitenkamp. Austin, 1979.

Selle, Götz von, ed. *Die Matrikel der Georg-August-Universität zu Göttingen 1734–1837.* Veröffentlichungen der Historischen Kommission für Hannover, Oldenburg, Braunschweig, Schaumburg-Lippe und Bremen, pt. 9, vol. 3. Hildesheim, 1937.

Sheridan, Francis C. *Galveston Island, Or a Few Months Off the Coast of Texas: The Journal of Francis C. Sheridan, 1839–1840.* Edited by Willis W. Pratt. Austin, 1954.

Smithwick, Noah. *Evolution of a State: Or Recollections of Old Texas Days.* Edited by Nanna Smithwick Donaldson. Austin, [1900?].

Sommer, Carl von. *Bericht über meine Reise nach Texas im Jahre 1846. Die Verhältnisse und den Zustand dieses Landes betreffend.* Bremen, 1847.

Sörgel, Alwin H. *Für Auswanderungslustige! Briefe eines unter dem Schutze des Mainzer Vereins nach Texas Ausgewanderten.* Leipzig, 1847.

Spieß, Werner, ed. *Personen- und Ortsregister zum Bd. 1, Album Academiae Helmstadiensis . . . 1574–1636.* Veröffentlichungen der Historischen Kommission für Niedersachsen, 9. Hannover, 1955.

Steinert, W. *Nordamerika, vorzüglich Texas im Jahre 1849. Reisebericht. Ein Buch für Auswanderer, besonders für Auswanderungslustige.* Berlin, 1850.

Stiff, Edward. *The Texan Emigrant. Being a Narration of the Adventures of the Author in Texas and a Description of the Soils, Climate, Productions . . . of That Country.* Cincinnati, 1840.

Storck, Adam. *Ansichten der Freien Hansestadt Bremen und ihrer Umgebung.* Frankfurt am Main, 1822.

Strubberg, Friedrich Armand [pseud. Armand]. *Friedrichsburg, die Kolonie des deutschen Fürsten-Vereins in Texas.* Leipzig, 1867.

———. *Die Fürstentochter.* 3 vols. Hannover, 1872.

———. *Saat und Ernte.* 5 vols. Leipzig, 1866.

Texas in 1840. Or the Emigrant's Guide to the New Republic. [. . .] By an Emigrant Late of the U.S. Introd. Rev. A. B. Lawrence, New Orleans. New York, 1840.

Treu, Georg. *Das Buch der Auswanderung. Enthaltend eine Sammlung der wichtigsten in den süddeutschen Staaten, in Bremen und in Nordamerika erschienen Verordnungen und diplomatischen Aktenstücke, der Bekanntmachungen der deutschen Gesellschaften, des Texas-Vereins . . . Nebst zweckdienlichen Ratschlägen für Auswanderer. Ein zuverlässiger Ratgeber für Auswanderungslustige, Juristen, Agenten und Geschäftsmänner, welche mit dem Auswanderungswesen in Berührung kommen.* Bamberg, 1848.

United States Census Bureau. *The Seventh Census of the United States 1850. . . . A Statistical View of Each of the States.* Washington, 1853.

Verzeichnis der bremischen Seeschiffe für das Jahr 1844. Bremen, [1844?]. Copy in the University Library, Bremen.

Verzeichnis der bremischen Seeschiffe für das Jahr 1845. Bremen, [1845?]. Copy in the University Library, Bremen.

Wagner, Maria, ed. *Was die Deutschen aus Amerika berichteten 1828–1868.* Stuttgart, 1984.

Wappäus, Johann Eduard, ed. *Deutsche Auswanderung und Kolonisation.* Leipzig, 1846.

———, ed. *Deutsche Auswanderung und Kolonisation.* 1. Fortsetzung: *Deutsche Auswanderung nach Sud-Amerika.* Leipzig, 1848.

Weser-Zeitung, Die (Bremen), February 8 and 10, 1846.

White, Gifford, ed. *The 1840 Census of the Republic of Texas.* Austin, 1966.

———. *1840 Citizens of Texas.* Austin, 1984.

———. *1830 Citizens of Texas.* Austin, 1983.

Wied-Neuwied, Prince Maximilian Alexander Philipp. *Reise in das Innere Nordamerika in den Jahren 1832 his 1834.* 2 vols. Koblenz, 1839–1841.

Williams, Villamae, ed. *Stephen F. Austin's Register of Families.* Reprint. Baltimore, 1989.

Willkomm, Ernst. *Die Europa-Müden. Modernes Lebensbild.* 1838. Reprint. Göttingen, 1968.

Witte, August. *Kurze Schilderung der Vereinigten Staaten von Nord-Amerika nach ihren statistischen, politischen und commerciellen Verhältnissen, so wie in Ansehung der Sitten und Lebensweise für Einwohner nebst ausführlichen Vorsichtsregeln für Auswanderer nach eigenen Beobachtungen und Erfahrungen.* Hannover, 1833.

Wrede, Friedrich W. von. *Lebensbilder aus den Vereinigten Staaten von Nordamerika und Texas.* Kassel, 1844.

Young, J. H. *New Map of Texas with the Contiguous American and Mexican States.* Philadelphia, 1836. Copy located in Map Division, New York Public Library.

Zimmermann, Paul, ed. *Album Academiae Helmstadiensis*, pt. 2, vol. 1: *1574–1636.* Veröffentlichungen der Historischen Kommission für Hannover, Oldenburg, Braunschweig, Schaumburg-Lippe und Bremen, 9. Hildesheim, 1926. For *Personen- und Ortsregister*, SEE Spieß, Werner.

C. Secondary Works

Abel, Wilhelm, ed. *Handwerkgeschichte in neuer Sicht.* Göttingen, 1970.

Achelis, Johann, and Hans Achelis. *Die Familie Achelis in Bremen 1579–1921.* Bremen, 1921.

Achilles, Walter. *Die Lage der hannoverschen Landbevölkerung im späten 18. Jahrhundert*, Veröffentlichungen der Historischen Kommission für Niedersachsen und Bremen, 34. Hildesheim, 1982.

Adams, Willi Paul. "Die Assimilationsfrage in der deutschen Einwanderungsdiskussion 1890–1930." *Amerikastudien* 27 (1982): 275–291.

———. *The German-Americans: An Ethnic Experience.* Translated by L. J.

Rippley and Eberhard Reichmann. Publications of the Max Kade German-American Center of Indiana University-Purdue University at Indianapolis. Bloomington, Ind., 1993.

Adams, Willi Paul, ed. *Die deutschsprachige Auswanderung in die Vereinigten Staaten: Berichte über Forschungsstand und Quellenbestände*, Materialien des John F. Kennedy Instituts der Freien Universität Berlin, 14. Berlin, 1980.

Addington, Wendell G. "Slave Insurrections in Texas." *Journal of Negro History* 35 (1950): 408–434.

Aptheker, Herbert. *American Negro Slave Revolts*. New York 1963.

Assion, Peter, ed. *Der große Aufbruch: Studien zur Amerikaauswanderung*. Hessische Blätter für Volks- und Kulturforschung, Neue Folge 17. Marburg, 1985.

Atherton, Lewis E. *The Pioneer Merchant in Mid-America*. Columbia, Mo., 1939.

———. *The Southern Country Store 1800–1860*. Baton Rouge, La., [1949].

Aubin, Hermann, and Wolfgang Zorn, eds. *Handbuch der deutschen Wirtschafts- und Sozialgeschichte*. 2 vols. Stuttgart, 1971–1976.

Auerbach, Inge. "Auswanderung aus Kurhessen 1832–1866." In *Der große Aufbruch: Studien zur Amerikaauswanderung*, edited by Peter Assion. Hessische Blätter für Volks- und Kulturforschung, Neue Folge 17. Marburg, 1985.

Auspurg, Dagmar. "Deutsche Einwanderung nach Texas im 19. Jahrhundert." Staatsexamensarbeit, Bochum University (1977).

Bade, Klaus J. "Altes Handwerk, Wanderzwang und 'gute Polizey:' Gesellenwanderung zwischen Zunftökonomie und Gewerbereform." *Sozial- und Wirtschaftsgeschichte* 69 (1982): 1–37.

———. "Deutsche Überseeauswanderung und -einwanderung im 19. und frühen 20. Jahrhundert." *Archiv für Sozialgeschichte* 26 (1986): 480–487.

———. "Massenwanderung und Arbeitsmarkt im deutschen Nordosten von 1880 his zum 1. Weltkrieg: Überseeische Auswanderung, interne Abwanderung und kontinentale Zuwanderung." *Archiv für Sozialgeschichte* 20 (1980): 265–323.

Bade, Klaus J., ed. *Auswanderer-Wanderarbeiter-Gastarbeiter: Bevölkerung, Arbeitsmarkt und Wanderung in Deutschland seit der Mitte des 19. Jahrhunderts*. 2 vols. Ostfildern, 1984.

———. *Deutsche im Ausland. Fremde in Deutschland: Migration in Geschichte und Gegenwart*. Munich, 1992.

Baer, Willis N. *The Economic Development of the Cigar Industry in the United States.* Lancaster, Pa., 1933.

Baker, T. Lindsay. *Ghost Towns of Texas.* Norman, Okla., 1986.

Bancroft, Hubert Howe. *History of the North Mexican States and Texas.* The Works of Hubert Howe Bancroft, 14–15. 2 vols. San Francisco, 1884–1889.

Barba, Preston A. *The Life and Works of Friedrich Armand Strubberg.* Americana Germanica, 6. [Philadelphia], 1913.

Bargmann, Robert. *Bremens Wollhandel.* Bremen, 1941.

Barkan, Elliott R. "Race, Religion, and Nationality in American Society: A Model of Ethnicity — From Contact to Assimilation." *Journal of American Ethnic History* 14 (1995): 38–75.

Barker, Eugene C. "The Annexation of Texas." *Southwestern Historical Quarterly* 50 (1946): 49–74.

———. *The Life of Stephen F. Austin, Founder of Texas, 1793–1836: A Chapter in the Westward Movement of the Anglo-American People.* 2d ed. Austin, 1949.

Barr, Alwyn. *Black Texans: A History of Negroes in Texas, 1528–1871.* Austin, 1973.

Baughman, James P. "The Maritime and Railroad Interests of Charles Morgan, 1837–1885. A History of the 'Morgan Line.'" Ph.D. diss., Tulane University, 1962.

Barnstone, Howard. *The Galveston That Was.* New York, 1966.

Benjamin, Gilbert G. *The Germans of Texas.* Philadelphia, 1909. Also published in: *German-American Annals,* n. s., 6–7 (1908–1909).

Benjamin, Steven M. "The Texas-Germans: A Working Bibliography." *Occasional Papers of the Society for German-American Studies,* 8 (1980): 91–116.

Berkner, Lutz K. "Peasant Household Organization and Demographic Change in Lower Saxony (1689–1766)." In *Population Patterns in the Past,* edited by Ronald D. Lee. New York, 1977.

Berlin, Ira, and Herbert G. Gutman. "Natives and Immigrants, Free Men and Slaves: Urban Workingmen in the Antebellum American South." *American Historical Review* 88 (1983): 1175–1200.

Bernecker, Walther L. *Die Handelskonquistadoren: Europäische Interessen und mexikanischer Staat im 19. Jahrhundert.* Wiesbaden, 1988.

Bessel, Georg. *Bremen. Geschichte einer deutschen Stadt* (3. Aufl., Bremen, 1955.

Beutin, Ludwig. *Bremen und Amerika: Zur Geschichte der Weltwirtschaft und der Beziehungen Deutschlands zu den Vereinigten Staaten.* Bremen, 1953.

———. *Gesammelte Schriften zur Wirtschafts- und Sozialgeschichte.* Edited by Hermann Kellenbenz. Cologne, 1963.

———. "Wesenszüge des bremischen Tabakhandels." *Der Schlüssel. Bremer Beiträge zur deutschen Kultur und Wirtschaft* 2, no. 5 (1937): 1–7.

Biesele, Rudolph L. *The History of the German Settlements in Texas, 1831–1861.* Austin, 1930.

Biggers, Don H. *German Pioneers in Texas: A Brief History of Their Hardships, Struggles, and Achievements.* Fredericksburg, Tex., 1925.

Binkley, William C. *The Expansionist Movement in Texas, 1836–1850.* Berkeley, 1925.

Bippen, Wilhelm von. *Geschichte der Stadt Bremen.* 3 vols. Bremen, 1892–1904.

Blum, Jerome. *The End of the Old Order in Rural Europe.* Princeton, 1978.

Bodnar, John. *The Transplanted: A History of Immigrants in Urban America.* Bloomington, 1987.

Bohmbach, Jürgen. "Niedersachsen im Ausland: Auswanderung" and "Niedersachsen auf dem amerikanischen Kontinent." In *Zwischen London und Byzanz: Die geschichtlichen Territorien Niedersachsens in ihren Beziehungen zum Ausland,* pp. 111–119. Veröffentlichungen der Niedersächsischen Archivverwaltung, Beiheft 23. Göttingen, 1979.

Bohner, Theodor. *Der deutsche Kaufmann über See. 100 Jahre deutscher Handel in der Welt.* Berlin, 1939.

Bonham, Dora Dietrich. *Merchant to the Republic.* San Antonio [1958?].

Bonnet. "Texas und deutsche Familienforschung." *Familiengeschichtliche Blätter* 26 (1928): 48–50, 136–139.

Borchardt, Knut. *Wachstum, Krisen, Handlungsspielräume der Wirtschaftspolitik: Studien zur Wirtschaftsgeschichte des 19. und 20. Jahrhunderts.* Göttingen, 1982.

———. "Zur Frage des Kapitalmangels in der 1. Hälfte des 19. Jahrhunderts in Deutschland." *Jahrbücher für Nationalökonomie und Statistik* 173 (1961): 401–421.

Bosse, Georg von. *Das deutsche Element in den Vereinigten Staaten unter besonderer Berücksichtigung seines politischen, ethischen, sozialen und erzieherischen Einflusses.* Stuttgart, 1908.

Bowen, Frank C. *A Century of Atlantic Travel, 1830–1930.* Boston, 1930.

Bowman, Shearer D. "Antebellum Planters and *Vormärz* Junkers in Comparative Perspective." *American Historical Review* 85 (1980): 779–808.

————. *Masters and Lords: Mid-Nineteenth Century U.S. Planters and Prussian Junkers*. New York, 1993.

Brakensiek, Stefan. "Agrarian Individualism in North-Western Germany, 1770–1870." *German History* 12 (1994): 137–179.

Brazoria County Federation of Women's Clubs, ed. *History of Brazoria County*. [Angleton, Tex.?], 1940.

Bremische Biographie des 19. Jahrhunderts. hg. v. der Historischen Gesellschaft des Künstlervereins. Bremen, 1912.

Brenner, Peter J. *Reisen in die Neue Welt: Die Erfahrung Nordamerikas in deutschen Reise- und Auswandererberichten des 19. Jahrhunderts*. Tübingen, 1991.

Bretting, Agnes. *Soziale Probleme deutscher Einwanderer in New York City 1800-1860*. Wiesbaden, 1981.

Bretting, Agnes, and Hartmut Bickelmann. *Auswanderungsagenturen und Auswanderungsvereine im 19. und 20. Jahrhundert*. Von Deutschland nach Amerika: Zur Sozialgeschichte der Auswanderung im 19. und 20. Jahrhundert, 4. Stuttgart, 1991.

Bromwell, William J. *History of Immigration to the United States*. New York, 1856.

Brown, John Henry. *History of Texas from 1685 to 1892*. 2 vols. St. Louis [1892–1893?].

Brownell, Blaine A., and David R. Goldfield. *The City in Southern History: The Growth of Urban Civilization in the South*. Port Washington, N.Y., 1977.

Bruchey, Stuart, ed. *Cotton and the Growth of the American Economy, 1790–1860: Sources and Readings*. New York, 1967.

Buchholz, Friedrich. *Geschichte von Bockenem*. Hildesheim, 1843.

Bugbee, Lester G. "The Old Three Hundred." *Texas State Historical Association Quarterly* [subsequently *Southwestern Historical Quarterly*] 1 (1898): 108–117.

Burgdörfer, Friedrich. "Die Wanderungen über die deutschen Reichsgrenzen im letzten Jahrhundert." *Allgemeines Statistisches Archiv* 20 (1930): 161–196, 383–419, 537–551.

Campbell, Randolf B. *An Empire for Slavery: The Peculiar Institution in Texas, 1861–1865*. Baton Rouge, 1989.

Campbell, Randolf B., and Richard G. Lowe. *Wealth and Power in Antebellum Texas*. College Station, Tex., 1977.

Carlson, A. L. *A Monetary and Banking History of Texas: From the Mexican Regime to the Present Day, 1821–1929*. Fort Worth, 1930.

Carson, Gerald. *The Old Country Store*. New York, 1965.

Chipman, Donald E. *Spanish Texas, 1519–1821*. Austin, 1992.

Clark, Joseph Lynn. *The Texas Gulf Coast: Its History and Development*. 4 vols. New York, 1955.

Cohn, R. L. "Mortality on Immigrant Voyages to New York, 1836–1853." *Journal of Economic History* 54 (1984): 289–300.

Coleman, D. C. "Proto-Industrialization: A Concept Too Many." *Economic History Review* 2d ser., 26 (1983): 425–448.

Conze, Friedrich. *Die Familie Conze aus Elze*. Berlin, 1941.

Conze, Werner. *Die liberalen Agrarreformen Hannovers im 19. Jahrhundert*. Hannover, 1947.

Conzen, Kathleen Neils. "Germans." In *Harvard Encyclopedia of American Ethnic Groups*, edited by Stephan Thernstrom, pp. 405–425. Cambridge, Mass., 1980.

———. *Immigrant Milwaukee, 1835–1860: Accommodation and Community in a Frontier City*. Cambridge, Mass., 1976.

———. "The Writing of German-American History." *Immigration History Newsletter* 12, no. 2 (1980): 1–14.

Creighton, James A. *A Narrative History of Brazoria County*. [Angleton, Tex.], 1975.

Curlee, Abigail. SEE ALSO Holbrook, Abigail Curlee.

Curlee, Abigail. "The History of a Texas Slave Plantation, 1831–1863." *Southwestern Historical Quarterly* 27 (1922): 79–127.

———. "A Study of Texas Slave Plantations, 1822–1865." Ph.D. diss., University of Texas, Austin, 1932.

Dane, Hendrik. *Die wirtschaftlichen Beziehungen Deutschlands zu Mexiko und Mittelamerika im 19. Jahrhundert*. Cologne, 1971.

Day, James M. *Jacob de Cordova: Land Merchant of Texas*. Waco, Tex., 1962.

Denecke, Dietrich. "Die sozio-ökonomische Gliederung südniedersächsischer Städte im 18. und 19. Jahrhundert: Historische-geographische Stadtpläne und ihre Analyse." *Niedersächsisches Jahrbuch für Landesgeschichte* 52 (1980): 25–38.

Deutsches Geschlechterbuch (Genealogisches Handbuch bürgerlicher Familien). Vol. 17, Görlitz, 1910; vol. 158, Limburg, 1971.

DeVoto, Bernard. *The Year of Decision: 1846*. Boston, 1943.

Dinnerstein, Leonard, and David M. Reimers. *Ethnic Americans: A History of Immigration and Assimilation*. New York, 1975.

Dobie, J. Frank. *The Flavor of Texas*. Dallas, 1936.

———. *Tales of Old-Time Texas*. Boston, [1955?].

Doebner, Richard. *Aus Bockenems Vergangenheit. Vortrag gehalten im Bürger-Verein zu Bockenem.* Hildesheim, 1894.

Doerries, Reinhard R. *Iren und Deutsche in der Neuen Welt: Akkulturationsprozesse in der amerikanischen Gesellschaft im späten neunzehnten Jahrhundert.* Vierteljahrschrift für Sozial- und Wirtschaftsgeschichte, Beiheft 76. Stuttgart, 1985.

Duckwitz, Arnold. *Denkwürdigkeiten aus meinem öffentlichen Leben von 1841 bis 1866. Ein Beitrag zur bremischen und deutschen Geschichte.* Bremen, 1877.

Dun & Bradstreet. *Dun & Bradstreet: The Story of an Idea.* [New York?], 1968.

Duval, J. C. *Early Times in Texas.* Austin, 1892.

Dyer, J. O. *The Early History of Galveston*, Part 1. Galveston, 1916.

Eisenhour, Virginia. *Galveston: A Different Place.* 2d ed. Galveston, 1984.

Elliott, Claude. "Union Sentiment in Texas, 1861–65." *Southwestern Historical Quarterly*, 50 (1947): 449–477.

Eltis, David. "Free and Coerced Transatlantic Migrations. Some Comparisons." *American Historical Review* 88 (1983): 251–280.

Engelsing, Rolf. *Bremen als Auswandererhafen 1683–1880*, Veröffentlichungen aus dem Staatsarchiv der Freien Hansestadt Bremen, 29. Bremen, 1961.

———. "Ein Reisebericht von 1842. Bremen im Urteil eines Anhängers des Jungen Deutschlands." *Bremisches Jahrbuch* 48 (1962): 375–402.

———. "Die wirtschaftliche und soziale Differenzierung der deutschen kaufmännischen Angestellten im In- und Ausland 1690–1900." In *Zur Sozialgeschichte deutscher Mittel- und Unterschichten*, edited by Rolf Engelsing. Göttingen, 1973.

Entholt, Hermann. "Bremens Handel, Schiffahrt und Industrie im 19. Jahrhundert (1815–1914)." In *Hamburg, Bremen, Lübeck: Die Hansestädte*, by Otto Mathies et al. Die deutsche Wirtschaft und ihre Führer, 5. Gotha, 1926.

Erhorn, Irmgard. *Die deutsche Einwanderung der Dreissiger und Achtundvierziger in die Vereinigten Staaten und ihre Stellung zur nordamerikanischen Politik: Ein Beitrag zur Geschichte des Deutschamerikanertums.* Übersee-Geschichte, 9. Hamburg, 1937.

Erickson, Carolyn R., and Frances T. Ingmire, eds. *First Settlers of the Republic of Texas: Headright Land Grants Which Were Reported as Genuine and Legal by the Traveling Commissioners, January 1840.* 2 vols. Nacogdoches and St. Louis, 1982.

Bibliographical Essay and Bibliography

Ernst, Robert. *Immigrant Life in New York City, 1825–1863*. New York, 1949.

Esslinger, Dean R. *Immigration and the City: Ethnicity and Mobility in a Nineteenth-Century Midwestern Community*. Port Washington, N.Y., 1975.

Etzler, T. Herbert. "German-American Newspapers in Texas: With Special Reference to the Texas *Volksblatt*, 1877–1879." *Southwestern Historical Quarterly* 51 (1954): 423–431.

Exley, Jo Ella Powell, ed. *Texas Tears and Texas Sunshine: Voices of Frontier Women*. College Station, Tex., 1945.

Fairchild's Dictionary of Textiles. Edited by Stephen S. Marks. New York, 1959.

Faltin, Sigrid. *Die Auswanderung aus der Pfalz nach Nordamerika im 19. Jahrhundert. Unter besonderer Berücksichtigung des Landkommissariates Bergzabern*. Frankfurt am Main, 1987.

Faust, Albert B. *The German Element in the United States*. 2 vols. Reprint. New York, 1969.

Hans Fenske. "Die deutsche Auswanderung." *Mitteilungen des Historischen Vereins der Pfalz* 76 (1978): 183–220.

————. "Die deutsche Auswanderung in der Mitte des 19. Jahrhunderts: Öffentliche Meinung und amtliche Politik." *Geschichte in Wissenschaft und Unterricht* 25 (1973): 221–236.

Ferenczi, Imre. "Proletarian Mass Migration." In *International Migrations*, edited by Walter F. Willcox, vol. 1 of 2 vols. New York, 1929–1931.

Flügel, Heinrich. *Die deutschen Welthäfen Hamburg und Bremen*. Jena, 1914.

Focke Museum (Bremen). *Das alte Bremen*. Leipzig, 1922.

Fornell, Earl W. *The Galveston Era: The Texas Crescent on the Eve of Secession*. Austin, 1961.

————. "The German Pioneers of Galveston Island." *American German Review* 22, no. 3 (1956): 15–17.

Frantz, Joe B. "The Mercantile House of McKinney & Williams, Underwriters of the Texas Revolution." *Bulletin of the Business Historical Society* 26 (1952): 1–18.

Freeden, Hermann von, and Georg Smolka, eds. *Auswanderer: Bilder und Skizzen aus der Geschichte der deutschen Auswanderung*. Berlin, [1937?].

Freie Hansestadt Bremen: Werden, Vergehen und Wiederaufbau 1564–1947. Schriften der Bauverwaltung Bremen, Ergänzungsheft. Bremen, 1947.

Freitag, Friedrich. *Rund um Bockenem: Geschichtsbilder aus dem Amber-*

gau, 2. Teil. n.p., [1978?]. New ed. of *Vom Hainberg zum Weinberg: Geschichtsbilder aus dem Ambergau*. Volkersheim über Derneburg, 1953.

Fuchs, Konrad. "Zur Auswanderungsproblematik in Deutschland im 19. Jahrhundert." In *Festschrift für Eberhard Kessel zum 75. Geburtstag*, edited by Heinz Duchardt and Manfred Schlenke. Munich, 1982.

Gebauer, J. H. *Geschichte des Handels und des Kaufmannstandes in der Stadt Hildesheim*. Bremen, 1950.

―――. *Geschichte der Stadt Hildesheim*. 2 vols. Hildesheim, 1922–1924.

Gelberg, Brigit. *Auswanderung nach Obersee: Soziale Probleme der Auswandererbeförderung in Hamburg und Bremen von der Mitte des 19. Jahrhunderts bis zum 1. Weltkrieg*. Hamburg, 1973.

Genovese, Eugene D. *The Political Economy of Slavery: Studies in the Economy and Society of the Slave South*. New York, 1966.

Giesecke, Albert. *Über Ursprung, Alter, Bedeutung, Geschichte und Verbreitung der Namen Giesecke, Gieseke, Giseke, Giske, Geske, Jeske, Geschke, Jeschke, Gyzycki, Giese, Geisel und ähnlicher Formen*. Dresden, 1923.

Gillhoff, Johannes. *Jürnjakob Swehn, der Amerikafahrer*. 1917. Berlin, 1920.

Gillhoff, Johannes, and Theodor Gillhoff. *Mine Markow, der neue Amerikafahrer*. Berlin, [1957?].

Gish, Theodore, and Richard Spuler, eds. *Eagle in the New World: German Immigration to Texas and America*. College Station, Tex., 1986.

Gläbe, Friedrich. *Die Unterweser: Chronik eines Stromes und seiner Landschaft*. Bremen, 1963.

Gordon, Milton. *Assimilation in American Life: The Role of Race, Religion, and National Origins*. New York, 1964.

Gouge, William M. *The Fiscal History of Texas*. Philadelphia, 1852.

Gracy, Alice D., Jane Summer, and Emma G. Gentry, eds. *Early Texas Birth Records, 1838–1878*. 2 vols. Austin, 1969–1971.

Graff, Paul. *Geschichte des Kreises Alfeld*. Hildesheim, 1928.

Gras, N. S. B. *Businessmen and Capitalism: An Introduction to Business History*. New York, 1939.

Grether, Andreas, and Sabine Scheuermann. "Rückwanderung aus Amerika. Zum Problem der Rückkehr aus der Fremde." In *Der große Aufbruch: Studien zur Amerikaauswanderung*, edited by Peter Assion. Hessische Blätter für Volks- und Kulturforschung, Neue Folge 17. Marburg, 1985.

Griffin, S. C. *History of Galveston, Texas: Narrative and Biographical*. Galveston, 1931.

Gröpner, Klaus. *Im Winter brach der Regenbogen: Der deutsche Treck nach Texas*. Vienna, 1978.

Gruenwald, Kim M. "Settling the Old Northwest: Changing Family and Commercial Strategies in the Early Republic." Ph.D. diss., University of Colorado, 1994.

Gruhne, Fritz. *Auswandererlisten des ehemaligen Herzogtums Braunschweig ohne Stadt Braunschweig und Landkreis Holzminden 1846–1871. Quellen und Forschungen zur Braunschweigischen Geschichte*, 20, 1971.

Grünzweig, Walter. *Das demokratische Kanaan: Charles Sealsfields Amerika im Kontext amerikanischer Literatur und Ideologie*. Munich, 1987.

Guillet, Edwin C. *The Great Migration: The Atlantic Crossing by Sailing Ships since 1770*. 2d ed. Toronto, [1963?].

Günther, Friedrich. *Der Ambergau*. Hannover, 1887.

Gutman, Herbert G. *Work, Culture, and Society in Industrializing America: Essays in American Working-Class History*. New York, 1976.

Hamerow, Theodore S. *Restoration, Revolution, Reaction: Economics and Politics in Germany, 1815–1871*. Princeton, 1958.

Hammond, M. B. *The Cotton Industry: An Essay in American Economic History*, pt. 1: *The Cotton Culture and Cotton Trade*. Publications of the American Economic Association, n. s., 1. New York, 1897.

Hammond, Theresa Ann Mayer. "American Paradise: German Travel Literature from Duden to Kisch." Ph.D. diss., University of California at Berkeley, 1977.

Handlin, Oscar, ed. *Immigration as a Factor in American History*. Englewood Cliffs, N.J., 1959.

———. *The Uprooted: The Epic Story of the Great Migrations That Made the American People*. 1951. 2nd. ed. Boston, 1973.

Hansen, Harry, ed. *Texas: A Guide to the Lone Star State* [*The Federal Writers' Project Guide*, new ed.]. New York, 1969.

Hansen, Marcus Lee. *The Atlantic Migration, 1607–1860: A History of the Continuing Settlement of the United States*. 1940. Reprint. New York, 1961.

———. *The Immigrant in American History*. Edited by Arthur M. Schlesinger. New York, 1964.

Harvard Encyclopedia of American Ethnic Groups. Edited by Stephen Thernstrom. Cambridge, Mass., 1980.

Hauschild, Henry J. *The Runge Chronicle: A German Saga of Success*. Austin, 1990.

Hawgood, John A. *The Tragedy of German-America: The Germans in the United States of America during the Nineteenth Century and After.* New York, 1940.

Hayes, Charles W. *Galveston: History of the Island and the City.* 2 vols. 1879. Reprint. Austin, 1974. All copies of the first edition of 1879 were destroyed in a fire; the reprint is a corrected edition of the surviving proofs.

Hazen, Edward. *Popular Technology: Or Professions and Trades.* 2 vols. New York, 1843.

Heinen, Hubert. "German-Texan Attitudes toward the Civil War." *Yearbook of German-American Studies* 20 (1985): 19–32.

Henson, Margaret Swett. *Samuel May Williams: Early Texas Entrepreneur.* College Station, Tex. [1976?].

Herbst, Albert. *Die alten Heer- und Handelsstraßen Südhannovers und angrenzender Gebiete.* Göttingen, 1926.

Hershberg, Theodore, et al. "Occupation and Ethnicity in Five Nineteenth-Century Cities: A Collaborative Inquiry." *Historical Methods Newsletter* 7 (1974).

Hertneck, Fr. *Kampf um Texas.* Leipzig, [1941?].

Heyne, Bodo. "Über bremische Quellen zur Auswanderungsforschung." *Bremisches Jahrbuch* 41 (1944): 159–169.

Hieke, Ernst. *Zur Geschichte des deutschen Handels mit Ostafrika. 1. Teil: Das hamburgische Handelshaus Wm. O'Swald & Co. 1831–1870.* Hamburg, [1939].

Hinueber née Ernst, Caroline von. "Life of German Pioneers of Early Texas." *Texas State Historical Association Quarterly* [subsequently *Southwestern Historical Quarterly*] 2 (1899): 5, 227–232.

Historical and Biographical Record of the Cattle Industry and Cattlemen of Texas and Adjacent Territory. 1894. Reprint. New York, 1959.

Hochstadt, Steve. "Migration in Preindustrial Germany." *Central European History* 16 (1983): 195–224.

Hoerder, Dirk, ed. *Labor Migration in the Atlantic Economies: The European and North American Working Classes during the Period of Industrialization.* Westport, Conn., 1985.

———. "The Traffic of Emigration via Bremen/Bremerhaven: Merchants' Interests, Protective Legislation, and Migrants' Experiences." *American Ethnic History* 13 (1993): 68–101.

Hogan, William, R. *The Texas Republic: A Social and Economic History.* Norman, Okla., 1946.

Holbrook, Abigail Curlee. SEE ALSO Curlee, Abigail.

Holbrook, Abigail Curlee. "Cotton Marketing in Antebellum Texas." *Southwestern Historical Quarterly,* 71 (1970): 431–455.

———. "A Glimpse of Life on Antebellum Slave Plantations in Texas." *Southwestern Historical Quarterly* 16 (1973): 361–383.

———. "Robert Mills." In *Handbook of Texas,* edited by Walter P. Webb et al. 3 vols. Austin, 1952–1976.

Holtmann, Antonius, "Snares for the Genealogist and the Historian. A Critique." *Newsletter of the Society for German-American Studies* 14 (1993): 17–24.

Höver, Otto. "Bremische Segelschiffe und ihre Reeder 1840–1914." *Jahrbuch der Bremer Gesellschaft von 1914* (1928–1929): 10–14.

———. *Von der Galiot zum Fünfmaster: Unsere Segelschiffe in der Weltschiffahrt 1780–1930.* Bremen, [1934].

———. *Von der Kogge zum Clipper: Zur Entwicklung des Segelschiffs.* Hamburg, [1948].

Huber, Armin O. "Frederic Armand Strubberg, Alias Dr. Shubbert: Townbuilder, Physician, and Adventurer, 1806–1889." *West Texas Historical Association Yearbook* 38 (1962): 37–71.

Huck, Jürgen. "Bürgermeister und Rat der Stadt Elze 1627–1793. Mit Nachrichten zur Entwicklung der Elzer Ratsverfassung." *Norddeutsche Familienkunde* 3 (1954): 52–56.

———. "Elze, die Stadt der Brände." *Niedersachsen. Zeitschrift für Heimat und Kultur,* 1949, no. 4: 133–135.

———. "Elzes Weg vom Dorf zur Stadt." *Alt-Hildesheim. Zeitschrift für Stadt und Stift Hildesheim* 27 (1956): 37–41.

———. "Landbesitzer der Stadt Elze von 1671." *Norddeutsche Familienkunde* 3 (1954): 12–14.

———. "Das Post -und Fernmeldewesen in der Stadt Elze." *Archiv für deutsche Postgeschichte* (1972), no. 2: 117–132.

———. "Die Stadt Elze im 16., 17. und 18. Jahrhundert." *Unsere Heimat. Blätter für Heimatgeschichte, Volks- und Naturkunde* [Gronau] 15, no. 1 (1967).

Hutchinson, E. P. *Immigrants and Their Children, 1850–1950.* New York, 1956.

Hvidt, Kristian. *Flight to America: The Social Background of 300,000 Danish Emigrants.* New York, [1975?].

Hyer, Julien. *The Land of Beginning Again: The Romance of the Brazos.* Atlanta [1953?].

Jacobs, Jane. *Cities and the Wealth of Nations: Principles of Economic Life.* New York, 1985.

Jäger, Helmut, ed. *Methodisches Handbuch für Heimatforschung in Niedersachsen*, Veröffentlichungen des Instituts für Historische Landesforschung der Universität Göttingen, 1. Hildesheim, 1965.

James, Marquis. *The Raven: A Biography of Sam Houston.* Indianapolis, 1929.

Jennett, Elizabeth Le Noir, ed. *Biographical Dictionary of the Texan Conventions and Congresses, 1812–1845.* n.p., [1941?].

Jerome, Harry. *Migration and Business Cycles*, National Bureau of Economics Publications, 9. New York, 1926.

Jeschke, Jörg. *Gewerberecht und Handwerkswirtschaft des Königreichs Hannover im Übergang 1815–1866: Eine Quellenstudie.* Göttingen, 1977.

Johnson, William R. *A Short History of the Sugar Industry in Texas*, Publications of the Texas Gulf Coast Historical Association, vol. 5, no. 1. Houston, 1961.

Jones, Fred Mitchell. *Middlemen in the Domestic Trade of the United States, 1800–1860.* Urbana, 1937.

Jones, Maldwyn Allen. *American Immigration.* Chicago, 1960.

Jordan, Terry G. "The German Element in Texas." In *Texas and Germany: Crosscurrents*, edited by Joseph Wilson. Rice University Studies, vol. 63, no. 3. Houston, 1977.

———. *German Seed in Texas Soil: Immigrant Farmers in Nineteenth-Century Texas.* Austin, 1966.

———. "The Pattern of Origins of the *Adelsverein* German Colonists." *Texana* 6 (1968): 245–257.

Justman, Dorothy Eckel. *German Colonists and Their Descendents in Houston, including the Usener and Allied Families.* Quanah, Tex., 1974.

Kamphoefner, Walter D. "German-Americans and Civil War Politics: A Reconsideration of the Ethnocultural Thesis." *Civil War History* 37 (Sept. 1991): 232–246.

———. "Texas Germans and Civil War Issues: The Evidence from Immigrant Letters." *Journal of the German-Texan Heritage Society* 13, no. 1 (1991): 16–23.

———. "Umfang und Zusammensetzung der deutsch-amerikansichen Rückwanderung." *Amerikastudien* 33 (1988): 291–307.

———. *Westfalen in der Neuen Welt: Eine Sozialgeschichte der Auswanderung im 19. Jahrhundert.* Münster, 1982. U.S. ed.: *The Westfalians: From Germany to Missouri.* Princeton, 1987.

Kappe, Gustav. *Die Unterweser und ihr Wirtschaftsraum: Formen und Kräfte einer Landschaft am Strom.* Bremen, 1929.

Kattner, Lauren A. "Growing Up and Town Development: Social and Cultural Adaptation in a German-American Town." Master's thesis, University of Texas at Dallas, 1987.

Kaufhold, K. H. "Handel und Industrie 1800–1850." In *Handbuch der deutschen Wirtschafts- und Sozialgeschichte,* edited by Hermann Aubin and Wolfgang Zorn, vol. 2 of 2 vols. Stuttgart, 1971–1976.

Kaufmann, Wilhelm. *Die Deutschen im amerikanischen Bürgerkriege.* Munich, 1911.

Kazal, Russell. "Revisiting Assimilation: The Rise, Fall, and Reappraisal of a Concept in American History." *American Historical Review* 100 (1995): 437–471.

Keil, Hartmut. "German Workers in Nineteenth-Century America: Working-Class Culture and Everyday Life in an Urban Industrial Setting." In *America and the Germans: An Assessment of a Three-Hundred-Year History,* edited by Frank Trommler and Joseph McVeigh, vol. 1 of 2 vols. Philadelphia, 1985.

Keil, Hartmut, ed. *German Workers' Culture in the United States, 1850–1920.* Washington, 1988.

Keil, Hartmut, and John Jentz, eds. *German Workers in Industrial Chicago, 1850–1910: A Comparative Perspective.* DeKalb, Ill., 1983.

Kellenbenz, Hermann. "Der Bremer Kaufmann. Versuch einer sozialgeschichtlichen Deutung." *Bremisches Jahrbuch* 51 (1969): 19–49.

———. "Zur Frage der konsularischen diplomatischen Verbindungen und die Handelsverträge der Hansestädte mit überseeischen Staaten im 19. Jahrhundert." *Bremisches Jahrbuch* 49 (1964): 219–224.

———. "Verkehrs- und Nachrichtenwesen, Handel, Geld —, Kredit- und Versicherungswesen 1800–1850." In *Handbuch der deutschen Wirtschafts- und Sozialgeschichte,* edited by Hermann Aubin and Wolfgang Zorn, vol. 2 of 2 vols. Stuttgart, 1971–1976.

———. "Zahlungsmittel, Maße und Gewichte seit 1800." In *Handbuch der deutschen Wirtschafts- und Sozialgeschichte,* edited by Hermann Aubin and Wolfgang Zorn, vol. 2 of 2 vols. Stuttgart, 1971–1976.

Kempen, Wilhelm van, "Übersee-Auswanderer aus dem Raum Göttingen 1847–1876." *Norddeutsche Familienkunde* 9 (1961): 274–288.

Keyser, Erich. *Niedersächsisches Städtebuch.* Stuttgart, 1952.

King, Dick. *Ghost Towns of Texas.* San Antonio, 1953.

Kivisto, Peter, and Dag Blanck, eds. *American Immigrants and Their Gen-*

erations: *Studies and Commentaries on the Hansen Thesis after Fifty Years*. Urbana, 1990.

Klaube, Manfred. *Der Ambergau im 19. Jahrhundert und in der Gegenwart*. Bockenem, 1973.

———. *Die Stadt Bockenem 1847 im Jahr des Großen Brandes und die Gegebenheiten in den Jahren davor und danach*. Bockenem, 1988.

Klein, Ruth (Thierfelder). *Lexikon der Mode: Drei Jahrtausende europäischer Kostümkunde*. 3 vols. Baden-Baden, [1950].

Kloss, Heinz, ed. *Atlas der im 19. und frühen 20. Jahrhundert entstandenen Siedlungen in den USA*. Marburg, [1975].

———. *Um die Einigung des Deutschamerikanertums: Die Geschichte einer unvollendeten Volksgruppe*. Berlin, 1937.

———. "German-American Language Maintenance Efforts." In *Language Loyalty in the United States: The Maintenance and Perpetuation of Non-English Mother Tongues by American Ethnic and Religious Groups*, edited by Joshua Fishman. New York, 1978.

Klotzbach, Kurt. *Wagenspur nach Westen: Deutsche Pioniere in Texas*. 4. Aufl. Göttingen, 1976.

Klüber, Karl Werner. "Wiedergefundene Bremer und Hamburger Auswandererlisten." *Genealogie* 15 (1966): 329–332.

Knösel, H. "Vor Hundert Jahren ausgewandert: Auswandereragenturen gab es in Alfeld, Elze und Sack." *Alfelder Zeitung* (Alfeld), January 11, 1965.

Köllmann, Wolfgang. "Bevölkerungsgeschichte 1800–1970." In *Handbuch der deutschen Wirtschafts- und Sozialgeschichte*, edited by Hermann Aubin and Wolfgang Zorn, vol. 2 of 2 vols. Stuttgart, 1971–1976.

———. "Versuch des Entwurfs einer historisch-soziologischen Wanderungstheorie." In *Soziale Bewegung und politische Verfassung: Beiträge zur Geschichte der modernen Welt*, edited by Ulrich Engelhardt, Volker Sellin, and Horst Stuke. Stuttgart, 1976.

Köllmann, Wolfgang, and Peter Marschalck. "German Emigration to the United States." *Perspectives in American History* 7 (1973): 499–554.

Konwiser, Harry M. *The Texas Republic Postal System*. New York, 1913.

Kossok, Manfred. "Die Bedeutung des spanisch-amerikanischen Kolonialmarktes für den preußischen Leinwandhandel am Ausgang des 18. und zu Beginn des 19. Jahrhunderts." In *Hansische Studien: Heinrich Sprömberg zum 70. Geburtstag. Forschungen zur Mittelalterlicher Geschichte*, 8. Berlin, 1961.

———. "Zur Geschichte der deutsch-lateinamerikanischen Beziehungen

(Forschungs- und Periodisierungsprobleme)." *Hansische Geschichts-blätter* 82 (1964): 49–77.

―――. "Preußen, Bremen und die 'Texas-Frage' 1835–1845." *Bremisches Jahrbuch* 49 (1964): 73–104.

―――. "Prussia, Bremen, and the 'Texas Question,'" *Texana* 3 (1965): 227–269.

Kraus, Gerhard. "Der Bockenemer Stadtplan von 1843." *Alt-Hildesheim: Jahrbuch für Stadt und Stift Hildesheim* 45 (1974): 45–50.

―――. *Im Schatten der Heiligen Allianz. Deutschland und Lateinamerika 1815–1830. Zur Politik der deutschen Staaten gegenüber der Unabhängigkeitsbewegung Mittel- und Südamerikas.* Berlin, 1964.

Kresse, Walter. "Die Auswirkungen der Handelsverträge der Hansestädte mit amerikanischen Staaten auf die Hamburger Schiffahrt." *Zeitschrift des Vereins für Hamburgische Geschichte* 60 (1974): 139–146.

―――. "Die hanseatische Reederei im 18. und 19. Jahrhundert." *Hansische Geschichtsblätter* 93 (1975): 89–99.

Kriedte, Peter, Hans Medick, and Jürgen Schlumbohm. *Industrialisierung vor der Industrialisierung: Gewerbliche Warenproduktion auf dem Lande in der Formationsperiode des Kapitalismus.* Göttingen, 1977.

―――. "Sozialgeschichte in der Erweiterung—Proto-Industrialisierung in der Verengung? Demographie, Sozialstruktur, moderne Hausindustrie: eine Zwischenbilanz der Proto-Industrialisierungs-Forschung." *Geschichte und Gesellschaft* 18 (1992): 70–87, 231–255.

Kruse, Hans, ed. *Deutsche Briefe aus Mexiko. Mit einer Geschichte des Deutsch-Amerikanischen Bergwerkvereins 1824–1838. Ein Beitrag zur Geschichte des Deutschtums im Auslande.* Veröffentlichungen des Archivs für Rheinisch-Westfälische Wirtschaftsgeschichte, 9. Essen, 1923.

Kulikoff, Allan. *The Agrarian Origins of American Capitalism.* Charlottesville, 1992.

Kulischer, Alexander, and Eugen Kulischer. *Kriegs- und Wanderzüge: Weltgeschichte als Völkerbewegung.* Berlin, 1932.

Die Kunstdenkmale der Provinz Hannover, series 10, vol. 2: *Der Kreis Marienburg.* Hannover, 1910; series 26, vol. 2: *Der ehemalige Kreis Gronau.* Hannover 1939.

Lack, Paul D. "Slavery and the Texas Revolution." *Southwestern Historical Quarterly* 89 (1985): 181–202.

Lane, Elizabeth. "History of Brazoria County." Master's thesis, Texas College of Arts and Industries, Kingsville, 1948.

Lathrop, Barnes F. *Migrations into East Texas.* Austin, 1949.

Laurie, Bruce. *Artisans into Workers: Labor in Nineteenth-Century Europe.* New York, 1989.

Laurie, Bruce, Theodore Hershberg, and George Alter. "Immigrants and Industry: The Philadelphia Experience, 1850–1880." In *Philadelphia: Work, Space, Family, and Group Experience in the Nineteenth Century,* edited by Theodore Hershberg. New York, 1981.

Lenz, Louis. "Texas Money." *Southwestern Historical Quarterly* 51 (1953): 175–180.

Levine, Bruce C. "Free Soil, Free Labor, and *Freimänner*: German Chicago in the Civil War Era." In *German Workers in Industrial Chicago, 1850–1910: A Comparative Perspective,* edited by Hartmut Keil and John B. Jentz. DeKalb, Ill., 1983.

———. "In the Heat of Two Revolutions: The Forging of German-American Radicalism." In *"Struggle a Hard Battle": Essays on Working-Class Immigrants,* edited by Dirk Hoerder. DeKalb, Ill., 1986.

———. *The Spirit of 1848: German Immigration, Labor Conflict, and the Coming of the Civil War.* Urbana, 1992.

Lich, Glen. "German Emigration Contracts in the General Land Office." *Texas Library* 38 (1976): 19–21.

———. *The German Texans.* San Antonio, 1981.

———. "Sealsfield's Texas: Metaphor, Experience, and History." *Yearbook of German-American Studies* 22 (1987): 71–79.

Lich, Glen, and Dona B. Reeves, eds. *German Culture in Texas: A Free Earth. Essays from the 1978 Southwestern Symposium.* Boston, 1980.

Linde, Hans. "Das Königreich Hannover an der Schwelle des Industriezeitalters." *Neues Archiv für Niedersachsen* 24 (1951): 413–443.

———. "Proto-Industrialisierung: Zur Justierung eines neuen Leitbegriffs der sozialgeschichtlichen Forschung." *Geschichte und Gesellschaft* 6 (1980): 103–124.

Lindeman, Moritz. "Zur Geschichte der älteren Handelsbeziehungen Bremens mit den Vereinigten Staaten von Nordamerika." *Bremisches Jahrbuch* 10 (1878): 124–146.

Lindemann, Ann, James Lindemann, and William Richter, eds. *Historical Accounts of Industry, Texas, 1836–1986.* New Ulm, Tex., 1986.

Linn, John J. *Reminiscences of Fifty Years in Texas.* 1883. Reprint. Austin 1935.

Löbe, Karl. *Das Weserbuch.* Hameln, [1968?].

Lonn, Ella. *Foreigners in the Confederacy.* Chapel Hill, N.C., 1940.

Luebke, David. "German Exodus: Historical Perspectives on the Nineteenth-Century Emigration." *Yearbook of German-American Studies* 20 (1985): 1–17.

Luebke, Frederick C. *Germans in Brazil: A Comparative History of Cultural Conflict during World War I.* Baton Rouge, 1987.

———. *Germans in the New World: Essays in the History of Immigration.* Urbana, 1990.

Lüntzel, Hermann Adolf. *Die bäuerlichen Lasten in Fürstentume Hildesheim.* Hildesheim, 1830.

Mahrenholtz, Hans. "Auswanderer aus dem Landdrosteibezirk Hildesheim." *Norddeutsche Familienkunde* 7 (1958): 110–115.

———. "Über den Umfang der Auswanderung aus Niedersachsen." *Norddeutsche Familienkunde* 7 (1958): 80–82.

Marienbach, Bernard. *Galveston: Ellis Island of the West.* Albany, 1983.

Marschalck, Peter. *Deutsche Überseewanderung im 19. Jahrhundert: Ein Beitrag zur soziologischen Theorie der Bevölkerung.* Stuttgart, 1973.

———. "Der Erwerb des bremischen Bürgerrechts und die Zuwanderung nach Bremen um die Mitte des 19. Jahrhunderts." *Bremer Jahrbuch* 66 (1988): 295–305.

Massengill, Fred I. *Texas Towns.* Terrell, Tex., 1936.

McComb, David G. *Galveston: A History.* Austin, 1986.

———. *Houston: The Bayou City.* Austin, [1969?].

Mentz, Brígida von, et al. *Los Pioneros del imperialismo alemán en Mexico.* Mexico City, 1982.

Merk, Frederick. *Slavery and the Annexation of Texas.* New York, 1972.

Meyer, Heinrich [pseud. H. K. Houston Meyer]. *Konrad Bäumlers weiter Weg: Ein Texas-Deutscher Roman.* Stuttgart, 1938.

———. *Was bleibt: Bemerkungen über Literatur und Leben, Schein und Wirklichkeit.* Stuttgart, 1966.

Meyer, Hildegard. *Nordamerika im Urteil des deutschen Schrifttums bis zur Mitte des 19. Jahrhunderts: Eine Untersuchung über Kürnbergers "Amerika-Müden".* Übersee-Geschichte, 3. Hamburg, 1929. Has an excellent bibliography.

Meyer zu Selhausen, Hermann. *Die Schiffahrt auf der Weser.* Stuttgart, 1911.

Mikoletzky, Juliane. *Die deutsche Amerika-Auswanderung des 19. Jahrhunderts in der zeitgenössischen fiktionalen Literatur.* Tübingen, 1988. Has an excellent bibliography.

Miller, Edmund T. *A Financial History of Texas.* Austin, 1916.

Mitchell, Robert D. *Commercialism and Frontier: Perspectives on the Early Shenandoah Valley.* Charlottesville, Va., 1977.

Mittelhäußer, Käthe, ed. *Der Landkreis Alfeld (Regierungsbezirk Hildesheim). Kreisbeschreibung nebst Raumordnungsplan und statistischem Anhang.* Die Landkreise in Niedersachsen, Reihe D, 14. Bremen-Horn, 1957.

Moltmann, Günter. "American-German Return Migration in the Nineteenth and Early Twentieth Centuries." *Central European History* 13 (1980): 378–392.

———. "Die deutsche Amerikaauswanderung im 19. Jahrhundert." In *". . . nach Amerika!" Auswanderung in die Vereinigten Staaten,* by Wolfgang Hell et al. Aus den Schausammlungen des Museums für Hamburgische Geschichte, 5. Hamburg, 1976.

———. "Die deutsche Auswanderung in überseeische Gebiete. Forschungsstand und Forschungsprobleme." *Der Archivar* 32 (1979): 57–66.

———. *Von Deutschland nach Amerika: Sozialgeschichte der Auswanderung im 19. und 20. Jahrhundert.* Wiesbaden, 1979.

———. "Das Risiko der Seereise. Auswanderungsbedingungen im Europa-Amerika-Verkehr um die Mitte des 19. Jahrhunderts." In *Festschrift für Eberhard Kessel zum 75. Geburtstag,* edited by Heinz Duchardt and Manfred Schlenke. Munich, 1982.

Moltmann, Günter, ed. *Deutsche Amerikaauswanderung im 19. Jahrhundert: Sozialgeschichtliche Beiträge.* Amerikastudien, 44. Stuttgart, 1976.

Molyneaux, Peter. *The Romantic Story of Texas.* New York, 1936.

Mönckemeier, Wilhelm. *Die deutsche überseeische Auswanderung: Ein Beitrag zur deutschen Wanderungsgeschichte.* Jena, 1912.

[Möring, Maria]. *Joh. Achelis & Söhne Bremen: Export-Import.* [Bremen, 1976?].

Moore, James Talmadge. *Through Fire and Flood: The Catholic Church in Frontier Texas, 1836–1900.* College Station, Tex., 1992.

Morrison, Andrew, ed. *The Industries of Galveston.* Galveston, 1887.

Mottek, Hans, et al. *Wirtschaftsgeschichte Deutschlands.* 3 vols. Berlin, 1959–1975.

Muir, Andrew F. "The Destiny of Buffalo Bayou." *Southwestern Historical Quarterly* 47 (1943): 91–106.

———. "Railroad Enterprise in Texas, 1836–1841." *Southwestern Historical Quarterly* 47 (1944): 339–370.

Muir, Andrew F., ed. *Texas in 1837: An Anonymous Contemporary Narrative.* Austin, 1958.

Müller, Richard, "Deutsche Dörfer in Texas." *Familiengeschichtliche Blätter* 35 (1937): 279–286.

Bibliographical Essay and Bibliography

Müller, Siegfried. "Gesellenwandern in der ersten Hälfte des 19. Jahrhunderts, dargestellt am Beispiel Hannovers." *Historisches Jahrbuch* 107 (1987): 77–93.

Müller, Wilhelm. "Von den großen Stadtbränden Bockenems, seinen Archivquellen und dem Bürgerverzeichnis von 1531–69." *Alt-Hildesheim* 28 (1957): 43–47.

Nadel, Stanley. *Little Germany: Ethnicity, Religion, and Class in New York City, 1845–1880.* Urbana, 1990.

Neusinger, Edward W. "The Monetary History of the Republic of Texas." *Southwestern Historical Quarterly* 57 (1953): 82–90.

Newman, J. Wilson. *"Dun & Bradstreet": Established in 1841 for the Promotion and Protection of Trade.* New York, 1956.

Newsome, W. L. "The Postal System of Texas." *Southwestern Historical Quarterly* 20 (1916): 102–131.

Newton, Lewis W., and Herbert P. Gambrell. *A Social and Political History of Texas.* Dallas, [1932?].

Nord, Ludolf. *Die Stadt Bockenem 1131–1931: Mit einer Betrachtung über die geschichtliche Entstehung des Ambergaus.* Hildesheim, 1931.

Obermann, Karl. "Die deutsche Auswanderung nach den Vereinigten Staaten im 19. Jahrhundert. Ihre Ursachen und Auswirkungen (1830 bis 1870)." *Jahrbuch für Wirtschaftsgeschichte* 17, no. 2 (1975): 33–55.

Oberschelp, Reinhard. *Niedersachsen 1760–1820: Wirtschaft, Gesellschaft, Kultur im Land Hannover und Nachbargebieten.* 2 vols. Hildesheim, 1982.

Ohe, Werner von der. "Bayern im 19. Jahrhundert — ein Entwicklungsland? Möglichkeiten und Grenzen des Beitrags der vergleichenden Sozialforschung." In *Aufbruch ins Industriezeitalter*, vol. 1: *Linien der Entwicklungsgeschichte*, edited by Claus Grimm. Munich, 1985.

Pessen, Edward. "How Different from Each Other Were the Antebellum North and South?" *American Historical Review* 85 (1980): 1119–1149.

Peters, Fritz. "Über bremische Firmengründungen in der 1. Hälfte des 19. Jahrhunderts (1814–1847)." *Bremisches Jahrbuch* 36 (1936): 306–361.

Pferdekamp, Wilhelm. *Deutsche im frühen Mexiko.* Stuttgart, 1938.

———. *Auf Humboldts Spuren: Deutsche im jungen Mexiko.* Munich, 1958.

Pickrell, Annie D. *Pioneer Women in Texas.* Austin, 1929.

Piore, Michael. *Birds of Passage: Migrant Labor and Industrial Societies.* Cambridge, 1980.

Pitsch, Franz Josef. *Die wirtschaftlichen Beziehungen Bremens zu den Ver-*

einigten Staaten von Amerika bis zur Mitte des 19. Jahrhunderts. Veröffentlichungen aus dem Staatsarchiv der Freien Hansestadt Bremen, 42. Bremen, 1974.

Platter, Allen A. "Educational, Social, and Economic Characteristics of the Plantation Culture of Brazoria County, Texas." Ph.D. diss., University of Houston, 1961.

Pletcher, David M. *The Diplomacy of Annexation: Texas, Oregon, and the Mexican War.* Columbia, Mo., 1973.

Pohlmann, M. "Vorkommen und Herkunft des Familiennamens Pohlmann." *Norddeutsche Familienkunde* 6 (1957): 254–257.

Potts, Lydia. *The World Labour Market: A History of Migration.* Translated by Terry Bond. London, 1990.

Prüser, Friedrich. "Der Bremer Überseekaufmann. Vorläufer und Wegbereiter." *Der Schlüssel. Bremer Beiträge zur deutschen Kultur und Wirtschaft* 10 (1938): 425–436.

———. "Vom Bremer Überseekaufmann." *Abhandlungen und Vorträge [der Bremer Wissenschaftlichen Gesellschaft]* 14 (1940).

Prüser, Friedrich, and Fritz Peters. *Die Freie Hansestadt Bremen*, Familiengeschichtliche Wegweiser durch Stadt und Land, 18. Neustadt a. d. Aisch, 1953.

Prüser, Friedrich, and Wilhelm Treue, eds. *Beiträge zur bremischen Firmengeschichte.* Tradition, Beiheft, 5. Munich, 1966.

Prüser, Jürgen. *Die Handelsverträge der Hansestädte Lübeck, Bremen und Hamburg mit überseeischen Staaten im 19. Jahrhundert.* Veröffentlichungen aus dem Staatsarchiv der Freien Hansestadt Bremen, 30. Bremen, 1962.

Puryear, Pamela Ashworth, and Nath Winfield. *Sandbars and Sternwheelers: Steam Navigation on the Brazos.* College Station, Tex., [1976?].

"Quellen zur Niedersächsischen Familienforschung [im] Staatsarchiv Bremen." *Niedersächsisches Familien-Archiv* 6 (1917–1918): 3–5.

Ransleben, Guido E. *A Hundred Years of Comfort in Texas. A Centennial History.* San Antonio, 1954.

Rauers, Friedrich. *Bremer Handelsgeschichte im 19. Jahrhundert.* Bremen, 1911.

———. *Geschichte des Bremer Binnenhandels im 19. Jahrhundert: Namentlich unter den alten Verkehrsformen und im Übergang.* Bremen, 1913.

———. "Zur Geschichte der alten Handelsstraßen. Versuch einer quellenmäßigen Übersichtskarte." *Petermanns Mitteilungen aus Justus Perthes' geographischer Anstalt* 52 (1906): 49–59.

————. *Vom Wilden zum Welttraumfahrer: Die Geschichte des Verkehrs von den Anfängen bis zur Gegenwart.* Edited by Joachim Vosberg. Bad Godesberg, 1962.

Reden, Friedrich Wilhelm Otto Ludwig Freiherr von. *Allgemeine vergleichende Handels- und Erwerbs-Geographie und Statistik. Ein Handbuch für Kaufleute, Fabrikanten und Staatsmänner.* Berlin, 1844.

————. *Das Königreich Hannover statistisch beschrieben. Zunächst in Beziehung auf Landwirtschaft, Gewerbe und Handel.* 2 vols. Hannover, 1839.

Reeves, Dona B. "German Galveston: A Personal Narrative." *Schatzkammer der deutschen Sprache, Dichtung und Geschichte* 17 (1991): 111–118.

Reeves, Dona B., and Glen Lich, eds. *Retrospect and Retrieval: The German Element in Review. Essays on Cultural Preservation.* Ann Arbor, 1978.

Reichstein, Andreas. *Der texanische Unabhängigkeitskrieg: Ursachen und Wirkung.* Berlin, 1984. Translation: *Rise of the Lone Star: The Making of Texas.* Translated by Jeanne R. Willson. College Station, Tex., 1989.

Reineke, Karl. "Die familiengeschichtlichen Quellen im bremischen Staatsarchiv." *Familiengeschichtliche Blätter: Monatsschrift für wissenschaftliche Genealogie* 28 (1930): 390–395.

Renner, Johann Georg Friedrich. *Aus der Geschichte der Stadt Osterode am Harz.* 1833. Reprint. Osterode am Harz, 1977.

Reppmann, Joachim. *"Freiheit, Bildung und Wohlstand für Alle!" Schleswig-Holsteinische "Achtundvierziger" in den USA 1847–1860,* Schriften zur schleswig-holsteinische Amerikaauswanderung. Wyk auf Föhr, 1994.

Reps, John W. *The Making of Urban America: A History of City Planning in the United States.* Princeton, 1965.

————. *Town Planning in Frontier America.* Princeton, 1969.

Richter, Klaus. "Die Auswanderungsquellen der hansestädtischen Archive." *Der Archivar* 32 (1979): 49–51.

Robinson-Zwahr, Robert. *Die Bremerverwandtschaft in Deutschland und Texas.* 2 vols. Quanah, Tex., 1979.

Rogers, Mary Nixon. "A History of Brazoria County, Texas." In *A History of Brazoria County, Texas* [and two other works], by Travis L. Smith et al. Houston, 1958.

Rosenberg, William von. *Kritik der Geschichte des Vereins zum Schutze der deutschen Auswanderer nach Texas.* Austin, 1894.

Rosenberg-Tomlinson, Alma von. *The von Rosenberg Family of Texas.* Boerne, Tex., 1949.

Rüthnick, Richard. "Das Geschlecht Achelis." *Der Schlüssel: Bremer Beiträge zur deutschen Kultur und Wirtschaft* 1, no. 5 (1936): 37–41.

Saalfeld, Dietrich. "Handwerkereinkommen in Deutschland vom ausgehenden 18. Jahrhundert bis zur Mitte des 19. Jahrhunderts." In *Handwerksgeschichte in neuer Sicht,* edited by Wilhelm Abel. Göttingen, 1970.

Scale, Martha. "Zur Entwicklung von Handwerk und Industrie in einer niedersächsischen Kleinstadt in der ersten Hälfte des 19. Jahrhunderts. Dargestellt am Beispiel der Stadt Alfeld." In *Handwerksgeschichte in neuer Sicht,* edited by Wilhelm Abel. Göttingen, 1970.

——. *Geschichte der Stadt Alfeld (Leine) in neuer Sicht.* Alfeld, 1973.

Schaefer, Hans-Ludwig. *Bremens Bevölkerung in der ersten Hälfte des 19. Jahrhunderts.* Veröffentlichungen aus dem Staatsarchiv der Freien Hansestadt Bremen, 25. Bremen, 1957.

Scheben, Joseph. *Untersuchung zur Methode und Technik der deutschamerikanischen Wanderungsforschung.* Bonn, 1939.

Scheffel, Fritz. *Deutsche suchen den Garten der Welt: Das Schicksal deutscher Auswanderer in Texas vor 100 Jahren.* Stuttgart, 1937.

Schmitz, Joseph W. *Texan Statecraft, 1836–1845.* San Antonio, 1941.

——. *Thus They Lived.* San Antonio, 1935. 2d ed., new title: *In the Days of the Republic.* San Antonio, 1960.

Schnath, Georg. *Hannover und Westfalen in der Raumgeschichte Nordwestdeutschlands.* Veröffentlichungen der Wirtschaftswissenschaftlichen Gesellschaft zum Studium Niedersachsens, Reihe A: Beiträge, 19. Hannover, 1932.

Schöberl, Ingrid. *Amerikanische Einwanderungswerbung in Deutschland 1845–1914.* Stuttgart, 1990.

Schramm, Percy Ernst. "Die deutschen Überseekaufleute im Rahmen der Sozialgeschichte." *Bremisches Jahrbuch* 49 (1964): 31–54.

Schroeder, John H. "Annexation or Independence: The Texas Issue in American Politics, 1836–1845." *Southwestern Historical Quarterly* 89 (1985): 137–164.

Schuchalter, Jerry. "Charles Sealsfield's 'Fable of the Republic.'" *Yearbook of German-American Studies* 24 (1989): 11–25.

——. "*Geld* and *Geist* in the Writings of Gottfried Duden, Nikolaus Lenau, and Charles Sealsfield: A Study of Competing America-Paradigms." *Yearbook of German-American Studies* 27 (1992): 49–73.

Schüppen, Franz. *Charles Sealsfield. Karl Postl: Ein österreichischer Erzähler der Biedermeierzeit im Spannungsfeld von Alter und Neuer Welt.* Frankfurt am Main, 1981.

Bibliographical Essay and Bibliography

Schwebel, Karl H. "Bremer Kaufleute im Auslande." In *Bremen-Bremer-haven: Häfen am Strom*. 7. Aufl., publ. by Gesellschaft für Wirtschaftsförderung Bremens. Bremen, 1966.

Schwedler, Ferdinand A. von. "Deutsche Einwanderer in Texas (USA) 1844." *Genealogie* 17 (1968): 154–158.

Scott, Franklin D. *The Peopling of America: Perspectives on Immigration*. American Historical Association Pamphlet, 241. Washington, 1984.

Shook, Robert W. "The Battle of the Nueces, August 10, 1862." *Southwestern Historical Quarterly* 66 (1962): 31–42.

———. "German Migration to Texas, 1830–1850. Causes and Consequences." *Texana* 10 (1972): 226–243.

Sibley, Marilyn McAdams. *The Port of Houston: A History*. Austin, [1968].

Siegemann, Theodor, and Wilhelm Schramme. *Geschichte der Stadt Gronau*. Gronau, 1931.

Sievers, Kai Detlev, ed. *Die deutsche und skandinavische Amerikaauswanderung im 19. und 20. Jahrhundert*. Studien zur Wirtschafts- und Sozialgeschichte Schleswig-Holsteins, 3. Neumünster, 1982.

Sitterson, J. Carlyle. *Sugar County: The Cane Sugar Industry in the South, 1753–1950*. Lexington, Ky., [1953?].

Smith, Justin H. *The Annexation of Texas*. New York, 1941.

Smith, Travis L. *Steamboats on the Brazos*. In *History of Brazoria County* [and two other works], by Travis L. Smith et al. Houston, 1958.

Smolka, Georg. "Auswanderung und Kolonisationsprojekte im Vormärz." In *Staat und Gesellschaft: Festschrift für Günther Küchenhoff*, edited by Franz Mayer. Göttingen, 1967.

Sollors, Werner, ed. *The Invention of Ethnicity*. New York, 1989.

Steilen, Diedrich. *Die Niederweser*. Monographien zur Erdkunde, 37. Bielefeld and Leipzig, 1928.

Stolarik, M. Mark, ed. *Forgotten Doors: The Other Ports of Entry to the United States*. Philadelphia, 1988.

Streeter, Thomas W., ed. *Bibliography of Texas, 1795–1845*. 5 vols. Cambridge, Mass., 1960.

Strobel, Abner J. *The Old Plantations and Their Owners of Brazoria County, Texas*. In *A History of Brazoria County* [and two other works], by Travis L. Smith et al. Houston, 1958.

Struck, Wolf-Heino. "Die Auswanderung aus Hessen und Nassau in die Vereinigten Staaten." *Nassauische Annalen* 89 (1978): 78–114.

Struve, Adam. "Artisans among Galveston-Bound Immigrants, 1846–1850." Typescript. 1985. This essay exploits recently published passenger lists.

―――. "Economic Mobility among Foreign-Born Artisans in the Ante-bellum Lower South: The Case of Galveston, Texas." Typescript. 1986.

Struve, Walter. "German Merchants, German Artisans, and Texas during the 1830's and 1840's." *Yearbook of German-American Studies* 23 (1988): 91–103. Reprinted in *Journal of the German-Texan Heritage Society* 11, no. 1 (1989): 35–38.

―――. *Die Republik Texas, Bremen und das Hildesheimische: Ein Beitrag zur Geschichte von Auswanderung, Handel und gesellschaftlichem Wandel im 19. Jahrhundert. Mit den Briefen eines deutschen Kaufmanns und Landwirts in Texas 1844–1845.* Quellen und Darstellungen zur Geschichte Niedersachsens, 96. Hildesheim, 1983.

Swierenga, Robert P. "List upon Lists: The Ship Passenger Records and Immigration Research." *Journal of American Ethnic History* 10 (1991): 42–53.

Szymanski, Hans. *Die Anfänge der Dampfschiffahrt in Niedersachsen und den angrenzenden Gebieten von 1817 bis 1867.* Schriften der wirtschaftswissenschaftlichen Gesellschaft zum Studium Niedersachsens, Neue Folge, 67. Hannover, 1958.

Tarlton, Dewitt T. "The History of the Cotton Industry in Texas, 1820–1850." Master's thesis, University of Texas, Austin, 1923.

Tausend Jahre Bremer Kaufmann: Aufsätze zur Geschichte bremischen Kaufmannstums, des Bremer Handels und der Bremer Schiffahrt. Aus Anlaß der Marktgründung durch Erzbischof Adaldag 965. Bremen, 1965.

Taylor, Philip. *The Distant Magnet: European Emigration to the U.S.A.* New York, 1971.

Texas Department of Agriculture. *Year Book, 1909.* Texas Department of Agriculture Bulletin, 13. Austin.

Thistlethwaite, Frank. "Migration from Europe Overseas in the Nineteenth and Twentieth Centuries." In *XI Congrès International des Sciences Historique,* vol. 5: *Histoire Contemporaine,* pp. 32–60. Stockholm, 1960)

Thomas, Brinley. *Migration and Economic Growth: A Study of Great Britain and the Atlantic Economy.* National Institute of Economic and Social Research, Economic and Social Studies, 12. Cambridge, 1954.

―――. *Migration and the Rhythm of Economic Growth.* Manchester School of Economics and Social Studies, 19. Manchester, 1951.

Thompson, Laurence S. "German Travellers in the South from the Colonial Period to 1865." *South Atlantic Bulletin* 37 (1972): 64–74.

[Tiling, Moritz?]. "Die Deutschen in Texas vor der Massen-Einwanderung im Jahre 1844." *Deutsch-Texanische Monatshefte* 11 (1906–1907): 9–

15, 48–54, 88–92, 128–129, 199–203, 232–237, 272–277, 313–318, 358–365, 400–405; 12 (1908): 10–14, 45–51, 87–92, 120–124.

Tiling, Moritz. *History of the German Element in Texas from 1820 to 1850. And Historical Sketches of the German Texas Singers' League and Houston Turnverein from 1853 to 1913.* Houston, 1913.

Tilly, Richard H. "Capital Formation in Germany in the Nineteenth Century." In *Cambridge Economic History of Europe*, vol. 7, pt. 1. Cambridge, 1978.

Tolzmann, Don H. *German-Americana: A Bibliography.* Metuchen, N.J., 1975.

Treue, Wilhelm. *Niedersachsens Wirtschaft seit 1760: Von der Agrar- zur Industriegesellschaft.* Hannover, 1964.

Trommler, Frank, and Joseph McVeigh, eds. *America and the Germans: An Assessment of a Three-Hundred Year History.* 2 vols. Philadelphia, 1985.

Turner, Frederick Jackson. *The Frontier in American History.* 3d ed. New York 1958.

———. *Frontier and Section: Selected Essays.* Edited by Ray Allen Billington. Englewood Cliffs, N.J., 1961.

Ültzen-Barckhausen, Johannes. *Bremische Schiffahrt vor 100-200 Jahren in ihrer Bedeutung für bremische Handels, Firmen- und Familiengeschichte.* Leipzig, 1933.

United States Works Progress Administration, Texas. *Texas Newspapers, 1813–1939.* Houston, 1941.

Vagts, Alfred. *Deutsch-amerikanische Rückwanderung: Probleme, Phänomene, Statistik, Politik, Soziologie, Biographie, Jahrbuch für Amerikastudien,* Beiheft 6. Heidelberg, 1960.

Ventker, August Friedrich. *Stüve und die hannoversche Bauernbefreiung.* Oldenburg, 1935.

Verdenhalven, Fritz, ed. *Alte Maße, Münzen und Gewichte aus dem deutschen Sprachgebiet.* Neustadt an der Aisch, 1968.

Virtanen, Keijo. *Settlement or Return: Finnish Emigrants, 1860–1930, in the International Overseas Return Migration Movement.* Finnish Historical Society, Studia Historica, 10. Helsinki, 1979.

van Ravenswaay, Charles. *The Arts and Architecture of German Settlements in Missouri: A Survey of a Vanishing Culture.* Columbia, Mo., 1977.

Wachsmuth, Wilhelm. *Geschichte von Hochstift und Stadt Hildesheim.* Hildesheim, 1863.

Wächter, Hans-Helmut. *Die Landwirtschaft Niedersachsens vom Beginn des 19. bis zur Mitte des 20. Jahrhunderts.* Bremen, 1959.

Walker, Mack. *Germany and the Emigration, 1816–1885.* Cambridge, Mass., 1964.

Wallace, John Melton, ed. *Gaceta to Gazette: A Check List of Texas Newspapers, 1813–1846.* Austin, 1966.

Wallerstein, Immanuel. *The Modern World System.* 2 vols. New York, 1974–.

Ward, Forrest E. "Pre-Revolutionary Activity in Brazoria County." *Southwestern Historical Quarterly* 64 (1960): 212–231.

Wätjen, Hermann. *Der deutsche Anteil am wirtschaftlichen Aufbau der Westküste Amerikas.* Leipzig, 1942.

———. *Aus der Frühzeit des Nordatlantikverkehrs: Studien zur Geschichte der deutschen Schiffahrt und deutschen Auswanderung nach den Vereinigten Staaten bis zum Ende des amerikanischen Bürgerkriegs.* Leipzig, 1932.

———. "Zur Geschichte der bremischen Südseefischerei in 19. Jahrhundert." *Bremisches Jahrbuch* 25 (1914): 138–166.

Webb, Walter P. *The Great Frontier.* Boston, 1952.

———. *The Texas Rangers: A Century of Frontier Defense.* 2d ed. Austin, 1965.

Webb, Walter P., et al., eds. *The Handbook of Texas.* 3 vols. Austin, 1952–1976.

Weber, Adolf Paul. *Deutsche Pioniere. Zur Geschichte des Deutschtums in Texas.* 2 vols. San Antonio, 1894.

Weber, David J. *The Spanish Frontier in North America.* New Haven, 1992.

Weber, Paul C. *America in Imaginative German Literature in the First Half of the Nineteenth Century.* 1926. Reprint. New York, 1966.

Weems, John Edward. *Dream of Empire: A Human History of the Republic of Texas, 1836–1846.* New York, 1971.

Wheeler, Kenneth W. *To Wear a City's Crown: The Beginnings of Urban Growth in Texas, 1836–1865.* Cambridge, Mass., 1968.

Whisenhunt, Donald W. *Chronology of Texan History.* 2 vols. Burnet, Tex., 1982–1986.

Wiedenfeld, Kurt. *Die nordwesteuropäischen Welthäfen London, Liverpool, Hamburg, Bremen, Amsterdam, Antwerpen, Havre in ihrer Verkehrs- und Handelsbedeutung.* Veröffentlichungen des Instituts für Meereskunde und des geographischen Instituts, 3. Berlin, 1903.

Willcox, Walter F., ed. *International Migrations.* 2 vols. New York, 1929–1931.

Williams, Elgin. *The Animating Pursuits of Speculation: Land Traffic in the Annexation of Texas.* New York, 1949.

Wilson, Joseph, ed. *Texas and Germany: Crosscurrents.* Rice University Studies, vol. 63, no. 3. Houston, 1977.

A Window to the Past: A Pictorial History of Brazoria County, Texas. [Brazoria], 1986.

Winfrey, Dorman H. "Genealogical Research in Texas State Archives." *Texas Libraries* 22, no. 3 (1960): 80–83.

Winkel, Harald. "Der Texasverein: Ein Beitrag zur Geschichte der deutschen Auswanderung im 19. Jahrhundert." *Vierteljahrschrift für Sozial- und Wirtschaftsgeschichte* 55 (1968): 348–372.

Winston, James E. "Notes on Commercial Relations between New Orleans and Texan Ports, 1838–1839." *Southwestern Historical Quarterly* 34 (1930): 91–105.

Witthöft, Harald. *Umrisse einer historischen Metrologie zum Nutzen der wirtschafts- und sozialgeschichtlichen Forschung: Maaß und Gewicht in Stadt und Land Lüneburg, im Hanseraum und im Kurfürstentum/Königreich Hannover vom 13. bis zum 19. Jahrhundert.* 2 vols. Göttingen, 1980.

Wittich, Werner. *Die Grundherrschaft in Nordwestdeutschland.* Leipzig, 1896.

Wittke, Carl. *The Utopian Communist: A Biography of Wilhelm Weitling.* Baton Rouge, La., 1950.

Woodman, Harold D. *King Cotton and His Retainers: Financing and Marketing the Cotton Crop of the South, 1800–1925.* Lexington, Ky., 1968.

Woodson, Leroy H. *American Negro Slavery in the Works of Friedrich Strubberg, Friedrich Gerstäcker, and Otto Ruppius.* Catholic University of America Studies in German, 22. Washington, 1949.

Wooster, Ralph A. "Foreigners in the Principal Towns of Antebellum Texas." *Southwestern Historical Quarterly* 66 (1962): 208–220.

———. "Wealthy Texans [in] 1870." *Southwestern Historical Quarterly* 74 (1970): 24–35.

Wortham, Louis J. *A History of Texas: From Wilderness to Commonwealth.* 5 vols. Fort Worth, 1924.

Wright, Carroll D. *History and Growth of the United States Census.* Washington, 1900.

Wyman, Mark. *The Immigrants Return to Europe, 1880–1930.* Ithaca, N.Y., 1994.

Yoakum, Henderson. *History of Texas.* 2 vols. New York, 1856.

York, Miriam Corff. *Friedrich Ernst of Industry*. Giddings, Tex., 1989.

Zang, Gert, ed. *Provinzialisierung einer Region: Regionale Unterentwicklung und liberale Politik in der Stadt und im Kreis Konstanz im 19. Jahrhundert. Untersuchungen zur Entstehung der bürgerlichen Gesellschaft.* Frankfurt am Main, 1978.

Zorn, Wolfgang. "Sozialer Wandel in Mitteleuropa 1780–1840. Eine vergleichende landesgeschichtliche Untersuchung." *Kölner Zeitschrift für Soziologie und Sozialpsychologie*, Sonderheft 16 (1972): 343–356.

INDEX

Note: This index does not include the data from the Chart of the Giesecke Family.

abolitionism and Germans, 76–77
acculturation, 3–4, 7
  See also assimilation
Achelis, Rebekka *Antoinette. See* Basse,
  Rebekka *Antoinette* née Achelis
Achelis, Thomas (1766–1841), 31
Achelis, Thomas (1807–1872), 31
Achelis & Sons, Joh., 155n17
Ackerbürger (term), 21
Ackerbürgerstadt (term), 18
Adelsverein (Verein zum Schutze
  deutscher Einwanderer in Texas [As-
  sociation for the Protection of German Immigrants in Texas]), 4–5, 51,
  143n13, 160n30
  founding and activities, 46–50
  names of *Adelsverein* colonists, 60–
    61, 167n12
  and passenger ships, 190n33–34,
    193n83
Adriance, John, 86–87, 95
African Americans, 3, 42, 47, 70
  as craftsmen, 105
  See also Negroes; slaves
agricultural reforms
  in Germany, 25–26
  in Hannover and Hildesheim areas,
    25–26
agriculture
  in Brazoria County, 73–74, 92–97

cotton, 82–86
in Germany, 18, 21, 75–76, 78,
  153nn38–39
as source of capital for other invest-
  ments, 25–26
in Texas, 74–75
See also cotton; farmers; land; plan-
  tations; slaves
Ahlers (German in Brazoria), 80, 94,
  103, 122
Ahlers, Gerhard, 180n80
  See also Ahlers (German in
    Brazoria)
Ahlers, Hermann, 180n80
  See also Ahlers (German in
    Brazoria)
Ahlers, J. H., 180n80
  See also Ahlers (German in
    Brazoria)
Ahlfhausen, Ahlshausen, 180n80
alcoholic beverages, 86
Alfeld (*Amt* [District])
  emigration from, 30, 62
Alfeld (town), xiv, 14, 23–24
  emigration from, 155n11
  linen industry in, 24, 123, 188n14
Alfhausen, 180n80
Allendorf (Hessen), 157n43
alliances through marriage, 189n22
Allsfeld. *See* Alfeld; Alsfeld

Alsace, Alsatians, 50
Alsfeld (Hessen), 24
    emigration from, 62
Alshausen, 180n80
Ambergau, 18
    See also Bockenem
Amsterdam, 34, 49
An[c]ker, 197
Angleton, Texas, xv, 73
Antoinette (brig), 122, 179n60, 187–188n3
Antwerp, 49
Apollo (brig), 135
architecture. *See* houses, frame, German reaction to
archives, xiii–xiv, 199–200
Argentina, 41
aristocrats, German, 75, 78, 111
    See also Junkers
Armand. *See* Friedrich Armand Strubberg
artisans, 5
    in Bockenem, 23
    in Brazoria County, 105–107
    displacement in Germany, 102
    in Elze, 23–24
    emigration from Germany, 102–106
    in Galveston, 105–106
    in Galveston County, 185n151
    German, in Texas, 101, 103–108
    in Hannover (Kingdom), 12, 14
    neglect by scholars, 114
    in New Braunfels, Texas, 184
    in New Orleans, 106
    in Southern United States, 105
    in United States, 102
    See also individual occupations
assimilation, 3–4, 7
    See also acculturation
Association for the Protection of German Immigrants in Texas (*Verein zum Schutze deutscher Einwanderer in Texas*). See *Adelsverein*
Austin, Stephen F., 42–43, 44, 67
Austin, Texas, 45, 79

Austin's Colony, 42–45, 67, 97
"Austin's Old Three Hundred," 98
Austria, 39
Austrians in Texas, 50

Bad Sooden-Allendorf, 157n43
bakers, 107
Baltimore
    German emigrants in, 63
    as immigrant port, 48, 60, 61, 62, 161n38
barrel makers. *See* coopers
barrels, 197
Basse, Christoph *Carl*, 21, 22, 31, 137, 152n18, 189n22
    failure to write, 123, 126
Basse, Friedrich Heinrich, 31, 189n22
Basse, *Marie* Henriette Sophie. *See* Giesecke, *Marie* Henriette Sophie née Basse
Basse, Rebekka *Antoinette* née Achelis, 31
Basse, *Sophie* Friederike Christine née Sander, 137, 189n22
Basse family
    Bremen branch, 31, 189n22
Bastrop, Baron de (Philipp Bögel), 44
Bastrop, Texas, 44, 55
Behr, Ottomar von, 103
Belgium, 43
bells, animal, 85
Benjamin, Gilbert G., 76
Berlin, Ira, 105
Beyer, Moritz, 74
Biebrich, 46
Biedermeier period, 8–9
Bielefeld, 190n43
Bielefeld, linen, 127
Biesele, Rudolph L., 76
Bilderlahe (*Amt* [District]), 24
birthplaces in census returns and ship passenger lists, 199
blankets, 86
    horse, 85
    saddle, 126

Bockenem, xiv, 18–19
  emigration from, 30, 63, 152n20
  See also Ambergau
Bocris, G. C., 35
Bodenwerder, 188n19
Bögel, Philipp. *See* Bastrop, Baron de
Bohemia, 4
bookbinders, 106
books, 86
boots, 86
bourgeoisie
  in Germany, 5, 8–9, 13–16
  in Texas, 5
  See also *Ackerbürger*; patricians
bourgeois society, development, 9, 91–92, 109–111
Bowie knives, 86. *See also* knives
Bracht, Victor, 172n41
brandy, 80
  See also alcoholic beverages
Brauer, August Wilhelm Ludolph, 178n49
  See also Brauer & Son, C. L.
Brauer, Carl Ludwig, 178n49
  See also other entries under Brauer
Brauer, J. A., 178n49
  See also Brauer & Son, C. L.
Brauer & Son, C. L., 113, 120, 133, 134, 178n49
  and cotton trade, 89, 179n60, 188n5, 189
  letter to Charles A. Giesecke, 122
  letter to Friedrich Giesecke, 194n87
  ships of, 187n3, 189n21, 190n34
  and tobacco trade, 94
Braunschweig. *See* Brunswick (city) and (duchy)
Brazil, 41, 56, 158n5
  declaration of independence from Portugal (1822), 39
Brazoria, Texas (town), 43, 54, 59
  as commercial center, 87, 88
  descriptions by travelers, 67–71, 73, 80–81
  Germans in, 72, 80

history neglected, 109
links with New Orleans, 68
population size, 170n16, 171n20
See also Brazos County; Brazos River
Brazoria County, Texas, 68
  cotton prices, 123–124
  Germans in, 72
  population (1844), 171n20; (1847), 73
  shift from cotton to sugar cane, 101, 124
  shops, 84
  shortage of women, 81
  slavery in, 73–74
  sugar plantations, 74, 124
Brazos Ports, 54, 67
Brazos River, 44, 45, 67, 70, 73, 80
  and commerce, 71
  sailing ships on, 66
  steamers on, 54, 71
Bremen, xiv, 5
  cigar manufacturing and trade, 34, 36, 193n71
  cotton trade, 36, 89–92
  development as port, 32, 34–35
  as emigrant port, 29–30, 33, 61, 156n25
  and Galveston, 9–10
  and hinterland, 32–33, 156n25
  imports, 40, 90
  Low German language in, 191n60
  merchants in Texas, 5–6, 41
  scheduled service to New Orleans, 48
  ships seeking cargo in Galveston, 122
  tobacco trade, 34–35, 193n71
  trade with Mexico, 40
  See also Bremerhaven; commercial treaties; Hanseatic cities
Bremerhaven, 29
bricklayers and brickmasons, 105, 106
  See also masons
Britain. *See* Great Britain

Bromme, Traugott, 103
Brower & Co., John H., 86
Brunswick (city), 129
Brunswick (duchy), 17, 19
  and *Adelsverein*, 46
  emigration from, 48
Buffalo Bayou, 55, 71
butchers, 105, 107
Büttner, Johann, 74, 172n42

cabinetmakers, 106
Caldwell, Texas, 55
calfskins, 122
  See also hides; skins
calico, 126, 133
capital, 25–26
  formation, 153n37
  inadequate, 16, 112–113
capitalism, 92–93, 109
  and frontier, 9
  See also bourgeoisie; bourgeois soci-
    ety; commerce; merchants
cargo manifests, inward, 178n49
carpenters, 105, 106
carters. *See* freight haulers
Catholics, German
  in Brazoria, 72
  in Hildesheim area, 20
  and Low German language, 191n60
  in Texas, 50
  See also under Galveston
cattle, 69
Central America, 158n7
chain migration, 63
  See also emigration; migration
chains for harnesses, 85
chalk, 134
Chile, 39, 41
cigars, cigar making, cigar trade, 125
  in Brazoria, 94–95
  in Bremen, 34
  Cuban, 180n81
  Havanas, 95, 132
  in Industry, Texas, 189–190n32
  Regalias, 131, 193n71–72

techniques, 131
  in Texas, 95
  See also tobacco
Circassian fabric, 133, 193n75
citizenship in German towns
  levels and purchase of, 14–16
Civil War in United States, 43
class. *See* social class
clipper ships, 7
clothing, 86
Coburg and *Adelsverein*, 46
cochineal, 39
Coleto Creek, 45
Colorado River, 44, 45
Columbia, Texas, 39, 54, 68, 69, 73,
  86, 95
  population (1844), 171n20
commerce
  between Hanseatic cities and North
    America, 32
  between Texas and Europe, 87
  See also commercial treaties; guilds;
    names of individual cities, states,
    and countries
commercial capitalism. *See* capitalism
commercial freedom, 104–105, 110
commercial treaties
  between Belgium and Texas (1840),
    43
  between France and Texas (1839), 43
  between Great Britain and Texas
    (1840), 43
  between Hanseatic cities and Texas
    (1844), 51
  between Hanseatic cities and United
    States (1827), 32
  between Netherlands and Texas
    (1840), 43
  See also tariffs and tariff policy; indi-
    vidual cities and states
commission business, 84
communications problems, 112, 121,
  123
confectioners, 106
Conze, Friedrich, 152n14

Conze, Werner, 152n14
coopers, 102, 105, 106, 132
coppersmiths, 102, 106
cotton
    factors, 87, 91
    press, 88
    prices, 91, 123–124
    See also cotton trade; textiles
cotton trade, 89–90, 92
country store
    concept, 84
    See also Giesecke, Edward (Ernst
        Eduard), store in Brazoria
craftsmen. *See* artisans
Cuba, 43, 56, 95
culture, internationalization of, 8–9
Curlee-Holbrook, Abigail, 86, 89
Czechs, 3

Daingerfield, William Henry, 51
Danes, 73
darning needles, 85
Davis, Jefferson, 98
Davis, Jesse Kincheloe, 182n107
Davis, Sarah Mary. *See* Giesecke,
    Sarah Mary, née Davis
Davis, Thomas Kincheloe, 97, 181n97
day laborers. *See* laborers, day; workers
deaths, early and migration. *See* mor-
    tality of emigrants
deerskins, 122
    See also hides; skins
Delius, F. and E. (firm), 94
Dethard, Johann (brig). *See* Johann
    Dethard (brig)
Deutscher Bund. See German
    Federation
Dickinson's Bayou, 80, 185n151
Dietrich, Francis (Franz), 79
Dirks, Christian Friedrich Ernst. *See*
    Ernst, Friedrich
distilleries, distillers, distilling of alco-
    holic beverages
    in Kingdom of Hannover, 101
    in Mississippi and Ohio Valleys, 101

in Texas, 100–101
    See also artisans; brandy; coopers;
        coppersmiths; rum; whiskey
Doby, Li[e]sette. *See* Giesecke,
    Li[e]sette née Doby
Douai, Adolf, 77
drums, 86
Dübel, Wilhelm, 62
Duden, Gottfried, 44, 160n22
Dun, R. G. & Company, xv, 175n14
    See also Dun & Bradstreet Corpora-
        tion; Tappan, Lewis
Dun & Bradstreet Corporation, 82
    See also Dun, R. G. & Company
Dunt, Detlef (Detlev Jordt), 44–45,
    154n1 *See also* Jordt, Detlev
duties. *See* tariffs
dye stirring poles, 39
Dyel [?], Godfried, 62
dyestuffs, 39

Edward, D. B., 68–69
elderberry blossoms, 122
Electoral Hesse. *See* Hessen
ell, 197
Elze, xiv
    emigration from, 30, 62, 63, 65,
    location, 118
emetics, 85
emigrant guides
    for Germans, 27, 44, 74, 102–103,
        154n2
    plagiarism by authors, 170n14
emigrant letters as historical sources,
    200–201
emigrant ports used by Germans, 34
emigrants,
    mortality. *See* mortality, of emigrants
    social origins, 30–31
emigrant ships, 193n74
emigration
    agents, 103–104
    costs from Germany to North
        America, 27, 43
    handbooks for, 44–45, 74, 83

and newspapers, 20
ports and routes, 29
returnees. *See* migration, return
to South America, 40–42
See also Adelsverein; emigrants; immigration; migration; specific places, countries, and regions
empresarios, 42
England. *See* Great Britain
Erath, George Bernard, 68
Erie Canal, 61
Ernst, Friedrich (Christian Friedrich Ernst Dirks), 44, 45, 180n81, 189–190n32, 193n71

factors, 84, 87
See also cotton, factors; merchants
Falcke family, 21
family
alliances, 189n22
disintegration of, 16
and oral traditions as sources, 97–98, 164–165n2
farmers, 7, 62–63
in Texas, 5, 110
See also agriculture; peasants; plantations and planters
farming implements, 85
females. *See* women
Ferdinand (brig), 125, 130
figs, 136
fishing hooks, 85
flax, 18
See also linen
Fleischmann, C. L., 83, 113
flintlocks, 85
flutes, 85, 127
foot (measure), 197
France
commercial treaty with Texas (1839), 43
scheduled steamer service with Galveston, Texas, and New Orleans, 56
See also French

freedom of trade. *See* commercial freedom
freight
charges, 86
hauling overland in Germany, 17, 32
French
in Texas, 50
See also France
Freudenthal, J. W., 91
Friedrich William III, King of Prussia (1797–1840), 46
frontier
and capitalism, 9
in North America, 7, 9
in Texas, 85, 92
fruit trees, 86
furniture, 86
furs. *See* hides; skins
Furtwängler, Philipp, 24

Galveston, 3, 5, 45
and Bremen, 9–10
cooperation with Houston, 55
cotton exports to Bremen, 90, 179n60
development as harbor, 5
exports, 77
German artisans in, 62
German Catholics in, 50, 162n50
hinterland of, 77
opposition to statehood, 56
passenger service with Europe, problems, 164n14
population, 56, 171n20, 171n24
scheduled ship lines with France, 54; with New Orleans, 54; with New York
ties to New Orleans and New York, 56
See also Bremen, commerce with Galveston; with Houston
Galveston Bay, 67, 71,
proposed canal to the Brazos, 72
Galveston Bay and Texas Land Company, 159n15
Gandersheim, 17, 19

gardeners, 105
Gautier, Dr. P. W., 125, 190n36
general store. *See* country store
Georgia, 28
Gerlach, Johann, 63
German-Americans
    migrants to Texas, 50
German emigration, 33, 41
Germania (German Society in New
    York), 45
German language and dialects
    maintenance in Texas, 3–4
    See also Low German
German literature, depiction of emi-
    gration, 29, 149n9
German migration
    to Latin America, 40–41
    to Pennsylvania, 44
    to Poland and Russia, 28
    and slavery, 74–77, 99
    to Texas, 159n19
    to Texas, beginning, 41; 43–44
    from United States to Texas, 159n19
    See also Texas
Germany, North, 8, 14–15
Gevelsberg, 128, 191n53
Giesecke family
    in Bockenem, 17–19
    in Bremen, 31, 156n20
    in Elze, 22–23
    in Gittelde, 17, 150–151nn1–2
    in Texas, 43
Giesecke, Adolf, 150n1
Giesecke, Asa A., 165n2
Giesecke, Charles A. (Anton Carl)
    (1811–1864/65), xiii–xiv, 6, 66,
    166n4
    arrival in Texas, 59, 64
    birth, 21
    cigar making, 94–95, 131, 189–
        190n32
    complaints about brother Edward,
        81, 121
    confirmation in Bockenem (1825),
        165n2

correspondence, xiii, 83, 120
cotton trade, 91
death, 113
diction, 121
dissolution of partnership with
    Eduard Giesecke, 129
distilling, 100, 101
exports, 91, 92, 134–135, 137, 166n5
farm, 80
imports, 86, 165n2
linens, 64
marriage, 136
as "planter," 92–93, 96, 136
property in Texas, 59, 96–97
requests artisans, 132
and slavery, 75–76, 80, 93
as stock raiser, 95
tobacco cultivation and trade, 80,
    94–95
use of imported German labor, 101–
    103
    See also wares
Giesecke, Christian August, 18, 151n7
Giesecke, Christoph *Carl* (1845–
    1926), 113, 119–120, 137, 189n22
    birth, 193n81
    christening, 194n92
    in United States, 165n2
Giesecke, Edward (Ernst Eduard)
    (1815–1856), 6, 23, 66
    arrival in Texas, 65–66
    assets, 84
    birth, 21
    confirmation in Bockenem (1829),
        165n2
    death, 84
    debts, 134–135, 136
    in letters of Charles A. Giesecke, 121
    loss, 125, 130
    store in Brazoria, 73, 79, 80, 81, 82–
        83
Giesecke, Ernst *Eduard*. *See* Giesecke,
    Edward
Giesecke, Friederike (Riecke), 21–22,
    112

failure to write, 123
as speaker of Low German, 130
wax for, 134, 136
Giesecke, Friedrich (Fritz) (1809–
1865), 6, 23, 119
arrival in Texas, 64–66
birth, 21
confirmation in Bockenem (1823),
165n2
criticized by brother Charles, 121
death, 113
as emigration agent, 102–103
marriage, 31, 174n10, 189n22
shipping mark, 179n58
Giesecke, Fritz. *See* Giesecke, Friedrich (Fritz)
Giesecke, Heinrich Friedrich, 17–19,
21, 22
Giesecke, Jack P., 165n2
Giesecke, Johann Jürgen, 150n1
Giesecke, Johann Zacharias, 150n1
Giesecke, Li[e]sette née Doby, 81, 84,
174–175n10, 191n60
Giesecke, Luise *Amalie* née Sander,
19, 22–23
Giesecke, *Marie* Henriette Sophie née
Basse, 31, 189n24
Giesecke, *Marie* Sophie Henriette. *See*
Struve, *Marie* Sophie Henriette née
Giesecke
Giesecke, Riecke, *See* Giesecke, Fried-
erike (Riecke)
Giesecke, Sarah Mary née Davis, 97,
136
Giesecke, *Thomas* Davis, 88
Giesecke, Widow. *See* Giesecke, Luise
Amalie, 19
Gillespie County, Texas, 76
Gisch, Theodor, xv
Gittelde, 17–18
Glauber's salt (sodium sulfate crystals)
used in dyeing textiles and also as ca-
thartic), 85
Gloystein, Nicholas, 155n19

Gloystein, Tilman, 31, 155n19
Golden Star (*Güldener Stern*) Inn in
Elze, 19
goldsmiths, 63
Goliad, Texas, 45
Göttingen, 35
Great Britain
commercial treaty with Texas ratified, 43
diplomatic recognition of Republic
of Texas, 43
Great Lakes, 29, 61
Gronau, 21, 195n99
craftsmen from, 63
emigration from, 62, 63
Gronau-Poppenburg (*Amt* [District]),
24
emigration from, 30
Groschen, 197
Grote, 197–198
Guadalupe River, 3
guidebooks for emigrants to Texas, 74,
86, 102–103, 107
guilds
in Bockenem, 18–19, 23
in Elze, 22–23, 186n161
in Germany, 102
in Kingdom of Hannover, 13, 25,
102
See also trade, restrictions
Güldener Stern. See Golden Star
Gulf of Mexico, 42
Gülich, Gustav von, 13
gumbo, 136
gunpowder, 86
Gutman, Herbert G., 9, 105

Haesloop (ship captain), xvi,
123
Hagedorn, Hermann, 114
Hagedorn & Prusner (firm), 92
Haidmanschester, 190n48
Hamburg, 36, 40
See also Hanseatic cities

Hamelin (Hameln), 114
hammers
pick, 85
shingling, 128
Hanau, 35
handbooks for emigrants from Germany, 45, 85
Handlin, Oscar, 7
Handwerk, Handwerker. See artisans
Hannover (city), xiv
emigration from, 48
Hannover (electorate and kingdom), 19–20
emigration from, 28–30, 61–63
linen industry in, 25
southern region, 78
Hanover. *See* Hannover
Hanse. *See* Bremen; Hamburg; Hanseatic cities; Lübeck
Hanseatic cities, 15, 51–52
commerce with Mexico, 39–40; with Spanish America, 32; with Texas, 52; with United States, 32
See also under Bremen; Germany; Hamburg; Lübeck
Hanseatic League. *See* Hanseatic cities
Hapsburg Empire, 50, 111
See also Austria, Austrians in Texas
hardware, 85
harnesses, 85
Harrisburg, Texas, 55
Harz Mountains, 17
Harz region, 18, 48
emigration from, 48
See also Harz Mountains
hats, 85
Havana, 178n49
cigars, *See* cigars, Havanas; tobacco
Heimatforscher, xiv–xv
See also history, local
herbs, medicinal, 39
Hercules (bark), 194n87
Herman[n], Missouri, 47

Hess, Philipp, 62
Hesse, Nicholas, 14, 16, 102
Hesse. *See* Hessen; Hessen-Darmstadt; Hessen-Kassel; Nassau
Hessen, 46, 48
See also Hessen-Darmstadt; Hessen-Kassel; Nassau
Hessen-Darmstadt, 46, 102
See also Hessen; Hessen-Darmstadt; Hessen-Kassel; Nassau
Hessen-Kassel, and *Adelsverein*, 46
"Hessian" soldiers as immigrants, 28
hides, 91, 92, 179n61
market for in Texas, 133
See also skins
Hildesheim (area), xiv, 19, 20
emigration from, 30, 48, 61, 107
and Low German language, 191n60
Hildesheim (town)
emigration from, 48, 79
Hill Country of Texas, 3–4, 50
Hinze, Friedrich August, 168n29
See also Vinze, Carl Adolph
hired women, German in America, 62
history, local, xiv
hoes, 85
hogsheads, 198
costly in Texas, 137
Höhne, Friedrich, 106
Holbrook, Abigail, 86, 89
Holstein, 44
Holy Alliance, 39
Holy Roman Empire, 20
Horn, Anton Friedrich, 152n14
Horn, *Henriette* Sophie née Sander, 137, 152n14, 195n99
Horn, Johann Alhardt, 21, 137, 152nn14–15, 195n99
horses
bits, 85
bridles. *See* bridles, horse
Horst
emigration from, 192n66

Houston (town), 3
  in 1844, 71
  Germans in, 45
  hinterland of, 55
  population 56, 164n19, 171n20,
    171n24
  See also Galveston
Houston, Sam, 51
Huck, Jürgen, 13
Hudson River, 61

imaginative literature as historical
  source, 149n9, 161n38
Immermann, Karl, 78
immigration. *See* emigrants, emigration; migrants, migration
indigo, 39
industrialization
  and emigration, 6
  in Germany, 25
Industry (town), Texas, 44
  See also Dunt, Detlef; Ernst,
    Friedrich
Irish
  linen, 127
  in Texas, 50
iron teeth for harrows, 85
iron wares, 39

Jews,
  in Elze, 23
  as emigrants from Europe, 33, 63–
    64
jew's harps, 86
Jockusch, J. W., 88, 176n19
Johann Dethard (brig), 135
Johnson, Lyndon Baines, 4, 145–
  146n4
Jones, Anson, President of Texas,
  192n66
Jordan, Terry G., 77
Jordt, Detlev (pseud. Detlef Dunt), 44–
  45, 68. *See also* Dunt, Detlef
Junkers, 111
  See also aristocrats, German

Kallehem [?], J. P., miller from
  Gronau, 63
Kapp, Friedrich, 73
Kassel, 79
Kauffman (firm), 88, 113, 126, 129,
  134, 168n20. *See also* under
  Kauf[f]man[n]
Kauf[f]man[n], Eduard, 63, 111, 131,
  133, 168n20
  purchasing tobacco with Edward
    Giesecke, 135
Kauf[f]man[n], Julius [J. F.], 62, 111,
  168n22,24, 176n19
Kauffman & Co., Julius, 168n22
  See also Kauffman (firm)
Kauffman & Runge (firm), 111
Kiel, 44
Klaener, D. H., 168n24
knives, 85–86, 127–128
Kruse, Friedrich, 150n1
Kulenkampff, Brothers (firm), 89
Kulikoff, Allan
Kümmelwasser (caraway liqueur), 135

laborers, day, 75
La Grange, Texas, 55
land
  speculation, 42, 46–47, 159n15
  in Texas, 42, 45–46, 88, 93
Landdrostei (term), 20
language maintenance
  See German language and dialects,
    maintenance in Texas
Latin America
  Wars of Liberation, 39
  See also Central America; South
    America; West Indies; and specific
    countries
"Latin farmers," 5
Lauenau, 103, 189n26
Lausitz, emigrants from, 48
lead, 85
leather. *See* tanneries; tanning
Le Havre, 60
Lehnhoff, Conrad, 108, 186n161

letters, of emigrants, 119–120, 200–201
See also Giesecke, Charles C., letters
Lewis Tappan & Co. *See* Tappan,
Lewis & Co.
Liebenau, 35
Ligardi, F. de (merchant), 179n58
linens,
from Alfeld, 153n29
from Bodenwerder, 123
German, 25
German to Mexico, 39–40
German to New Orleans, 59,
178n55
ordered by Charles A. Giesecke, 85
from Osnabrück, 188n14
Silesian, 129
See also textiles, textile trade
line of settlement. *See* frontier
Linnen-Legge (Leinenlegge),
153nn29–30
Liverpool, 29, 36, 87
local history. *See* history, local
Lower Lausitz. *See* Lausitz
Lower Saxon State Archives
Hannover, xiii
Low German language, 130, 191n60
Lowood Plantation, 88
Lübeck, 15
Lüdering & Co., 193n83

maids, German in America, 62, 63
Manchester (fabric), 128
Manhattan. *See* New York City
Mariengroschen, 198
marriage alliances. *See* alliances
through marriage
Maryland, Germans in, 28
masons, 106
Matamoros, Mexico, 40
McKinney & Williams (firm), 55, 88,
89, 91
See also Williams, Henry H.
Mecklenburg, 8, 189n22
emigrants from, 8, 33, 48, 81, 130,
191n60

medications, 86
Meiningen, 46
Melchers & Co., C., 194n87
"melting pot" theory, 9
merchant
concept, 5, 8, 176n19
neglect by scholars, 114
merchants, 5–6, 8–9
and frontier, 9–10
German, 5, 9; in Mexico, 39, 41–42
in Germany, 13–16, 149n10
guidebooks for, 83
marriages, 189n22
surplus in Germany, 13, 112
See also names of individuals and
firms
Metternich, Clemens Prince von, 39
Meusebach, John O. [Otfried Hans
von Meusebach], 47
Mexican Americans, 3
Mexicans
in Texas, 56, 70
Mexico
declaration of independence from
Spain (1821), 39
exports, 39
and German commerce, 39–40
German firms in, 41
and German merchants, 41
Texas policy, 42
treaties of commerce and friendship
with German states, 40
See also commerce; merchants; and
names of firms
Mexico, Gulf of. *See* Gulf of Mexico
Mexico, Republic of, 5
Mexico City, 41
Meyer, Chr., 123
Meyer, Christ. (linen dealer in Bre-
men), 188n13
Meyer, Heinrich (German philologist
and novelist), 99
Meyer, Heinrich (shoemaker from
Gronau), 63
Michener, James, 3

migrant, migration, 4, 7
  and economic conditions, 6–7,
    147–148n15
  Germans to Russia, 28
  regional patterns, 4, 146–147n10
  return, 6–7, 63–64
  and social class, 4–5, 114, 146n8
  See also migrants, migration
military officers and emigration, 102
Mill Creek, Texas, 44, 45
Miller, Rev. James A., 72, 171–172n30
millers, 62, 107
Mills, David G., 87, 88, 124
Mills, Robert, 55, 81, 87, 88, 89
  death, 113
  fortune, 88
Mills (firm), 88, 125, 130, 135,
    177n38, 179n61
  warehouse, 84, 122
  See also Mills, David G.; Mills,
    Robert
Mississippi River, 61
Missouri, 14, 44, 63
mobility, geographic
  restriction in Hannover, 153n36
molasses, 101, 124
Monroe, James, 98
Monroe Doctrine (1823), 39, 41
Moore, Francis, 71
Morgen (German land measure), 198
mortality, of emigrants, 49–50,
    162nn41, 43
mousseline de laine (fabric), 128
Münsterland, emigrants from, 28
musical instruments, 39
music and bourgeois culture. *See* piano

Nadel, Stanley, 4
Nankeen (fabric), 127
Napoleon III, 43
Nassau (duchy), 46
  emigrants from, 28, 48
Navasota, 55
needles, Schwabacher, 126

Negroes, 124, 126, 130, 133–134. *See
  also* African Americans; slaves
Neptun[e] (bark), 129, 130, 189n21
  bound for Texas, 133, 168n20,
    193n74
  and cotton trade, 89, 125, 194n87
Netherlands
  recognition of the Republic of Texas,
    43
Neu-Braunfels, Texas. *See* New Braunfels, Texas
Neuss, xiv
New Braunfels, Texas, 81, 184n133
Newell, Chester, 69
New Orleans,
  arrivals of Gieseckes, 23, 59
  and Brazoria, 68
  commerce, 53
  and cotton trade, 90
  and German immigrants, 44, 48, 63
  and German merchants, 16, 85
  as immigrant port, 48, 60, 61, 62, 65,
    161n38
  intercourse with Brazoria, 68
  role in cotton trade, 90
  scheduled ship service with Bremen,
    48
  scheduled ship service with France, 56
New York (steamer), 169n43
New York City, 44, 45
  German merchants in, 16
  as immigrant port, 48, 60, 61
New York State, Germans in, 28
Niemann, Eliza, 194n90
Niemann, Fräulein, 136, 194n90
Niemann, Frederica (sp?), 194n90
Niemann, Theresia, 194n90
Nienburg, 35, 114
nobility. *See also* aristocrats, German;
  Junkers
Northeim, 35
North Germany. *See* Germany, North;
  and names of specific places and
  districts (Alfeld; Bockenem; Boden-

werder; Bremen; Elze; Göttingen; Hannover; Harz Mountains; Hessen; Hildesheim; Holstein; Kiel; Mecklenburg; Münsterland; Oldenburg; Osnabrück; Osterode; Waldeck; Westphalia)

Norwegians
    as emigrants, 7
    in Texas, 50
Nötzel, Klaus, 150n1
Nürnberg, 35

Odessa, 29
officers. *See* military officers
officials and emigration, 102
Ohio, 62
okra, 136
Olbers (ship), 192n66
Oldenburg (city and duchy), 44
    emigrants from, 28
Olmstedt, Frederick Law, 76, 84
Osnabrück
    linens, 188n14
    See also linens
Osterode am Harz, 119
O'Swald (firm), 149n12

padlocks, 126
painters, house, 106
Palatinate, 35
Paris, 102
passenger lists. *See* ship passenger lists
patricians in Germany, 13
Peach Point Plantation, 89, 94
peasants, 7–8
    German, 5, 75
    See also farmers
pelts. *See* hides; skins
Pennsylvania "Dutch." *See* Pennsylvania Germans
Pennsylvania Germans, 4, 28
Perry, James F., 93–94
Pessen, Edward, 179n63
Philadelphia, 178n49

physicians, 106
piano, 136
    and bourgeoisie, 186n14
pianomakers, 106
Pilsbury, Thomas, 130, 191n61
Piore, Michael, 107
planes, carpenter's, 85. *See also* tools, importing
plantations and planters (terms), 93, 179n19
    See also farmers and farms
Plathner, Fritz, 150n1
Plattdeutsch. See Low German language
playing cards, 86
Pohlmann, Adolph, 103, 124–125, 132, 184n138
    departure, 136
    and wares, 123, 128, 129, 130
Pohlmann, H., 192n66
Pohlmann, Heinrich Christoph Conrad, 192n66
Polk, James K., United States President, 192n66
Poppenburg, domain
    See Gronau-Poppenburg (District)
Postl, Karl. *See* Sealsfield, Charles
potatoes, sweet, 125
precapitalist society, 91–92
prices, in Texas, 85
printers, 106
Prussia
    and *Adelsverein*, 46
    commerce with Mexico, 40
    linen industry, 40
    Treaty of Commerce and Friendship with Mexico (1827), 40
push-pull factors. *See* emigration

Quakenbrück, 180n80
Quarterly Abstract
    as source, 64–65, 163n36
    See also ship passenger lists
Quintana, Texas, 54

Reden, F. W. O. L. Freiherr von, 25, 35
Red River, 90
Refugio, Texas, 79
Regalia cigars, 193n71–72
regionalism and migration, 4, 146–147n10
See also settlement patterns
Reichstaler, 198
Restoration era in Europe and migration, 14
return migration. *See* migrants; migration, return
Rheingau, 35
Rhine Province. *See* Prussia, Rhine Province
rhubarb, 85, 129
Richter, C. A. (merchant), 180n75
Richter, Johann Heinrich, 180n75
Richter & Krebs, 180n75
   Richter, Carl Friedrich August, 180n75
Richter (firm), 123, 124, 130, 131
rifles, 86
Rio de Janeiro, 178n49
Rock [?], Frederick, 62
Rølvaag, O. E., 7
Roman Catholic Church. *See* Catholic Church
ropemakers, 105, 108
Rosenberg Library (Galveston, Texas), xv
Rotterdam, 34
ruling class, of Texas, 42
rum making
   in Bockenem, 18
   Jamaican, 135
   Puerto Rican, 124
   smuggling, 135
   in Texas, 101, 129
   West Indian, 135
   See also distilleries, distillers, distilling of alcoholic beverages
Rumpff, Victor, 51
Runge, Julius, 168n20
Russia, 28

Sachsen-Anhalt, emigrants, 48
saddle blankets. *See* blankets, saddle
San Antonio, 70, 77
San Bernard River, 67
Sander, Anton Christian, 20–22
Sander, Bodo Christoph, 98
Sander, Henriette Sophie. *See* Horn, Henriette Sophie née Sander, 20–21
Sander, Lieutenant Colonel, 21
Sander, Luise *Amalie. See* Giesecke, Luise *Amalie* née Sander
Sander, Sophia Dorothea, née Sander, 20–21
Sander, Sophie Friederike Christine. *See* Basse, Sophie Friederike Christine née Sander
Sander family
   Bremen branch, 31, 155n15
   and Conze family, 152n14
San Felipe administrative area, 68
Saxony, 3
Scherpf, G. A., 170n14
Schilling, 198
Schlecht, Friedrich, 75
Schleswig-Holstein. *See* Holstein
Schmidt, H. (goldsmith from Alsfeld), 63
Schulte, Gerhard, 63
Schumacher & Co., 89
Schürhof (firm) in Gevelsberg, 128, 191n53
Schwabach, 190n41
Scotch-Irish. *See* Irish
Scots, in Texas, 50
sealing wax. *See* wax, sealing
Sealsfield, Charles (Karl Postl), 4, 67
Seele, Hermann, 79–81, 82, 92
serfdom, 111
ship passenger lists as historical sources, 59–60, 199–200
shipping costs, 86
   See also *Quarterly Abstract*
shirting, 127
shoemakers, 23–24, 63, 105, 106

shoes from Germany, 85, 125
Silesian linens. *See* linens, Silesian
silver, 39
silversmiths, 106
skins, 91, 92, 179n61
   See also hides
slavery
   abolition in Mexico (1829)
      in Brazoria County, 73–74
   expansion in United States, 43
   in Texas, 42–43, 74
slaves
   clothing of, 188n14
   rental of, 135
   revolts and unrest in Texas, 77
   in Texas, 42, 47, 50, 56, 88
   value of, 84
   See also African Americans
Smith, Morgan L., 86–87, 176n37
smuggling, 53, 133, 135
   See also rum
social class
   and migration, 4–5, 114, 146n8
socks, defective, 122, 127, 190n45
soils, in Texas, 69
Solms Braunfels, Prince Carl of, 5, 47,
   50, 80
Sommer, Captain Carl von, 154n2
South America
   immigration of Germans, 40–41
   as source of raw materials (leather)
      for Elze, 24
   See also Latin America
Spanish-speaking Texans, 3, 47
steamers and steamships, 7, 54–56,
   71
Steinert, W., 172n41
Steurt, J. McNeal, 188n6
Stewart, Charles B., 188n6
Stewart, Dr., 188n6
Stiege, 191
Stiff, "Colonel" Edward, 69, 86
stirrups, 85
St. Joseph-on-the-Brazos, Brazoria,
   Texas, 72

St. Mary's Church, Freeport, Texas,
   171n30
stock. *See* cattle; livestock
stockings, 85
stock raising, 95, 97
Stolzenau, 35
storekeeper, term, 176n19
stores. *See also* country store; Giesecke,
   Edward
Strubberg, Friedrich Armand, 74–75
Struve, *Marie* Sophie Henriette née
   Giesecke, 120
Struve, Walter (1871–1929), 119, 120
"Stuart" house, 122
sugar and sugar cane, 74, 100–101,
   124
   See also molasses
Swedes, in Brazoria County, 73
sweet potatoes, 125
Swiss and Swiss Germans
   in Brazoria County, 72
   in Texas, 50, 200

tailors, 62, 105
Tampico, Texas, 56
tanneries, tanners, tanning, 24, 65
Tappan & Co., Lewis, 82–83
tariffs, tariff policy, 53
   Texas, 86, 100
   United States, 25, 43, 100, 111, 133
   See also commercial treaties
Texas
   commerce, 51–53
   distribution of wealth, 95–96
   early German settlers in, 3, 43–48,
      79
   entry into United States, 130, 132–
      133
   exports, 52–53
   German colonies in, 4
   German farmers in, 5
   German immigration, 43–45
   Germans in, 47–48, 50
   imports, 52–53
   pipes in, 86

plebiscite favoring entry of Texas into United States, 43
population (1841), 47–48; (1850), 50
ruling class, 32
See also Adelsverein; cattle; commercial treaties; cotton; *empresarios*; land grants; plantations and planters; slavery; slaves; sugar; tobacco; world market
Texas, Republic of (1836–1846), 3
Texas, statehood, consequences, 192n66
Texas State Archive, Austin, Texas, xv
textiles, textile business, and textile industry, 36
textile trade in Texas, 133
in Bockenem, 18
See also cotton goods; linens; woolens
Thaler, 198
Thuringia, emigration from, 48
Tiling, Moritz, 173n53
tobacco, tobacco farming, tobacco trade, 91
in Allendorf, 157n43
in Bockenem, 18
in Brazoria County, 133
cutter, German in Galveston, 133
factory in Bockenem, 18
Göttingen, 35
Hanau, 35
Havana, 95, 131, 132, 178n49
Hessen, 35, 157n43
leaf, 122
Liebenau, 35
Nienburg, 35
Northeim, 35
Nürnberg, 35
Palatinate, 35
prices and other market conditions, 130, 131, 133
Rheingau, 35
Stolzenau, 35

Texas, 126, 131, 189–190n32
use of scraps, 124
Wanfried, 157n43
along the Werra, 157n43
along the Weser, 35
West Indian, 131
See also cigars
tools, importing, 86, 128
towns. *See* under cities and towns; commerce; guilds; merchants; trade
transatlantic crossings, 7
travel literature, German, 63
Travis, William Barret, 98
treaties, commercial. *See* commercial treaties
Trinity River, 55
trousers, linen, 122
twine, flax, 85
Tyler, John, United States President, 192n66

Uhrlaub, Georg, 62
Unkraut & Son (firm), 187
upholsterers, 106
Upper Lausitz. *See* Lausitz

vanilla, 39
Van Ravenswaay, Charles, 102–103
Varner, Martin, 93, 100, 182n106
Varner's Creek, 93
Velasco, Texas, 54, 73, 91, 98, 179n61
Vera Cruz, 56
Verein zum Schutze deutscher Einwanderer in Texas. See Adelsverein
Viëtor & Achelis (firm), 31
Vinze, Carl Adolph, 63
See also Hinze, Friedrich August
violins, 86
violin strings, 85

Waldeck (principality)
and *Adelsverein*, 46
emigrants from, 28
Wanfried, 157n43

wares
  from Germany requested or received
    by Charles A. Giesecke, 59, 120,
    126–129, 133–134, 190n35
  shipped by the Gieseckes from
    America, 120, 122, 179n61,
    194n87
Washington County, Texas, 95
Washington-on-the-Brazos, Texas, 71, 79
watchmakers, 106
Wätjen, D. (firm), 48, 94
Wätjen & Co., D. H. (firm), 48, 94
wax, sealing, 134, 136
Webb, Walter Prescott, 9
Weiser, Father Jacob, 72 n171
Wends, 3
Werra River, 157n43
Weser (brig, schooner brig), 91, 122,
  187n3, 189n21, 192n66, 193n71
Weser River
  navigability, 29, 32
  See also Bremen; Bremerhaven

West Columbia (formerly Columbia),
  Texas, 181n94
West Indies, 56
Westphalia (area), 190n43
Westphalia (Kingdom of), 19
wheelwrights, 105
whiskey, 124, 133
Williams, Henry H., 89. *See also* Mc-
  Kinney & Williams (firm)
Winston-Salem, 28
Wolfenbüttel, xi, 19
women, shortage of in Texas, 81, 97
woolens and wool trade. *See* textiles,
  textile business, and textile industry
world market, 74, 77–78, 86
Wrede, Captain Friedrich W. von,
  160n28
Württemberg (kingdom)
  and *Adelsverein*, 46
  emigrants, 48
Wussken [?], Christine, 63

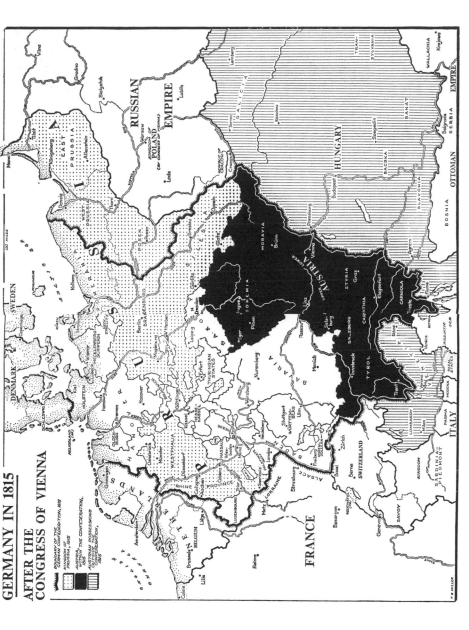

1. Map of Germany in 1815. From Hajo Holborn, *A History of Modern Germany*, 3 vols. (New York: Alfred A. Knopf, 1959–1969), vol. 2. Reproduced with permission of Hannah Holborn Gray.

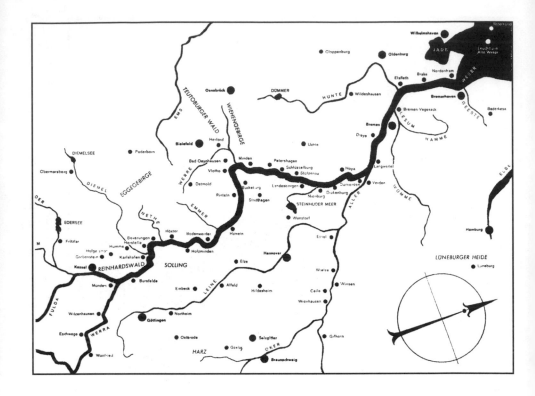

2. Northwestern and North Central Germany.

Section of a map showing many of the towns mentioned in the text. They include Hildesheim (south of the Hanover); Elze and Gronau (east of Hildesheim); Bockenem (south of Hildesheim); and Anfeld (southeast of Bockenem). Among the other places on this map mentioned in the text, but not as prominently, are Bodenwerder, Hameln (Hamlin), Stolzenau, and Nienburg—all on the Weser River; Bremen and Bremerhaven; Brunswick (Braunschweig); Osnabrück and Bielefeld in the northwest; Northeim and Osterode near the Harz Mountains; and Hamburg to the east.

3. Bockenum.

The St. Pankratius Church before the Great Fire of 1847. Courtesy Rudi Meller, Bockenem.

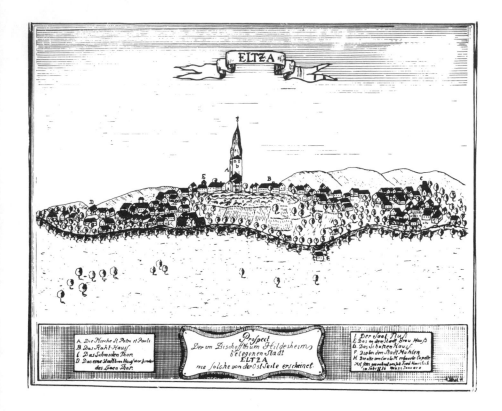

4. Elze.

Engraving of 1736 after a drawing by Johann Friedrich Haarstick. From D. E. Baring, *Beschreibung der Saale im Amt Lauenstein* (Lemgo, 1744).

5. The Giesecke-Sander House in Elze (now Hauptstraße 47).

From a photo also showing the inhabitants, about 1910. The exterior of the building had been altered by the addition of tiles. Courtesy Karl Mundhenke, Frankfurt am Main.

6. The Main Marketplace in Hildesheim (much as it was in the middle of the nineteenth century).

Courtesy New York Public Library.

7. The Horns of Gronau. Photographs of Oil Portraits.

7.1. Henriette Sophie Horn, née Sander (1780–1858), Aunt of Charles A. Giesecke and His Brothers.

7.2. Her Husband, Johann Alhardt Horn (1767–1851). Courtesy Retired Bank director Klaus Nötzel, Bonn-Bad Godesberg.

8. Large German Freight Wagon on the Bremen Route, 1853.

From Friedrich Rauers, *Geschichte des Bremer Binnenhandels im 19. Jahrhundert. Namentlich unter den alten Verkehrsformen und im Übergang* (Bremen, 1913).

9. Emigrant Ships in Bremerhaven ca. 1840.

From a lithograph. From Otto Höver, Von der Galiot zum Fünfmaster: Unsere Segelschiffe in der Weltschiffahrt 1780–1930 (Bremen, [1934]).

Der Riesenkrahn in Bremerhaven. Nach einer Zeichnung von K. Geißler.

10. Giant Crane in Bremerhaven (mid-nineteenth century).
Courtesy New York Public Library.

11. Bremen ca. 1852.
Courtesy New York Public Library.

Für deutsche Auswanderer

Zeichnung aus den Fliegenden Blättern, um 1847

„Unter den Schiffsrhedern und Expeditenten herrscht ein reger Wettstreit, den Auswanderern die Reise auf das angenehmste zu machen. Die ihnen überwiesenen Schiffsräume sind hell, luftig und bequem, so daß keine Gelegenheit gegeben ist zur geringsten Klage."

12. German Caricatures of Emigration and Commerce.

12.1. 1847. The text reads: "Lively competition prevails among shipping companies and expediters to make the journey of emigrants pleasant. The rooms on the ships are bright, well ventilated, and comfortable; there is no reason for the slightest complaint."

Volkswirtschaftslehre für Jedermann

Freihandelsystem für Deutschland / Jahr der Beglückung

Steindruck aus Frankfurt a. M. 184

Import und Export.

Zu deutsch: Waaren herein! Menschen hinaus

12.2. 1848. The caption reads: "Import and Export. In plain language, wares in, people out!" The left gate is labeled "Out," the right "In."

Both from Hermann von Frieden and Georg Smolka, eds., *Auswanderer: Bilder und Skizzen aus der Geschichte der deutschen Auswanderung* (Berlin, [1937?]).

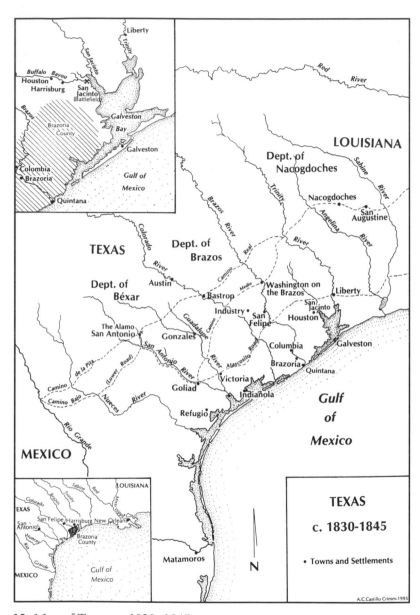

13. Map of Texas ca. 1830–1845.
Courtesy of Carolina Castillo-Crimm.

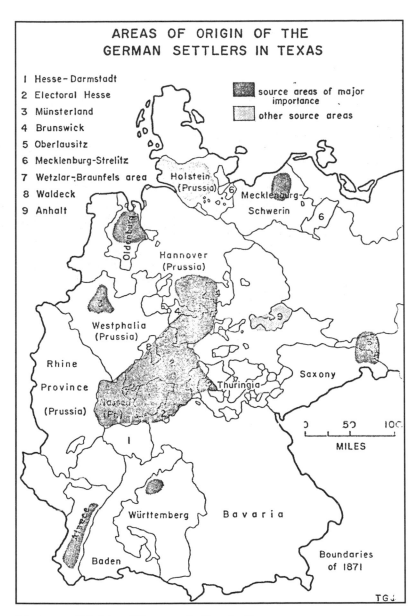

14. Areas of Origin of German Settlers in Texas.

From Terry G. Jordan, *German Seed in Texas Soil: Immigrant Farmers in Nineteenth-Century Texas* (Austin, 1966). Courtesy Professor Jordan and the University of Texas Press.

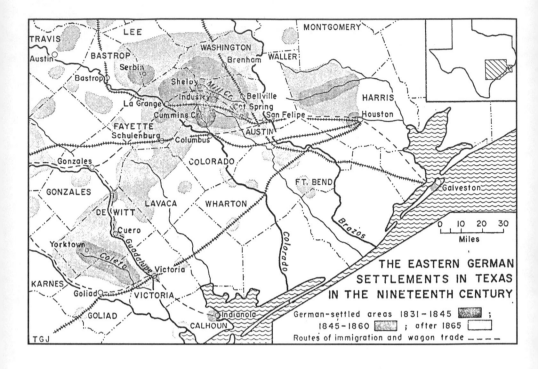

15. The Eastern German Settlements in Texas in the Nineteenth Century.

From Terry G. Jordan, *German Seed in Texas Soil: Immigrant Farmers in Nineteenth-Century Texas* (Austin, 1966). Courtesy Professor Jordan and the University of Texas Press.

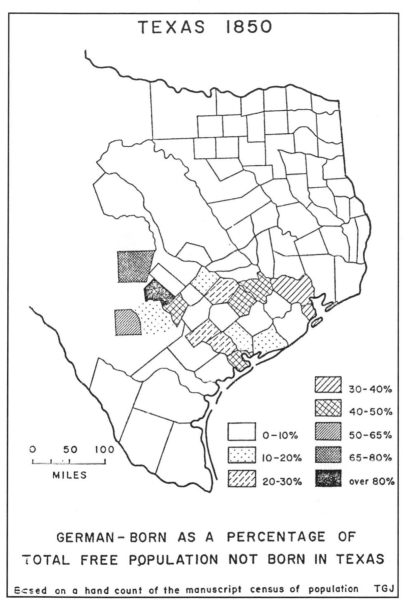

TEXAS 1850

30-40%
40-50%
0-10%
50-65%
10-20%
65-80%
20-30%
over 80%

0   50   100
MILES

GERMAN - BORN AS A PERCENTAGE OF
TOTAL FREE POPULATION NOT BORN IN TEXAS

Based on a hand count of the manuscript census of population   TGJ

16. German-Born as a Percentage of the Total Free Population Not Born
in Texas.

From Terry G. Jordan, *German Seed in Texas Soil: Immigrant Farmers in
Nineteenth-Century Texas* (Austin, 1966). Courtesy Professor Jordan and
the University of Texas Press.

17. Galveston ca. 1839.

From Edward Stiff, *The Texan Emigrant. Being a Narration of the Adventures of the Author in Texas and a Description of the Soils, Climate, Productions . . . of That Country* (Cincinnati, 1840).

18. Galveston ca. 1846.

From Carl von Sommer, *Bericht über meine Reise nach Texas im Jahre 1846. Die Verhältnisse und den Zustand dieses Landes betreffend* (Bremen, 1847).

19. From Charles A. Giesecke's Correspondence with His Brother Friedrich.

All letters in the possession of the author.

19.1. Address Fold of Letter of March 16, 1844. Transmitted from Texas to Elze via Bremen.

19.2. Address Fold of Letter of February 18, 1845, from Texas to Elze via New Orleans, Liverpool, and Le Havre. A Liverpool stamp is on the rear of this letter, as is Charles A. Giesecke's seal.

19.3. First Page of the Letter of February 10, 1845.

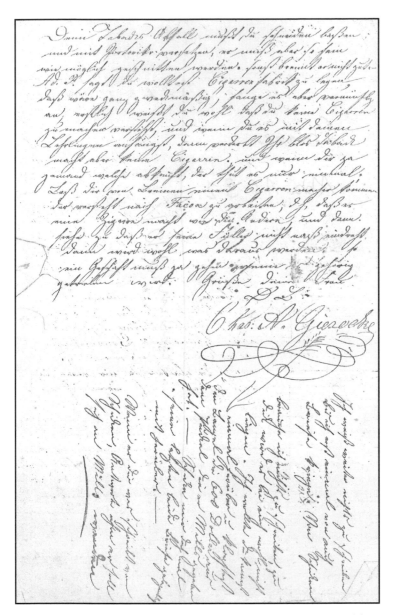

19.4. Preliminary conclusion of the Letter of February 10, 1845, with a Fine Example of Charles A. Giesecke's Signature.